**Coping with
U.S.-Japanese
Economic
Conflicts**

Coping with U.S.-Japanese Economic Conflicts

Edited by

I.M. Destler
Carnegie Endowment for
International Peace

Hideo Sato
Yale University

LexingtonBooks
D.C. Heath and Company
Lexington, Massachusetts
Toronto

Library of Congress Cataloging in Publication Data

Main entry under title:
    Coping with U.S.-Japanese economic conflicts.

    Contents: "Introduction" by I.M. Destler and Hideo Sato—"The U.S.-Japanese steel issue of 1977" by Hideo Sato and Michael W. Hodin—"The politics of U.S.-Japanese auto trade" by Gilbert R. Winham and Ikuo Kabashima—"Agricultural trade: the case of beef and citrus" by Hideo Sato and Timothy J. Curran—[etc.]

    1. United States—Foreign economic relations—Japan—Case studies—Addresses, essays, lectures. 2. Japan—Foreign economic relations—United States—Case Studies—Addresses, essays, lectures. 3. United States—Commerce—Japan—Case studies—Addresses, essays, lectures. 4. Japan—Commerce—United States—Case studies—Addresses, essays, lectures. I. Destler, I.M. II. Sato, Hideo, 1942-   .
HF1456.5.J3C66   382'.0973'052   81-47897
ISBN 0-669-05144-6   AACR2

Published simultaneously in Canada

Printed in the United States of America

International Standard Book Number: 0-669-05144-6

Library of Congress Catalog Card Number: 81-47897

Contents

Preface

This book treats five politically volatile economic issues that arose between 1977 and 1981. Its case chapters trace the development of U.S.-Japanese difficulties in steel trade, automobiles, agricultural products, telecommunications equipment, and macroeconomic policy coordination, concluding with how these specific issues were resolved. The opening and closing chapters provide broader background information and analyses, including prescriptions as to how officials in both governments can manage better the future economic conflicts that will inevitably arise.

The book began in early 1980, when the Japan-United States Economic Relations Group, known informally as the wise men, asked us to study how recent bilateral economic disputes had risen to political prominence and how such disputes might best be managed and contained. After developing a common analytic framework, working separately, we each conducted or contracted for studies of the five cases, because each of us was originally charged with investigating his own nation's policymaking. Thus, Ikuo Kabashima and Hisao Mitsuyu joined Sato in writing original papers on Japanese policymaking on four of the issues, and Yasushi Hara provided important analysis and advice on the NTT dispute. Timothy J. Curran, Michael W. Hodin, and Gilbert W. Winham joined Destler in doing parallel studies of the U.S. side of these issues. We then gleaned from these studies specific recommendations for the wise men to consider when preparing their report of January 1981 to the president of the United States and the prime minister of Japan.

After consulting with our collaborators, we agreed that the Japanese and U.S. case studies were complementary and mutually reinforcing, so we decided to merge them. In each case chapter, the author listed first undertook to blend the two original papers into a single, coherent account and analysis. (For the NTT article, Curran served as sole author and drew on Hara's contribution and his own previous investigation of the issue in Tokyo.) The result, we believe, is a truly binational study, drawing on interviews in both capitals as well as on public sources. We have published it expeditiously, while the issues are relevant; we hope, however, that the conclusions have broader application.

Our debts are many. The study was initiated and financed by the Tokyo and Washington offices of the Japan-United States Economic Relations Group. Therefore, we are grateful to Ambassadors Nobuhiko Ushiba and Robert Ingersoll, the group's co-chairmen, and to Tadashi Yamamoto and Jack B. Button, its executive directors, for their initial encouragement and support and for their cooperation as we moved toward publication. Yamamoto also provided an indispensable Tokyo base for Sato at the

Japan Center for International Exchange. Destler is grateful to Thomas L. Hughes, president of the Carnegie Endowment for International Peace, for his cooperation with Destler's involvement in this study. Carnegie also provided facilities in the Washington office for Curran, who, in addition to writing two cases, provided superb overall backstopping and research support for the U.S. side of the study, which was conducted in the spring and summer of 1980. We both owe a particular debt to Sato's Yale colleague, Hugh Patrick, one of the wise men, who was a stimulating and constructive critic and who generously allowed Sato to draw on the preliminary findings of their joint Yale project.

Finally, we are grateful to Alease Vaughn for her indispensable help in making sure that successive drafts were typed expeditiously and accurately and in providing broader administrative support.

I.M.D.
H.S.

Coping with U.S.-Japanese Economic Conflicts

1   Introduction

I.M. Destler and
Hideo Sato

In November 1977, a U.S. trade official led an economic mission to Tokyo to urge changes in Japanese policies. The purpose was to avert what U.S. officials saw as a threatening crisis in bilateral economic relations. He was chosen, in part, for his modest rank and low-key personal style, because the United States's objective was to press issues strongly but privately. Instead, the mission provoked a media storm in Tokyo—so much of a storm that, when the emissary called upon Prime Minister Takeo Fukuda, he was greeted with the words, "I am happy to meet the most famous man in Japan." The immediate result was to make conflict more visible and acute.

In early 1979, senior U.S. and Japanese officials had to work very hard to prevent a summit conference from being poisoned, for the Japanese, by a dispute over whether Japan's national telephone company would procure sophisticated equipment from U.S. and other non-Japanese manufacturers. This issue had not even been prominent the year before, but suddenly it became, to Americans, a symbol of Japan's closed market, and, to Japanese, an example of outrageous U.S. pressure.

In early 1977, U.S. steel companies pressed a campaign against imports from Japan and sought quantitative limits on them. Their counterparts in Japanese industry were quite amenable to enforcing such limits. Yet the issue nonetheless ballooned politically, bringing enormous political pressure on Congress and the Carter administration throughout the summer and the fall and a concomitant rise in anti-Japanese political rhetoric.

In December 1978, Japanese Prime Minister Masayoshi Ohira declared that his country would fall short of attaining its economic growth target. This was consistent with the consensus of economists, yet it triggered a sharply critical letter from President Jimmy Carter accusing Japan of abandoning her international commitments.

Throughout 1980 and into 1981, U.S.-Japanese trade politics were dominated by the matter of automobiles. With domestic employment and sales plummeting, the president of the United Auto Workers, Douglas Fraser, flew to Tokyo to seek restraint on Japanese exports and on the construction of Japanese auto plants in the United States. Others joined in the pressure, only to have the U.S. International Trade Commission rule, in October, that the U.S. industry was not eligible for import relief under current U.S. law.

In all five of these episodes, the economic issues between Japan and the United States were intrinsically difficult. In all five, they were rendered more complicated by the specific evolution of politics and decision-making in one country or both. This book seeks to shed light on how and why these complications arose and what might be done about them in the future.

Much of the drama—the noise—in U.S.-Japanese economic relations is inevitable. Both countries are active democracies, and they are also the world's two largest market economies. Democracy spawns controversy, particularly over issues that matter. And trade often matters a great deal—to producers, to workers, and to consumers. With over 300,000 layoffs in the U.S. auto industry in 1980, and with Japanese car imports totaling $8.4 billion in value and 21 percent of the U.S. market in volume, it would be a miracle if automobiles had not become an important political issue in the United States.

Some of the noise is desirable. Dealing with changing economic realities requires frequent, sometimes painful policy adjustment in both Washington and Tokyo. Such change is unlikely to occur without a healthy dose of political contention, within each country and sometimes between the two. Citizens in both countries need to understand that a certain amount of friction is normal, and they must learn to live with it. Policy conflict is often a necessary ingredient in the process of coping with and resolving bilateral issues.

Yet the frequency and intensity of U.S.-Japanese trade conflict is deeply troubling. From 1969 to 1971, bilateral economic relations were dominated by a bitter textile wrangle over Japanese exports that totaled only 4 percent of her textile production and only one pecent of U.S. textile consumption. In the 1977-1980 period, there was an epidemic of economic conflicts—over color televisions, steel, beef and citrus, telecommunications, automobiles, nuclear processing, macroeconomic policy coordination, and economic sanctions toward Iran.

Each of these conflicts became, for a time,a focus of strong controversy in at least one country, and each threatened to spill over to affect broader relations and policies. This is exactly what happened in 1971, when bitterness over textiles pervaded the Nixon White House, encouraging rebuffs to Tokyo on other issues and threatening Senate ratification of the Okinawa reversion treaty. The relationship reached its postwar nadir, symbolized by the U.S. threat of invoking the Trading with the Enemy Act with regard to its major East Asian ally see (Destler, Fukui, and Sato, 1979). There was no comparable breakdown of relations in 1977-1980, although it seemed possible more than once. However the cumulative impact of recent disputes has been to give the impression of "unceasing acrimony," as Ambassador Nobuhiko Ushiba recently put it (Ushiba, 1980, p. 2). And this, we are convinced, has been anything but healthy and desirable.

Persistent, high-visibility trade conflict generates bitterness in both countries: Japanese are bitter about what they see as constant U.S. pressure and self-righteousness; Americans are bitter about what they perceive as Japanese relentless exporting and covert protection of imports. It can render particular issues enormously more difficult to resolve as national positions become polarized and government leaders fear that compromise will be viewed, in the glare of publicity, as a sign of weakness. It fosters stereotypes—of the "unfairness" of Japanese trade practices or the "laziness" of U.S. workers.

What can be done, then, to mute this pattern? How can the two countries achieve a more constructive approach to U.S.-Japanese economic relations, as President Carter and Prime Minister Ohira urged at their May 1979 summit meeting? This book addresses the problem through close examination of recent experience. Specifically, we present case analyses of five representative recent issues—steel, automobiles, agricultural products, telecommunications equipment, and macroeconomic policy coordination. Each draws on research in Tokyo and in Washington in order to highlight the perspectives and interests of both countries. Each addresses a common set of questions—about how the issue rose to political prominence, the specific interplay of interests on both sides, and the path to the resolution of the issue.

Each case—and, more generally, U.S.-Japanese trade conflicts—must be understood within broader contexts. One central cause of such conflict in the sixties and seventies was, of course, the enormous expansion of bilateral trade and its shifts in composition. Another factor was the erosion of the postwar international system dominated by the cold war. A third was the different approaches the two nations took to trade-policy management. A fourth was the peculiar psychology of postwar U.S.-Japanese relations and its inconsistency with current economic realities. Finally, there was the specific situation that decision makers confronted in 1977—a world economy shaken by OPEC, severe inflation, and a deep recession followed by a shaky recovery.

Each of these broader, background factors deserves brief, separate treatment before we turn to the cases that form the heart of this book.

The Trade Explosion

In 1960, the United States exported $1.4 billion in goods to Japan and imported $1.1 billion in goods. In 1980, the United States exported $20.8 billion and imported $30.7 billion in goods. Some of this enormous increase can be explained by inflation.[1] But there remains a fivefold real increase in U.S. exports to Japan, and a sevenfold real increase in imports, over this twenty-year period. This increase far outstripped the growth of overall U.S. production.[2]

The trade balance also shifted dramatically—from a consistent surplus in the United States's favor through 1964 to a steady and growing deficit thereafter, reaching a peak (using U.S. data) of $11.6 billion in 1978 (see table 1-1 below).

There was also a remarkable change in the composition of Japan's exports. Textiles dropped from 30.4 percent of her worldwide total in 1960 to 6.7 percent in 1975, while over this same period iron and steel rose from 9.6 to 18.7 percent and machinery (including autos and ships) rose from 25.5 to 53.8 percent (Rapp and Feldman, 1979, pp. 104-105). In automobiles, Japanese sales to the U.S. market rose from 2,000 cars in 1960 to 313,000 cars in 1970 to 1.9 million cars in 1980. The composition of U.S. exports to Japan remained, by contrast, relatively constant and concentrated in primary goods.

Each of these factors contributed to bilateral trade friction. Increased volume meant a greater impact on more domestic markets, causing predictable reactions from those adversely affected. The bilateral imbalance and the divergent commodity compositions of exports and imports also tended to exacerbate trade relations.

To a considerable extent, friction is inevitable given the two nations' overall situations. Being a nation lacking vital natural resources and large

Table 1-1
Trade Balance Data
(billions of dollars)

Year	Global Current Account Position		Bilateral Merchandise Trade Balance		Total Trade	
	U.S.	Japan	U.S. Data	Japan Data	U.S. Data	Japan Data
1970	2.3	2.0	− 1.2	1.5	10.5	10.5
1971	− 1.4	5.8	− 3.2	3.4	11.3	11.6
1972	− 5.8	6.6	− 4.1	4.0	14.0	13.9
1973	7.1	− 0.1	− 1.3	1.3	18.8	17.5
1974	2.1	− 4.7	− 1.7	1.9	23.0	23.5
1975	18.3	− 0.7	− 1.7	1.0	20.8	20.8
1976	4.4	3.7	− 5.3	5.5	25.7	25.7
1977	− 14.1	10.9	− 8.0	8.6	29.1	30.1
1978	− 14.3	16.5	−11.6	10.7	37.3	38.7
1979	− 0.8	− 8.8	− 8.6	7.6	43.8	44.4
1980[a]	0 to +5	−13 to −15	− 9.9	NA	51.0	NA

Sources: Reprinted from Japan-United States Economic Relations Group, *Report of the Japan-United States Economic Relations Group* (Prepared for the president of the United States and the prime minister of Japan, January 1981), p. 17. Current account: United States—*Survey of Current Business* Japan—*Balance of Payment Monthly* Bilateral Merchandise Trade: United States *Department of Commerce, Bureau of Census. FT 990* Japan—*Balance of Payment Monthly.*

Note: The United States has a deficit in bilateral trade, Japan a surplus.

[a]Estimated.

arable land, Japan has to depend heavily on imports to meet its domestic demand for minerals, fuels (oil alone taking up about 40 percent of its import bill), and important agricultural and forestry products such as wheat, soybeans, corn, and lumber. In order to earn the necessary foreign exchange to import these materials, Japan has to export as many manufactured products as possible. The United States happens to provide the world's largest and most prosperous market for manufactured products and it also happens to be the largest exporter of agricultural and forestry products. Although the United States is also a major exporter of manufactured goods, its share of the Japanese import market for manufactured goods has been declining from 39 percent in 1972 to 29 percent in 1978 (GAO, 1979, p. 15). Consequently, major Japanese exports to the United States consist of manufactured products that are largely high technology, whereas agricultural products and raw materials are a large part of U.S. exports to Japan. What the Japanese supply is also more likely to be available from competing U.S. firms. As Philip Caldwell of Ford Motor Company put it: "Look at the types of trade between the U.S. and Japan: What is it that Japan has that we are vitally required to have? The answer is zero."[3]

This situation is hard for Americans to abide. A generally balanced congressional report concludes that, judging by the data, "(aircraft excluded) we are a developing nation supplying a more advanced nation—we are Japan's plantation: haulers of wood and growers of crops, in exchange for high technology, value-added products . . . this relationship is not acceptable" (*United States-Japan Trade Report*, 1980, p. 5).

The trade imbalance adds to the difficulty. Combined with Japan's history of protecting her markets, it reinforces the view that the trade is a one-way street in Japan's favor and makes it difficult for U.S. officials to be accommodating to Japanese arguments without undermining their own credibility at home. Of course, as the same congressional group put it, "from an economic point of view, a bilateral merchandise trade deficit should not be an object of great concern as long as a nation's worldwide current account is in rough balance. This economic truth, however, is a political falsity" (*United States-Japan Trade Report*, 1980, p. 3).

Erosion of the Postwar International System

Another factor contributing to the U.S.-Japanese trade conflict is the erosion—at least until recently—of the bipolar international system. During the height of the cold war in the 1950s and early 1960s, the United States was primarily concerned with the cohesion of the Western coalition against the Communist bloc. Thus, U.S. leaders went out of the way to be generous and patient with Japan and other Western industrial states. Free trade among the nations of the free world was emphasized, with the U.S. government often deflecting domestic pressures for protection from imports originating in the allied countries. With the U.S. economy strong and healthy, the United States could afford to practice this benevolent policy. The allies, for their part, shared enough of the anti-Communist ideology to defer to U.S. leadership, and they welcomed, of course, the opportunity to expand their exports. Indeed, the United States not only provided a relatively open market for Japanese products but also allowed Japan "to engage in severe import and foreign exchange restrictions on goods, services, and capital."[4]

However, as cold-war tension subsided in the latter half of the 1960s, the United States began to deemphasize its patron role, becoming more and more sensitive and attentive to domestic interests. It became less and less patient with its allies over bilateral or intrabloc conflicts. This coincided with the relative decline of the macroeconomic position of the United States in the world and the declining U.S. competitiveness in specific industries. C. Fred Bergsten wrote (1971, p. 625):

> Support for continued liberal trade policies on foreign policy grounds has . . . been sharply eroded. . . . the generally reduced fear of a threat to our security from the communist world—in the industrialized or lower-income countries—renders our society increasingly unwilling to inflict economic pain on important (domestic) groups to promote our overall foreign policy.

At the same time U.S. allies became more self-assertive and less willing to defer to U.S. policy and leadership. This trend was reinforced by the serious problems of inflation and recession, which confronted most Western industrial states in the wake of the 1973 OPEC oil embargo, and by the subsequent problem of recovery and stagflation. Compared to military or security issues, economic issues involve a larger number of domestic actors (including special-interest groups and their proxies in the legislature), which makes it more difficult for governments to balance domestic politics and foreign policy.

Ironically, a combination of several factors—including the relative economic decline of the United States, floating exchange rates, and the quantitative increase in economic transactions across national boundaries—has made the international economic system far more interdependent than before. Domestic groups have become more assertive and influential at the very time the need to coordinate economic policies among Western industrial states has become even greater.

Contrasting Approaches to Trade Policy

A third contributor to trade conflict is differences in national trade policies and institutions. Both countries have developed highly effective governmental trade organizations, but the U.S. organization has traditionally performed a brokering function—balancing competing interests—in order to maintain a relatively open national and international trade regime. Japan, by contrast, has given priority to improving its balance of trade, especially with regard to export expansion.

U.S. manufacturers have long enjoyed a large and prosperous home market and have been oriented primarily toward this market. In the early postwar period, moreover, they could export easily, almost as an afterthought, and the national trade balance was consistently in the black. Thus, government trade policymakers focused not on improving this balance but rather on maintaining and expanding an open international market for all countries, through international agreements, and on minimizing U.S. trade restrictions through careful brokering with import-affected interests and their advocates in Congress. The policymaking system that evolved—a U.S. trade representative (the Office of the Special Trade Representative until 1980) in the president's executive office who balanced domestic and international concerns; special procedures and institutions, including the independent U.S. International Trade Commission (USITC) that weighed import relief claims; and strong congressional committees that controlled general trade legislation but preferred to defer to the executive and the USITC in particular product cases—was well-suited to these goals.

Japan, by contrast, began its postwar recovery with an absolute need to export in order to survive and with a persistent balance-of-payments constraint on its growth. It was logical, therefore, that Japan's government place primary trade-policy responsibility with the same agency that is responsible for industrial growth—the Ministry of International Trade and Industry (MITI). For most of the postwar period, MITI naturally gave priority to promoting exports and restraining imports. Japan's continuing need to import primary products (including 99 percent of its oil) provides a contemporary impetus in this direction. Thus, as a U.S. observer noted in 1979 (Samuelson, pp. 1072-1073):

> The gap between America's efforts to sell Japan and Japan's efforts to sell America is striking. According to Japan's MITI, Japanese companies have 764 trading offices in the United States with 20,844 workers; the comparable U.S. representation in Japan is 162 officers and 1,901 employees. But even these numbers may understate the difference, because the Japanese in the United States probably speak English and are better schooled in Americana than their U.S. counterparts are in the Japanese language and customs.[5]

In both countries, the 1970s brought some institutional adjustment. The MITI became considerably more free-trade oriented, reflecting Japan's enormous stake in open world markets and her partners' growing pressure for reciprocal market access. The U.S. trade reorganization implemented in 1980 placed greater priority on the promotion of U.S. exports. Yet contrasting trade institutions and perspectives continue, contributing to each side's frustrations in dealing with the other. Americans look for a more aggressive Japanese commitment to trade liberalization, at home and worldwide. Japanese see U.S. lags in industrial innovation and export promotion as the cause of much bilateral woe.

In Japan, the seventies brought a weakening of the overriding government-business consensus in support of high investment and rapid growth. Inflation, oil shocks, and the rise of competing social priorities have complicated the government's economic policymaking, leading to what some have labeled "immobilism." Thus, the U.S. image of "Japan, Inc.," misleading a decade ago, is even more inappropriate today.

In the United States, the same period saw a rise in the visibility of protectionist pressures and a stronger advocacy of import relief by affected industries and their allies in Congress. This did not mean that Congress imposed specific statutory restrictions on particular products; in practice, the legislative branch employed its trade-policy power sparingly. However, the executive branch was necessarily more sensitive to congressional views, particularly during the multilateral trade negotiations, because the result required congressional approval.

Psychology of Postwar U.S.-Japanese Relations

What further exacerbates bilateral economic conflicts is the outmoded yet persistent expectations that date from the first two postwar decades, the period of U.S. dominance and Japanese dependence. As noted earlier, the United States's postwar economic policy toward Japan was based on the assumption that the United States needed to help its weak Asian protégé recover and develop economically as a way of deterring Communist subversion and control. Now Japan has become a major economic power in its own right and the traditional cold-war rationale has all but disappeared in U.S. policy toward Japan. That is why the United States has come to treat Japan as an economic competitor. Yet old expectations and perceptions of each other die hard. Some Americans still tend to look on Japan as a protégé that should acquiesce to U.S. wishes. Now confident and proud of their economic achievements, the Japanese strongly resent such presumption on the part of Americans. At the same time, some Japanese still find it difficult to rid themselves of their sense of dependence on the United States as well as their image of the United States as rich and almighty, and they tend to be unusually impatient with or unsympathetic to the actual economic difficulties facing their former patron.

Americans see Japan as not only accumulating bilateral trade surpluses but also outcompeting the United States in many traditional U.S. industries, including steel, electronics, and automobiles. For some Americans, it is unthinkable that the United States would lose free competition to its Asian protégé, and they are attracted to the argument that Japan must be resorting to unfair competition.[6] This in turn irritates the Japanese, who feel they are being blamed for their hard work and efficiency—for living out the Protestant work ethic.

It is true that the United States is economically more important to Japan than vice versa. While Japan's trade in goods and services with the United States constituted 26.1 percent of its total trade in 1978 (down from 30.9 percent in 1955), the United State's trade with Japan was 12.2 percent of its total in the same year (up from 4.1 percent in 1955) (Patrick, 1980, p. 10). The Japanese economy is only one-half of the U.S. economy (although income per capita is now roughly equal) and there is still some absolute difference between the two countries in terms of their various economic capabilities. However, Japan is growing and moving faster than the United States (see table 1-2).

It is this speed of Japanese growth that seems most alarming to U.S. officials and industrialists. As a U.S. journalist wrote, "Japan's economic success has shaken American self-confidence and destroyed the foundation of a father-son political kinship" (Samuelson, 1979, p. 1068). All this creates a psychological climate not necessarily conducive to rational, cool-headed management of economic issues between the two countries.

Both U.S. and Japanese policymakers still largely subscribe to free-trade principles and understand the importance of the overall bilateral relationship. Yet they have difficulty upholding this cause of free trade or the

Table 1-2
Comparative Economic Data for Japan and the United States, 1975-1979
(in percent)

Year	Growth Rate in Real GNP		Growth in Output Per Hour in Manufacturing		Ratio of Savings to Disposable Personal Income		Ratio of Gross Domestic Fixed Capital Formation to GNP	
	United States	Japan	United States	Japan	United States	Japan	United States	Japan
1975	−1.3	1.4	5.1	−3.9	7.7	22.5	16.3	32.2
1976	5.9	6.5	4.4	8.1	5.8	22.4	16.4	31.0
1977	5.3	5.4	3.0	4.6	5.0	21.2	17.2	30.0
1978	4.4	6.0	.5	7.9	4.9	21.4P	18.0	30.5
1979	2.3	6.0	1.5	8.3	NA	NA	17.7P	31.7P

Source: Reprinted from *United States-Japan Trade Report* (Washington, D.C.: U.S. Government Printing Office, 5 September 1980), p. 8. Based on international Monetary Fund, International Financial Statistics, and U.S. Department of Commerce; International Economic Indicators. Contained in "Anti-Inflation Policies in Japan," Dick Nanto, CRS, Library of Congress, May 20, 1980, Rept. No. 80-ICOE.

alliance when dealing with specific economic issues because of the changing configurations of domestic politics in each country.

The Situation in 1977

If these were some of the general factors affecting U.S.-Japanese trade relations in the late seventies, what was the particular policy environment at the start of the period this book treats? Each country had a new government— Takeo Fukuda became Japan's Prime Minister in December 1976, twenty-seven days before Jimmy Carter's presidential inauguration. The United States had led the advanced industrial countries in recovering from the deep recession of 1974-1975, but the strength of domestic demand was generating a growing trade deficit. Japan's recovery path was quite different. For three years, Japan's economy had been squeezed very tight to thwart inflation, which had reached 24 percent in 1974. The resulting weak domestic demand and slow growth stood in sharp contrast to the remarkable double-digit average annual real growth experienced between 1960 and 1973. By 1977, inflation had been controlled and recovery was underway, but it was led by exports, the general rise of which was triggering concern among Japan's trading partners.

Particularly important to U.S. policymakers was the need to complete the multilateral trade negotiations (MTN) and have the results of that approved by Congress. In scope, the MTN was the most ambitious of the series of postwar rounds to reduce trade barriers: it sought not mainly tariff cuts but agreements on international codes to limit nontariff trade distortions like subsidies and "buy national" government procurement policies. The talks, formally inaugurated in 1973, made little progress in their first three years, but Carter's aggressive trade representative, Robert Strauss, succeeded in winning an international commitment to achieving substantial results and a schedule for their achievement. This meant, however, increased U.S. pressure on trading partners for important concessions, increased governmental sensitivity to the plight of import-impacted domestic industries (which might threaten MTN ratification), and increased concern with any overall trends in trade that might make it appear that the United States was being outdone or taken advantage of. The growing bilateral imbalance with Japan was foremost among such trends, and the remarkable burgeoning of Japan's worldwide trade and current account surpluses in 1977 and 1978 further increased the concerns of the United States.

Yet, while Japan's trading partners saw these surpluses as unwelcome results of Japanese economic power, the view in Tokyo was different. There, for Fukuda, the economic malaise, the weakness of domestic demand, was the core policy problem—the need was to stimulate home-market economic activity without rekindling inflation. It was the weakness of this market that was enlarging the trade gap, because it both limited import demand and channeled production into overseas markets. However, this perception of weakness made Japanese officials less able to initiate the sorts of trade-policy actions that the United States believed were called for by Japanese strength.

Together with the broader factors outlined, the particular policy environment of 1977 was an important general source of U.S.-Japanese trade conflict. Yet attention to these broad contextual factors, essential though it is, does not yield answers to important specific questions—about why and how particular issues escalated into major sources of political tension. Nor does it offer useful clues about how such tension might be avoided or minimized in the future. Why was the product area of prime contention in 1977-1978 not automobiles but citrus products—for, which the value of existing trade flows was less than one-hundredth as great? Why did U.S. officials end up intruding deeply into Japanese domestic economic policymaking,and why did some Japanese appear to welcome this intrusion? How was it that no major political explosion or impasse, such as the conflict over textiles in 1971, resulted? What did officials in both countries do right this time?

To shed light on questions like these is the purpose of this book. It treats the five most prominent U.S.-Japanese economic issues of 1977-1980, divided into three broad categories. The following sections in this chapter will introduce these issues.

However, a type of economic conflict *not* addressed in this book is that which arises from the tension between national economic interests and the political-strategic policies of at least one country—usually the United States. The United States asks that Japan, as an ally, curtail certain economic transactions or put them at risk; Japan sees serious economic costs if it complies with this request. A historical example was the United States's concern in the fifties about Japanese trade with the Peoples Republic of China. More recently, Japan's priority to energy security has repeatedly been in conflict with other U.S. policy objectives: in 1973, when Japan's diplomatic tilt in the Arab-Israeli conflict complicated Kissinger's effort to inaugurate peace talks (Nau, 1980); in 1977, when Japanese plans to undertake experimental nuclear reprocessing at the Tokai Mura plant came up against President Carter's nonproliferation policy; and most dramatically in December 1979, when expanded Japanese economic relations with Iran appeared to undercut the United States's efforts to get its hostages back home.

This latter case posed particular dangers for bilateral relations, because here the attentive audience was the broad U.S. public preoccupied with the hostage drama, and what they heard was the administration's denunciation of the Japanese for rushing to buy Iranian oil after the U.S. had halted its purchases and for going overboard to help Iran cope with the United States's freeze of its assets. Fortunately, the issue quickly faded, with U.S. officials embarrassed by the way it had surfaced and by the shaky factual basis for their assertions, and with the Japanese embarrassed by how their oil purchases appeared. But it suggested the likely volatility of such issues in the future.

Types of Issues

The most recent U.S.-Japanese trade conflicts can be divided into three distinct types, each with its own political pattern. The first, historically the most familiar, arises from the reaction of a U.S. industry to Japanese success in penetrating its market. The second begins with the U.S. government's efforts to secure the relaxation or removal of specific Japanese import barriers. The third arises from the United States's broader concern with the overall trade imbalance, bilateral and worldwide, and its resulting efforts to influence Japanese macroeconomic policies.

1. *U.S. Imports from Japan.* Rising imports in a particular product category cause a U.S. industry to seek protection or other U.S. government action. The executive branch seeks to respond, at least partially, to industry demands, because of the merits of the case, pressure from Congress, a presidential political commitment, or some other motivation. If the competing U.S. and Japanese industries take strong, irreconcilable positions, and their governments support them, the issue can prove extremely contentious, as did the textile negotiations of 1969-1971.

Recently, issues regarding imports have arisen concerning color televisions (and consumer electronics generally), steel, and automobiles. None of these led to major conflict between the two governments from 1977 to 1980, but each generated strong pressures and spilled over into broader trade policies and relations. The steel and automobile cases are the subject of case studies in this book.

2. *U.S. Exports to Japan.* A second pattern of conflict, particularly evident in recent years, has come from the United States's efforts to expand the Japanese market for products where U.S. producers believe they have significant comparative advantage. Typically, this kind of issue initially comes to prominence not from the pressure of an industry seeking a future gain, but from U.S. executive-branch officials—usually in the context of a broader negotiation, such as the MTN. At first, the issue may be raised quietly, with U.S. officials dissatisfied with the Japanese response. Thereafter, the pressure becomes stronger and more public, with U.S. interest groups and congressional allies joining in the campaign with the executive branch's encouragement (and sometimes orchestration).

In the period from 1977 to 1980, the primary issues falling into this category were agricultural commodities and high-technology manufactured goods. Particularly important cases included Japanese imports of beef and citrus products (treated in chapter 4) and the U.S. demand that the procurement of Japan's public corporation, Nippon Telephone and Telegraph (NTT), be opened up to non-Japanese firms (the subject of chapter 5).

3. *The Trade Imbalance and Japanese Growth Policy.* Specific trade negotiations in 1977 and 1978 took place in the context of an unprecedented overall trade imbalance. The bilateral deficit in Japan's favor grew from $5.4 billion in 1976 to $8 billion in 1977 and $11.6 billion in 1978—each figure setting a record. Worldwide, Japan's current account surplus increased from $3.7 to $10.9 to $16.5 billion over this same period, and U.S. trade worldwide was in a record deficit.

To cope with these problems, U.S. officials sought not only removal of Japanese import barriers but changes in Japanese macroeconomic policies, which they considered partially responsible for the imbalance. This effort is the subject of chapter 6.

Summaries of Cases

Chapter 2: Steel (by Hideo Sato and Michael W. Hodin)

In 1977, the U.S. steel industry was in difficulty—its domestic market showed no long-term growth trend, but imports were rising and export prospects were limited by world steel overcapacity and the United States's inability to compete on price. Moreover, Japanese steel sales in the United States had risen sharply in 1976 in response to the increased demand that recovery from the recession had generated.

The industry responded by mounting a campaign to restrict imports, and the campaign was targeted particularly at Japan. Steelmen linked their trade problems to unfair practices of foreign firms and governments, particularly subsidies (though they lacked hard, current evidence of such practices in Japan) and sought relief under U.S. statutes combating such practices. They particularly sought quantitative limits on imports, such as had existed under a U.S.-Japanese-EEC voluntary restraint agreement in existence from 1969 through 1975. Specifically, in October 1976, the American Iron and Steel Institute (AISI) filed a formal complaint under the 1974 Trade Act's provision for unjustifiable or unreasonable foreign trade practices. The AISI charged that Japanese producers were diverting shipments from Europe to the United States. The Gilmore Steel Corporation, a small Oregon firm, followed in February 1977 with an antidumping suit against five major Japanese steelmakers. In the meantime, U.S. industry and labor officials were urging their Japanese counterparts to conclude orderly marketing agreements limiting Japanese sales to the U.S. market.

Increasingly the industry worked with congressional allies in pressuring the Carter administration to take action against imports. The administration could not ignore such pressure, because it was engaged in pushing through the multilateral trade negotiations (MTN). The MTN agreements required congressional approval, and this would have been difficult to obtain if a major industry, such as steel, had stood in opposition.

Japanese steelmakers thought the AISI emphasis on unfair trade practices was basically unfounded, at least insofar as they were concerned. They prided themselves on their modern, efficient, internationally competitive plants. However, while they abhorred the charges and the legal actions, they took the campaign as evidence of the U.S. industry's seriousness in seeking import controls. The major Japanese firms were quite willing to contemplate an intergovernmental orderly marketing agreement (OMA). Unlike their counterparts in textiles, electronics, and many other industries, Japanese steel leaders had been extremely sensitive to the United States's criticisms for a variety of reasons, including their indebtedness to the United States for postwar assistance as well as their fear of losing their large share of the U.S. market. Indeed, Yoshihiro Inayama of Nippon Steel, head of the Japan Iron and Steel Federation (JISF), was known as "Mr. Cartel" for his emphasis on the need for export restraint.

Officials at the Ministry of International Trade and Industry (MITI) were sympathetic to the JISF view that an orderly marketing agreement was desirable; they saw the initiation of negotiations, however, as up to the United States, and they found the Carter administration extremely reluctant to take this course. The administration had just negotiated an OMA with Japan for color televisions and one with Korea and Taiwan for shoes, and it had no wish for more such agreements. Moreover, it saw quantitative restrictions as an invitation to the U.S. industry to raise its prices, exacerbating inflation. Thus, the administration took no action as the issue heated up through the spring, summer, and early fall. Industry charges of Japanese unfairness, meanwhile, were highlighted in the Japanese press, generating considerable resentment.

Finally, the U.S. steel industry forced the issue by generating what some called a "firestorm" on Capitol Hill. In September, senators and representatives from producing states formed steel caucuses; the combination of their pressure and plant closings generated front-page attention. The campaign received further impetus when the Treasury Department made a preliminary determination in favor of the Gilmore suit, at least partly because the Japanese firms, arguing operational confidentiality, declined to supply cost-of-production data the Treasury needed to enforce the U.S. law. President Carter responded by forming an interagency task force headed by Undersecretary of the Treasury Anthony Solomon, who was to provide the strong leadership on this issue that the government had previously lacked. Then, on October 13, Carter met with industry and labor leaders and promised vigorous pursuit of antidumping investigations (by now, U.S. steel had filed a suit of its own). In exchange, the industry dropped its call for quotas.

The use of U.S. antidumping laws as a solution was anathema to the Japanese, who argued that these laws themselves were unfair because of how they defined dumping. Europeans were, if anything, even less receptive to this approach. Over the next month, in consultation with Europeans and Japanese, the Solomon task force worked out an alternative, innovative trigger price mechanism (TPM) that was to be enforced unilaterally by the United States but with foreign cooperation. Minimum import prices would be set for different categories of steel, and these prices would be based on the costs of the world's most efficient producers—the Japanese. If products entered the United States at prices below these, the Treasury would itself initiate an antidumping investigation. In the meantime, however, industry antidumping suits would be withdrawn.

In short-run political terms, the TPM was a striking success. The U.S. industry got some protection; the Japanese industry got an orderly U.S. import regime plus official recognition of its role as world pacesetter (although the TPM itself discriminated in favor of less efficient producers, particularly in the European Community (EC), and the Japanese share of the U.S. market declined significantly in 1978). The U.S. government got both a quieting of the political storm and some de facto control over steel prices. And when the MTN came before Congress in 1979, steel senators and representatives voted in favor of it.

Chapter 3: Automobiles (by Gilbert R. Winham and Ikuo Kabashima)

In the 1970s, U.S. automobile imports doubled, rising from 1.26 million in 1970 to 2.32 million in 1979. The Japanese share of these imports tripled, as Japan's automakers—who had sold mainly to domestic buyers in the sixties—moved aggressively onto the world stage. For most of the decade, the political response of U.S. automakers and labor was muted. The companies' main earnings were from sales of large cars at home and from plants overseas, neither of which was directly threatened by small-car imports. The United Auto Workers (UAW), the most liberal of the United States's large unions, did express growing concern, but it mainly sought to persuade Japanese companies to open plants in the United States. Thus, despite their central importance to both national economies, automobiles did not figure prominently in either the substance of the MTN agreements or the politics of their ratification by the U.S. Congress.

However, as the decade ended, an automobile crisis suddenly emerged. Revolution in Iran triggered a round of oil-price increases by OPEC countries, driving U.S. gasoline prices higher and bringing temporary but well-publicized shortages and gasoline lines. What had been a gradual shift toward small cars in consumer preferences was suddenly accelerated, and U.S. automakers were unready to meet this demand. Recession compounded their problems, as did the spreading view that U.S.-built cars were inferior in quality to Japanese imports. Chrysler was saved from immediate bankruptcy by special government loan guarantees; Ford and General Motors also suffered record losses; and industry employment dropped by 29 percent.

By early 1980, automobiles had become the most important trade issue facing the Carter administration and the hottest U.S.-Japanese issue. In February, UAW President Douglas Fraser, frustrated by the limited success of previous calls for Japanese investment, made a well-publicized trip to Japan, where he argued not only for Toyota and Nissan to build plants in the United States (Honda had already announced plans to do so), but for restraint in Japanese car exports to the U.S. Market. Then and subsequently, MITI leaders sought to persuade Toyota and Nissan to invest, but with only limited success. They also moved reluctantly to the view that some form of export restraint might be necessary, but they hesitated to act without U.S. initiative. Without official U.S. participation in import restraints, the Japanese might be vulnerable to action under U.S. antitrust laws barring restraint of trade. Moreover, the MITI needed a formal U.S. request as leverage with the auto companies, who were reluctant to restrain exports—partly because of intense competition among them—and over whom the MITI's power was limited.

The immediate U.S. response to UAW pressure was stated by U.S. Trade Representative Reubin Askew's congressional testimony in March: the United States was opposed to quotas, but it strongly supported Japanese investment. As the issue heated up, it became intertwined with the electoral campaign, with President Carter in urgent need of UAW support. Divisions within the U.S. government grew, with Transportation Secretary Neil Goldschmidt supporting quotas and the Office of the U.S. Special Trade Representative (USTR) unable to establish clear primacy on the issue. The two governments did negotiate some further liberalization of Japanese auto-import policies, such as eliminating tariffs on auto parts (automobile tariffs, as high as 50 percent in 1967, had already become zero in 1978) and making it easier for U.S. manufacturers to meet Japanese product standards. In the critical U.S. market, however, the action was forced on June 12 when the UAW petitioned the U.S. International Trade Commission for relief under the escape-clause provision of U.S. trade law, claiming that imports caused serious injury to the industry and urging sharp, temporary import cutbacks to provide relief. The Ford Motor Company joined in the petition.

By this time, the automobile issue had become one of the most visible U.S.-Japanese trade issues of the postwar period. Pressure from congressional sources increased, although it took the form of hearings and general resolutions aimed at influencing the U.S. administration—and the Japanese—rather than legislation for a statutory solution. President Carter, after a thorough interagency review, stopped in Detroit (en route to Prime Minister Ohira's funeral) to announce a $1 billion relief program for the auto industry, grandly packaged as the beginning of a close-knit, permanent partnership between Washington and Detroit as part of a broad new industrial policy. He also urged the ITC to expedite its investigation of the UAW petition. The commission did so, but it decided to make its findings known after, not before (as Carter had asked), the fall election.

On November 10, the ITC voted against the UAW and Ford by a three-to-two vote. All commissioners concluded that the auto industry had suffered injury, but the majority found that imports were a less important cause then recession, high interest rates, and the shift in the consumer demand from large to small cars. Thus, under the law, they could not recommend import restrictions.

This negative finding deprived Carter of clear authority to negotiate restraints with Japan. The House of Representatives responded by passing, in December, a resolution granting the president this authority, but it was easy for Senate opponents to block this resolution in the waning days of the session. However, John Danforth and Lloyd Bentsen, senior members of the Senate Trade Subcommittee, introduced a quota bill in January and said they would press for its enactment unless restraints on Japanese exports were achieved. There was, in fact, evidence of some de facto restraint in late 1980: MITI Minister Rokusuke Tanaka had explicitly forecast reduced sales on September 17, a statement immediately and favorably acknowledged by President Carter. But with sales of U.S.-made cars remaining sluggish into 1981, pressure for more formal restrictions continued, making autos the first major trade problem confronted by the Reagan administration.

Initially, the leaders in the new administration split visibly on whether there should be any trade restrictions, very much as the Carter administration had split. However, by April 1981, the administration was clearly seeking an export-restraint arrangement that would be undertaken and implemented by Japan alone. In form, this result was achieved on May 1 when the MITI announced it would apply an overall quota of 1.68 million cars to 1981 exports, down from 1.82 million in 1980. But the Japanese succeeded in getting the United States to share responsibility for this outcome. In fact,

U.S. Trade Representative William Brock flew to Tokyo to discuss (not negotiate) the arrangement as it was being put into final shape and announced. His communications with congressional leaders led to the immediate shelving of the Danforth-Bentsen quota bill.

This "nonagreement," as it was quickly labeled, cooled the immediate political crisis, but a longer-run structural problem remained. Japanese and U.S. automakers had approached the world market in opposite ways: General Motors and Ford had approached it by investing and producing overseas; Toyota and Nissan had approached it through home-based manufacturing and exports. The auto crisis of 1979-1981 suggested there might be enduring political limits to the Japanese firms' approach—their overseas sales were vulnerable in a way that sales of cars produced abroad by U.S. firms were not.

*Chapter 4: Agriculture (by Hideo Sato
and Timothy J. Curran)*

The agricultural trade issue of 1977-1978, which particularly concerned beef and citrus, arose in the context of the MTN and an enormous bilateral trade imbalance. Although beef and citrus involved only a tiny fraction of the total bilateral trade, the United States focused on the Japanese import quotas on these products, which came to be seen as symbols of the closed Japanese market. Beef and oranges represented two of the twenty-seven residual import quotas Japan still maintained against GATT rules. (The negotiations did not address U.S. beef-import quotas, or disease-control regulations barring the import of Japanese mandarin oranges to all but six U.S. states.)

At first, beef and citrus, among other products, were simply mentioned by U.S. officials as possible import-liberalization items for consideration by the Japanese government. Failing to obtain sufficient Japanese response to this and other proposals, the United States intensified its pressure in the late fall of 1977, starting with the trade mission, headed by STR General Counsel Richard Rivers, in November.

The Japanese strongly resisted the demand for full import liberalization. Japanese farmers enjoy considerable political power because of their close association with the ruling Liberal Democratic Party (LDP) and a skewed electoral district system that favors rural areas. They are also effectively organized under the name of Nokyo (Agricultural Cooperative Association). Moreover, Japanese citrus growers faced a serious problem of overproduction, and beef-cattle farmers were still recovering from the damage they had suffered in 1973-1974, when the doubling of beef imports was followed by a drastic reduction of domestic demand in the wake of the

OPEC oil embargo. However, under strong U.S. pressure, Agriculture Minister Ichiro Nakagawa acceded to discussions of incremental import expansion.

In January 1978, an agreement was reached as part of broader negotiations between STR Robert Strauss and Minister for External Economic Affairs Nobuhiko Ushiba. Japan consented to a threefold increase in its annual import quota for fresh oranges, a fourfold increase in its citrus-juice quota, and a threefold increase in the hotel-beef quota.

This Strauss-Ushiba agreement did not end the issue, however. Instead, it whetted the appetite of U.S. domestic producers for Japanese concessions. Believing that the issue had been settled once and for all, Japanese producers mounted emotional resistance to renewed U.S. pressure for liberalization of Japanese beef and citrus imports in the spring and summer of 1978.

In July, the United States agreed to shelve its demand for full liberalization and suggested specific trade-expansion figures. Japanese officials thought that this U.S. compromise offer might lead to prompt settlement. But the Nakagawa-Strauss talks in September proved otherwise. A press leak about the July concession alarmed U.S. producers, who had been kept in the dark about it. Moreover, charges of alleged profiteering and scandal among privileged Japanese fruit importers circulated among U.S. citrus growers, strengthening their determination to press for maximum concessions from Tokyo. So Strauss, needing to respond to competing demands from Florida and California orange growers, toughened the U.S. position, to the surprise and disappointment of Japanese officials. Another series of talks ensued at both political and working levels, and it was not until mid-November that Ministry of Agriculture, Forestry, and Fisheries (MAFF) Economic Affairs Bureau Director Nobuo Imamura and Deputy STR Alonzo McDonald arrived at a tentative agreement formula in the course of their Geneva talks.

In early December, Ministers Nakagawa and Ushiba met in Tokyo with Ambassador Mike Mansfield and Deputy STR Alan Wolff with the aim of concluding the issue. There Wolff made one more attempt to get the Japanese to discuss a timetable for liberalization—but to no avail. The two sides concluded the talks—basically along the line of the Imamura-McDonald formula—on December 5, just hours before Prime Minister Takeo Fukuda and his cabinet stepped down as a result of Fukuda's unexpected loss to Masayoshi Ohira in the party's primary election. According to the agreement, Japan's annual importation of fresh oranges, orange juice, and high-quality beef would, by 1983, be roughly double the amounts promised in the Strauss-Ushiba agreement in January, with the understanding that post-1983 trade expansion would be a subject of future intergovernmental discussion.

Japanese beef and citrus producers acquiesced in the settlement between the two governments, and U.S. producers, basically happy with the results, subsequently endorsed the MTN package.

Chapter 5: Nippon Telephone and Telegraph (NTT)
Procurement (by Timothy J. Curran)

During the MTN negotiations for a code on government procurement, the United States requested that Japan place purchases by its state-owned public corporations, including Nippon Telephone and Telegraph Company (NTT), under the code's open bidding procedures, allowing foreign firms to compete for that business. The Japanese resisted the United States's request, arguing that most telephone systems follow closed procurement practices similar to Japan's. Detailed and complex negotiations throughout late 1978 and early 1979 failed to bring a solution. As the dispute festered, it became entangled with preparations for summit meetings to be held in May and June 1979. Many feared that a major confrontation would be sparked when a highly publicized series of negotiations collapsed in March and April.

The NTT confrontation began in Geneva. In the summer of 1978, the United States offered to open about $16 billion of its government contracts to open bidding, while the EC offered about $10.5 billion and the Japanese offered about $3.5 billion. Arguing that this Japanese offer was disproportionately low, the U.S. officials requested that Japan add to it the purchases of its three public corporations. Of these, NTT was the largest, with procurement totaling $3 billion. At this point, U.S. interest focused on NTT because of the amount of the company's purchases, not because of their high-technology content.

The Japanese were unable to comply with the request. NTT used a closed, negotiated system of procurement and made 97 percent of its purchases from a small family of Japanese suppliers. Contrary to the initial assumption of U.S. government officials, the central government in Japan did not exercise direct control over the public corporations, particularly NTT, which had developed a number of formal and informal means to insulate itself from central authority. NTT was determined to resist open procurement in order to protect its relationships with local suppliers and prevent the possible leakage of high-technology secrets. Its power to resist was increased when the job of pressing for industry concessions was given to the Ministry of Foreign Affairs, which lacked expertise and credibility in this area of policy.

As the NTT stalemate continued, the issue became intertwined with broader U.S. criticism of Japan's trade practices. Two groups in particular, the Commerce Department's staff supporting the U.S.-Japan Trade

Facilitation Committee and the House Ways and Means Committee's Task Force on U.S.-Japan Trade, focused on NTT's restrictive buying practices. In November 1978, three task-force members visiting Tokyo called at NTT headquarters to request greater access to its high-technology procurement. The meeting was unproductive, and the U.S. representatives returned to the United States angry at what they saw as NTT's extreme inflexibility. They began to call NTT a symbol of Japan's closed market. In their widely publicized report of January 1979, issued in both Japan and the United States, they labeled NTT procurement policies "one of the sorest points in our bilateral trade." Citing the overall imbalance in telecommunications trade, they added: "Since telecommunications is one of the industries 'of the future,' this type of one-sided and unfair trade competition is particularly serious" (*Task Force Report*, 1979, p. 33).

As negotiations continued in 1979, U.S. negotiators increasingly stressed the technological importance of this issue—the focus shifted from the amount of NTT's purchases to the content of those purchases. But the Americans did not specify which particular high-technology goods they most wished NTT to open to competitive bidding, although they felt their general emphasis was clear. This lack of specificity weakened the hand of the Ohira government in Tokyo, which had begun belated but very determined efforts to pressure NTT into making some concessions to U.S. demands.

Tension increased as the NTT negotiations became entangled with the approaching bilateral and multilateral summit meetings. The most serious clashes took place on the eve of the May 1979 Carter-Ohira meeting in Washington, when Japanese offers, which contained increased access to NTT's contracts but still lacked certain high-technology items, were rejected by U.S. trade officials, resulting in a widely publicized stalemate. With just hours to spare before the start of the bilateral summit, a procedural solution was reached that set a common negotiating objective and postponed future negotiations until after the summit. In June 1979, Robert Strauss and Nobuhiko Ushiba signed an interim agreement on NTT, in which the two countries agreed to negotiate for a settlement by December 31, 1980, on the basis of "mutual reciprocity . . . in access opportunities to each other's markets." The United States, in the meantime, indicated that it would deny Japanese firms access to U.S. contracts under the MTN government procurement code unless a satisfactory deal on NTT was achieved.

Finally, in December 1980, the two governments reached an agreement that would open all NTT procurement to bidding by U.S. firms; the technologically most sophisticated products, however, were to remain outside the GATT government procurement code. In early 1981, the Motorola Company succeeded in winning a fairly important NTT contract.

*Chapter 6: Macrodiplomacy (by I.M. Destler
and Hisao Mitsuyu)*

The Japanese surplus of 1977-1978 had its roots in the inflationary explosion earlier in the decade. Spurred by a combination of expansionist economic policies and the OPEC oil shock of 1973-1974, Japan's consumer price index for 1974 jumped 24.3 percent over the previous year's, and the wholesale price index rose 31.4 percent. Senior LDP leader Takeo Fukuda was installed as government economic czar to combat this inflation. He maintained very tight monetary and fiscal policies through the end of 1975, more than a year after the onset of worldwide recession, and price stability was restored. The wholesale price index, for example, rose by only 1.9 percent in Japan's fiscal year (JFY) 1975 (April 1975 to March 1976) and by only 5.5 percent in JFY 1976.

A side effect of these policies was to delay Japan's recovery from recession. When recovery came, it was led by exports, resulting in a substantial current-account surplus—$4.7 billion in JFY 1976. When Fukuda became prime minister in December 1976, he declared his intention to right this balance by strengthening domestic demand, and his JFY 1977 budget called for expanded spending in public works. However, Japanese private economists questioned whether investment and consumer spending would grow enough to make the key targets (7 percent economic growth, and a current-account deficit of $700 million) attainable.

U.S. recovery from the recession had, by contrast, been relatively rapid, and the Carter administration's economic officials came to power determined to accelerate it further. To promote international balance, they pressed the "locomotive thesis: that the three strong advanced industrial economies (West Germany, Japan, and the United States) should stimulate demand and draw in imports, pulling the weaker economies along. Vice-President Walter Mondale sounded this theme in his postinauguration trip to Europe and Japan. The United States and its allies, the United Kingdom in particular, continued to urge stronger Japanese (and German) growth at the London economic summit of May and at OECD and IMF meetings that summer and early fall. They also pressed the Ministry of Finance and the Bank of Japan not to prevent the yen's value from rising. (The United States was convinced it had done so in 1976 by intervening heavily in foreign exchange markets.) The yen did move sharply upward in 1977—from 289 in January to 277 in April, 266 in July, and 240 by year's end.

However, Japan's growth rate lagged and the surplus, contrary to government projections, was rapidly rising. The United States increasingly saw this surplus as a major international problem (viewing Japan as a drag on world economic recovery) that threatened to become, in combination with specific trade disputes and the growing U.S. deficit, a U.S. political problem. When State and Treasury Department officials raised the issue at subcabinet bilateral talks in September, their Japanese counterparts neither challenged the U.S. definition of the problem nor took clear action to address it.

The rise of the yen, however, was fueling discontent with Fukuda's economic policies in the Japanese business community. So the United States turned up the pressure, encouraged by some Japanese, who saw external pressure as useful in their internal economic policy struggle. MITI officials in particular were expansionist-minded, while Finance people adamantly resisted. In late November, a U.S. mission presented a number of specific trade and economic policy demands—including a 7 to 8 percent growth target for JFY 1978—and its visibility and pressure were magnified by the Tokyo media. In subsequent weeks, Fukuda reshuffled his cabinet to put expansionists in key positions, and his government adopted the 7 percent growth target, planning to achieve it with record deficit spending. The growth target was incorporated in the Strauss-Ushiba joint statement of January 1978; also incorporated in the statement was a prediction, which some Americans read as a promise, of marked diminution of the current-account surplus.

The statement calmed the political waters, but, despite the new Japanese policy goals, growth lagged and the surplus grew. It reached $14 billion for JFY 1977, and figures for the spring and summer indicated it might be even larger in 1978. At the Bonn summit of July 1978, the United States won a reiteration of the growth target (paired with a similar German pledge), and a promise from Fukuda to adopt a supplementary stimulus package if needed. One was adopted in September. Meanwhile, the United States was bowing out as a locomotive. Inflation was accelerating well beyond the U.S. government's predictions, the dollar was plummeting, and Carter promised at Bonn to combat inflation and to pursue an effective energy policy. This promise was followed by a major dollar-defense initiative in November: a sharp tightening of U.S. monetary policy and an international program of exchange-market intervention in which Japan was a major participant.

In December 1978, Masayoshi Ohira upset Fukuda in the LDP presidential primary. In his first press conference as prime minister, Ohira announced that Japan was abandoning the 7 percent growth target as unreachable. Washington's reaction was sharp. Officials were frustrated by the persistent Japanese surplus, exhausted by a series of difficult bilateral trade negotiations, and worried about congressional action on the MTN in 1979. Carter dispatched a strongly critical letter to Fukuda, which was read (probably incorrectly) as a threat that he might not attend the Tokyo economic summit scheduled for June 1979. The Japanese who saw the letter were, in turn, shocked and angered by it.

Fortunately, both sides then moved away from confrontation. A group of U.S. economic forecasters visited Tokyo in January and concluded that, unlike previous years' Japanese government current account projections, the one for JFY 1979 (anticipating marked improvement) was plausible. And Japan's current account balance did, at long last, move rapidly from surplus to deficit. By the May 1979 bilateral summit, it was possible to put national macroeconomic policy commitments in more general, reciprocal form. It was then agreed that both the Japanese surplus and the U.S. deficit were not appropriate, but that there had been significant reduction of both in recent months. Japan would foster domestically led growth and continue to open up her markets; the United States would reduce inflation, restrain oil imports, and promote exports. The period of visible macroeonomic policy conflict was over.

Conclusion

These brief summaries suffice to give the reader some initial sense of the cases this book treats—why they were important and how they played themselves out. Chapters 2 through 6 tell their fuller stories. In so doing, they provide the base for our conclusions, presented in chapter 7.

Notes

1. U.S. economic statistics suggest that the average price of exported goods nearly tripled during this period and the average price of imports nearly quadrupled (see table B-3 in *Economic Report of the President*, January 1981, p. 237). The statistics in the text are drawn from U.S. Commerce Department data, unless other sources are cited.

2. Real U.S. GNP doubled between 1960 and 1980. Real Japanese GNP in 1980 was about five times its real GNP in 1960.

3. Peter Behr, "Ford Chairman Restates Need for 3-year Limit on Japanese Auto Imports," interview in *The Washington Post*, 2 November 1980. Reprinted with permission.

4. Hugh T. Patrick, "The Economic Dimensions of the United States-Japanese Alliance: An Overview," unpublished paper, Yale University, 1980, p. 6. Reprinted with permission.

5. Robert J. Samuelson, "U.S., Japan Find Old Relationships Have Unraveled," *National Journal*, 30 June 1979, pp. 1072-1073. Reprinted with permission.

6. For a cogent elaboration of this point, see Angel, "Japan's Most Serious Economic Problem in the U.S., 1979.

References

Angel, Robert C. "Japan's Most Serious Economic Problem in the U.S." Washington, D.C.: United States-Japan Trade Council, 1979.

Bergsten, C. Fred. "Crisis in U.S. Trade Policy." *Foreign Affairs*, July 1971, pp. 619-634.

Destler, I.M.; Sato, Hideo; Clapp, Priscilla; and Fukui, Haruhiro. *Managing an Alliance: The Politics of U.S.-Japanese Relations*. Washington, D.C.: Brookings Institution, 1976.

Destler, I.M.; Fukui, Haruhiro; and Sato, Hideo. *The Textile Wrangle: Conflict in Japanese-American Relations, 1969-1971*. Ithaca and London: Cornell University Press, 1979.

Japan-United States Economic Relations Group. `Report of the Japan-United States Economic Relations Group`. Prepared for the president of the United States and the prime minister of Japan, January 1981.

Nau, Henry R. "Japanese-American Relations During the 1973-1974 Oil Crisis." In *Oil and the Atom: Issues in U.S.-Japan Energy Relations*, edited by Michael Blaker. New York: East Asian Institute, Columbia University, 1980.

Patrick, Hugh T. "The Economic Dimensions of the United States-Japan Alliance: An Overview." Unpublished paper, Yale University, 1980.

Rapp, William V., and Feldman, Robert A. "Japan's Economic Strategy and Prospects." In *Japan and the United States: Challenges and Opportunities*, edited by William J. Barnds. New York: New York University Press (for the Council on Foreign Relations), 1979.

Samuelson, Robert J. "U.S., Japan Find Old Relationships Have Unraveled." *National Journal*, 30 June 1979, pp. 1068-1079.

U.S., Congress, House, Subcommittee on Trade of the Committee on Ways and Means, *Task Force Report on United States-Japan Trade*, 95th Cong., 2d sess., 1979.

_____ . *United States-Japan Trade Report*. Washington, D.C.: U.S. Government Printing Office, 5 September 1980.

U.S. General Accounting Office. *United States-Japan Trade: Issues and Problems*. Washington, D.C.: U.S. Government Printing Office, 21 September 1979.

Ushiba, Nobuhiko. "United States-Japan Economic Relations: Bilateral Problems and Global Responsibilities." Speech delivered at the Annual Meeting of the American Bar Association, Honolulu, August 1980.

The Washington Post, 2 November 1980.

The U.S.-Japanese Steel Issue of 1977

Hideo Sato and
Michael W. Hodin

In the recent past, U.S.-Japanese trade issues have followed a familiar pattern. First, growing Japanese imports cause the domestic industry to seek protection through the U.S. government. Then, the U.S. government approaches the Japanese government to accept some type of trade restraint, often voluntary export restraint. The Japanese government refuses to comply due to domestic industry opposition, and the issue is progressively politicized the longer it remains unresolved.

In 1977, increasing Japanese steel imports did cause the U.S. industry to seek U.S. government actions in reducing imports, but intergovernmental negotiations in the traditional sense did not ensue. The U.S. government never formally asked the Japanese government for export restraint. Typically, Japanese and U.S. industries maintain incompatible or contradictory interests that cause the two governments (each representing domestic industry interests) to clash or, at least, to go through difficult negotiations in search of a mutually acceptable compromise between domestic and alliance interests. However, unlike in the textile wrangle of 1969-1971 and in the more recent color-television issue, the competing U.S. and Japanese industries did not take strong, irreconcilable positions. Nevertheless, steel became a major source of trade friction between Japan and the United States in 1977. It was not until December that the tensions between the two countries began to ease. It was then that the Carter administration announced it would establish a trigger price mechanism (TPM) for controlling the prices of foreign steel imported into the U.S. market.

This study will examine closely how steel became a major source of bilateral tension in 1977, with special focus on the politics of policymaking in both countries and the interaction between them. It will begin with a concise account of the U.S. industry's efforts to limit foreign steel imports during the decade preceding 1977 and with a brief overview of the economic and political setting in which the steel issue developed that year.

Sato's contribution to this chapter draws substantially on data collected for his joint project with Hugh Patrick, "The Political Economy of U.S.-Japanese Relations." He is grateful to Patrick for allowing him to use the data as well as for giving him useful comments on his draft.

Background to the Issue

By the late 1960s, it had become clear that the U.S. steel industry no longer enjoyed the competitive advantage to which it had become accustomed before and after World War II. In a broader sense, the steel industry in the immediate postwar period did not have to think much about the subtleties and nuances of international trade: for them, there was no particular reason to waste political capital on a U.S. policy toward imports and exports. Instead, they were able to engage in a general support of the popular free-trade position: to help build up Europe and Japan. And why not? Strong, competitive, knowledgeable U.S. industries such as steel were then affected little by the fledgling industries of Japan and West Germany. The industry operated at or near peak capacity except during occasional recessions. There was enough demand at home—for automobiles, construction, and refrigerators, for example—to persist in believing the theory that smaller markets abroad were not worth the effort. Others could supply those markets and, besides, the industrial development of Japan and Europe was synonymous with patriotism and security.

Indeed, the country's foreign-policy elite had already interpreted economic growth in war-torn Europe and Japan as a necessary and integral part of building a web of strong democracies. U.S. policy in those days not only supported the growth of the Japanese and West European industrial economies, but actually promoted them as part of the building of U.S. security arrangements in the post-World War II period. In particular, the development of basic industries such as steel was considered necessary by all if those security arrangements were to be long-lasting and effective.

Thus, steel and similar industries were complacent in their attitude toward markets outside the United States and, in general, to international trade. That complacency was implicitly encouraged by the foreign-policy assumptions of the period. So the steel industry failed to integrate into its long-term strategic planning the possibility that the rate of growth of the U.S. market would decline and that the competitive advantage of others would grow concomitantly. If they had taken this into account, other attitudes might have prevailed and different policies might have followed. One course might have been to invest abroad or to begin to export—in short, to penetrate other markets. But the industry did not do that (see table 2-1).

As others became stronger and the competition grew, the industry was forced to struggle with smaller shares of the home market. In 1977, steel imports into the United States comprised about 18 percent of apparent domestic consumption, considerably higher than the 5 percent level experienced at the beginning of the sixties and also substantially more troublesome to the industry than the 10 percent level reached in the mid-

Table 2-1
U.S. Steel Mill Products, 1958-1978
(in thousands of tons)

Year	Domestic Shipments[a]	Exports[a]	Imports[a]	Apparent Domestic Consumption[a]	Imports as a Percent of Apparent Domestic Consumption
1958	59,914	2,823	1,707	58,798	2.9
1959	69,377	1,677	4,306	72,096	6.1
1960	71,149	2,977	3,359	71,531	4.7
1961	66,126	1,990	3,163	67,299	4.7
1962	70,552	2,013	4,100	72,639	5.6
1963	75,555	2,224	5,446	78,777	6.9
1964	84,945	3,442	6,440	87,943	7.3
1965	92,666	2,496	10,383	100,553	10.3
1966	89,995	1,724	10,753	99,024	10.9
1967	83,897	1,605	11,455	93,667	12.2
1968	91,856	2,170	17,960	107,646	16.7
1969	91,877	5,229	14,034	102,682	13.7
1970	90,798	7,062	13,364	97,100	13.8
1971	87,038	2,027	18,304	102,515	17.9
1972	91,805	2,073	17,681	106,613	16.6
1973	111,430	4,052	15,150	122,528	12.4
1974	109,472	5,033	15,970	119,609	13.4
1975	79,957	2,953	12,012	89,016	13.5
1976	89,447	2,654	14,285	101,078	14.1
1977	91,147	2,003	19.306	108,450	17.8
1978	97,935	2,422	21,135	116,648	18.1

Source: Domestic shipments—American Iron and Steel Institute: exports and imports—U.S. Department of Commerce. All of these are as reported in the *Survey of Current Business,* various issues.
[a]Apparent Domestic Consumption = Domestic Shipments − Exports + Imports.

sixties. The low prices that accompanied the increased market percentage further undercut the U.S. steel industry's profitability.

Predictably, different reasons are offered by different groups to explain the industry's plight. Some blame the steel labor agreements, citing in particular the long strike of 1959, which ensured ever-spiraling labor costs that the industry could afford less and less. Others emphasize the costs of government-imposed environmental and health and safety regulations, especially since these regulations come at a time when capital shortages needed for modernization already posed serious problems. Still another view holds that the industry itself mismanaged its investments and research and development and, therefore, did not modernize to the degree it now seems evident it might have. Indeed, this latter argument points to the industry's complacency, born of success, as well as to its failure to perceive the prospects of a Japanese industrial success in international markets, including the United States. In a move that was thought prudent at the time, the risks involved with new technology and processes were left to the newer entrants in Japan, West Germany, and the smaller companies at home. Thus, the large capital investments that were needed to modernize the industry were not committed. This view argues that the U.S. steel industry seemed to be content with producing for home consumption and presumed continued preeminence here.

All of these views hold some truth. However, to understand the events of 1977, one must also look at the changing state of the world steel market since the 1960s. By 1977, the growth in steelmaking capacity had far outpaced demand, which lead to a condition of global overcapacity and oversupply. Steelmaking capacity in the industrial world went from about 400 million net tons in 1967 to about 550 million tons in 1976, while consumption remained about the same, slightly less than 300 million net tons (Central Intelligence Agency, 1977). Moreover, the structural dilemma of overcapacity had been exacerbated in the 1974-1977 period by an especially slow rate of growth in Europe, the United States, and Japan. Complicating matters still further was the uneven rates of recovery following the recession of 1974-1975. As the United States began to recover in 1975-1976 with more rigor than its trading partners, it acted as a kind of magnet, attracting steel that was being produced elsewhere but that was in less demand in those other markets. It was such global overcapacity, exacerbated by conditions associated with the 1974-1975 recession and its aftermath, that contributed to the surge in imports into the United States in 1976, thus setting the stage again for U.S. industry campaigns to limit foreign steel imports.

Indeed, the 1977 issue was preceded by earlier U.S. industry efforts to limit foreign steel imports. And, as we shall see in our study of the 1977 issue, earlier efforts were also focused in large measure on encouraging congressional allies to pressure the executive branch into making policies that would limit imports. In 1967, Representative Thomas Burke of Massachusetts and Senator Vance Hartke of Indiana submitted an omnibus bill providing for mandatory import quotas on a number of products, including steel. As a preemptive move, however, the State Department negotiated a three-year voluntary restraint agreement (VRA) with Japanese and European steel exporters. The VRA went into effect on January 1, 1969, and was then extended in 1972 for another three years. The industry, of course, supported these agreements, as did the foreign producers involved, on the theory that it gave them the least bad deal by ensuring substantial market percentages for their product.

Among those unhappy with the VRA, however, were consumer groups in the United States, who believed then, and argue still, that a cheaper product, no matter its origin, ought not to be denied the U.S. consumer. In addition to their opposition to the VRA on these economic grounds, the consumer groups also voiced the concern that such agreements merely legitimized and made easier an industry's ability to control prices and, therefore, markets.

Thus, in October 1972, the Consumers Union of the United States brought an antitrust suit against the State Department, the domestic steel industry, and foreign steel producers, charging that the parties to the VRA violated the Sherman Act by conspiring to restrain foreign commerce. The U.S. Court of Appeals upheld the State Department's authority to negotiate the agreement and dismissed an expression by the district court suggesting that there was an antitrust violation. (The counsel agreed to withdraw the antitrust issue from the case because it would have required protracted litigation.) However, this case led the major parties involved to believe that the VRA should not be renewed when it expired in early 1975. There were other courses that U.S. industry and labor could pursue, however, to prevail upon their government to restrain foreign imports. One such course was made available by the Trade Act of 1974.

In July 1975, U.S. specialty steel (alloy steel and stainless steel) producers, backed by the United Steelworkers of America (USW), filed a petition for relief from imports under the escape-clause provision of the Trade Act of 1974. In January 1976, the International Trade Commission (ITC) ruled in favor of the industry. It recommended that import quotas be imposed for a five-year period on a product-by-product basis. Upon receipt of this recommendation, President Ford instructed Special Trade Representative (STR) Frederick B. Dent to negotiate orderly marketing agreements (OMA)—intergovernmental voluntary restraint agreements that did not risk antitrust violations—with principal exporting nations.

After three months of negotiations, the Japanese government agreed to limit specialty steel exports to the United States to 66,400 tons (instead of the 63,500 tons recommended by the ITC) for the twelve-month period from June 1976 to June 1977, with 3 percent annual increases in each of the two subsequent years. However, because the European countries refused to accept an OMA, the president imposed three-year mandatory quotas, with Japan given the bilaterally negotiated quota and the EEC given 2,000 tons below the ITC-recommended quota of 34,000 tons for 1976-1977. At about the same time, the Europeans persuaded six major Japanese steel producers to agree to voluntarily limit shipments of general steel products to the EEC to 1.2 million tons for the coming year—a 23.9 percent reduction from the previous year (Adams and Dirlam, 1979, pp. 98-101). Thus, in spite of opposition to import restraint in the United States by consumerist groups, by 1976 the U.S. government had taken specific actions that legitimized some form of import restraint and had entered into arrangements with its major trading partners in Europe and Japan. In these earlier efforts, dating from 1968, and again in 1977, it was abundantly clear that the influence of groups opposed to import restrictions—consumerists, steel importers, and the like—would not prevail.

The U.S. Steel Lobby and the 301 Complaint

Ever since the U.S. steel industry began to face foreign competition in the U.S. market in the 1960s, it had focused on unfair trading practices of the Japanese and Europeans (rather than on its failure to modernize or to control spiraling labor costs) as the elemental factor leading to its troubled condition. U.S. steelmakers contended that they were being undersold by foreign producers because these producers benefited from government subsidies. Moreover, they argued that the low prices at which Japanese and European steel was being sold in the U.S. market effectively initiated a price war that undercut their profitability. These arguments were used in their anti-import campaigns of 1967-1968 and again in the 1976-1977 period. This time, the steel lobby used an additional tactic: it developed a finely tuned strategy designed to pressure the executive branch where it was most vulnerable—the multilateral trade negotiations. Indeed, the existence of these negotiations, and the attendant desire to achieve liberalization, seems, ironically, to have eventually led U.S. policymakers to take more of an accommodationist view toward the steel lobby's pressure than they might have otherwise. (From the viewpoint of U.S. policymakers, it always came down to saving the MTN, and the stronger lobbies, among which steel must be counted, were therefore able to exercise strong leverage in two ways. First, the 1974 Trade Act provided for the creation of an advisory committee, thereby creating the institutional network for communication between representatives from industry and labor and the administration. Second, it called on the president to "negotiate by sectors" to achieve, "to the maximum extent feasible, export opportunity for U.S. products equivalent to the opportunities afforded to the importation of similar products" in the U.S. market. The Senate Finance Committee's report on the act, moreover, cited steel as one of the sectors lending itself to this approach.)

After the specialty steel dispute of 1975, the first effort by the U.S. steel industry to pressure the executive branch about imports came in October 1976 in the form of a 301 complaint filed with the Office of the Special Trade Representative. The 301 provision of the Trade Act of 1974 had been specifically intended to deal with foreign practices and policies that adversely affect the U.S. economy, including distortions of trade that result from foreign governmental arrangements. The suit filed by the American Iron and Steel Institute (AISI) appealed for relief from imports, charging that six major Japanese steel producers' voluntary export restraint agreement with the EEC was an unfair, unreasonable, and discriminatory practice clearly actionable under Section 301 of the act because it diverted their steel shipments from Europe to the United States.

On the face of it, the AISI complaint seemed fully justified—Japanese exports to the U.S. market were increasing rapidly in 1976. Indeed, between

January and October 1976 steel imports from Japan were 33.7 percent above the import level of the corresponding period in 1975. Could this increase really be attributed to Japan's steel export restraint agreement with the European community? In light of the movement of Japanese exports to the EEC during this period, the increase in Japanese exports to the United States seems to have been more a function of Japan's quick response to the improvement of the U.S. economy, which resulted in increased steel demand. (Despite the absence of VRAs or mandatory import quotas on shipments of general steel products to the United States after 1974, foreign steel imports to the U.S. market did not dramatically increase, mainly because of the stagnant demand situation following the October 1973 oil embargo by OPEC. Japanese steel exports to the United States actually declined in 1975, as did European steel exports to the U.S. market.) In fact, as shown by the graph in figure 2-1, the decline in Japanese steel exports to the EEC between 1975 and 1976 was almost negligible compared to the increase in Japanese exports to the United States in the same period (0.023 million tons versus 2.14 million tons).

Nevertheless, Yoshihiro Inayama, chairman of the Nippon Steel Corporation and head of the Japan Iron and Steel Federation (JISF), immediately issued a statement that sympathized with the U.S. industry's position but that did not directly respond to the AISI charge itself. "It is quite natural," he said, "for the U.S. industry to try to protect its own interests, and we should not merely criticize its recent move as contrary to the spirit of free trade." He then pointed out the importance of maintaining orderly exports and expressed the Japanese industry's willingness to restrain exports to the United States (as well as to the European Community) through an intergovernmental agreement, if necessary. (The reasons for the Japanese industry's sensitivity to U.S. criticisms are discussed below.)

On the other hand, officials in the Ministry of International Trade and Industry (MITI) did try to refute the AISI charge directly during bilateral working-level steel discussions in early December. They argued that the impact of the Japanese export restraint agreement with the European Community was minimal in view of the fact that a very low European demand had made it even more difficult for Japan to fulfill the agreed quota. They also contended that the AISI charge was not applicable because the Japanese government was not directly involved in the six domestic steelmakers' export restraint agreement.

After the AISI appeal to the STR, no formal U.S. government push for Japanese restraints on steel exports to the United States came in 1976, in part because the Ford administration was on its way out. Even though the Carter administration announced, in January 1978, the discontinuance of its review of the AISI complaint because of lack of sufficient evidence, the 301 case did serve to alert U.S. trade-policy bureaucrats to the plight

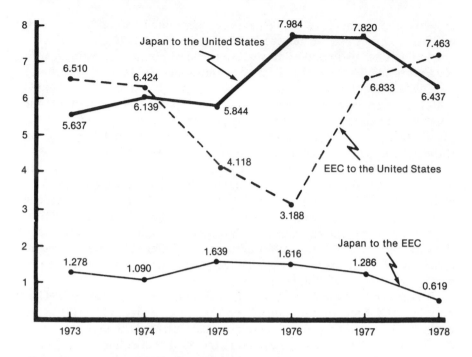

Source: U.S. Department of Commerce.

Figure 2-1. Steel Exports to the United States and the EEC by Country of Origin, 1973-1978 (unit: million tons)

of the domestic steel industry, thereby setting the atmosphere in which the new administration began considering the steel-trade issue.

The Japanese Industry's Readiness to Cooperate

Upon entering office in January 1977, the Carter administration came under strong pressure from the domestic steel industry. The industry put particular emphasis on limiting imports from Japan, which, in 1976, had increased 37 percent over the previous year, accounting for 14 percent of apparent domestic consumption. During his Tokyo visit in early February, Vice-President Mondale did express the new administration's concern about the increasing steel (and color-television) imports from Japan, but he fell short of proposing any specific measure to deal with the problem. Nevertheless, this was a sufficient signal for the Japanese steel industry. On February 5, the president of Nippon Steel, Eishiro Saito, and seven other steel executives proposed to MITI Minister Tatsuo Tanaka that the

Japanese government open intergovernmental steel negotiations with the United States with a view toward concluding an OMA. They suggested the OMA approach mainly because they were afraid the Japanese industry's unilateral export restraint might violate U.S. antitrust laws.

Indeed, ever since the steel issue first arose with the United States in 1967, the Japanese industry had been more or less willing to restrain exports to the U.S. market. Had it not been for antitrust considerations, it is entirely likely that the VRA would have been renewed in 1974. The Japanese industry's willingness to restrain exports was also evident in Inayama's statement in regard to the AISI's 301 appeal (noted earlier).

What explains the Japanese industry's position? Why is this particular industry not as resistant as most other industries, including textiles and electronics, to export restraint? Four interrelated reasons are usually included in the various explanations given by steel experts, both inside and outside the industry: (1) the interdependent nature of the industry, (2) indebtedness to the United States, (3) profit motives, and (4) fear of losing a U.S. market share. It is important to understand each of these motives in a bit more detail because they shaped the Japanese response to the issue and, therefore, the resolution eventually reached.

1. The Japanese steel industry is heavily dependent on suppliers of various materials, including iron ore and coking coal, and buyers of related products (steel is used in most manufactured products) in different countries. Keenly mindful of such international interdependence, Japanese steelmakers believe they cannot afford to antagonize any major supplier or buyer in any country.

2. In the postwar period, the United States generously and cheaply provided Japan with needed technology and materials, and so the Japanese steel industry is very much indebted to the United States for its current status as the world's major steel exporter. This debt of gratitude is real and is reflected in Japan's willingness to bend and compromise to U.S. interests, but it has not always worked to their advantage. It is also conditioned by the correct assumption that steel is still considered a basic and necessary industry in the United States, and, unlike other industries (such as shoes or leather apparel), its demise would not be tolerated.

3. Quantitative export restraint often helps to raise steel prices and thus proves profitable to steel exporters; at the very least, they seldom suffer major losses as a result of export restraint.

4. The United States is not only the biggest market for steel, but also the single most reliable market in the world. In view of the large size and the prosperous nature of the U.S. economy, it is very easy for Japanese steel exporters to find customers. If one customer stops buying steel, it is easy to find another customer. In most other markets, it is difficult to find such flexibility. Consequently, Japanese steelmakers want to keep a certain share

of the U.S. market, even if they can sell the same steel products at higher prices elsewhere. Unrestrained exports will unnecessarily induce antidumping and other strict protectionist actions in the United States, possibly resulting in a major reduction or loss of the Japanese share of the U.S. market.

Of course, relative emphasis given to these factors varies from people to people. Inayama, known as Mr. Cartel because of his strong belief in the importance of export restraint, singles out one reason (Japan's indebtedness to the United States) as most important. Most other steel executives give greater weight to the interdependence factor and to the fear of losing the market share. Critics of the industry usually point up the profit motive as most relevant.

In any case, due to whatever combination of these reasons, a consensus developed among Japanese steel producers, particularly among six major integrated steelmakers (Nippon Steel, Nippon Kokan, Kawasaki Steel, Sumitomo Metal, Kobe Steel, and Nisshin Steel), concerning the need for maintaining orderly exports to the United States. The strong leadership exercised by Inayama in the industry seems to have reinforced this industry position.

The MITI, too, had been moving in that direction in recent years. But, as a government agency, it tended to work under the assumption that the Japanese industry need not implement voluntary export restraint, or the Japanese government need not initiate OMA negotiations, unless the U.S. government formally asked for such restraint or negotiations. MITI officials also feared that one industry's easy resort to export restraint might induce the United States to ask for similar restraint by other Japanese industries.

Ironically, quantitative export restraint, which the Japanese industry was willing to accept, was exactly what had been asked for by U.S. steel executives and labor leaders, including Edgar B. Speer, Chairman of the U.S. Steel Corporation (and, during 1977, chairman of the AISI) and Lloyd McBride, president of the USW. It is certainly not the lack of convergent interests between the Japanese and the U.S. industries that made news headlines. "Had it not been for the antitrust laws," Inayama once said, "Japanese and American steelmakers could get together and settle bilateral steel-trade problems very smoothly."

Gilmore Files an "Antidumping" Suit

Although Japanese steelmakers did not particularly mind their U.S. counterparts calling for an intergovernmental agreement to restrain Japanese steel imports to the United States, they abhorred another kind of action—antidumping suits. The Gilmore Steel Corporation, a small steelmaker in Portland, Oregon, had a head start in this campaign on February 28 when it filed an antidumping suit with the Treasury Department against five major Japanese steelmakers. Gilmore Steel charged that Nippon Steel, Nippon Kokan, Kawasaki Steel, Sumitomo Metals, and Kobe Steel were selling carbon steel plates $77 below the average U.S. domestic price per ton and must be dumping steel in the U.S. market. (According to an MITI official, Gilmore was notorious for its tendency to file legal suits against foreign steel producers and, therefore, its antidumping suit should not have been taken seriously by the Treasury Department.) So, on March 29, the Treasury Department began an investigation into the Gilmore charge.

Although Gilmore was a small company, the timing of the investigation meant that the Treasury's determination could well affect all Japanese carbon-steel-plate exports to the United States. Japanese steelmakers were also disturbed by what they regarded as a peculiar definition of dumping—a definition that the United States would apply and that came from the revision of U.S. trade law in the Trade Act of 1974. Traditionally, dumping had been defined as the sale of a product in significant quantities in export markets at prices below those of the home market. The 1974 Trade Act revised this, however, to take into account conditions where home-market prices were below average production costs. In such cases, the U.S. statute now said that the fair value of exports must be calculated according to constructed value, or the sum of direct production costs, 10 percent overhead, and profit equal to 8 percent of total costs. Dumping was thus defined as the sale below unit costs plus 8 percent, which meant that, if the exporter was losing money at home because of a recession or other source of market decline, he could not take the same approach in foreign markets. According to this definition then, exporters were much more likely to be charged with dumping. In this situation, they would be forced either to raise their steel prices high enough to avoid further dumping allegations and cut their competitive edge accordingly or to stop exports altogether. Thus, an antidumping suit could be an effective means to limit foreign steel imports.

The Gilmore case was also a manifestation of a particularly serious concern among U.S. steelmakers on the West Coast about growing Japanese steel imports. In 1976, Japan's share in the U.S. steel market as a whole was about 8 percent, but among seven Western states (California, Arizona, New Mexico, Utah, Oregon, Washington, and Idaho) it was as much as 27 to 28 percent—well beyond the 20 percent ceiling that had been more or less tolerated as the Japanese share in the past. Most of the U.S. companies in the area were small and, except for Kaiser Steel, which had four aging oxygen blast furnaces (BOFs), had no BOFs. Consequently, they were no match for major Japanese integrated steel-makers. The five major Japanese companies had been resorting to selfrestraint in their exports to this area since the last quarter of 1976 in order to avoid flooding the market. Other countries, including South Korea, had begun to take advantage of the situation by increasing steel exports to this area. However, the Japanese remained the main target of criticism.

The AISI Publishes Its "White Paper"

Meanwhile, the AISI and the USW were organizing major nationwide campaigns to enlist support for their cause. Their short- and middle-range strategies included efforts to achieve quantitative import control (through an OMA or an appeal based on Article 301 of the Trade Act of 1974) or to limit imports through antidumping suits. Their ultimate goal was to attain a multilateral sectoral agreement to organize steel trade under GATT auspices, along the lines of the multifiber arrangement (MFA) on textiles.

(Although the trade route, and import restraint in particular, comprised the larger proportion of their efforts, it should also be noted that the AISI and the USW simultaneously pursued other policy directions as well. Relaxation of environmental regulations so capital could be directed toward equipment and plant-modernization programs, faster depreciation write-off schedules, and government-loan guarantees were three policy areas also addressed by the steel industry's campaign. Indeed, as we shall see below, the Solomon Report, which came to represent the blueprint for the Carter administration's steel policy, provided policy recommendations for each of the industry's concerns—increased availability of capital, relaxation of environmental regulations, and, primarily, of course, restraints on imports.)

The AISI held its general meeting on May 26 and adopted a report entitled "Economics of International Steel Trade" that had been prepared by Putnam, Hayes, and Bartlett, Inc. The report charged that foreign suppliers (including the Japanese) had discriminatory pricing practices between home and export shipments; that various types of direct and indirect aids by national governments had led to large-scale capital expansion; and that pressures existed to export at prices below full unit costs in order to help pay for this substantial investment. Among other things, this adoption showed that, in light of the Gilmore suit, other major nationwide steel companies would begin collecting the data and developing the evidence to file their own antidumping suits.

The Japanese, however, had a different view of what constituted dumping. Indeed, this difference of perspective, which stemmed in no small part from the data one chose to accumulate, as well as how one chose to interpret the data, dramatizes how tensions between nations can be exacerbated over international trade issues. International trade is not a simple matter of economics; it is subject to the subtleties, nuances, and complications of political economy. The U.S. industry, as indicated in the discussion about Gilmore, started from the premise, legitimized by U.S. trade laws, that dumping could be considered to have occurred if the product was being sold below the constructed value, as defined in the Trade Act of 1974. Within that context, much of what they did they considered to be in keeping with what U.S. trade law defined as fair trade. At the same time, of course, the Japanese believed that the U.S. industry was asking their government for something that was not supported by either fair or acceptable standards of international trade, but was simply an excuse for assistance in an area where they had lost their competitiveness.

Thus, finding the AISI allegations subject to numerous factual errors and misrepresentations, the Japanese industry decided to prepare its formal rebuttal. In addition, because Japanese industry leaders interpreted the latest AISI move as a manifestation of the serious intent of the U.S. industry to seek import control, these leaders renewed their call for intergovernmental negotiations to work out an OMA. However, the MITI maintained its position that the Japanese government should not initiate a move in that direction without a formal approach from the U.S. government. For the time being, MITI officials thought it necessary to feel out the U.S. government's position at a meeting of the special OECD Ad Hoc Steel Group, which was scheduled to take place in Paris in late July.

At about this time, the U.S. industry and labor campaign against Japanese steel imports quickly developed momentum. In many parts of the country, AISI Chairman Speer was giving speeches in which he emphasized the crisis state of the domestic steel industry and argued it was largely a result of the flooding of low-priced Japanese steel imports. The steel industry's campaign to educate the public and government officials as to what it regarded as unfair and illegal practices by Japanese exporters benefited from the more general disfavor with which U.S. labor and industry viewed the Japanese. The U.S. bilateral trade deficit with Japan was increasing at unprecedented rates, and the affected industries were not at all reluctant to gang together in admonishing the Japanese. For example, during their Tokyo visit, Jacob Clayman of the AFL-CIO and other U.S. labor leaders told Japanese steel executives and labor leaders to limit steel exports to the United States through an OMA because of a serious unemployment problem in the U.S. steel industry.

The steel industry campaign continued in other ways as well. It soon became known that U.S. Steel, the largest U.S. steel company (with about 30 percent of the domestic share), was preparing to file with the Treasury Department a major antidumping suit against all Japanese steel products coming into the U.S. market. Again, the particular tensions between the United States and Japan were ever too apparent. Because European steelmakers were much less efficient than their Japanese counterparts and, therefore, much more likely to have dumped steel in the United States, one may wonder why the U.S. industry was focusing its attack on Japan. It is true that Japan was the single largest foreign exporter of steel to the United States, with approximately a 52 percent share of the total U.S. steel imports in 1976. However, it also seemed true that Speer and other U.S. steel leaders were effectively using Japan as a scapegoat to propagandize their case for import control. Making Japan, rather than a European country, a scapegoat was easier because U.S. steel industry leaders' ties were much less close with Japanese steel leaders than with their European counterparts. Singling out Japan as the main target of criticism was also politically useful because public opinion in the United States was growing more critical of Japan because of the enormous bilateral trade imbalance. In the context of the MTN, news of Japanese nontariff barriers to trade increasingly made headlines in major U.S. newspapers. Thus, Japan was seen by many Americans as a nation reaping the benefits of free trade but not sufficiently sharing the responsibilities as a leading economic power. As a Washington observer put it at the time, "It has become politically popular to take on Japan." And the steel industry was willing to exploit the unpopularity of Japan.

Prevailing Views among Carter Aides

As we have seen, Japanese steel producers were seriously concerned about the intensifying U.S. steel industry and labor campaigns against Japanese steel imports and had been prepared to implement an OMA as soon as the two governments could negotiate one. However, by the summer of 1977, the Carter administration still had not reached a consensus on precisely how to cope with the steel problem. They only knew what they did not want, and for good reason: The administration that had just concluded an OMA with Japan on color-television imports was generally reluctant to handle steel in the same way or through any other quantitative import restrictions. It was believed that, because the steel industry was an oligopoly, quantitative import restrictions would give U.S. steel producers an additional incentive to raise prices. (The industry's tendency to raise steel prices was reinforced in 1973 when it signed an experimental negotiating agreement (ENA) with the USW. In effect, the industry promised to maintain (and further raise) the extraordinary high level of wages for U.S. steelworkers in return for the union's pledge not to strike nationwide and for its implied promise to help the industry lobby for protection from foreign competition.) Administration officials (Undersecretary of State Cooper, Assistant Secretary of the Treasury Bergsten, and Treasury Secretary Blumenthal) wished to avoid

higher prices because that situation would have contributed to the inflationary spiral already seriously burdening the domestic economy. Indeed,
between January 1960 and December 1968, a period when imports were
soaring, the compositive steel price index rose 4.1 points (0.45 points per
year)—compared to an increase of 26.7 points (6.67 points per year) in the
four years between January 1969 and December 1972, when the Japanese
and EEC steel producers were implementing the VRA with the U.S. State
Department (Controller General, 1974, p. 23). The wholesale price index of
steel compared to that of total manufacturing is shown in figure 2-2.

On the other hand, many officials in the executive branch who normally
would have opposed government protection, in whatever form and almost
under any conditions, were reluctant to take such a position in view of their
greater concern for the completion of trade liberalization under the MTN.
They were willing to allow assistance in the case of steel in exchange for the
steel industry's support for the MTN. This view was understandably strong
in the STR, which was centrally in charge of the MTN. STR officials were at
first divided between those who wanted to take the OMA approach and
those who were opposed to any kind of quantitative import control on the

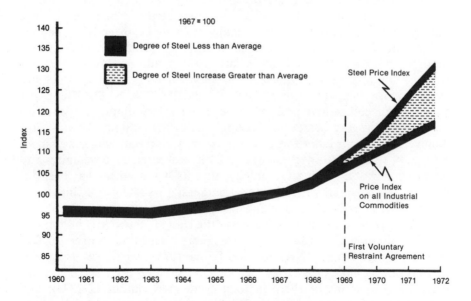

Source: Prepared by GAO from information obtained from the Department of Labor Bureau
of Labor Statistics.

Figure 2-2. Comparison of Wholesale Price Index for Industrial Commodities and Steel Mill Products

grounds that such an action would be inflationary. Eventually, the latter group held sway, with Strauss coming out against the quantitative approach in late July. As one story goes, Strauss, who had handled the OMA negotiations on color-televisions, came to detest the idea of such quantitative control after learning about the complexity involved in its enforcement. He also realized that the steel issue was a much more difficult and messier one than the color-television issue and that the Treasury might as well handle it. After all, Strauss did not like Blumenthal, who had opposed his nomination as special trade representative.

The Japanese Industry Responds
to the AISI Report

On July 18, two days before the meeting of the OECD Ad Hoc Steel Group in Paris, the Japanese steel industry made public its formal rebuttal to the earlier AISI report. The rebuttal, a paper entitled "U.S.-Japan Steel Trade: Basic Views on Current Issues," was prepared by the Japan Iron and Steel Exporters Association and emphasized that the Japanese industry's cost competitive position did not come from any grandiose scheme, any manipulation of steel trade and pricing, or any subsidies. (A former U.S. Treasury official observed in 1978: ". . . there seems to be little evidence that government subsidies play a major role in exporters' competitive thrusts into the U.S. market. The sharp drop in U.S. import prices which occurred in 1975 and then again in early 1977 should not be attributed to subsidies but to the effects of excess capacity in a world industry which has become more competitive over time" [Crandall, 1978, p. 8].) The paper stated: "Our competitive position comes from a very simple fact—our industry is the lowest cost steel producer in the world; that it has the most productive, industrious labor force; that it uses raw materials and energy more efficiently than any other country; that it pioneered in developing and adopting new steelmaking technology; that its management has been innovative in all aspects of steel trade—marketing, handling and shipping." Specifically, it emphasized that Japan was investing more money annually in steel facilities and equipment than was the United States ($3.7 billion versus $3.2 billion in 1975); Japan was using more blast furnaces over 2,000m^3 than the United States (37 versus 5 as of June 1975); Japan was using continuous casting more extensively then the United States (31.1 percent versus 9.1 percent in terms of share in total crude steel output in 1976); and Japan's annual crude steel production per steelworker was higher than the United States's (515 tons versus 321 tons in 1976).

The OECD Ad Hoc Steel Group met in Paris on July 20-21. Director Kiyoshi Takahashi of the MITI's International Economic Affairs Department and other Japanese representatives did discuss the bilateral steel trade problem with their U.S. counterparts. However, the U.S. side did not have any definitive position, except that it was not particularly interested in pushing quotas. The U.S. representatives did not speak in one voice, either. The only consensus between the two sides at the time was that the issue would be settled within a multilateral framework. As noted earlier, the U.S. steel industry had been seeking an international sectoral arrangement for steel within the GATT framework and after the fashion of the MFA for textiles. Some members of the U.S. government—particularly those in the STR and the Commerce Department—were supportive of that approach as a way to ensure the industry's support for the MTN. The Japanese and the Europeans, however, were unalterably opposed. Thus, the governments agreed that steel discussions were to be pursued in the OECD instead.

Japanese industry leaders were relieved to learn during the OECD meeting that there was no particular hint of the Americans and the Europeans ganging up on Japan in the name of orderly steel trade, but they still feared that such a united front against Japan might be formed in the fall. As an example of what was to come, Britain had already decided to charge antidumping duty on Japanese imports of steel, which the Janpanese thought unfair.

Japan Refuses to Provide Cost Data

The first sign of confrontation between the governments of the United States and Japan regarding steel surfaced in late July, when the Japanese steel industry refused to submit steel production-cost data to the Treasury Department, which had been requesting such data for its investigation of the Gilmore case. The Treasury had been asking for data on production costs as well as on domestic and export prices. The Japanese industry agreed to provide price data but refused to submit data on product-by-product costs. The request for cost data was unusual and unprecedented, and no producer would have willingly provided such data. Industry leaders thought that the United States was using the antidumping suit as a pretext to obtain production secrets about the world's most efficient steel industry. The Japanese feared that, once the Treasury obtained such data, there was no guarantee that the U.S. industry might not somehow get hold of it as well. Not satisfied with the Japanese industry's explanation about operational confidentiality, the Treasury continued to press for Japanese production-cost data (domestic and export price data had been submitted), asking the Japanese government to persuade the domestic industry. The Treasury communicated its warning to Ambassador Fumihiko Togo in Washington, stating that the amicable settlement of the steel issue depended entirely on the Japanese. But the Japanese government itself had been opposed to the submission of such cost data, advising the industry not to comply with the Treasury's request. Industry leaders were facing a dilemma. To clear themselves of the dumping charge, they needed to cooperate with the Treasury, but at the same time they felt they could not do so without threatening operational confidentiality. They particularly feared that, if they provided cost data on steel plate for the Gilmore case, they might be asked to submit cost data on all other steel products for future antidumping cases, including the impending U.S. Steel suit. If they did not provide such data, then U.S. industry leaders could say that the Japanese had admitted their own guilt by not cooperating with the Treasury investigation. Moreover, without cost data from the Japanese industry, the Treasury might have to depend on the less reliable data available in the United States. If they looked on the earlier AISI report as any indication of what was to come, Japanese steel leaders could not have had much confidence in the Treasury investigations unless they provided data. As expected, the Japanese refusal to provide cost data was conveniently interpreted by U.S. producers as an admission of dumping. The refusal also forced Treasury personnel to make their own assessment of Japanese steelmaking costs, as mandated by the Trade Act of 1974.

Amaya Visits the United States

MITI officials were deeply worried about the negative impact of the unresolved steel issue on the overall U.S.-Japanese economic relationship. Ambassador Mansfield had been warning that the issue might be further politicized and needed to be resolved before giving additional impetus to widespread antidumping and antiimport campaigns in the United States. However, these officials were at a loss as to how the issue might be resolved best. They were sandwiched between the Japanese industry, which wanted voluntary export restraint, and the U.S. government, which was opposed to such a quantitative approach. All the while, the U.S. government was increasingly being pressured by the industry and labor, who, by late summer, began to play hardball with the MTN. Under these circumstances, and without being asked to do so by the United States, Naohiro Amaya, MITI's Director of the Heavy Industries Bureau, decided to pay a visit to the United States to explore the ways and means of settling the issue with the U.S. government. Amaya believed that it was important for the Japanese side to take an initiative in an early resolution of the issue. By taking on the task early, he also thought he could prevent further complications and the involvement of more officials and more government agencies in the issue.

Amaya left for the United States on August 3. During his several days' stay there, he saw various U.S. government officials, including Under-Secretary of the Treasury Anthony M. Solomon and his subordinate, Bergsten, Cooper of the State Department, and Richard Heimlich of the STR. It became clear from these talks that the U.S. government was definitely not interested in the quantitative approach and was more inclined to support a kind of price-oriented approach. On the whole, U.S. officials were still uncertain as to the exact approach to be taken. Although they said they were against a quantitative solution, they thought they had to be careful not to leave the impression that it was all right for Japan to export as much steel to the U.S. market as it was capable of doing. They did recognize, however, that the Japanese were sensitized to the problem and were acting in order to avoid criticism. Amaya also saw some U.S. industry and labor leaders, including Speer of the AISI and Clayman of the AFL-CIO. These leaders were still determined to pressure the Japanese into quantitative export restraint.

Upon his return to Tokyo, Amaya reported on his trip to Inayama and told him about the U.S. government's opposition to Japan's voluntary export restraint through an OMA or otherwise. Inayama refused to believe him, saying that the U.S. government would definitely push for such a quantitative approach. (Inayama's conviction that the United States wanted Japan's voluntary export restraint came from his informal conversations with Speer at international steel meetings, in which the latter repeatedly expressed the U.S. industry's preference for the quantitative approach.)

The Raging Firestorm against Imports

Despite, or because of, the lack of support for import restrictions on the part of the Carter administration, U.S. industry and labor leaders and their supporters intensified their campaigns against steel imports. In his article in an AISI journal, Speer called for intergovernmental negotiations to restrain imports. Lloyd McBride of the USW repeated his call for steel-import restrictions in his New York speech on August 15. In early September, twenty-five U.S. mayors from steel-producing districts formed a "Steel City League" to lobby for the protection of the domestic steel industry.

All of this would have meant very little had the steel industry and the steelworkers not been successful in mobilizing the U.S. Congress behind their position. It was through congressional pressure that the Carter administration was convinced of the urgency of a serious response to the steel industry's problems. It is also important to recognize that neither the Congress nor the steel lobby really wanted policy from Congress. Instead, Congress was expected to lobby for constituent interest with the administration. It performed this role in a manner similar to the way that lobbyists represent their clients' interests to Congress. The House and the Senate each used its institutional powers quite effectively but neither ever actually acted as an instituion per se. In this way, they avoided the ultimate responsibility for trade matters, a decision that had been made explicitly and implicitly over and over again since the experiences associated with the Smoot Hawley Tariff in 1930. Congressmen are too aware that it is highly unlikely that they won't find both sides of an issue in their district and will lose somewhere. Indeed, during the entire period of the steel issue, the Congress never once acted as a body, only as individuals and in relatively narrow instances. Moreover, this perspective fit well with what the steel lobby thought of as its best approach. The steel lobby knew that policy had to come from the administration, and it was the administration, of course, that had this power. It held the authority to negotiate agreements to limit imports.

Thus, congressional authority could be used for pressure, but the steel lobby realized that, as a practical matter, the law-making process would be too cumbersome and unwieldly and not very conducive to attaining a quick response. Unless organized, however, congressional energies, even over a specific issue such as steel, can be diffuse, and therefore can lose a good deal of their effectiveness. The tactics used by the steel lobby to ensure the appropriate organization and attention of Congress were cleverly pointed.

Thus, the cause of the sudden congressional interest in the steel issue can be traced to well-orchestrated, several-pronged lobbying efforts by the steel lobby, including the Steel City League's efforts in local communities across the United States. Predictably, the lobbying efforts were directed especially at representatives and senators from steel states, notably, Ohio, Pennsylvania, West Virginia, New York, and Illinois. For instance, Charles Vanik, chairman of the House Ways and Means Subcommittee on International Trade, and a representative from Ohio, was an obvious target for congressional lobbying. The results were several hearings, held by Vanik and others, where congressmen began speaking to the administration.

Indeed, congressional pressure on the administration grew in direct proportion to the amount of pressure the steel lobby put on them, either by knocking on their doors and asking for help or by closing down more plants. The common thread that justified the link between job losses, steel-lobby pressure on the Congress, and congressional pressure on the administration was the well-documented fact that imports were steadily rising. There was enough evidence available—indications of the findings of anti dumping in the Gilmore suit and in the AISI documents, for example—to suggest that the rise in imports was a result of unfair trade by the Japanese as well as by the Europeans. This evidence, however much disputed by the Japanese, still provided the means by which the steel lobby could win a number of allies in important places such as the U.S. Congress.

It was not surprising, then, when Congressman Charles Vanik met with Amaya in Tokyo on September 16 and suggested that the Japanese steel industry unilaterally restrain its steel exports to the United States. Nor was it surprising when, on that same day, across the Pacific, Senators Jacob K. Javits and Daniel Patrick Moynihan of New York sent a letter to Strauss, recommending intergovernmental negotiations with prinicpal steel-exporting countries based on a sectoral approach similar to the one used for negotiating the MFA on textiles.

These calls for import control and forms of orderly marketing arrangements coincided with the publishing of some bad news about the domestic industry in major U.S. newspapers The Youngstown Sheet and Tube division of the Lykes Corporation announced that it would severely cut back operations at its Youngstown, Ohio, plant, permanently furloughing 5,000 production workers. The Bethlehem Steel Corporation and the Armco Steel Corporation, both among the industry's top five producers, announced the closing of shops and the elimination of 8,000 jobs in Johnstown, Pennsylvania, Lackawana, New York, and Middletown, Ohio. Alan Wood, a small but venerable steel producer near Philadelphia, had gone into bankruptcy earlier in the year and had to auction off its plant piece by piece because no single buyer could be found. Both the AISI and the USW used these plant closings to dramatize the plight of the domestic industry through media exposure; full-page advertisements as well as stories recounting the effects of high unemployment in concentrated regions of the United States appeared in major U.S. newspapers. Some of the plant closings themselves may have been announced intentionally to put pressure on the government for import control as well as for relaxing various government regulations. "One theory prevalent in steel circles these days," wrote Winston Williams in *The New York Times* on September 25, "is that the companies consider 1977 a lost year for profits anyway, so that they have decided to take all their lumps during the current slump." The dramatization of the impact of foreign imports and the government's role in controlling unfair trade, which allegedly led to those increased imports, may also have been a useful excuse to close down old, inefficient plants with minimum opposition from the USW; the USW could, thus, direct the focus of its rage from industry to government.

Finally, on September 19, what the Japanese industry had feared most became a reality. U.S. Steel filed with the Treasury a major antidumping suit against the six largest Japanese steel companies (Nippon Steel, Nippon Kokan, Sumitomo Metals, Kawasaki Steel, Kobe Steel, and Nisshin Steel). It was alleged that these companies were dumping their excess steel products (including steel plate, shapes, pipes, hot-rolled and cold-rolled sheets, and galvanized steel) at distress prices in the United States. The suit specifically charged that the Japanese steelmakers were selling their steel products at 23 percent below production costs. At the same time, the administration sent its STR ambassador, Robert Strauss, to testify before the House Ways and Means Committee. He told Representative Vanik's Subcommittee on International Trade that: (1) the government was in the midst of studying a possible resolution of the issue; (2) import quotas or voluntary restraint resulting in quantitative restrictions would not be feasible in the short run; (3) the steel trade issue should be settled as a price problem and quantitative control would be considered only when all other solutions had been exhausted; and (4) an international mechanism for adjusting world steel trade would be necessary in the long run, and the government intended to explore this path with Japan and the European community within the framework of the OECD.

The day before the suit was filed, anticipating U.S. Steel's move, Chairman Inayama of the Japan Iron and Steel Federation stated in a press conference that the Japanese industry was prepared to resort to unilateral export restraint before the end of the year, hoping that the current issue would be settled before the Treasury Department took up the U.S. Steel case. As soon as the U.S. Steel suit was formally filed, Japanese industry began its preparations for implementing the unilateral export restraint.

Because Japanese industry leaders believed that U.S. Steel resorted to this suit because the U.S. government was not receptive to the quantitative approach, they hoped that, if they restrained their exports unilaterally, U.S. steel would withdraw its antidumping suit. However, consent among the Japanese steel industry was by no means automatic. Inayama and the other industry leaders' immediate concern was whether they could get smaller domestic steel companies to go along with such unilateral export restraint. (There were three types of small and medium-size Japanese steel firms: (1) those that were under the control of the major firms; (2) those that were under the control of big trading companies, such as Mitsui and Mitsubishi; and (3) those that were independent of either the major steel companies or the major trading companies. The first two types were relatively more cooperative than the third with regard to these smaller companies, the major firms were counting on the MITI to supervise and coordinate policy.) Market conditions had changed substantially since the 1968-1974 period, when Inayama was able to obtain industrywide agreement on export restraints with relative ease. By 1977, most of the small and medium-size Japanese steelmakers who had depended largely on the domestic market before 1974 had, by 1977, come to export large volumes of steel due to a slack in domestic demand. They were interested, by 1977, in keeping the large U.S. market open and flexible. Thus, it was only among the six major steel companies, which could accommodate more easily to changes in export-market availability, that consensus could be easily attained in regard to export adjustments. The six major steel firms alone could go ahead with unilateral export restraint, but it would not be sufficiently effective because the other domestic steelmakers' export share was increasing: the six major firms and other Japanese firms exported 4 million tons and 1.18 million tons, respectively, in 1975, but in 1976 the corresponding figures were 4.8 million tons and 2.6 million tons, respectively.

Once again, a problem in perception resulted. The Japanese industry's eagerness to resort to voluntary export restraint was interpreted by some Americans as an admission of guilt. "The Japanese are afraid of what might happen in this case," said one brokerage-house executive referring to the U.S. Steel suit. "Why else would they voluntarily agree to limit their exports to six million tons a year instead of eight million?"

So, with no particular policies coming from the Carter administration and with only promises by Strauss to consider further study, and with most leaders in the U.S. industry and USW believing that they indeed had a strong case against foreign steel, the steel lobby began stepping up pressures on the Congress to force action from the administration. This resulted in the formation of Senate and House steel caucuses. Understandably enough, the formation of both the Senate and House steel caucuses were a result of the steel lobby's pressure on key senators and congressmen, who, in turn, encouraged their colleagues to help them help their constituents. Because there was no noticeable opposition to the steel lobby's pressures, countervailing forces in the Congress, which might have weighed against one coleague providing another with help, did not exist.

The House steel caucus was formed on September 22, 1977, and its Senate counterpart was formed six days later, not coincidentally at about the same time that thousands of layoffs and plant closings were making headlines. Both caucuses were created through the urging of "Dear Colleague" letters by those senators and congressmen most affected by the layoffs—in the Senate, Metzenbaum and Glenn of Ohio, Heinz of Pennsylvania, and Randolph of West Virginia; and, in the House, Representatives Carney and Vanik, both of Ohio.

The House steel caucus sent its resolution to the president in late September:

> That the President direct his Special Trade Representative for Trade Negotiations immediately to undertake international efforts to seek restraints on exports of steel to the United States under section 107 of the Trade Act of 1974. [U.S. House Steel Caucus, Resolution 1, 1977]

From the Senate steel caucus came similar commitments, also during that last week in September:

The Senate reaffirms its support for existing laws restricting unfair or sub-
sidized competition from imports, particularly the Antidumping Act of
1921 and the Trade Act of 1974, and urges the President to direct federal
agencies, particularly the Treasury and the Office of the Special Trade
Representative, to enforce vigorously and aggressively existing laws to prevent cases of dumping, trade discrimination, and other forms of unfair
competition that have an adverse impact on the American steel industry.
[U.S. Senate Steel Caucus, Resolution 1, 1977]

These resolutions, and a host of other pieces of legislation endorsed by a
great many representatives and senators, were all the more effective in view
of the administration's commitment to the MTN. Congressional mobiliza-
tion in support of the steel lobby's position was seen by the Carter
administration as a preview of potential congressional stonewalling on the
MTN agreement if influential lobbies such as the steel one were not
satisfied. It was a coalition that could have wrecked the MTN because of the
unusual congressional procedures that required all or nothing approval of
the MTN once the administration submitted it to the Congress.

Contributing still further to the raging firestorm in the United States
over the steady increase of steel imports was the Treasury Department's
announcement regarding the Gilmore antidumping suit. On September 30,
the Treasury Department informed the Japanese embassy in Washington
that it was planning to make a formal announcement on October 3 of its
preliminary determination in favor of the case brought by Gilmore Steel.
The Treasury ruled that carbon steel plate imported from Japan was being
sold in the United States at less than fair value, with a dumping margin
estimated at an average of around 32 percent. Thus, according to the provisions of U.S. trade law, as of October 3, importers of the Japanese plate
were required to post a bond equivalent to 32 percent of the declared value
of new shipments to show that the money was available to pay the higher
duties, if necessary. This itself could have been a deterrent to new shipments.

Japanese industry leaders were surprised at the Treasury Department's
preliminary ruling and attributed it to their refusal to provide the cost data.
Industry advocates contended that, in reaching the decision, the Treasury
"simply combined two pieces of information contained in anti-dumping
petitions of American steel companies; namely, the plate cost 'coefficient'
(the ratio of the plate cost to the average cost of all steel products) of
Japanese producers estimated by Gilmore Steel and the translated financial
reports of Japanese steel firms supplied by U.S. Steel" (Mueller and
Kawahito, 1979, p. 9). Various U.S. studies that subsequently became
public concluded that the Japanese had a substantial cost advantage,
perhaps sufficient to offset importation costs. Among them was a study by
the Federal Trade Commission, which found a Japanese cost advantage of

more than $85 in 1976 or 1977. At the least, it came to be generally agreed by U.S. analysts that "the Japanese may have had a $65 to $70 per ton advantage over the United States before the yen began to appreciate in 1977" (Crandall, 1978, p. 6). Their studies did not, however, alter the Treasury ruling, which represented U.S. authority on these matters.

Quite predictably, the Treasury's preliminary ruling on the Gilmore case was used by the U.S. steel industry to their advantage. It was now possible for the AISI and the USW to state with conviction that what they had been saying all along was true. U.S. Steel issued a statement declaring that unfair trade practices had been giving foreign producers "an advantage [resulting] in the loss of almost 20 percent" of the U.S. steel market *(The New York Times,* 4 October 1977). At least within the broad spectrum of the U.S. policymaking process, the politics had clearly swung to the side of the steel lobby. Even the Treasury Department, notably a promoter of free trade, provided implicit support.

This situation brought on understandable protestations by the Japanese industry. In fact, the Japanese did not issue their formal protests with the U.S. government until October 6, and it was not until October 25 that they issued their formal protest with the GATT Dumping Prevention Committee. On October 6, the Japanese government issued a formal complaint to the U.S. government with regard to the earlier Treasury ruling on the Gilmore case. The government protest, hand-delivered by Ambassador Togo to Solomon, stated that (1) it was regrettable that the antidumping issue had occurred in spite of the Japanese willingness to settle the issue flexibly; (2) the antidumping issue should not be used to restrict imports; and (3) a dumping determination should be made by comparing domestic and export prices and should not be based on the constructed value as such. Though the protest seemed not to have much effect on the U.S. policy process, it was apparently issued at that time to affect President Carter's meeting with U.S. industry leaders, which was scheduled for the next week.

Carter Forms the Solomon Task Force

As the Carter administration increasingly came under pressure from the domestic steel lobby, it tried to separate this difficult steel issue from other international trade and economic issues. Thus, the idea was to take the steel solution out of the MTN per se, even though the two were inextricably tied in everyone's mind. Similarly, although the steel issue was related to U.S.-Japanese economic and trade relations, the topic was separated from others in the highly visible and controversial U.S.-Japanese trade talks that took place during 1977.

Within the executive branch, there was a steel steering committee, comprised of representatives from the STR and the Treasury, State, Commerce, and Labor Departments, which had been meeting on an ad hoc interagency basis. Essentially, their mandate was to consider those issues in the steel sector that affected the MTN. As the domestic political crisis began to unfold throughout the latter part of 1976 and into 1977, it became evident that the steel steering group would play a role other than overseeing the MTN process. By September 1977, the Carter administration recognized that an even more specialized task force was also needed to address the immediate and specific domestic political issue. It was determined that the ad hoc steel group was not equipped to respond to the quick-moving pace of the domestic situation. In addition, there was significant political mileage to be gained from creating a new committee. The president could announce publicly his concern and interest in the issue and point to the specific action being taken. Accordingly, the president asked Undersecretary of the Treasury Anthony Solomon to develop a steel plan that would respond appropriately to the issue. In effect, the president had given the steel steering group a special mandate and had appointed Solomon to head it: "We are addressing the steel industry with a multidepartmental approach," the president said in a press conference held on September 29, 1977.

There were several reasons why a member of the Treasury Department was chosen to head the task force. First, in the White House and at the secretary and assistant-secretary levels of policymaking in the departments, it was already clear that whatever specific policy did evolve would be a variation on the antidumping theme (this will be discussed further below). Since the Treasury had jurisdiction over the administration and was responsible for the enforcement of antidumping laws, it was natural that the lead go to the Treasury Department.

The Treasury's key role was reinforced by several other factors. The bureaucratic-politics model seemed to apply in reverse: no one really wanted the issue, but someone had to take it. The fact that the Treasury had jurisdiction over the dumping laws gave logic to a move that was based on a gut reaction: As noted earlier, Strauss did not want much to do with the steel issue. He was having a hard enough time trying to negotiate a multilateral trade agreement without taking specific responsibility for the highly politicized steel issue. In short, it was assumed to be a no-win situation, and, for Strauss, could only make the selling of the MTN that much more difficult. Moreover, Strauss could argue that, if he did accept the lead of this group, the steel issue would be linked to the MTN, which was something to be avoided.

A third reason the Treasury was chosen relates to the administration's perception of that department as the most balanced of the departments. Once the STR was eliminated as the agent with prime responsibility, the only other serious possibilities—the Commerce or State Departments—would be suspect by one or another group: Because it was generally believed that the Commerce Department favored domestic industry, it would not be trusted by the foreigners. On the other hand, industry and labor distrusted the State Department because they believed that it would always lean toward the international. In fact, both these perceptions describe with great accuracy how these two bureaucracies tend to operate. At least institutionally, the Treasury was believed by all to be less biased and therefore more representative of an objective administration position.

A final, but very important, reason the responsibility to lead the group went to the Treasury was Secretary Solomon himself. Most of the officials who had been representing their respective agencies at both the interagency meetings in Washington and the international ad hoc meetings at the OECD in Paris realized that, because of a fortunate coincidence, Anthony Solomon had an appropriate background for this position. As assistant secretary of state, he had been largely responsible for negotiating the voluntary restraint agreement for steel in 1968; therefore, he knew the issue firsthand, was familiar with industry and labor leaders in the United States and abroad, and was well-respected by his counterparts at the STR, the State Department, and the Commerce Department and by the administration's economists as well. He was sophisticated both in the politics of international trade and in the economics of the issue. Still, there were important differences between the situation in 1968 and the one a decade later for which Solomon was again expected to develop a resolution. Critically, the difference was in the type of solution considered: in 1968, as indicated above, the Johnson administration negotiated export restraint agreements; now the solution was to be a variation on the antidumping theme in the form of a price solution. This solution came about as a result of several events.

First U.S. Steel's antidumping suit against the Japanese steel producers and the Treasury ruling on the Gilmore case encouraged other U.S. steelmakers to prepare similar suits against European steelmakers. Previous to the Treasury ruling, the Georgetown Steel Corporation had already filed an antidumping complaint regarding merchant rods from France. Bethlehem Steel, the second largest U.S. steelmaker, had began its preparations to file a major antidumping suit against steelmakers in the European community.

Second, on October 13, President Carter met with U.S. industry and labor leaders, including Chairman Speer of the AISI and McBride of the USW, in what turned out to be a blessing of the antidumping approach. Also attending the meeting were Strauss, Blumenthal, Solomon, and several members of the congressional steel caucus. After listening to an impassioned presentation by Speer on the plight of the domestic industry because of illegally dumped imports, the president was quoted (in the November 3 issue of *The New York Times*) as saying: "I have not been aware of this derogation of duty until just this week. We're going to do something about it, but we need your help." He then expressed his opposition to the idea of concluding VRAs with the Japanese and the Europeans and his administration's intention to enforce the antidumping laws. He apparently encouraged, if not invited, domestic steelmakers to file antidumping complaints.

Significantly, after the meeting, industry and labor dropped their call for quotas—a condition they agreed to in exchange for strict enforcement of the antidumping laws, but one that surprised congressional leaders such as Charles Vanik, who had introduced, on behalf of the industry, legislation for quotas and who was informed of the agreement by the press. (Even as late as mid-October, representatives of the Senate and House steel caucuses (now including some 150 members) were urging President Carter to approve quantitative import control through OMAs, indicating the confusion between what industry and labor were negotiating with the administration and the pressures they continued to urge their representatives in Congress to apply.)

So it began: the steel industry filed petitions against foreign producers, about whom they had been accumulating ample evidence during 1977. The industry filed twenty-three petitiions against foreign steel exporters. Among the petitions filed was one by National Steel, the third largest U.S. steelmaker, which was filed on October 20 against twenty-nine producers in six European countries (Britain, West Germany, France, Belgium, Italy, and the Netherlands).

The Carter administration, however, had not really thought through how they were going to cope with a number of antidumping cases. It did not have the staff ability to handle so many cases. The office in charge of antidumping investigations in the Treasury was very small—only ten persons or so. A more serious concern was one of policy: how to avoid a major political confrontation with Europe. Many U.S. officials were beginning to realize that the Japanese were indeed the world's most efficient producers and that their dumping problem, if anything, would not be widespread. However, it was becoming increasingly clear that there had been large-scale dumping by European firms.

During this period, the European steel industry suffered at least as badly as the U.S. industry from old and inefficient plants and, therefore, from the structural shifts in world wide production and trade patterns. As in the United States, there was great political tension as a consequence of actual or threatened plant closings and layoffs, and in many sections of France, Belgium, Italy, and Great Britain the tensions were far worse than those in the United States. These conditions quite often led to the making of government policies to maintain production levels and to halt the rising unemployment levels. Thus, it was apparent to many officials in the U.S. government that strict enforcement of the antidumping laws would find a number of European steel producers guilty of dumping in the U.S. market and would thereby constrain European trade to the United States. By some accounts, European steel would then have been all but excluded from entry into the U.S. market. These same officials feared that the consequences of such constraints on European trade would force the European firms to cut back production, leading to further unemployment and, finally, to increased political strains.

Under such circumstances, several quite plausible and wholly unattractive consequences were feared: First, there was good reason to believe that such conditions would have led to a virtual stalemate of the multilateral trade talks. As in the United States, the European steel industry constituted a significant political force. Second, even if the MTN could somehow be kept alive, it was all but certain that the economic burdens on the Europeans would lead to political pressure for a protectionist backlash in a range of other sectors, industrial as well as agriculture. The latter was a particularly sensitive area for the U.S. government and one against which it could not afford politically to allow the Europeans to erect trade barriers.

Moreover, the 1977 period was one when Eurocommunism seemed to be gaining ground and when European communist and/or socialist parties were likely to be the greatest beneficiaries of political and social strains from increased unemployment. The strikes in France occurring at about this time dramatized the dimensions of this issue only too clearly and pointed to the special sensitivities of labor in the well-organized steel sector. Thus, the exacerbation of an already unstable political and economic environment was to be avoided.

Because of these circumstances, U.S. officials involved in steel policy began to believe that, if the United States were going to take the antidumping route, it then needed some price-related mechanism to lighten the burden on the part of the Treasury and possibly to help avoid a political confrontation with Europe.

The variation on the antidumping theme had its origins at a meeting of the OECD Ad Hoc Steel Group that was held from September 29 to 30 in Paris. (It was not until October 21, 1978, that an International Steel Committee was formally established within the OECD.) Deputy Assistant Secretary of the Treasury John Ray, who was attending the meeting, broached an idea that might possibly resolve the dilemma—an idea that had previously been suggested by a number of people both within and outside the Solomon task force. It was an embryonic version of what was later developed into the trigger price mechanism. Ray and his State Department counterpart, William Barraclough, met privately with the Japanese to obtain their response. The Japanese seemed quite glad of the idea, indicating that they were willing to do anything to solve the problem. The Japanese officials took this idea back to Tokyo, and it was apparently in response to the U.S. representatives' approach in Paris that MITI Minister Tanaka submitted, in early October, a letter to Ambassador Mansfield expressing the Japanese government's interest in what was then called the price-assurance system. In Washington, Solomon assigned a member of his staff, Frank Vukmanic, to work out the details.

Toward the Adoption of the TPM

While the Solomon task force was working out the details of a possible settlement plan, the domestic firestorm over steel continued to rage. The pace quickened, with different policy alternatives promoted in different circles, manifesting what by then had become a situation wrought with both frustration and confusion. For example, on October 4, twenty-seven freshmen in Congress submitted a resolution to President Carter, urging him to renew the ongoing OMA on specialty steel with Japan and the European community. Then, on October 11, in Pittsburgh, Pennsylvania—the heart of the U.S. steel country—McBride appealed to Carter to negotiate a voluntary export restraint agreement with Japan and the European Community. On October 12, the U.S. Senate adopted a resolution calling for an active application of the antidumping rules. (It should be stated, however, that the specialty-steel issue and the big-steel issue were kept separate in terms of policy direction, even though they were linked in the industry's public posture as being part of the general trade dilemma with which it has to cope.)

As a result of numerous U.S. antidumping suits filed against foreign steelmakers, it had by this time become clear to most members of the bureaucracy that the antidumping solution was unworkable for precisely the reasons mentioned above. In fact, the Carter administration had been getting panicky. U.S. industry and labor were seeking remedy under the antidumping act—a solution wholly unacceptable to the Japanese and the Europeans and increasingly unpalatable to the administration for foreign-policy reasons. On the other hand, Congress seemed to be calling for everything, either through letters, floor debates, or the introduction of legislation.

While in the United States these different types of policy solutions were being called for, the Japanese domestic industry still intended to proceed with unilateral voluntary export restraint. The MITI, however, was opposed to this. On October 20, Amaya met with President Eishiro Saito of Nippon Steel and advised against such export restraint until the U.S. government further clarified its position on the issue. At this late date, Japan's unilateral export restraint was also discouraged by the U.S. industry. U.S. Steel President David Roderick has stated in an interview with a *Nihon Keizai* correspondent that the U.S. steel industry would not withdraw its antidumping suits against the Japanese steelmakers, even after the later resorted to voluntary export restraint.

While debates were going on for or against voluntary export restraint, the Gilmore antidumping suit (its initial filing in early spring as well as the subsequent ruling by the Treasury) had a de facto effect of reducing Japanese steel exports to the United States by the end of October. President Saito of Nippon Steel said the need to post bond and uncertainty about what Carter administration policy would emerge toward the steel problem had forced Nippon Steel to cut back its exports to the United States. According to a U.S. steel executive, the Japanese producers had pulled back and this had brought some new orders to domestic producers. He added, however, that steel producers in Europe and third-world countries such as Korea and Taiwan were going after the customers lost by the Japanese. In fact, Japanese steel-plate exports, which had been subject to the Treasury investigation for Gilmore, had been practically terminated, and major Japanese steel produces were virtually suspending shipments of other steel products covered by the U.S. Steel suite—70 percent of all Japanese steel exports to the United States—for the January-March 1978 period.

Trying to respond to all these different views, Solomon's task force considered a number of different policy directions. Solomon's office had looked at quotas, tariffs, and tariff-rate quotas. It appears that virtually nothing was excluded before the decision to go with a trigger price system was made.

Their mandate, really, was to produce a plan that would defuse the domestic political steel crisis—to convince the steel industry that the administration was serious about helping it. It was, therefore, to be a plan that would address all of the steel industry's problems—modernization, environmental regulation, and trade. Clearly, however, major efforts were directed at the trade issue. Thus, on November 4, *The New York Times* published a story on a forthcoming report by the Solomon task force. It stated that under a plan being worked out by the task force, "Foreign steel mills would be permitted to sell without penalties in the American market at 5 percent below a reference price (or a trigger price) based on production costs of Japanese steel companies." This was what became known as the trigger price mechanism.

The TPM was new, and then again it was not new. It was based on the antidumping concept, which had been around for over fifty years. Also, it was intended to put constraints on the flow of unfairly traded imports—certainly something that had been tried before. In addition, its central feature, self-initiation of antidumping procedures, was nothing new: under traditional antidumping laws, the enforcing agency (then the Treasury, but now the Commerce Department) had always been authorized to initiate antidumping procedures without a petition having been filed by an outside party. However, the way in which the TPM's self-initiation procedure was to work was new. Indeed, it was the mechanics of this feature that made the TPM unique.

The central feature of the TPM was a base price, designated as the trigger price. Any imported steel selling at below the trigger price automatically signalled to those administration officials assigned the task of monitoring steel imports that an antidumping investigation should commence. Because dumping meant that sales were being made at below the cost of production, and because steel imports into the United States came from many countries, each with different economic conditions resulting in varying costs of production, the Solomon Report recommended that the most efficient producer's cost of production be used to determine the trigger price. This was worked out on the theory that the importing of steel priced below the most efficient producer's costs would surely be dumping and that an automatic commencement of an investigation, which implied a fair degree of certainty that dumping had occurred, would be justified. In any event, the cost of production of the Japanese, widely regarded as the most efficient producers of steel, was used.

Solomon's TPM addressed each of the administration's concerns; it also provided the necessary compromise between U.S. industry and the foreigners. First, the bureaucratic nightmare of investigating twenty or more antidumping petitions in such a short period was eliminated. Upon announcement of the TPM, the industry began to withdraw the antidumping petitions that had been filed in September and October. To prove still further his commitment to the plan, and to prove that the system could now cope with any number of countries exporting below the trigger price, President Carter provided for a Trigger Price Enforcement Office in the Treasury Department. The office had its own director, William A. Anawaty, who was promptly dispatched to Capital Hill, to industry and labor leaders, and to Europe and Japan to explain and win support for the TPM.

At the same time, the mechanics of the TPM took account of the perilous domestic economic conditions. Unlike the quantitative restraints used in 1968 and 1972, the pricing mechanism was able to relate the level of import reduction to the price behavior of the domestic industry and, therefore, ensure a degree of pricing discipline. It was made clear in the Solomon Report that the more sharply the domestic firms raised their prices, the smaller would be their recapture of the market. Thus, the trigger price mechanism was a way to keep unfairly priced imports to a minimum, boost profitability for domestic industry, and establish a lid on domestic prices as well: If a foreign producer sold at less than the trigger price (to be adjusted quarterly), it would be subject to sharply higher duties through the immediate application of antidumping penalties. However, because the price level was keyed to the most efficient foreign producer, not the U.S. price level, any price increase by the domestic industry would widen the spread between their prices and the trigger price, making the selling price of the import that much more attractive relative to their own.

Thus, the TPM applied a pricing mechanism to ensure that foreign producers were not selling at below fair cost of production, which would outcompete efficient domestic producers. The purpose was not simply to keep out low-cost imports; nor was it designed to keep out imports per se as quotas (quantative restraints) would have done. Rather, it was to keep out unfairly priced imports. As Secretary Solomon put it, there was no intention "to protect the industry against imports as such," the intention was only "to protect them against dumping."

Support for the TPM

Meanwhile, Japanese and Common Market officials were being briefed on the plan. Typically, there were separate discussions with the Europeans and the Japanese. Although they were not given an option to agree or disagree, both the Europeans and the Japanese seemed quite happy with the plan, which seemed more attractive than any other option.

The Carter administration did establish a system that discriminated in favor of the Europeans, clearly a political choice of conscious design. It was felt that Europe had a more severe adjustment problem than Japan, and that the TPM approach would help buy time for their adjustment process. It would not cost the Japanese anything, and it would give them what they wanted—peace and higher prices.

The Japanese were not bothered by the fact that the Europeans had a license to dump. Nor were the Japanese upset that they were not able to take full advantage of their superior competitive position—that is, by outcompeting the Europeans in the U.S. market. Japanese industry leaders feared that they would become too exposed as the predominant supplier in the United States. Moreover, they competed in different parts of the country—Japan on the West Coast and Europe on the East Coast. More important, for the Japanese, the Solomon plan was by far the better alternative to the regular U.S. antidumping procedures. If Japan wanted to avoid dumping charges based on the constructed value, it would have to sell steel products at prices higher than U.S. domestic prices. According to the new plan, Japan could raise export prices and at the same time still maintain some competitive advantages. More generally, the Japanese felt they risked charges of dumping no matter how they exported their steel products to the United States. It was felt that the new plan would relieve them of such fear and uncertainty.

Although MITI officials were favorable toward the price-related solution at the very inception of the idea, Japanese industry leaders were skeptical at first. Until the very end of October, they had adhered to the view that anything other than a quantitative solution would be unlikely to work.

For one thing, they had not been exposed to any such price mechanism and feared possible loopholes. They were also afraid that they might be asked to submit detailed product-by-product cost data for the implementation of the plan. In fact, it took a face-to-face meeting between Solomon and Inayama to dispel such fears on the part of the Japanese industry leaders. Both men had known and respected each other since they had first met in 1968, when Solomon was an assistant secretary of state. On his way back from Cuba in early November, Inayama stopped in Washington, D.C., to see Solomon at the latter's request (MITI officials had been urging Solomon to contact Inayama for some time). At that time, Solomon convinced the Japanese industry leader of the importance of Japanese industry agreement. Subsequently, the Japanese industry decided to give up the idea of resorting to industrywide unilateral export restraint.

In a meeting with Treasury officials in Washington on November 18, Hachio Iwasaki, director of the MITI's Iron and Steel Division, was told that Japan should submit its industry's average cost data for the purpose of determining the reference prices. He promised to submit such data within the year (the domestic industry subsequently agreed to comply). It was on that same day that Japan heard the good news that U.S. Steel was prepared to withdraw its antidumping suit against the Japanese steel producers if what was called the dumping surveillance system (or the reference price system) functioned properly. In explaining this system to the U.S. domestic industry, Treasury officials did not receive absolute commitments that the industry would not proceed with antidumping suits if imports came within the 5 percent range of the reference or trigger prices. However, there was a tacit understanding that they would not do so. Indeed, the U.S. government had made it clear that it would not administer the new system if companies persisted in antidumping petitions on the grounds that it could not handle both at once. Thus, a compromise had been found.

On December 2, Solomon attended a USW convention in Washington and formally disclosed the contents of his task-force report, which was submitted to President Carter on the same day. Part of the thirty-five-page report stated:

> We recommend that the Department of the Treasury in administering the Anti-dumping Act, set up a system of trigger prices, based on the full costs of production including appropriate capital charges of steel mill products by the most efficient foreign steel producers (currently the Japanese steel industry), which would be used as a basis for monitoring imports of steel into the United States and for initiating accelerated anti-dumping investigations with respect to imports priced below the trigger prices.

> . . . The "trigger" prices would be revised quarterly and would include transportation and insurance costs from Japan to each major importing region for each product group. The U.S. Customs Service monitoring

system would immediately alert the Treasury when steel was imported below the "trigger" price.

The Customs service would also collect, on a continuous basis, information concerning steel prices, costs of producing steel and the condition of the domestic industry. With this information, the Treasury could, if warranted, promptly initiate a "fast track" investigation of suspected dumping.

The "trigger price" system would not prevent any person, domestic or foreign, from exercising its rights under the law to file petitions or contest any decision of the Treasury Department under the law. Nor is it to be regarded as a "minimum price"-setting mechanism. Its sole function is to permit constant review of prices, and, if appropriate, expedited anti-dumping actions. Implementation of the "trigger price" mechanism should result in a substantial elimination of the injury the industry claims it is suffering due to imports at less than "fair value." This should, in turn, eliminate the need for the domestic steel companies to maintain pending or to file future dumping complaints.

The Task Force anticipates that as the world economy expands, current excess steel production will be eliminated and steel pricing practices in world markets will return to more normal patterns. Accordingly, the trigger pricing system will be subject to periodic review and will be ended when conditions warrant. [Solomon Task Force Report, 1977, pp. 2-3, 13]

The TPM was regarded as one part of a four-part program intended to help the U.S. steel industry. The other components were tax benefits, or faster depreciation (also under the administration of Treasury Department); easing of environmental restrictions (under the EPA); and the provision of loans on concessionary terms (through the Commerce Department). However, of the four, the TPM was supposed to have the most immediate impact, both economically and politically.

The greatest success of the task force was its ability to defuse the domestic political crisis that had been seething since late August 1977. Industry's qualified endorsement of the trigger price system led to the virtual end of individual congressmen's pursuit of legislative remedies, the beginning of the lobby's support for the MTN, and a remarkably prompt withdrawal of antidumping petitions. For instance, U.S. Steel withdrew its antidumping suit against six Japanese producers several days after the TPM went into effect on February 21, 1978.

Technically, the bills were still pending, and not all of the antidumping petitions were withdrawn; both were used over the course of the next year as a constant reminder to the administration that the industry still had rather strong leverage over it. Even those suits that were withdrawn were done so on the condition that they would be refiled immediately and given priority consideration if the TPM was not working.

In reality, however, industry executives hoped that they would not be forced to resort to the traditional antidumping petitions. Consider, for example, Lewis Foy's response to congressional inquiries when he testified on behalf of other industry executives: "We hope we can work with the TPM System to make it better." David Roderick, chairman of U.S. Steel, stated that the reference price would be "fair and enable the industry to compete with foreign producers." Indeed, over the next months, other presidents and chairmen of the major steel companies weighed in with varying degrees of support for the TPM. Bethlehem Steel issued a statement in late January that "extended appreciation to the administration and many members of congress who [had] recognized the problems which must be dealt with . . . to encourage and maintain a strong competitive steel industry in the United States." Bethlehem, along with other U.S. companies did question the accuracy of the Japanese cost of production—a central element in developing the actual trigger prices. There were also those who believed that the TPM was far less than the industry could have obtained had they pursued the antidumping suits as originally filed. The important point is that, however qualified, support was forthcoming.

The steelworkers offered their support as well. Like the industry's support, the steelworkers support was more for what the administration was trying to do, since no one knew if the system would actually work, than an unequivocal endorsement. For example, Lloyd McBride, president of the United Steelworkers of America, said:

> We regard the mere existence of the TPM as good since it puts the world on notice that the U.S. government cares about the health of the American steel industry and workers. In that regard, the TPM is beneficial, and it is certainly better than doing nothing. [Steelworkers' Legislative Appeal, 7 December 1977]

This view was also contained in the policy statement labor sent to Congress not one day after the Solomon Report became public. This referred to the broader set of issues contained in the report:

> We welcome the recommendations of the proposed Solomon Task Force as an important indication that the government has finally accepted the necessity of attaining our goal . . . to put our members back to work immediately and to assure them that they will have long-term protection against the loss of their jobs. [Steelworkers' Legislative Appeal, 7 December 1977]

Labor was also optimistic about the new prospects for the antidumping laws. At a March 1978 meeting of the Senate steel caucus, the United Steelworkers endorsed the concept of prompt antidumping relief encompassed in the reference price system, hoping it would ensure a fair market price for imported steel.

The steelworkers' statement went on to outline what they believed the details of the reference price ought to be if it was going to work. Inherent in the outline was approval of the concept and the intentions:

> The United States Steelworkers of America supports the President's steel industry plan as a significant first step toward a necessary long-range program for developing a stronger steel industry and a stronger economy. . . . The reference price mechanism in the President's program does provide a "fast track" remedy for the dumping problems, and therefore we accept it." [Steelworkers' Legislative Appeal, 7 December 1977]

The economic problems were still there—industry still could not meet its cash-flow demands, and the USW continued to live with an exceptionally high unemployment rate—but the domestic political crisis had been defused. Not incidentally, the Japanese industry remained more efficient and therefore more competitive than its U.S. counterpart. However, U.S. policymakers had developed a system that introduced into the steel trade a number of important elements: a degree of predictability (since the exporter would know that sales above trigger prices were likely to be safe from dumping investigations); a speeding up of the investigatory process for the domestic industry; protection against dumping without insulating the domestic industry from price competition; and a focus on price rather than quantity as the determinant of fair trade, helping to satisfy a number of the administration's concerns.

However, critics reasoned that "this scheme in effect puts a floor under the price of imported steel, and thus allows the domestic industry to increase prices without fear of competition" (Adams and Dirlam, 1979, p. 103). On December 9, *The New York Times* editorialized that the gains from the reference price system would be "possible only if the domestic producers resist the temptation to raise prices."

The U.S. steel industry did raise its prices by 5.5 percent on the average, apparently to put maximum pressure on the Carter administration to be generous in the trigger price shield. In any case, congressional and industry outcries against the Japanese steel producers (as well as the Europeans) quickly subsided, and the highly politicized U.S.-Japanese steel issue of 1977 virtually came to an end.

Epilogue

After the TPM was put into effect, Japanese steel imports to the United States steadily declined, a condition that had developed since early October as an effect of the Gilmore suit. Japanese producers were selling steel in the U.S. market slightly above the trigger prices, in part because the dollar value of Japanese steel products rose as the yen appreciated in relation to the dollar. Japan's six major integrated steel companies were also individually exercising self-restraint in their U.S. exports (without forming an export cartel) to make sure Japanese imports would not alarm the United States again. Some Japanese steel executives, including Inayama, believed that such export self-restraint was necessary because the TPM might not be sufficient to help the U.S. industry. Consequently, Japanese steel imports during 1978 declined about 17 percent and Japan's share of the U.S. steel import market dropped to 32 percent. A consensus gradually emerged among the six major Japanese firms that the United States might tolerate about 15 percent of its apparent domestic production to be from imports and that Japan's share could reasonably be expected to be about one-third of that. The decline in the volume of steel exports to the United States was not a painful experience for the Japanese steel industry, because profits actually increased rather than decreased during the implementation of the TPM.

In the meantime, European steel imports (and imports from Canada and third-world countries) had increased rapidly. As noted earlier, the TPM was designed to avoid a political confrontation with Europe by de facto approval of dumping. It was also based on a tacit understanding that U.S. steel companies would not file antidumping petitions against European steelmakers as long as their imports conformed to the TPM. However, with increasing imports from Europe, including those from countries that were, by any standards, selling at below cost of production, the domestic industry was getting impatient. Finally, in March 1980, U.S. Steel filed major anti-dumping complaints against steelmakers of seven European countries (France, Germany, Belgium, Luxembourg, Italy, Britain, and the Netherlands), all of which had trouble with steel overcapacity and unemployment. U.S. Steel charged that steel products, accounting for 75 percent of the 5.4 million tons European steel companies shipped to the United States in 1979, were being sold at less than fair value, or below the cost of production. The Commerce Department (to which the TPM jurisdiction had been moved from the Treasury as a result of the January 1980 trade reorganization) immediately suspended the TPM. The Commerce Department contended that the industry would otherwise be getting dual-track protection, which would increase the danger of inflationary steel-price increases, and that, in any event, they had violated their end of the 1977 bargain by filing antidumping suits. Secretary of Commerce Stanley Klutznick said the TPM could be reinstated under changed conditions. Subsequently, the Commerce Department announced that it had found sufficient basis in the complaints by U.S. Steel to initiate a formal investigation of whether European producers were selling steel in the United States at unfairly low prices.

As predicted earlier, the decision to reinstate the TPM was announced in late September in exchange for the withdrawal of the antidumping complaints. The new trigger prices, effective on October 21, were 12 percent above the prices suspended in March. The new TPM also had an antisurge provision, which still allowed domestic producers to resort to antidumping suits if it was found that an excessive amount of certain specific steel products were being imported, provided that the capacity utilization of domestic industry was 85 percent and aggregate import penetration was more than 13.7 percent of domestic consumption.

Conclusions

At the outset of this chapter, we asked why steel became a major source of tension between Japan and the United States, despite the fact that the competing U.S. and Japanese industries did not necessarily take strong, irreconcilable positions. Indeed, the U.S. industry wanted Japan's quantitative export restraint and that was exactly what the Japanese industry was prepared to do. Thus, both the U.S. and Japanese industries approached their own governments to negotiate an OMA. The Japanese government was inclined to support the domestic industry's position regarding export restraint. The United States, on the one hand, was inclined against the quantitative approach but did not know what else to do, except to allow the domestic antidumping process to take its own course. In short, the issue was never formally initiated by the U.S. government. Rather, it was initiated more indirectly through U.S. industry campaigns for quantitative import restrictions, which were publicized in the press, and through its antidumping suits against Japanese (and European) steel producers, which forced the Treasury Department to take some action.

More fundamentally, however, there was a difference of perspective between the two governments over how and in what policy areas the issue was considered. The Japanese considered the issue primarily in terms of its relations with the United States. It was, for Japan, an issue of access to the U.S. market. This was indicated by both their fervent desire not to be intransigent with regard to possible solutions and their readiness to reduce their share of the U.S. market to what they perceived would be acceptable to the U.S. industry.

The United States, on the other hand, considered the issue in broader terms in a number of different policy areas. This suggests that, almost no matter what the Japanese did, or proposed, from the United States' perspective, the issue was not going to go away so quickly.

There was, of course, the issue of bilateral relations with Japan. But even within that framework, the U.S. government was responding not only to the steel lobby, but to the industries—shoes, consumer electronics, textiles, and leather apparel, for example—that were also pressing for limits on imports. The steel lobby in Congress, for example, was made up of many more people than simply those representing steel states. The issue for the Carter administration went beyond steel to reflect more general dissatisfaction of those in the Congress and of an increasing number of people in the country who feared that the United States was losing its competitive edge as a result of unfair trade practices by its trading partners.

U.S. policymakers and the steel lobby considered the issue in terms of multilateral trade-negotiation politics. Many of the claims by the steel lobby were initially presented in the MTN context and were pursued in that forum. Not all of these claims necessarily addressed the particular U.S.-Japanese bilateral problems, although they tended to exacerbate and keep up front the tensions between the two nations.

Thus, the Carter administration considered the steel issue in terms of what it meant for the prospects of successfully completing the MTN. This suggests, therefore, that the issue would be a major factor in U.S. trade policy as long as the MTN negotiations ensued and, furthermore, that Japan would be held responsible for a good number of the problems. Whether this was justified is not the point; the fact is that U.S.-Japanese relations suffered during this period.

Finally, and possibly most importantly, however, is that, for the United States, the steel issue was far more than one of bilateral relations with Japan—it was considered in the framework of relations with Europe as well. From the United States's point of view, even if the Japanese had promised unilaterally to reduce their share of the U.S. market by significant percentages, there still would have been an issue for which a policy solution would have been necessary. Most of the data, including that presented in U.S. Steel's petition of March 1980, supported the industry's allegation that a number of Europeans were dumping steel on the U.S. market, and that it was both the political and legal responsibility of the U.S. government go take the necessary actions.

Nonetheless, the issue might have been defused somewhat even before the controversial Gilmore suit was filed had the U.S. government decided to go the quantitative route earlier. The Japanese industry expressed its willingness to accept voluntary export restraint as early as October 1976, immediately after the AISI issued an appeal to the STR for import relief on the basis of Article 301 of the Trade Act of 1974. True, Japan's voluntary export restraint would have contributed to the raising of U.S. domestic steel prices—as quotas usually do. But at least it might have prevented the anti-import firestorm in the fall of 1977, giving both governments time to study a longer-term solution within the framework of the OECD or elsewhere.

If the U.S. government was so opposed to the quantitative approach on the grounds that it would be inflationary, one might perhaps argue that it could have done at least one—or a combination—of several things. First the government could have exercised stronger leadership in championing the cause of free trade to dissuade the domestic steel lobby. However, the Carter administration could not afford to antagonize the steel lobby because of the MTN. Second, the administration could have tried to form the OECD steel committee much earlier (than October 21, 1978) to accommodate the domestic political pressure for sectoral negotiations. This might have diffused the issue somewhat, but probably not sufficiently to satisfy the U.S. steel lobby, which wanted immediate relief from imports. Third, the U.S. government could have offered a TPM-like solution much earlier. The problem here was the lack of staff knowledgeable about the Japanese steel situation within the U.S. government. Indeed, it was not until the fall of 1977 that there emerged consensus among the U.S. officials involved in steel policy that the Japanese were the world's most efficient producers. Moreover, only after these officials learned that the domestic industry was also going to file major antidumping complaints against the Europeans did they begin to look seriously for an alternative to the regular antidumping procedure. Lastly, the government could have developed domestic policy courses more quickly than it eventually did—through the Solomon program-by providing tax benefits, easing environmental restrictions, and providing loans on concessionary terms. Even so, it is likely that the industry would still have insisted on immediate relief from imports, because the leaders believed, in good conscience, that this was the essence of their troubled condition. A more basic problem, which relates to all other possible alternatives mentioned above, was that U.S. officials did not understand the seriousness of the issue at first, partly as a result of the ignorance of the new administration, and partly as a result of the low profile of the issue during its early stages.

Much of unnecessary politicization involved the noise surrounding the antidumping suits. The issue was progressively escalated, first after March 29, when the Treasury decided to take up the Gilmore case, and then at the end of September, when the unemployment issue dramatically brought Congress into the policy process. An air of bilateral confrontation emerged in late July, when the Japanese refused to provide their production-cost data to the Treasury. This refusal led to the Treasury's preliminary determination in favor of Gilmore, given the U.S. government's lack of expertise about the Japanese industry and its apparent dependence on the data provided by U.S. industry sources. In this sense, it would have been much better if the Japanese side had maintained closer communications with the Treasury and negotiated for a compromise solution instead of simply saying no to the U.S. government. For instance, Japan could have bargained for the substitution of the average-cost data (later made available for the TPM) for the detailed product-by-product data requested by the Treasury.

The U.S. steel industry played a major part in creating an image in the United States that the Japanese industry was unfairly exporting steel to the U.S. market. Japanese industry and MITI officials were troubled by the fact that Japan was singled out for criticism as a scapegoat by the U.S. industry. As noted above, the Japanese industry's willingness to accept voluntary export restraint and its refusal to provide cost data only reinforced this image of an unfair Japan by providing the U.S. industry with the convenient argument that the Japanese were admitting their own guilt. By the time Treasury officials began to realize that the Japanese were indeed the most efficient steel producers, the domestic firestorm had raged intensely and widely, causing substantial strain in U.S.-Japanese relations. The fact that the United States seemed to be lenient toward the European steel makers (particularly until late September) similarly disturbed some Japanese industry and government officials. As one MITI official put it, "The United States and the European community seem to have a special relationship at the expense of Japan."

Treasury officials did not resort to pressure tactics as such, nor did they particularly encourage the image of an unfair Japan in the course of the steel issue. They realized, especially after the Amaya mission in August, that the Japanese were sensitized to the problem and were trying to cooperate. However, the prolonged recession in the U.S. economy and growing bilateral trade imbalance was, naturally, conducive to the U.S. public's sentiment which was critical of Japan and the Japanese steel industry. Throughout 1977, the United States was engaged in economic talks with Japan (on color television, growth rate, tariff reductions, and beef and oranges) and the noise associated with these talks certainly affected the way in which the steel problem was seen by Americans. It would have been difficult for the U.S. public not to sympathize with the domestic steel industry, particularly when they learned about a series of plant closings and cutbacks which were widely reported in the U.S. press. There was no active consumer movement challenging the domestic industry campaigns, although the American Institute for Imported Steel did try to offer an opposition within the steel community, but they proved to be too small and too weak and, in the end, were ineffective. "Unemployed steelworkers are highly visible," said Milton Friedman, "but what about the 'invisible' consumer? Where the hell are the consumer advocates now that we need them?" (Berger, 1978, p. 134). Although consumers are potential beneficiaries of import competition, they do not usually have as strong an incentive as producers to organize themselves for protecting their interests; they often become free riders, expecting others to do the work for them. Besides, they are usually poorly informed about the benefits of competition. Thus, "consumers often favor protection and regulatory interference in the economy—against their own interests" (Amacher, Tollison, and Willet, 1979, p. 59). According to an opinion poll published by *The New York Times* on June 27, 1980, as many as seven out of ten Americans believed that, given a choice between higher unemployment or cheaper foreign goods, it was more important to protect jobs.

The U.S. press was effectively used by the domestic industry as a medium of its antiimport campaigns. The U.S. media did seem more susceptible to influence by domestic industry views than at other times. The wide and frequent coverage of the steel problem, while not always critical of foreign steel producers, did seem to help the domestic industry in presenting its case to the public. The Japanese press faithfully printed what was reported in the U.S. media and kept the Japanese public informed of how the issue was seen in the United States. Moreover, major Japanese newspapers remained basically critical of the U.S. industry and the Treasury (in regard to the antidumping cases). To no small degree, therefore, the press in both countries played a role in promoting an air of conflict between the two nations.

The TPM was a result of the United States's unilateral action and was preceded by informal discussions and consultations with Japan and the European community. It was necessarily a holding operation, intended as a way to give a breathing spell to the domestic industry, which was suffering from import competition, and it was supposed to be ended when conditions changed. For a time the system seemed to function well as a way to help the domestic industry. U.S. mills were able to operate at almost full capacity—well over 90 percent capacity on the average. At the same time, the Japanese industry was operating at around 70 to 75 percent capacity. "Domestic producers, protected by the minimum prices established under the trigger price system, were now free to raise list prices—so that they would be higher than import prices—to at least the extent of the accustomed differential between domestic and foreign prices" (Adams and Dirlam, 1979, pp. 104-105). Each quarter, the trigger prices were revised, which usually meant that the prices were raised as the dollar-translated Japanese steel-production costs went up with the rising value of the yen. This enabled the domestic industry to further raise its actual and list prices. The immediate cost of inflation as a result of the TPM, as computed in three different studies, ranged from $1 billion to $6 billion (Adams and Dirlam, 1979, p. 105).

However, steel exporters in Europe and third-world countries took advantage of this situation as well as Japan's self-imposed export restraint and steadily increased their shipments to the United States. Because their production costs were well above the Japanese costs, it often meant that they were exporting below costs. Finally, in March 1980, U.S. Steel decided to file major complaints against producers from seven European countries, charging that they were shipping steel to the U.S. market as unfairly low prices. This action forced the Commerce Department to suspend the TPM. At the same time, the Europeans reacted with the threat of a political and economic confrontation, which U.S. officials had tried so hard to prevent in 1977. (Curiously enough, the Japanese steel producers did not issue such a warning in regard to the Gilmore and U.S. Steel antidumping suits in 1977.)

The TPM was reinstated in September 1980, in exchange for the

the withdrawal of the U.S. Steel antidumping suit. Japanese steel leaders prefer the continuation of the TPM to the regular U.S.. antidumping procedure. Apparently, they do not intend to (and they should not) take advantage of the current situation and expand their share in the U.S. market beyond 5-7 percent, provided the share of total foreign imports is kept to around 15 to 20 percent. At the same time, they have been trying to diversify the markets for Japanese steel exports. At present, Japan's steel exports to the United States constitute about 17 percent of its total steel exports, and this percentage may go down even further as exports to other markets (such as China, Southeast Asia, and the Middle East) are expanded. Inayama and other industry leaders seem to believe that Japan should hold its annual steel production at around 110 billion tons (despite the present capacity of 140 million tons) and focus their future efforts on further technological improvements and rationalization. Such a policy should be encouraged.

If the Japanese industry can maintain this position, regardless of cyclical changes in the world demand-supply situation, another major conflict over steel trade between Japan and the United States may be avoided, or at least minimized. However, as long as the structural problems of global overcapacity and oversupply continue and as long as the U.S. industry remains noncompetitive, there will always be a possibility of conflict with steel-exporting countries—if not with Japan or even the European community, then with such newly industrializing countries (NIC) as Korea and Brazil.

Consequently, it will be essential for the steel industries in the United States and Europe to do everything possible to modernize and rationalize production by reducing capacity and/or investing in new and more efficient processes, such as continuous casting and computerization. It will also be necessary for these U.S. and European industries to conrol costs by, among other things, preventing wages from going up as fast as they have been. The U.S. government would also do well to help its industry endeavor by giving greater tax benefits, providing larger loans, and revitalizing the U.S. economy as a whole. This is easier said than done, and most observers remain pessimistic on this score. In any case, a strong and competitive U.S. steel industry would be not only in the interest of the United States but also in the interest of Japan and other Western democracies. The United States's instincts to promote the restructuring and building up of industrial bases in Europe and Japan, born in the postwar period, continue to apply, for reasons having to do with political freedom as much as economic strength. However, in the future, it will be increasingly important to deal with steel trade in the long-term and global perspective—either within the framework of the OECD or the GATT—so, during cyclical recessions, some order can be maintained in international steel trade while, at the same time, keeping the free-trade mechanism basically intact.

References

Interviews

Seventy-six interviews with government officials and steel-industry leaders in Japan and the United States were conducted between July 1978 and July 1980. In the text, direct quotations not specifically cited are taken from these interviews.

Newspapers

Asahi Shimbun, October 1976–December 1977.
Nihon Keizai Shimbun, October 1976–March 1978.
The New York Times, February 1977–October 1980.

Articles and Reports

Adams, Walter, and Dirlam, Joel B. "Unfair Competition in International Trade." In *Tariffs, Quotas & Trade: The Politics of Protectionism,* edited by Walter Adams, at al. San Francisco: Institute for Contemporary Studies, 1979.

Amacher, Ryan C.; Tollison, Robert D., and Willet, Thomas D. "The Divergence between Theory and Practice." In *Tariffs, Quotas & Trade: The Politics of Protectionism,* edited by Walter Adams, et al. San Francisco: Institute for Contemporary Studies, 1979.

Berger, Michael. "Hidden Dimensions in United States-Japan Trade." *Pacific Community,* vol. 9, no. 3 (April 1978), pp. 327-40.

Central Intelligence Agency. *World Steel Market—Continued Trouble Ahead,* (Washington, D.C.: Government Printing Office, May 1977).

Crandall, Robert W. "Competition and 'Dumping' in the U.S. Steel Market." *Challenge* (July-August 1978).

Controller General of the United States. "Economic and Foreign Policy Effects of Voluntary Restraint Agreements in Textiles and Steel," in *Report B-179342,* (Washington, D.C.: Government Printing Office, March 31, 1974).

Interagency Task Force on Steel (Solomon Task Force). *Report to the President: A Comprehensive Program for the Steel Industry,* December 6, 1977.

Japan Iron and Steel Exporters' Association. *U.S.-Japan Steel Trade: Basic Views on Current Issues.* Tokyo: The Overseas Public Relations Committee, July 18, 1977.

Mueller, Hans, and Kawahito, Kiyoshi. "The Recent American-Japanese Discord over the Steel Dumping Issue: An Examination of the Causes of the American Misconception, with Some Reference to Japanese Business Culture." Unpublished paper. Middle Tennessee University, 1979.

Putnam, Hayes, and Bartlett, Inc. "Economics of International Steel Trade." Prepared for the American Iron and Steel Institute, Washington, D.C., May 1977.

U.S. House Steel Caucus. "Resolution 1, September 26, 1977." Attached to a letter sent to President Carter signed by Charles J. Carney, Chairman of the House Steel Caucus.

U.S. Senate Steel Caucus. "Resolution 1, September 26, 1977." Attached to a letter sent to President Carter signed by Jennings Randorf, Chairman of the Senate Steel Caucus.

United Steelworkers of America. "Steelworkers' Legislative Appeal. December 7, 1977."

3 The Politics of U.S.-Japanese Auto Trade

Gilbert R. Winham
and *Ikuo Kabashima*

The year 1980 brought a severe trauma to the automobile industry in the United States. In an industry that directly or indirectly accounts for one out of every six manufacturing jobs in the United States, approximately 300,000, or 40 percent, of the labor force were progressively laid off over the spring months, and roughly double that number were idled in the auto-related industries. What appeared in January to be a recessionary downturn in an admittedly cyclical industry began, by mid-year, to look as if it could afflict lasting change on the automobile companies and their production and marketing infrastructure. Ford and General Motors suffered record losses, and goverment-loan guarantees were required to save Chrysler from imminent bankruptcy. Meanwhile, during the same period, sales of imported cars, particularly from Japan, reached record levels. The suddenness and magnitude of the downturn in autos shocked Americans and led to certain manufacturers and the United Auto Workers (UAW) applying strong pressure on the government to negotiate an export restriction with Japan.

Throughout 1980, the Carter administration resisted these demands, and the action came to a temporary halt in November, when the U.S. International Trade Commission (ITC) found that Japanese auto imports were not the principal cause of injury to the domestic industry and that the industry was not, therefore, entitled to temporary import relief under Article 201 of the Trade Act of 1974. However, the parties seeking protection, principally the United Auto Workers and the Ford Motor Company, continued to solicit direct congressional action. They also put pressure on the incoming Reagan administration. With the U.S. auto slump continuing into 1981, the new administration yielded by working out an arrangement, announced on May 1, by which Japan would cut back modestly on her sales for at least two years.

The economic stakes were high, and they remain so. The immediate concern in the United States is to restore productivity in the domestic auto industry. A corollary concern is that this not be done through government actions that damage U.S.-Japanese economic relations or that reduce the auto industry's incentive to adapt to long-run economic change. The Japanese stakes are substantial, too. Thoroughgoing protection for the U.S. in-

Kabashima is grateful to Mr. Atsushi Ogata for his capable research assistance.

dustry could do severe damage to the Japanese, whose position in the international market place is more fragile than is apparent from current sales statistics, because the U.S. small-car market, which they largely developed, is important to their overall performance. Moreover, unlike in the United States, the auto industry is crucial for the international economic health of the Japanese nation, because it is the single largest earner of foreign exchange in a nation that, in commercial terms, must export or die. The auto case has the potential to become a very difficult political issue in U.S.-Japanese relations, along the lines of the textile wrangle of 1969-1971 (Destler, Fukui, and Sato, 1979). To date, the issue has been handled better than textiles, but what is worrisome is that the enormous economic importance of the automobile industry for both countries could lessen the room for political cooperation in what is basically a competitive economic relationship.

To understand generally U.S.-Japanese economic relations, it is important to examine how and why the auto-trade problem between the United States and Japan generated serious political tensions. This chapter analyzes how the auto issue developed in 1980, treating (1) the background of the auto-trade problem; (2) the process of politicization of the issue; (3) negotiation channels between the two countries; and (4) the management of the problem. The chapter will compare the issue to other examples of U.S.-Japanese economic relations, principally the aforementioned textile case, and will evaluate the diplomatic methods that characterized the auto case to the end of 1980. An epilogue (under Winham's sole authorship) treats the May 1, 1981, export restraint arrangement and its broader significance.

Some Facts behind the Auto-Trade Problem

The U.S. Auto Industry

The U.S. automobile industry is composed of four domestic manufacturers, namely: General Motors, Ford, Chrysler, and American Motors. The first three produce a full line of automobiles and, in 1979, held approximately 45 percent, 20 percent, and 10 percent of the U.S. automobile market, respectively (U.S. House Committee on Ways and Means, 1980; *Ward's Automotive Yearbook*, 1980). A fifth manufacturer, Volkswagen, assembles automobiles in the United States, which is classified as domestic production for retail sales purposes.

The automobile industry is a major employer in the U.S. economy. One out of every twelve manufacturing jobs is directly tied to the industry. More important in numerical terms, however, are the related industries that depend on automobile manufacturers. For example, automobile production accounts for 56 percent of the rubber demand, 24 percent of domestic steel demand, and 15 percent of aluminum demand (Congressional Quarterly, 10 May 1980, pp. 1262-1266). In terms of employment, this accounts for an additional three or more workers in other industries for every auto worker. Still more workers are employed in automotive sales and service. The result is that malaise in the auto industry can produce a ripple effect that has a widespread and severe impact on the U.S. economy.

For the decade of the 1970s, the market for new automobiles in the United States averaged 10.1 million units per year. This figure ranged from a low of approximately 8.5 million units in the years 1970, 1974, and 1975 to highs of over 11 million in 1973, 1977, and 1978. The variation in these figures demonstrates the well-known cyclical nature of the industry. By 1980, the overall number of automobiles registered in the United States was estimated at 120 million units. This represents more than one automobile for every two Americans, which can be compared to ratios of one automobile to three people in Germany, one to four in the United Kingdom, and nearly one to six in Japan. One the basis of these figures, the U.S. market is normally regarded as a mature (that is, replacement) market.

Historically, imports have not been a significant factor in the U.S. market. By 1950, when imports stood at less than one percent of the domestic market, the U.S. auto industry was already a mature industry. The relative position of the "Big Three" was established and did not change over the succeeding three decades. Even the market share of these domestic firms remained relatively constant, with the major change over the thirty-year period being a drop by Chrysler from 18 percent to 10 percent.

The United States began to import automobiles in substantial numbers in the late 1950s, due largely to the popularity of the VW Beetle. By 1959, imports climbed rapidly to 10 percent of the U.S. market, but sales slumped in the early 1960s and did not reach the 10 percent mark again until 1969. From 1969 to 1979, sales figures for imports spiralled their way upward, until, at the end of the decade, they stood at nearly 22 percent, more than double the 1969 figure (see table 3-1). During this period, Japanese manufacturers, who commenced substantial exports to the United States in 1965, gradually overtook the German lead in the U.S. domestic market. In 1969, the Japanese shipped 18 percent of total U.S. imports; in 1975, this figure had climbed to 50 percent. By 1979, Japanese ascendancy was complete, and three out of every four imported automobiles (76.3 percent) were made in Japan.

The Japanese Auto Industry

The Japanese auto industry is composed of nine manufacturers, namely, in order of size of production: Toyota, Nissan (Datsun), Honda, Toyo Kogo,

Table 3-1
U.S. Retail Sales of Domestic and Imported Automobiles, 1965-1980

Year	Domestic	Imports[a]	Total	Import Penetration (percent)
1980[b]	6,578,309	2,395,036	8,973,345	26.7
1979	8,315,622	2,325,477	10,641,099	21.9
1978	9,307,578	2,000,500	11,308,078	11.7
1977	9,104,454	2,070,633	11,175,087	18.5
1976	8,606,573	1,492,595	10,099,168	14.8
1975	7,050,120	1,577,763	8,627,883	18.3
1974	7,331,946	1,408,947	8,740,893	16.1
1973	9,631,082	1,653,494	11,384,576	15.4
1972	9,321,502	1,616,196	10,937,698	14.8
1971	8,676,284	1,563,178	10,239,462	15.3
1970	7,115,537	1,280,359	8,395,896	15.2
1969	8,464,375	985,767	9,450,142	10.4
1968	8,624,819	779,220	9,404,039	8.3
1967	7,567,884	780,579	8,348,463	9.3
1966	8,376,993	658,123	9,035,116	7.3
1965	8,763,197	569,415	9,332,612	6.1

Source: Taken from U.S. Congress, House, Committee on Ways and Means, 96th Cong., 2d Sess., 1980, *Auto Situation: 1980*. Report of the Subcommittee on Trade (Washington, D.C.: Government Printing Office, 1980), p. 4.

[a]Excludes U.S. imports from Canada.

[b]Data for 1980 taken from *Japan Insight*, January 23, 1981.

Mitsubishi, Fuji, Daihatsu, Isuzu, and Suzuki. Of these firms, only the first two had a production capacity of over one million assembled vehicles per year by 1979. Their combined productivity, however, gave Japan a capacity of over 6 million passenger cars and a total production of all motor vehicles of over 9.6 million (Japan Automobile Manufacturers Association, 1980). In 1980, this figure rose to 7 million cars and 10.9 million motor vehicles, making Japan the largest producer in the world (Japan Economic Institute, 1981).

The Japanese auto industry presents one of the more dramatic success stories in modern commercial history. Barely operating at the end of World War II, it went from the production of 110 automobiles in 1946 to the prodution of over 6 million units by 1979. The export performance of the industry is equally startling. Japan did not begin exporting cars until 1956, and then it did not reach an export volume of over 5,000 units until 1958. From this point, exports rose rapidly until 1979, when Japan shipped well over 3 million automobiles abroad, about half of which went to the United States. The annual growth in Japanese production since 1956 has been significantly higher than that in the six other major producing countries—around 15 percent compared to the others' average of 4 percent. In absolute terms, by 1967, Japan outproduced all European Community (EC) countries and, by 1980, it outproduced even the United States (Ikema, 1980). Such rapid expansion could well be a future concern in the auto-trade dispute, because some hold the opinion that the production and export boom of the Japanese has not yet reached any natural limit, despite current disclaimers from the industry itself.

The government of Japan played a significant role in developing the Japanese auto industry. To protect the auto industry in its infant stage, the government employed various forms of trade barriers, which freed the industry of competition from more powerful foreign auto manufacturers. For example, as shown in table 3-2, Japan had much higher tariff rates than did the United States or the European community until the beginning of the 1970s. Today, however, Japan has no tariffs on either small- or large-size cars. The protectionist policies of the past have frequently invited criticism in the United States that the Japanese auto industry achieved high levels of competitiveness behind some of the highest protective walls in modern industrial history.

While insulating the industry from foreign competition, the government of Japan also encouraged improvements in auto technology, plant rationalization, and market organization. For example, in the 1950s, the Ministry of International Trade and Industry (MITI) encouraged Japanese manufacturers to improve their technology by making policies that favored joint ventures with foreign producers; in this way, Japanese manufacturers could absorb advanced technology from abroad. Because the MITI controlled all foreign licensing agreements and gurantees for remittance of royalties from Japan, it could insist that such guarantees would be continued only on the condition that 90 percent of the licensed parts were produced in Japan within five years. This policy permitted domestic manufacturers to perform, under license, knock-down assembly of foreign cars in Japan. The government also coordinated, and provided directly, financial assistance for the

Table 3-2
Japan, U.S., and EC Tariff Rates on Passenger Cars, 1967-1978
(in percentages)

Year	Japan Small Cars	Other Cars	United States	European Community
1967	40.0	28.0	6.5	22.0
1968	36.0	28.0	5.5	11.0
1969	36.0	17.5	5.0	11.0
1970	20.0	17.5	4.5	11.0
1971	10.0	10.0	4.0	11.0
1972	6.4	6.4	3.0	11.0
1978	0	0	3.0	11.0

Source: Comptroller General of the United States, *United States-Japan Trade: Issues and Problems* (Washington, D.C.: U.S. Government Printing Office, 1979), p. 44.

auto industry. Reconstruction loans from the Japan Development Bank were extended to car producers from 1951 to 1955, and this funding accounted for approximately 9 percent of the total investment of Japanese manufacturers. Accelerated depreciation rates, allowing depreciation of up to 50 percent, in a year were extended to the manufacturers. Finally, in the 1950s, direct subsidies of approximately $1 million were given to the Automobile Technology Association. The overall result of these actions was that the auto industry was able to build a solid base in Japan before it was tested in international competition, although MITI officials do admit that the rapid development of the industry did have a price in that high-priced low-quality domestically produced cars were, for a time, imposed on Japanese consumers.

Although such government policy had significant influence, the main cause of the rapid expansion of Japanese auto production was almost certainly Japan's rapid economic growth. In the past two decades, per capita national income has risen quite rapidly. Because the selling price of automobiles has not changed significantly during this period, the price of a car relative to per capita national income declined at a rapid rate. There seems to have been high correlation between the sales of automobiles and economic growth. By combining rapid expansion of domestic demand with rapid economic development and government policies to aid the industry, the Japanese auto industry expanded its production and achieved significant economies of scale in the early 1970s, with the number of man-hours required to produce an automobile cut by more than half.

Until about 1970, as figure 3-1 illustrates, the great bulk of Japan's auto production was sold domestically. However, once growth slowed in the home market, the Japanese automakers turned their attention to foreign markets, particularly the United States, which took approximately 40 percent of Japan's total exports. The export drive in the early 1970s coincided with Japanese auto manufacturers' achieving significant economy of scale, which allowed strong international competitiveness. Beside this price competitiveness, the high quality of Japanese cars also contributed to the expansion of auto exports. In a survey conducted for a trade journal in 1979, nearly half of the U.S. automobile engineers who responded rated that Japanese cars were the best quality, followed by German cars (U.S. House Committee on Ways and Means, 1980, p. 47). They commented that Japanese cars were of highest quality not because Japan possessed the best technology, but principally because it possessed the most disciplined workmanship on the production line.

Causes of the Present Problem

One source of the auto-trade problem was the oil crisis of 1973. After the oil crisis, U.S. consumer demand shifted from large cars to fuel-efficient

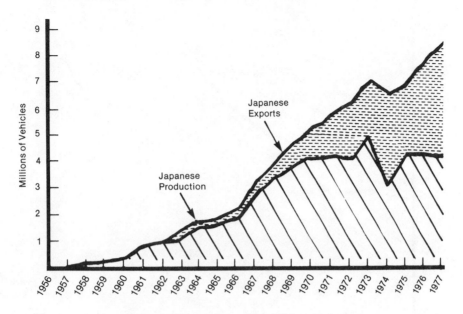

Source: The U.S. Comptroller General, *United States-Japan Trade: Issues and Problems.* (Washington, D.C.: U.S. Government Printing Office, 1979), p. 40.

Figure 3-1. Japanese Production and Exports of Cars, Trucks, and Buses, 1956-1977

small cars. The share of small-size cars in the U.S. market in 1972 was approximately 37 percent; it increased to 50.8 percent in 1975 (see figure 3-2). After 1975, consumption of small cars fell off, but the second oil crisis, in 1979, caused demand to increase once again, raising the market share to 56.6 percent.

The U.S. Big Three made some attempt to compete with foreign cars during the 1970s, notably with the introduction of General Motor's Chevette (and later the X-body cars, such as Citation), Ford's Pinto and Bobcat, and Chrysler's Omni and Horizon. However, their main emphasis was still on large cars because they were more profitable. Their continuing policy of emphasizing large cars failed to take into consideration the secular ˌshift in consumer demand, which occurred over the entire decade and resulted in the relinquishing of an increasing portion of market share to foreign producers. When the second oil crisis came in 1979, it sharply accelerated the shift to small cars, and Detroit was wholly unprepared for this sudden change. In 1979, the ratio of small cars to large cars sold in the United States jumped to 56 percent to 44 percent. In the first three months of 1980, the mix in favor of small cars became 64 to 36 percent. U.S. manufacturers did not have the small cars available to meet this new demand.

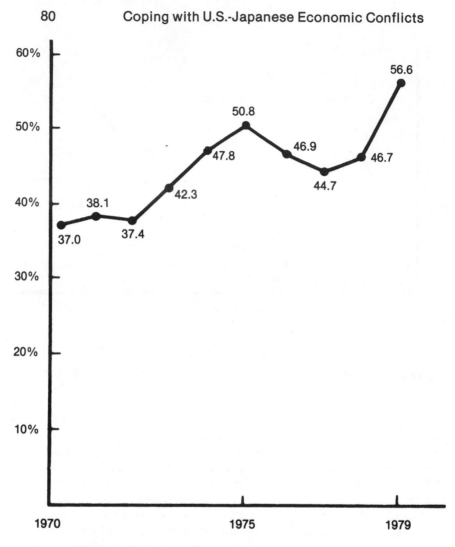

Source: U.S.-Japan Trade Council, Council Report No. 8, February 29, 1980.
Figure 3-2. Change in the Demand for Small-Sized Cars

In a market that averages about 10 million units per year, the U.S. manufacturers (including VW) were estimated to have the capacity to supply only
1.75 million small cars in 1980. The recent difference between the demand
for small cars and domestic output has been made up by imports, principally from Japan, while at the same time the domestic manufacturers have
been faced with large inventories, plant closures, and massive unemployment. It is interesting to speculate why a shift of comparable magnitude in
consumer preferences did not occur after the 1973 oil embargo and the

gasoline shortages it created. The answer is probably that the shortages were not followed by higher prices, so a skeptical public could dismiss the oil crisis as a temporary political phenomenon. In 1974, average U.S. gasoline prices, in constant dollars, posted only a 20 percent increase over the previous year, and thereafter they actually fell until 1979. However, in 1979, the oil emergency was followed by oil price decontrol. There was a steep rise in the real price of gasoline, which by December 1979 was 41 percent over the average price in 1978.

There has been a considerable thrust in public statements issued by both U.S. industry and government officials to affix blame on each other for the current situation. The case against the industry is that it failed to plan for and develop small-car production after the 1973 actions by the OPEC nations. The industry, it is argued, should have been able to foresee that gasoline prices would increase in the years following 1973, even if it could not predict exactly when, or how rapidly, they would rise. For its part, the industry has countered with the argument that government oil-pricing policies helped maintain the high demand for large cars, and that the automakers responded by producing large cars because they were the only ones the makers could sell. It is difficult to assess the industry's claim that, after 1974, low gas prices prevented it from further developing small fuel-efficient automobiles more effectively than it did. It is well known that the industry makes more profit on large cars than on small cars, in part because large cars can be more easily loaded with expensive accessories, such as automatic transmissions, air conditioning, and so forth. Therefore, the industry's claim has been subject to sharp criticism. Perhaps the most accurate judgment of this issue is that the government created the conditions wherein it was possible to put short-term gains ahead of more important long-run considerations, and the industry, in turn, behaved in precisely that way.

Politicization of the Auto Situation

The current crisis in automobiles arises in the context of a history of trade difficulties between the United States and Japan. Specific economic problems have had a tendency to escalate into more serious political confrontations between the two countries. The aforementioned textiles case was the most prominent example of this, but there have been other similar situations of strained relations, notably the case of color televisions (Metzler, 1979), the Strauss mission made in January 1978 in response to the adverse U.S.-Japanese trade balance (Destler, 1979), and the negotiations over the procurement policies of Japan's NTT (treated in chapter 5 of this book). In the 1980 automobile situation, which involved an industry of paramount importance, there were obvious dangers that the problem could become politicized to an extent that it might lead to a breakdown in the effort to maintain liberal trading relations between the United States and Japan.

Economic issues become politicized in U.S.-Japanese relations when they rise to prominence in one of the governments and cause officials in that government to make important demands on the other. According to the first part of this definition, the auto crisis clearly became politicized in 1980, because major actors in the United States ensured that the situation was (and continues to be) well-publicized, both at home and abroad. However, neither government made substantial demands on the other in 1980. To be sure, major figures in the U.S. government called upon Japanese to increase auto investment in the United States, but this demand was greeted with some sympathy, even in Japanese official circles. In comparison with the textile case, the auto issue proceeded more smoothly and with less difficulty for overall U.S.-Japanese relations, a point to which we will return later.

In this section, we will explore the process whereby certain actors sought to politicize the U.S. auto crisis and the various actions that were taken by members of the U.S. government and that have a bearing on this issue. In the following section, we will take up the concurrent interactions that occurred between the U.S. and Japanese governments.

UAW's Initiation

The group most responsible for initiating the auto dispute was the United Auto Workers. This is not surprising, because the UAW is the group most affected by the U.S. auto slump. Unlike Japanese workers, auto workers in the United States are treated as variable inputs and, therefore, are usually laid off when manufacturers face serious inventory build-ups. By November 1979, the number of laid-off workers reached 102,000, which galvanized the UAW leadership to publicize the issue.

In response to rising unemployment, the UAW urged Japan to invest in assembly plants in the United States in order to absorb part of the unemployment and reduce export of Japanese cars. Such urgings by the UAW were not a new phenomenon. Because of its historic free-trade principles, the UAW preferred to meet the problem of competition from Japanese exports through investment in the United States by Toyota and Nissan rather than through import restrictions. As early as 1975, UAW President Leonard Woodcock had strongly encouraged Japanese auto makers to invest in the United States. Subsequently, UAW Vice-President Pat Greathouse visited Japan to meet with the heads of Japanese auto manufacturers and urge them to build assembly plants in the U.S. (Mainichi, 29 June 1977). In March 1978 and June 1979, he again urged Toyota and Nissan to invest in the United States. However, his approach to the Japanese auto industry was too low keyed to produce any response from Toyota and Nissan. This failure to persuade Japanese manufacturers taught the current president of the UAW, Douglas A. Fraser, to take a different approach. His approach was to dramatize the issue in an attempt to apply pressure on Japanese auto manufacturers.

Fraser criticized the Japanese auto makers publicly on various occasions. On November 1, 1979, he declared that UAW members would boycott Japanese cars unless Toyota and Nissan built assembly plants in the United States. On January 13, 1980, at a press conference in Washington, Fraser told reporters that he was preparing a recommendation for legislation that would require automobile manufacturers who sold more than 200,000 cars in the United States to build assembly plants in that country. He claimed that this legislation had the general support of congressmen and senators, although there were no subsequent moves of any consequence in the Congress, despite the offer by Michigan's Senator Donald W. Riegle, Jr., to introduce the legislation proposed by Fraser (*Sankei Shimbun*, 13 January 1980).

In the initial stage of the automobile-trade dispute, two other developments were important from the Japanese perspective. On January 28, 1980, Ambassador Mike Mansfield made a speech at the Japanese press club warning that, unless Toyota and Nissan quickly decided to invest in the United States, the U.S. government might take very protectionistic actions. He reminded his audience that this was a presidential election year, and he described the present situation as particularly tense. Second, Chairman David M. Roderick of U.S. Steel also helped to escalate the auto-trade problem by saying that, according to research conducted by U.S. Steel, Toyota and Nissan were dumping their cars in the United States at prices 14 to 20 percent lower than the prices of cars sold in Japan. This statement was made in a lecture at the Detroit Economic Club on February 4, 1980. Toyota Motor Sales flatly denied Roderick's accusation (*Yomiuri Shimbun*, 5 February 1980). These two developments received a great deal of press attention in Japan.

On February 10, on the invitation of Ambassador Mansfield and Mr. Ichiro Shioji (chairman of both the confederation of Japanese Automobile Workers Associations and Nissan's Labor Union), Fraser went to Japan to urge Toyota and Nissan to build plants in the United States. Shioji undertook this initiative, which might have been expected to have had an adverse effect on Japanese labor, because he was a good friend of Fraser and was very sympathetic to the UAW problem. Shioji thought that inviting Fraser to Japan would improve both the Japanese government's and manufacturers' understanding of the U.S. problem and would thereby avoid emotional conflict. In addition, Shioji himself urged Toyota and Nissan to build plants in the United States.

With regard to this latter action, it is worth noting that Shioji took a more sympathetic view of the UAW position than did the Toyota labor leaders, probably because Shioji enjoyed greater autonomy from the Nissan management than the Toyota unionists enjoyed. The Toyota union leader, Shiro Umemura, took a more conservative view regarding employment security in Japan and pointed out that, if Toyota began to produce 200,000 cars in the United States, approximately 40,000 Toyota workers would become jobless. He further claimed that, even if Japanese automakers began construction of plants in the United States, it would be two to three years before they would contribute to relieving the unemployment among U.S. autoworkers. Despite his objections, he was not unequivocally opposed to Toyota's investment in the United States, although he placed priority on domestic employment.

On his arrival in Japan on February 10, 1980, Fraser immediately made his intentions clear in a press conference by stating: "I will tell the Japanese auto manufacturers and the government to restrict Japan's exports and to establish assembly plants in the United States." He proceeded to carry out his plans in a series of meetings with Japanese leaders and was accorded a VIP treatment that was unusual for such a private visit (*Nihon Keizai Shimbun*, 10 February 1980).

On February 12, Fraser met with President Takashi Ishihara of Nissan Motors Company. Ishihara apparently agreed that Japanese exports should be restricted, but he had doubts about overseas plants, despite the fact that Nissan was considering manufacturing small-sized trucks in the United States (*Nihon Keizai Shimbun*, 13 February 1980). Fraser knew of Nissan's planned investment in truck production, and he emphasized that Nissan should consider producing passenger cars as well, noting the large sales of Datsun sedans in the U.S. market.

The following day, Fraser met separately with Prime Minister Masayoshi Ohira and Minister of Foreign Affairs Saburo Okita. In the first meeting, Ohira suggested that some friction was probably inevitable due to the large trade between Japan and the United States, but that it was desirable to solve such problems early and in a spirit of understanding and cooperation. He added that, in this case, it was desirable that Fraser discuss the matter with those involved in order to initiate a cooperative approach to this problem. Fraser pointed out that the friction was due to increased Japanese exports and the concurrent increase in unemployment in the United States and that, although the UAW had supported free trade so far, if Japanese manufacturers failed to make their decisions on investment quickly, it might be forced to support restrictions on imports. If the UAW did this, it would have the support of many within the United States, who were asking for a quota system against Japan similar to that applied by the United Kingdom, France, and other European countries. This, Fraser agreed, would not be a good idea; from an economic point of view, investment in the United States would be a preferred solution to those arrangements that had been previously made in the case of steel trade. Ohira replied that the question of building plants in the United States should be dealt with from a global point of view, and he added that the Japanese government would do whatever was possible to help solve the problem.

In his meeting with Foreign Minister Okita, Fraser reiterated that the UAW was worried that the auto problem might produce frictions in U.S.-Japanese relations and that it hoped to solve the problem through accommodation rather than confrontation. He emphasized that the root of this problem was, essentially, the high unemployment rates in the United States and that the UAW's preferred solution to this problem was the Japanese manufacturers' investment in the United States—a solution similar to that undertaken by Volkswagen in the state of Pennsylvania—rather than import restrictions. In his response, Okita noted that demand in the U.S. market was shifting from larger to smaller cars, thereby causing a temporary increase in the sale of Japanese cars, but that U.S. manufacturers would regain their competitiveness once they started producing small-sized cars as their main products. Therefore, Japanese manufacturers were hesitant to invest in the United States because they feared the possibility of overcapacity in the U.S. market. Fraser replied that the increasing demand for small cars in the United States was not a temporary phenomenon and that, even though General Motors would expand its production of small cars by the spring of 1982 and Ford and Chrysler would strengthen their small-car production by the end of the current year, Japanese cars would nevertheless maintain their competitiveness because of their high quality. Fraser repeated the strong desire of the UAW to have Japanese manufacturers invest in the United States. Fraser added that Representative Charles Vanik would be holding a House Trade Subcommittee hearing on the auto problem within thirty days and that a rational arrangement had to be adopted quickly because the problem could get out of hand on account of the presidential election campaign in the United States.

On February 14, Fraser met with Japanese Trade Representative Takeshi Yasukawa, who echoed the sentiments previously expressed by the other Japanese officials; that is, that Japanese manufacturers had not made their decisions on investing in the United States because they were unsure whether Japanese cars would maintain their competitiveness indefinitely. Therefore, it was a better tactic to seek to encourage, rather than to force, Japanese manufacturers to invest in the United States. Furthermore, to put pressure on Japan and charge that Japan was exporting unemployment would indeed not solve anything. Yasukawa emphasized that Japan would welcome UAW cooperation, and he encouraged the UAW to provide whatever documentary evidence or other material it could to encourage the Japanese manufacturers to invest in the United States.

Fraser responded that Toyota and Nissan had been considering the possibility of U.S. investments for a long time, especially since examples had already been set by VW and Honda, and that the time was ripe for action. He agreed that the risk involved was great, but this was partially offset by the fact that Japanese manufacturers would have to invest much less than U.S. manufacturers would in the production of small cars. In any case, Fraser said, the demand for small cars was likely to continue to increase in the forseeable future. To assist Japanese manufacturers in locating in the United States, Fraser promised that the UAW would cooperate with the efficient Japanese production systems that manufactured high-quality cars, and he noted that U.S.-built Volkswagens were said to be better quality than those built in Germany. He further proposed that, as it had for VW, the UAW would assist Japanese manufacturers by making agreements on wages and other matters until the Japanese automakers turned a certain measure of profit.

Later on February 14, Fraser met with President Eiji Toyoda of Toyota Motor Company and reiterated his now-familiar request that Toyota plants be established in the United States. Toyoda replied that Toyota did not have much confidence that it could compete with U.S. manufacturers at the present time, although he indicated that the problem was under review by Toyota (*Nihon Keizai Shimbun*, 14 February 1980).

The visit to Japan apparently served Fraser's objectives. In a concluding press conference, Fraser said that he was more optimistic than before he had arrived in Japan that the Japanese government fully understood the United States's concerns and that Toyota and Nissan were seriously considering the establishment of plants in the United States. He did allow, however, that he perceived the response of Toyota to be more serious than that of Nissan (*Nihon Keizai Shimbun*, 15 February 1980), a move undoubtedly designed to bring further pressure on Nissan to establish passenger-car plants in the United States.

From an analytical standpoint, it is clear that Fraser's mission increased Japan's awareness of the U.S. problem. The trip probably had little impact on U.S. policymaking, although it did allow certain concerns on the Japanese side to be voiced and presumably incorporated into U.S. thinking. For one thing, the Japansese auto manufacturers made a convincing case regarding the difficulties of taking company action to reduce exports to the United States. If such restrictions were done through agreements between the automakers, they could be sued in the United States by their U.S. dealers on the basis of restraint of trade provisions in U.S. antitrust legislation. On the other hand, if they restricted exports unilaterally, there was no guarantee that other Japanese companies would follow suit, which could leave them in an exposed position in a very competitive overseas market.

A second problem that surfaced was that U.S. demands on the Japanese automakers were indeed inconsistent. For example, on February 4, the chairman of U.S. Steel charged Toyota and Nissan with dumping, which is, of course, selling products on foreign markets at prices below those charged in the domestic market. However at the same time, they were being accused by the U.S. Internal Revenue Service (IRS) of understating the revenue of their subsidiaries in the United States. The IRS claimed that the manufcturers were avoiding taxes by exporting from Japan to the United States at unreasonably high prices, thereby reducing the profits of the U.S. subsidiaries. It appears that the IRS formulates this argument on the basis of information that the Japanese companies had provided to defend themselves against a previous dumping charge and that this information had been used against them (*Asahi Shimbun*, 18 February 1980). Another example of inconsistency, and one that would confirm the fear of Toyota and Nissan regarding antitrust suits, involved a suit U.S. dealers brought against Honda for alleged failure to supply sufficient units to retailers. This vividly pointed out that the Japanese auto manufacturers were in a difficult position, with pressures on the one hand from the UAW to restrict exports and pressure on the other from dealers to increase them.

Role of the Media

Almost by definition, the media in Japan and the United States helped to politicize the auto-trade issue, because they assisted in its rise to prominence before their respective publics. Starting with Fraser's visit to Japan, both the Japanese and U.S. press gave wide coverage to the auto problem, perhaps magnifying the problem more than it actually warranted. The U.S. press, shown in figure 3-3, escalated its coverage enormously at about the time of Fraser's visit to Japan, and the press continued to give prominence to it and other U.S.-Japanese trade issues. And public opinion showed substantial support for trade restrictions. According to *The New York Times*/CBS news poll of June 26, 71 percent of Americans were in favor of "protecting jobs at the cost of higher prices on foreign products," while only 19 percent favored lower prices if some unemployment were the result (*The New York Times*, 27 June 1980).

Japanese newspapers also paid close attention to the automobile problem. Although they warned that Japan should act quickly, they tended to be somewhat critical of U.S. aggressiveness and said that the final decisions for investments should rest with the individual companies. Generally, they supported amicable relations and stressed the need to remove misunderstanding between the two countries. Despite these views of the Japanese press regarding the United States, the wide coverage of the problem led to a growing concern in Japan and helped to magnify the issue.

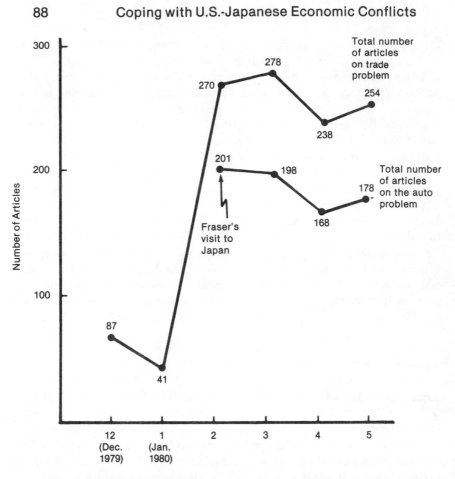

Source: Keizai Koho Centre, *Kaigai Tainichi Keizai Kankya Monitoring Monthly Report* (various issues), 1980.

Figure 3-3. U.S. Press Coverage on the Auto Problem

Congressional Action

By March 1980, public concern had galvanized action in Congress. Representatives Ronald M. Mottl and Bob Traxler introduced bills into the House that would impose quotas on imported automobiles and other vehicles. Both bills were referred to committee, and little action was subsequently taken. More significant were the Hearings on World Automobile Trade, held in early March by Representative Charles A. Vanik, chairman of the Subcommittee on Trade of the House Committee on Ways and Means. These hearings were especially timely in that they precipitated interagency decision making in the administration. They also, of course, allowed the automobile industry and associated experts to present data on the automobile crisis as the situation was still unfolding.

The testimony of major administration spokesmen, based on an inter-agency review of the automobile situation, reflected a rare degree of bureaucratic unity. The principal testimony was presented by U.S. Trade Representative Reubin Askew (elaborated upon by Deputy Robert D. Hormats) and by George C. Eads of the Council of Economic Advisors (CEA). This testimony was subscribed to by representatives of the Departments of State, Transportation, Energy, Commerce, and Labor and the Environmental Protection Agency. The testimony dealt foursquare with the issue of import restrictions. The economic analysis presented by Eads indicated that any effort by the government to help Detroit through either negotiated restrictions or outright controls would cost the U.S. economy far more than it would gain from increased production and employment in the United States. Using a model that assumed 1980 imports would be held to 1979 levels (a reduction of approximately 250,000 units from what was otherwise forecast), the CEA analysis projected the following results:

1. Increased consumer expenditures on automobiles by $1 to $2 billion.
2. Increased domestic employment by no more than 20,000 workers.
3. Increased oil imports by about one million barrels per year for up to ten years due to the decreased average fuel efficiency of U.S. models.

The figure of 20,000 workers included 5,000 from the automobile industry, with the remainder coming from auxiliary industries. It represented less than 3 percent of the number of automobile workers then on indefinite layoff. All told, the action projected would have cost the U.S. economy between $50,000 and $100,000 for each of the 20,000 jobs created.

The statements of Ambassadors Askew and Hormats dealt with the problem in broader perspective. The cause of the problem, they argued, was the sudden shift in consumer demand toward small, fuel-efficient quality automobiles, which occurred in response to the gas shortages and rising gas prices, both part of the ongoing energy crisis facing the United States. This shift was entirely understandable and was probably permanent. The U.S. industry was unprepared to meet this shift, partly because it had failed to draw the proper conclusions from the long gas lines, spot shortages, and sharply increasing world oil prices after 1973. This consuming public, which resisted energy conservation, also shared responsibility for this failure, and the government contributed to this misjudgment by maintaining artificially low domestic oil prices. In sum, the loss of market share by the U.S. companies was symptomatic of a much larger energy crisis facing the United States.

The Askew-Hormats testimony characterized the industry's situation as a transitional conversion problem and expressed confidence in the idea that U.S. automakers, already in the midst of the transition, would emerge better equipped to face foreign competition than ever before. The role of the government was not to restrict foreign imports, which would be costly and illegal under current law, but rather to encourage the United States's trading partners to conduct as open a regime as the United States did in matters of trade and investment. In the case of Japan, this would require efforts to encourage the Japanese to removing the remaining barriers to automobile imports from the United States and, particularly, to persuade the Japanese automobile industry to follow the precedent set by Volkswagen of building plants in the United States. The latter argument for investment was part of a more general approach to the management of the international economy. As Ambassador Hormats testified:

> The Administration believes as a matter of general policy, as stated by Governor Askew, that American interests are best served by an international system that allows investment, like trade, to flow freely—that is without artificial incentives, disincentives, barriers or conditions.

Within the framework of this policy, the administration would encourage the Japanese to invest in the United States, because it clearly had a market that would serve as a magnet for such investment. As Ambassador Hormats continued, "Companies which already have considerable sales in the United States, and know our market well, should give serious consideration to investing in production here" (Hormats, 1980, p. 189).

The policy that emerged from the hearings was clear-cut and widely shared among members of the administration. First, it rejected import restrictions as being against U.S. interests. Second, it sought to encourage economic investment in the United States by foreign, particularly Japanese, manufacturers. Third, it sought improved access for U.S. exports of automobiles and parts in foreign markets. At a time when restrictions against Japanese imports might have been expected, the U.S. policy appears to have been responsive to Japanese interests and concerns, but there is no evidence (based on the public record and personal interviews) that U.S. officials took much account of U.S.-Japanese trading relations in their policymaking on automobiles. U.S. policy was based wholly on an analysis of U.S. interests: If the government avoided a wrangle over automobiles so far, it was not because U.S. officials were consciously trying to avoid friction with Japan.

Separate U.S. Government Actions

Apart from the congressional hearings in the spring, the U.S. government became involved with the auto situation in three additional actions during the remainder of 1980. That these actions were wholly unrelated bears vivid testimony to the problem of achieving internal control over the actions of government—a problem especially threatening when those actions can have a deep significance for the management of external relations.

The first action involved the Customs Service of the Department of Treasury. In 1967, in response to an increase in poultry tariffs brought about by the commercial integration of the European community, the United States acted on its GATT rights and retaliated by raising its duty on light trucks to 25 percent. This action was part of the unfortunate trade dispute known as the chicken war. The target of U.S. retaliation was Germany, specifically Volkswagen, and the increased duty successfully stopped the small volume of trucks Volkswagen had been shipping to the United States. The response of VW over the ensuing years was to invest in the United States and to produce domestically trucks that would not be subject to the crippling duty. Japanese manufacturers, however, took a different route. The Japanese noted the tariff on truck parts was only 4 percent, which was consistent with the generally low U.S. tariffs on automotive products, and established assembly plants in the United States designed to carry out the final stage of truck production. The result was that the Japanese effectively exported trucks to the United States in two parts, truck chassis and truck bodies, paid a 4 percent duty, and then assembled and sold the trucks in the U.S. market.

As the volume of Japanese sales grew, demands increased, particularly from U.S. labor, to close the loophole in U.S. tariff law. The Customs Service finally studied the issue and, in May 1980, reached the technically correct decision that truck chassis indeed constituted trucks for the purpose of U.S. customs law, thereby raising the duty on truck chassis to the prohibitive level of 25 percent. The effects of this action were deeply ironic, leading *The Washington Post* to editorialize on May 28, 1980, about "the sweaty world of trade politics." The Big Three U.S. companies all imported Japanese chassis and sold them in the United States under their own name, so those supposedly protected by the duty had to pay it. The Japanese, who were not the target of the higher duty in the first place, faced a major new burden on their truck exports. The immediate beneficiary of the change was VW's plant in Pennsylvania, the only manufacturer of light trucks in the United States, which was owned by the same company against whom the increased tariff was directed over a decade ago.

The Customs action left President Carter some room to maneuver under U.S. law. He could allow the higher duty to go into effect, or he could reduce the 25 percent duty by up to two-thirds, either unilaterally or in negotiations with the Japanese. By early summer, the president was being advised by influential members of his administration that he should not hurry to revise the tariff downward, on the political grounds that it would appear to be rubbing salt in UAW wounds and fuel demands for more stringent import controls. The president acted on this advice. However sound this action may have been in terms of domestic politics (and even in terms of efforts to avoid more far-reaching restrictions), it nevertheless had an adverse effect on U.S.-Japan relations. Nissan Motors protested the action in a letter to Ambassador Askew and, in pointing out that Nissan was currently planning to establish a plant in the United States, claimed that the higher duty would "undermine the very basis" for the construction of the plan (*The New York Times*, 2 July 1980). On the face of it, this argument does not seem economically plausible, because high foreign duties that block exports are usually a reason for investing abroad. However, the higher tariff would impede imports of components by any U.S.-based Nissan plant, and it undoubtedly would disturb the political atmosphere surrounding the issue. As evidence for the latter point, there were suggestions from the auto industry in Japan that Japanese businessmen should withdraw some cooperative arrangements that the two countries had previously agreed upon (*The Wall Street Journal*, 25 July 1980).

The second of the three unrelated actions that occurred in the U.S. government took place in the Senate. In contrast with the Customs decision, which was technical and produced concrete results, the Senate action was political and largely symbolic. It consisted of a resolution introduced on June 18, 1980, by Senator Donald W. Reigle, Jr., of Michigan "to promote the competitiveness of the U.S. industry in the world automobile and truck markets' (*Congressional Record*, S7348-49). It was co-sponsored by eighty other senators and, obviously, passed overwhelmingly. The resolution took no action, hence it could be seen as a symbolic gesture rather than a serious attempt to do something about the problem. Its importance was that it revealed the way in which Congress perceived the problem, and the concerns that Congress might seek to protect should it later resort to legislation on the issue.

The resolution acknowledged that the present difficuly was "not self-correcting" and that it threatened to inflict "lasting structural deterioration and dislocation on the industrial base of the United States." It further acknowledged the importance of the problem by defining the automobile and truck industry as a "strategic national industry that is essential to the economic stability and national security of the United States." The resolution outlined the need to create an investment climate in which U.S. industry could rapidly convert to fuel-efficient automobiles, but it reserved its strongest language for the issue of unemployment: "It is in the national interest of the United States to reduce substantially the high level of unemployment . . ." *(Congressional Record,* S7348-49). The resolution called upon the administration, foreign governments, and foreign and domestic manufacturers and unions to take immediate action to reduce unemployment in the United States.

The resolution was significant because of what it did not say. It did not state a need to support individual automobile firms, even though Congress was engaged in just such an action with Chrysler. Nor did it mention taking action to change the trade deficit with Japan, although it deplored the trade deficit. By singling out unemployment, the resolution underscored what is perhaps obvious about normal trade relations, but what becomes inescapable in a time of crisis: In the modern international system, the real concern underlying trade issues regards relative levels of employment. The base of the present crisis is that U.S. workers are out of work while Japanese workers are enjoying a boom period through trade. The dilemma is that the tools of trade policy are either inadequate or inappropriate to handle the problem of unemployment. This is perhaps why U.S. leaders have focused as much as they have on securing Japanese investment in the United States.

The third unrelated action was an escape clause action, initiated on June 12, 1980, by the UAW and the Ford Motor Company, under Article 201 of the Trade Act of 1974. This action was filed with the International Trade Commission, and required the ITC to make a determination of whether Japanese imports constituted the principle cause of injury to the domestic industry. If the finding were affirmative, the ITC could recommend to the president of mix of actions (quotas, tariff increases and so forth) to reduce the threat. The president would then be at liberty to accept or reject the recommendation or to take alternative measures, but his actions would be subject to override by Congress. On November 10, the ITC finding on the injury question was announced as negative, and, consequently, no recommendations for increased trade restrictions were forwarded to the president.

The ITC's auto decision was perhaps one of the most significant the body had ever made and certainly one of the most politically sensitive. At the strong urging of the auto industry, President Carter had requested earlier that the ITC expedite its investigation, which would have necessitated a presidential decision at the height of the electoral campaign. The ITC did speed up its investigation slightly but not enough to return a decision before November 4, probably in an attempt to keep subsequent presidential action as objective and nonpolitical as possible. With regard to the substance of the case, the grounds on which the majority eventually decided were that the recession, higher oil prices, and shift in consumer tastes to small cars were the principal reasons for the current plight of the U.S. auto industry. Increased imports from Japan, the ITC concluded, were a reflection of those other causes, but not the principal cause of injury.

Negotiation Channels

The auto problem was the subject of extensive interaction between the U.S. and Japanese governments, as well as between other elements of the respective societies, such as union leaders and auto-company executives. This section will survey which officials and agencies took the lead in negotiating the problem and will examine how the problem became defined, both in the internal discussions that occured within capitals and in the various interactions that occurred between the two countries. Also of concern will be both governments' actions in the wake of negotiations.

Preparations for Negotiations: Japan

The MITI took the lead in the Japanese government in dealing with the automobile problem. Unlike in the textile conflict of the late 1960s and the early 1970s, MITI's position was very similar to the official stance taken by the U.S. government, namely, to seek to encourage Toyota and Nissan to build assembly plants in the United States. High-ranking officials of MITI conducted a series of meetings with Toyota and Nissan representatives to persuade them to invest in the United States, but the meetings were not successful. The MITI was inititally reluctant to undertake voluntary export restrictions because of the possibility that U.S.-based import dealers might sue Japanese manufacturers for not supplying enough cars or that U.S. consumer groups might charge that the practice was contrary to U.S. antitrust laws. After Fraser's visit to Japan, MITI officials realized that the auto problem had become politicized, and they hoped to get something settled before Prime Minister Ohira's visit to the United States in May. They were impatient at the prospect that nothing might be settled before then.

The MITI decided to send Vice-Minister Naohiro Amaya to the United States in early March to learn the viewpoints of the administration and the Congress on the automobile problem. On March 3, Amaya met with U.S. Trade Representative Reubin Askew, and he subsequently met with Secretary of Commerce Philip M. Klutznick, Undersecretary of State Richard Cooper, Congressmen Charles Vanik and James Jones, and Senators William V. Roth, Jr., and Adlai E. Stevenson, III *(Yomuiri Shimbun,* 6 March 1980). Several officials admitted that the rapid increase in Japanese car imports was due to the increasing demand for small cars, which U.S. manufacturers had failed to meet, and, therefore, the increase in imports had no direct relation to the increase in unemployment. However, the U.S. officials suggested that, because the automobile industry was so important to the United States, there was a strong possibility that protectionist trade laws would be established. Amaya reportedly mentioned five alternatives that might help to solve the auto problem: (1) investment and production in the United States by Japanese manufacturers; (2) voluntary restriction of exports by Japan; (3) restriction of Japan's exports through a bilateral agreement; (4) restriction of imports by laws passed by the U.S. Congress; and (5) encouragement of the importing of U.S. cars and parts to Japan (*Asahi Shimbun*, 8 March 1980). The Americans Amaya met preferred the first and fifth options. Askew particularly argued that, considering their high level of exports, Japanese manufacturers were at a stage where they could build plants and produce cars in the United States.

The MITI subsequently proposed that a working-level meeting be held in early April, before Prime Minister Ohira's upcoming visit to the United States. In preparing for this meeting, the Japanese government tried its best to persuade Toyota and Nissan to invest in the United States. Because similar attempts had been unsuccessful in the past, MITI Minister Yoshitake Sasaki himself undertook the task of dealing with the Toyota and Nissan executives. On March 14, Sasaki met with a vice-president of Toyota, Shigenobu Yamamoto, to press his request. He was unsuccessful; Toyota maintained its cautious attitude toward U.S. investments and countered Sasaki's request by bringing up such specific problems as labor quality and overcapacity in the U.S. market *(Yomiuri Shimbun,* 15 March 1980).

Aware of the difficulty of persuading Toyota and Nissan, as well as the limitations of time for settling the matter, the MITI changed its strategy in an effort to resolve the automobile problem. On March 15, the MITI announced that, in preparation for the working-level meeting, it would focus on Toyota's announced intention to build plants for the manufacture of small trucks. This seemed a good idea because those trucks were simple to assemble and would not have required a large investment by Toyota. Toyota's response to this approach was negative, which subsequently led Toshihiko Yano, vice-minister of the MITI, to publicly censure Toyota and Nissan for their unresponsiveness (*Asahi Shimbun*, 26 March 1980). Another alternative left to the MITI was to put more emphasis on the promotion of U.S. car imports. To do this, it was necessary to negotiate with other agencies of the government. The MITI began by seeking to persuade the Ministries of Finance and Transportation to eliminate remaining Japanese trade barriers (*Nihon Keizai Shimbun,* 13 March 1980). These included the commodity tax rate for large cars, tariffs on auto parts, and some import inspection procedures. The Ministry of Finance was disinclined to allow any tax reduction, although the MITI tried to convince the ministry by pointing out that commodity taxes on large cars were only 10 percent of the total commodity taxes on imported cars and that, if the number of imported cars increased, the amount collected would not decrease much. In the end, the MITI failed to persuade the ministry to accept any change, and negotiations between these two agencies reached a stalemate.

Preparations for Negotiations: United States

U.S. government involvement with the automobile crisis began in 1980 on an unauspicious note with the signing, on January 7, 1980, of the Chrysler Corporation Loan Guarantee Act of 1979. This act provided the corporation with $1.5 billion in federally backed loans, which were contingent on Chrysler's raising an additional $2 billion on its own. The act was controversial because it constituted a major step toward government participation in private investment decisions, but it was accepted by Congress when it appeared that the only alternative to government support was the bankruptcy of a major employer in the U.S. economy.

The act set up a Loan Guarantee Board designed to review Chrysler's investment plans and administer the loan arrangement. It also instructed the Department of Transportation to conduct a six-month study of the company's economic prospects and a further year-long analysis of the overall state of the automobile industry. As the crisis in the auto industry deepened, the latter task took on greater proportions than had been planned originally. Speaking in Detroit on January 15, Secretary of Transportation Neil Goldschmidt indicated that he would be leading an even more broadly conceived effort in the next nine months (Department of Transportation, August 1980). This effort was to include the participation of a number of federal agencies, including the Departments of Treasury, Commerce, Labor, Energy, Justice and the Interior, the Council of Economic Advisors, the Council on Wage and Price Stability, the Environmental Protection Agency, the Office of the U.S. Trade Representative, and the Office of Science and Technology Policy. Thus, as a result of the earlier action on Chrysler, the U.S. government already had interagency policy machinery established before the full impact of the 1980 downturn in the automobile industry was apparent to Washington. One part of this machinery, namely, the Office of the U.S. Trade Representative (USTR), took charge of the portion of the problem that dealt with trade, including, of course, the conduct of negotiations with the Japanese. In an effort to address the trade aspects of the auto crisis, USTR officials formulated demands in three areas relating to automobile trade: standards, Japanese import policy, and Japanese investment. More general U.S. demands in these areas had been well-aired during previous negotiations with the Japanese, particularly during the Tokyo Round Trade Negotiation, which had concluded in mid-1979. The automobile crisis gave the United States new ammunition to press old arguments, and the USTR particularly was quick to seize the opportunity. U.S. officials were further motivated by the self-serving (although probably valid) argument that pressure for import controls in Congress would be diminished if it could be demonstrated that Japanese officials were doing all they could to liberalize trade and investment on their side.

The matter of standards involved mainly the application of Japanese regulations to U.S. cars sold in Japan. These sales were very low volume, about 14,000 units per year, and, consequently, U.S. companies claimed that it is not profitable to build compliance with Japanese regulations into U.S. assembly-line production. As a result, U.S. cars sold in Japan must be modified upon arrival in Japan and prior to being sold, a process that is expensive, time consuming, and hence a deterrent to increased exports. U.S. companies, and the U.S. government, took the position that, for such a small volume of exports, Japan ought to accept U.S. practices if they comply with the intent, but not necessarily the letter, of Japanese regulations. For example, Japanese safety regulations require a small (30 millimeter) circular reflective disc to be mounted on the rear of automobiles. Would not the reflective surface of a Mustang, which is considerably larger, be sufficient to meet the regulation without further modification? Another issue involved different testing procedures for replacement catalytic converters. In both these cases, Japanese officials had previously been reluctant to make what appeared to be special exceptions for U.S.-made products. On the other hand, U.S. negotiators took the position that had won philosophical acceptance in the negotiation over the Standards Code in the Tokyo Round, namely, that regulations should be written to specify general performance criteria but not necessarily to specify the particular means by which the criteria are met.

The second demand dealt with Japanese import restrictions. As Japan's auto industry achieved international competitiveness, the Japanese government reduced the large barriers that had been erected in the 1950s, and, in 1978, they completely eliminated tariffs on fully assembled automobiles. However, tariffs on auto parts were still in force, and these became the target of U.S. trade officials. As a general principle, USTR officials sought to encourage Japanese manufacturers to use more U.S.-made parts in their final assembly, whether that assembly were accomplished in Japan or in possible future assembly plants in the United States. This issue was potentially significant for the U.S. auto industry as a whole, because production and employment in the replacement parts industry were even more depressed than in new-vehicle production and were not likely to improve simply through foreign investment in the United States (Raftery, 1980). As seen from the U.S. perspective, the task was to convince the government of Japan to remove any remaining import barriers to U.S.-made parts and to enlist that government's help in overcoming the resistance of Japanese automakers (who were resisting on the grounds of quality control) to buy U.S.-made parts or to authorize their use as replacements for vehicles sold in the United States.

The third demand was the familiar issue of Japanese investment in the United States. The U.S. perspective on this issue was influenced by the fact that overseas investment had been a long-established practice of U.S. auto manufacturers. However, Japanese firms have not followed the same pattern. The major firms, Toyota and Nissan (Datsun), have avoided committing themselves to building auto-manufacturing facilities in the United States, although Toyota does have a small-scale truck assembly plant in California, and, in May 1980, Nissan decided to build a similar plant in the Southeast or Great Lakes region (*The Washington Post*, 31 May 1980). Only Honda is firmly committed to building a passenger-car facility in the United States (Marysville, Ohio), but that is probably because it is a small company with only 8 percent of the Japanese market and with 40 percent of its production exported to the United States (in contrast to Toyota and Nissan, which export only 20 percent of their production to the United States).

U.S. officials recognized that there are numerous reasons why the Japanese have resisted investing in the United States. For one thing, the labor situation seemed much more problematic in the United States than in Japan, what with high wages, frequent strikes, and a standard of workmanship that is often perceived to be lower than Japan's. Another reason concerned suppliers: Japanese firms, especially Toyota and Nissan, have established intricate supply systems in Japan that allow them to assure the quality of their parts. Production in the United States would not offer the advantages of such arrangements. A third reason was the possibility that U.S. laws (for example, a requirement that minorities be represented on boards of directors) might force alterations in the management style of Japanese corporate executives. The U.S. response to these concerns was to emphasize that such problems are endemic in international business and that they are no worse than those U.S. companies faced in the process of going multinational. As one U.S. official put it in a personal interview: "If the Japanese are going to be players on the world scene, they must learn how to handle it. Sure, it [overseas production] is painful. It's one of the elements of being a multinational company." In its official position, the U.S. government practically couched the issue in terms of requiring Japan to invest in the United States as an exercise of good international corporate citizenship. As Ambassador Robert D. Hormats testified before Congress, the context of stating that U.S. policy was to encourage economically viable investment in the United States, "We fully expect that Japan will exercise responsibility by supporting our investment and trade objectives" (Hormats, 1980, p. 191).

Working-Level Negotiations

The working-level meeting initiated by the MITI took place in Washington, D.C., on April 7-9, 1980. Participating in this meeting were an interagency team from the U.S. federal government and, on the Japanese side (led by Shohei Kurihara, chief of the Machinery and Information Bureau of the MITI), a team from the MITI, Foreign Affairs, Transportation, and Finance. Two important principles were settled at this meeting. First, it was agreed that the Japanese government had done all it could to encourage Toyota and Nissan to invest in the United States and that, for the time being, the issue could no longer be profitably explored in government-to-government negotiation. Second, Japan undertook to simplify import procedures with the aim of increasing U.S. auto exports to that country. A further undertaking of the Japanese government was to send a semi-governmental mission to the United States to research the possibility of overseas investment by Japanese auto-parts manufacturers in that country. This move came in response to U.S. pressure to look at the whole range of auto production in an effort to alleviate U.S. unemployment.

On his return from Washington, Kurihara announced the results of his negotiations (*Nihon Keizai Shimbun*, 15 April 1980). He indicated that a subsequent meeting would be held to continue discussion on import procedures and to consider the problem of commodity taxes on large U.S.-made autos. He advanced the suggestion that, depending on the outcome of these discussions, it might not be necessary to include the auto crisis on the agenda of the upcoming meeting between Prime Minister Ohira and President Carter. Kurihara indicated his belief that it was now up to the U.S. administration to convince Congress that the Japanese government had done all it could to lessen the impact of the auto crisis on the United States.

On April 2, a team of congressmen visited Japan to study U.S.-Japanese trade relations while more formal negotiations between the two countries were going on at the working level. The team, including leading congressmen such as Jonathan B. Bingham, James Jones, and Charles Vanik, proposed measures to solve the automobile dispute between the two countries. These measures included using U.S.-made parts for Japanese cars as well as investment by Toyota and Nissan in the United States. In meeting with Kiyaoki Kikuchi, vice-minister for Foreign Affairs, Vanik warned that there was growing pressure within Congress to limit the flow of Japanese cars if the auto-trade problem were left unattended.

Kikuchi took the position that exporting of Japanese cars to the United States did not damage the U.S. economy but in fact helped to curb inflation, a position the U.S. administration itself had taken earlier. He also claimed there was no direct relation between the high rate of unemployment among auto workers and exports of Japanese cars. The team later met with President Ishihara and the executives of Nissan and strongly urged Nissan to invest in the United States. They conveyed to Nissan the tenseness of the political situation in the United States and suggested that protectionist-oriented legislation was becoming an increasingly likely course of action for the Congress to take.

On April 4, Nissan officially announced its decision to build a truck plant in the United States and presented the plan to its labor union. President Ishihara and Vice-President Masataka Okuma of Nissan left for the United States on April 9 to explain the plan to the Americans. The main points of the Nissan plan were as follows: (1) production would consist of one-ton trucks currently being sold in the U.S. market for leisure use; (2) purchase of the main assembly parts would be made, as much as possible, from U.S. manufacturers, even though two related auto-parts plants would be set up along with the Nissan plant; (3) more land than immediately needed would be bought to prepare for the later possibility of producing small cars; and (4) the new production system would relate to Nissan's plant in Mexico, which produces both trucks and cars. The Nissan mission did not discuss the auto-trade dispute, but their actions carried an obvious message. A UAW spokesman welcomed this action by Nissan and expressed the hope that Toyota would take similar action (*Asahi Shimbun*, 10 April 1980).

The Japanese Ministry of Foreign Affairs (MFA) also became involved in the preliminary intergovernmental discussions of the auto crisis. Essentially, the position of the MFA did not conflict with that of the MITI. As early as February 13, MFA officials had said that, in order to prevent the problem from becoming politicized, establishing plants in the United States would be inevitable. They particularly did not want this problem to have a negative impact on U.S.-Japanese relations, and they felt that, if the situation were left as it was, legal action would eventually be taken within the United States to demand that the Japanese manufacturers construct plants in the United States (*Nihon Keizai Shimbun*, 14 February 1980). However, one problem was that the MFA did not feel it had an accurate picture of the U.S. government's position. On March 5, Japanese Trade Representative Yasukawa, who was planning to meet with U.S. Trade Representative Reubin Askew in mid-March, met with Prime Minister Ohira. Yasukawa noted that, up to that point, the U.S. government had not formally asked Japan to take any action and that the Japanese were probably being overly influenced by Fraser of the UAW. He added that he would try to determine precisely the views of the U.S. government (*Sankei Shimbun*, 6 March 1980).

Subsequently, Foreign Minister Okita himself indicated that he would visit Washington from March 19 to 21, saying he desired an accurate understanding of the U.S. government's viewpoint on the automobile problem. He also indicated that he wanted to clarify the Japanese government's position that it was up to the manufacturers themselves to decide whether they should invest in the United States (*Nihon Keizai Shimbun*, 15 March 1980). On March 21, at a breakfast meeting including Okita, Askew, Secretary of the Treasury Miller, and Secretary of Commerce Klutznick, Askew reiterated that the U.S. government was opposed to import restrictions, but he added that, unless Toyota and Nissan moved quickly on the investment issue, the situation could become quite difficult. Klutznick said the U.S. government needed the support of Japan in fighting against rising protectionism within the United States. In response, Okita simply outlined the reasons Toyota and Nissan had given for not investing abroad, namely, that it was hard to forecast how long the present buoyant demand for Japanese cars would persist (*Yomuiri, Shimbun*, 22 March 1980).

High-Level Meetings

On May 1, 1980, Japanese Prime Minister Masayoshi Ohira made a brief visit to the United States in connection with a longer visit to both Mexico and Canada, to discuss possibilities for joint economic cooperation. It had been expected, particularly on the Japanese side, that Ohira's meeting with President Jimmy Carter would focus on global political issues, such as the Soviet invasion of Afghanistan, the Iranian hostage-taking, and the economic sanction that had followed both incidents. Similarly, it was not expected that the auto crisis would be raised at the Carter-Ohira meeting. Based on the assessments of both the MITI and the Japanese auto manufacturers, the Japanese government had concluded that the auto problem had been solved for the time being, because of Nissan's announced decision to build a small-truck plant in the United States and Toyota's engagement of several research institutions to conduct a study of investment prospects in the United States. Prior to leaving for the United States, Prime Minister Ohira had announced that he would not raise the auto issue with President Carter on the grounds that prior meetings at the working level had accomplished all that could be done for the time being (*Asahi Simbun,* 14 April 1980).

In spite of the optimism of the Japanese government, the conditions surrounding President Carter were not auspicious. Carter himself had agreed that unemployment in the United States was not caused by an increase in Japanese imports, but the auto-trade problem, coming at the same time as the frustrations produced by the situations in Iran and Afghanistan, created an impatient and even nationalistic mood toward Japan among elements of the

U.S. public. The UAW's actions and some Congressmen helped to fuel this mood. It was obvious that the president could not ignore the matter in a presidential election year, particularly given the electoral strength of the UAW. On the other hand, some of the import restrictions called for by the UAW would clearly raise inflation and energy consumption in the United States, and the president was equally committed to reducing the impact of these factors on the U.S. economy. To underscore this commitment, the editorials of major newspapers such as *The New York Times* and *The Washington Post* emphasized that it would be unwise to restrict imports of Japanese cars at the present time.

Prior to meeting with the president, Prime Minister Ohira held a breakfast meeting with leaders of the House and Senate. In this meeting, the Japanese government was sharply criticized for not taking the auto situation seriously, and Ohira felt constrained to defend his government on this point. In the following meeting with President Carter, the two leaders signed a scientific research agreement between the two nations and discussed political cooperation in connection with the situations in Iran and Afghanistan (*The New York Times,* 2 May 1980). Despite the earlier agreement at the working level not to discuss autos, the president raised the matter and incidentally proposed the coproduction of autos by U.S. and Japanese manufacturers. This idea was entirely novel to the Japanese, and it occasioned some speculation that the proposal had been made to gain the support of the UAW (*Nihon Keizai Shimbun,* 3 May 1980). It served to emphasize further the importance the Americans attached to Japanese investment in the United States.

President Carter met with Japanese leaders on two occasions following the Ohira visit. The first meeting, with Foreign Minister Okita, came at the Venice economic summit in June 1980, at which time Carter queried Okita about reports received in the United States that Japanese manufacturers were planning to increase plant capacity in Japan in order to boost exports even further. Okita denied any such plans. On the second occasion, President Carter visited Japan to attend funeral services for Prime Minister Ohira. He did not raise the subject of automobiles at this time.

To sum up, it would appear that the results of meetings at the head-of-government level produced little in the way of solution to the auto problem. The fact that the auto situation was raised in such meetings mainly served as a symbolic demonstration of the concern senior levels of government attached to the problem. However, they were not an effective vehicle for negotiating the issue, nor does it appear that the governments intended them to be.

A more productive mechanism of U.S.-Japanese interaction on the auto problem was meetings of senior trade officials. On May 10, 1980, a U.S.

trade delegation, headed by Ambassador Askew, arrived in Japan to negotiate both the auto and NTT issues, a meeting that had been requested by President Carter at the time of his earlier meeting with Prime Minister Ohira. Both governments prepared extensively for the meeting. For its part, the Japanese government decided to take several measures of import liberalization in an effort to remove charges by the U.S. side that Japan's internal market was still highly protected.

The U.S. mission met with Ambassador Yasukawa and other representatives of the MITI and the Ministries of Transportation and Finance. Askew repeated the U.S. concerns about Japanese investment in the United States, but he also expressed satisfaction with the U.S. investment plans of Nissan and Honda and the investment research being conducted by Toyota (*Asahi Shimbun*, 12 May 1980). The meeting produced a series of agreements with respect to auto trade, some of which had been initiated in Kurihara's meeting in Washington in April. The Japanese agreed to remove tariffs, ranging from 5 to 8 percent, on auto parts starting in fiscal year 1981. This did not include tariffs on tires, because the tire industry was still deemed to need protection. However, the tariff rate on tires was reduced. Further details were worked out regarding the Japanese mission to be sent to the United States to assess purchases of U.S. auto parts by Japanese manufacturers. The inspection procedures for U.S. imports into Japan were eased, particularly those for catalytic converters, although there was no change in the aforementioned requirement for safety reflection disks. One issue on which U.S. negotiations had pressed the Japanese was to alter the tax structure that made commodity taxes higher on large cars than on small cars. The Japanese government was unable to accomodate this request, although it did indicate that this would be the subject of further internal deliberation.

The Askew mission was generally regarded as successful within its parameters. The U.S. officials did not ask the Japanese to restrict exports, nor did the Japanese volunteer to do this. Several issues were taken up that admittedly did not lead to subsequent action. For example, the Japanese government indicated it would continue to press the manufacturers to increase investment in the United States, but its scope for effective action in this area was clearly limited. The Japanese requested that the U.S. team rescind the effects of the U.S. Customs action that caused the U.S. duties on small trucks to rise to 25 percent, but the president was subsequently unwilling to do this. It is obvious that the Askew mission did not convince one important constituent group in the United States, namely the UAW. Approximately one month after the Askew talks in Japan, the UAW filed the injury suit with the International Trade Commission, still aiming to seek a sharp reduction in Japanese auto imports.

Subsequent Actions: United States

Immediately following the Askew mission to Japan, President Carter held a White House meeting with top executives of the UAW and the five major U.S. auto manufacturers. He reported on the actions his administration and the Japanese government were taking on the auto problem. The session did not produce any policy changes (nor were any intended), but it did reveal a shift in White House thinking from criticism of the fuel-efficiency of U.S. products to a deep concern over the problems engulfing the industry. The president agreed to expedite the administration's study of the auto situation, and he gave the chairman of the group, Transportation Secretary Neil E. Goldschmidt, six weeks to present recommendations to the White House, after which the president would have a further meeting with the industry.

The president's action precipitated a second major round of interagency meetings in the U.S. government, although this time the discussions were more extended than those held earlier in the year, and they took into account a wider range of policies than import controls, which had been the focus of the previous meetings. The purpose of the Goldschmidt task force was to canvass the administration for policy options that could be used to help the auto industry and to present these options, with recommendations, to the White House Economic Policy Group (EPG). The involvement of the EPG promised that the suggestions forwarded to the president would be analyzed from the perspective of the politics as well as the economics of the problem.

The options produced by the Goldschmidt task force were recorded in a lengthy confidential memo and forwarded to the White House on July 2 (*The New York Times,* 28 June and 3 July 1980). The question of import controls was looked at once again. One possibility was that the president could seek congressional authority to negotiate a voluntary restraint agreement with the Japanese. A second was that an indirect signal could be sent to the Japanese to cut back on their own, an action that could be taken by the president without waiting for congressional authorization but that would be open to an antitrust suit if it were not done discreetly. A third course that was analyzed was provided for under Article 301 of the Trade Act of 1974, and called for the president to declare that Japan was trading unfairly and to institute retaliatory measures. This procedure had the advantage that the president could act unilaterally without Congress or the Japanese, but the action would be unjustified and would do extraordinary damage to U.S.-Japanese relations.

The options memo recommended against import controls, but it reflected greater division in the administration than had existed previously, largely because, at the cabinet level, controls were strongly supported by Secretary Goldschmidt. The White House, however, had received the analysis from the Council of Economic Advisors on what import controls would cost the U.S. economy. This analysis proved as persuasive with the EPG and the president as it had earlier with administration officials. In his later meeting with the auto industry, President Carter announced that he would not seek controls at that time, nor would he encourage the Japanese government to seek restraint by its industry.

Further actions were proposed for presidential consideration in the options memo, and these ranged from local to national to even international action. They included:

1. Assistance to communities affected by dislocation in the auto industry.
2. A federally sponsored retraining program to be initiated by the Labor Department.
3. Loan guarantees for auto dealers, to be arranged through the Small Business Administration under new rules yet to be worked out.
4. Relief from emission standards and other government regulations.
5. Tax relief through the accelerated depreciation of special tools used in automaking.
6. A request to the ITC for an accelerated finding on the UAW case.
7. An international conference on auto trade.

Many of the options presented constituted proposals that the administration would have considered in any case to counter the general economic recession in 1980. However, the options procedure forced attention onto those policies that would specifically benefit the auto industry and ensured that no measures readily available to the government would be overlooked.

Following the receipt of the options memo and an analysis of it by his staff, the president met in Detroit on July 8 with auto-industry representatives (*The New York Times* and *The Washington Post,* 9 July 1980). The president unveiled a $1 billion relief package for the industry, including $500 million in savings due to the reduction of high-altitude emission standards, up to $400 million in Small Business Administration loans to auto dealers, and $100 million in Economic Development Administration (EDA) aid to depressed communities. Tax relief was still under consideration, although it had encountered complications that had delayed its announcement at the July meeting. (One problem was the resistance of the Treasury and the Office of Management and Budget (OMB) to special provisions designed to help particular industries. Another was that tax relief would benefit only General Motors, because Ford and Chrysler were not earning enough profit to pay taxes.) At the political level, the president announced the creation of an auto-industry committee composed of representatives of business, labor, and the government, to assure a close-knit permanent partnership between Washington and Detroit. Following the meeting, the president left for Tokyo to attend the funeral of Prime Minister Ohira. He did not discuss the subject of automobiles with Japanese officials because he reportedly felt it inappropriate to raise the subject on such an occasion.

The Detroit meeting was well-received by the auto industry, even though little was done to provide short-run help for the industry. The relaxing of emission controls had been sought by the industry for some time as part of a general campaign against government regulation, but there were obvious limits as to how much the government could provide in this area, particularly because studies have shown that 84 percent of the production costs attributed to government regulations are related to fuel efficiency and are, in any case, demanded by the consumer. The real impact of the Detroit meeting seemed to be that the government and industry would cooperate on achieving common goals in the future, the most immediate being a fivefold increase in U.S. small-car production by 1983. It is apparent that both industrial and government leaders felt a new era had been opened up in government business relations. *The Washington Post* quoted White House Advisor Eizenstat as seeing the the the beginning of "a national industrial policy," while Chrysler Chairman Lee A. Iacocca countered, "We have taken a page from Japan's book" (*The Washington Post*, 9 July 1980).

Following the July meeting, no further major action was taken on the auto situation by the U.S. government during 1980. As would be expected the president became fully engaged in the electoral campaign during this period. In the administration, action was suspended pending the outcome of the ITC decision. Trade officials did engage in contingency planning in the event of an injury finding by the ITC, but this work was arrested by the ITC's negative findings. The ITC ruling ended any possibility of action by the outgoing Carter administration.

Subsequent Action: Japan

There was little likelihood that the Japanese government would take formal action on the automobile issue following the Askew mission. The problem was essentially a U.S. problem, and the Japanese government felt it had done all it could to alleviate the distress in the U.S. industry. However, the MITI continued its informal efforts to encourage Japanese manufacturers to invest in the United States and, as U.S. unemployment figures rose, to further encourage the automakers to restrict exports on a voluntary basis. The argument the MITI officials used was that the Japanese needed to not exacerbate the difficulties in the U.S. situation in order to forestall the U.S. government's resorting to export restrictions.

Apparently, the tactics pursued by the MITI had their effect. Officials at Toyota and Nissan began to realize that it was not likely that the automobile crisis would be calmed by the agreement made between Ambassadors Yasukawa and Askew. In addition, the UAW suit before the ITC put further pressure on Toyota and Nissan for action. According to a Japanese newspaper report which the company claimed was inaccurate, on June 25, Chairman Seishi Kato of the Toyota Auto Sales Company announced that Toyota would accept any export restriction decided upon by the U.S. and Japanese governments (*Asahi Shimbun*, 26 June 1980). Furthermore, Toyota decided to reduce its production for the second half of 1980 to about 1 million units, which was 7 percent lower than its initial estimate and the first such reduction since 1978 (*Nihon Keizai Shimbun*, 1 July 1980). On July 2, the Presidents of Toyota, Nissan, Honda, Mitsubishi, Toyo Kogyo, Isuzu, and Fuji Heavy Industries had a breakfast meeting to discuss the auto problem. They agreed that all they could do for the time being was to wait for the ITC's decision. The meeting, however, confirmed that they would follow the policy of orderly exporting, as had been suggested earlier by the MITI (*Yomuiri Shimbun*, 2 July 1980).

The most dramatic development on the Japanese side was the announcement by Toyota on July 9 that Toyota and Ford had agreed to produce small cars together. This agreement had apparently been worked out when President Petersen of Ford visited Japan on June 24. The plans called for using currently existing Ford plants in the United States. This announcement caught many parties by surprise, but the agreement was welcomed. The response by Ford to the announcement was rather cool, and the company said that it was too early to determine whether Toyota and Ford had reached an agreement, although Ford would welcome such an agreement. (According to government sources in Japan, it is probable that the Toyota announcement was leaked and not planned). Even if the Toyota-Ford plan were made, a problem might arise in relation to the U.S. antitrust laws. Because of the strong fear of monopoly in the United States, any market structure that might lead to monopoly is prohibited. For example, in the past, Hitachi and General Electric had tried to produce color televisions jointly, but they had not been permitted to by U.S. Department of Justice. Nevertheless, there was no doubt that this announcement somewhat relieved the tension that had been caused by the auto-trade problem between the two countries.

Management of the Auto Problem

The auto problem of 1980 was, and probably still is, potentially one of the gravest issues to bedevil U.S.-Japanese economic relations. The stakes involved in this issue are enormous. On the U.S. side, the problem involved the sudden collapse of an industry that reportedly accounts for up to one-sixth of the employment in the United States. On the Japanese side, the problem entailed the possible disruption of the export trade of an industry that earns up to one-sixth of the foreign-exchange earnings of Japan. Given the magnitude of the problem, and the precipitous and unexpected downturn in the U.S. industry, one would have expected the auto situation to have become a serious trade dispute between the two countries. Furthermore, this trade dispute could well have developed into a more generalized political dispute, with consequent damage to good relations between the two countries. Such a scenario has occurred in the past in U.S.-Japanese relations, and it is useful to examine why it did not occur in this instance.

There was no shortage of efforts to politicize the auto situation and to recommend actions that probably would have made the maintenance of amicable relations much more difficult. These efforts came principally from the UAW in the United States, which has suffered the most serious losses from the downturn in U.S. auto production. Some efforts to politicize the issue were also forthcoming from the U.S. Congress, in part from individuals such as Senator Donald Riegel, Jr., who sought controls against Japanese auto imports, and Charles Vanik, who sought mainly to examine and publicize the issue through the mechanism of congressional hearings. The press in Japan and the United States followed the issue closely and ensured that it rose to national prominence in both countries. In particular, the Japanese press gave careful coverage to events in the United States and to U.S.-Japanese negotiations, which meant that, on occasion, the blunter aspects of U.S. diplomacy, such as the sharp questioning of Prime Minister Ohira in the U.S. Senate, were made available to the Japanese public.

The reason why the auto situation in 1980 never became a difficult trade dispute between the United States and Japan is probably some combination of good fortune and good management. The good fortune is accounted for by the fact that the most difficult trade issue between the two countries, namely, import controls, never came up for negotiation in 1980. Had it done so, particularly early in the year, it is unlikely that the issue could have been resolved without some bitterness. On the other hand, the issues that were raised for negotiation were politically less difficult to deal with than import controls, but they were managed with considerable skill and sensitivity on the part of both countries.

The U.S. Government never defined the auto crisis as primarily a trade problem, that is, a problem for which the tools of trade policy would be the appropriate governmental response. This is because the major tool of trade policy (import controls) would have produced less benefits for the U.S. economy (in terms of employment created) than costs (in terms of greater fuel consumption and increased inflation). Even this aspect of the decision had its fortuitous aspects. It is, of course, entirely to the credit of the Carter administration that it conducted the analysis necessary to determine the economic trade-offs of the issue instead of adopting the politically simple solution of restricting Japanese cars regardless of whether it was an economically sensible policy for the United States. It was also chance that the automobile, which was the subject of the crisis, happened to be a product that, unlike color televisions or textiles, consumes large amounts of scarce energy resources. Therefore, no matter how important the automobile was to the U.S. economy, it was subsumed in an even larger problem facing the U.S. government. It would have been difficult indeed for the Carter administration to have convinced the nation, and the world, that it was serious about energy conservation had it restricted imports of fuel-efficient foreign cars and forced U.S. consumption toward domestic gas guzzlers.

The major trade decision of the 1980 auto crisis was the decision of the U.S. administration not to seek import controls on foreign cars. This decision was largely a unilateral one the U.S. government reached in the first quarter of 1980. Once made, the decision was not changed subsequently, although the United States did suggest that it welcomed Japanese export restraint. The decision was made on the basis of the needs of the U.S. economy, and there is little evidence that a concern over the U.S.-Japanese trade relationship was introduced, let alone was pivotal, in the United States's decision making. As it was, the decision proved to be extraordinarily beneficial for U.S.-Japanese relations, particularly if one considers what might have happened had it gone the other way. Had the administration decided on controls, it likely would have had to negotiate precise import figures with the Japanese, which would not have been easy to do if significant cutbacks were contemplated. The Japanese government, and particularly the Japanese automakers, were not receptive to voluntary restraint agreements early in the year. Even though they became more sympathetic to the idea by the end of 1980, substantial reductions might have required the United States to use crude pressure tactics —without any certainty of success. Furthermore, the prospect that a voluntary agreement might have been illegal under U.S. law (a prospect that undoubtedly would have stiffened Japanese resistance) would have increased the frustration of U.S. officials and put additional strains on the negotiation process. As an alternative to negotiation, the administration might have chosen to act unilaterally by seeking import-control legislation from Congress, but this would have posed a whole new set of political problems— domestically and in relation to Japan.

Once the United States removed the quota issue from the bilateral agenda, it then moved to negotiate a series of residual issues with the Japanese. The most important of these issues was Japanese investment in auto production in the United States, an issue that U.S. officials at all levels brought up with tiresome repetition in successive meetings with their Japanese counterparts. In retrospect, it is probable that the U.S. insistence on this point stemmed from two factors. One was a genuine belief that the Japanese automakers have benefitted enormously from the liberal policies of the United States on auto imports, and that they have thus incurred a tacit obligation to follow up their strong export performance with investments in auto production. The second factor was more political. The administration had rejected the demand for import controls by the powerful UAW, and, consequently, it was especially important that it be supportive of the other major demand this group had made. For their part, the Japanese government appeared to handle the demand for investment with considerable sophistication. On the one hand, the government could not order the Japanese automakers to invest in the United States, and pointing this out to the U.S. officials helped to dispel certain U.S. beliefs about monolithic economic control in Japan. On the other hand, the Japanese government had considerable scope in its influence on industry and could simultaneously maintain a sympathetic and helpful dialogue with the United States; it appeared to handle both tasks with some success. The government essentially sided with the U.S. administration in encouraging particularly Toyota and Nissan to build plant capacity in the United States, and it took the lead in promoting the acceptance of U.S.-made auto parts for Japanese production. These actions helped the administration make the case that it was doing all it could to improve the prospects for the recovery of the auto industry.

There were a number of times when the handling of the auto problem was decidedly different from the handling of other problems in U.S.-Japanese trade relations, particularly the handling of the textile issue of 1969-1971. The latter case has been subjected to extended analysis and a number of observations have been distilled about why relations became as strained as they did (Destler, Fukui, and Sato, 1979). It is useful to examine some of these observations to see how the procedures employed in the auto situation helped to produce a more favorable outcome for U.S.-Japanese relations.

The textile dispute stemmed in large measure from the political commitment President Richard Nixon had made to secure relief for the textile industry from Japanese imports. From this commitment flowed two implications: first, that textiles were a special case of trade policy and not subject to the ordinary bureaucratic procedures of analysis and policy making; and second, that the outcome would have implications for the president's reputation as a bargainer. In the auto case, President Carter declined to make a political commitment to the auto industry and, as a result, his subsequent relations with the Japanese were not burdened with the implications that Nixon's commitment had created. The Carter administration treated autos as an ordinary issue of economic policy, which is to say it analyzed the problem from the standpoint of national interest prior to deciding on policy. That this procedure permitted President Carter to manage the problem better than the textiles issue was managed seems indisputable, and this better management probably would have been the case even if the administration had decided in favor of import controls on autos. What is interesting to speculate is whether the president might have fared better at the polls in November had he taken a strong stand against Japanese imports. On this point, interviews give some evidence that White House advisors felt public opinion was unequivocally in support of import controls ("the politics of this thing are all one way"), but this might have been an attempt to make the president's position look more principled than it actually was. The fact is that any import restrictions on cars would have increased the cost of auto transportation for the U.S. consumer, and this prospect would undoubtedly have caused a sharp reaction from consumer groups. It is worth noting that, in the fall campaign of 1980, neither presidential candidate took a strong position in favor of import controls on autos, although Reagan did end up promising to seek Japanese restraint. This suggests that the issue may not have been all that easy to manipulate for political advantage.

A second point of comparison between the textile and auto cases can be found in the style of U.S. executive decision making. In the textile dispute, the U.S. executive branch was deeply divided over policy, and the resulting bureaucratic politics ensured that inconsistent signals were sent to Japan, with the result that uncertainty and misunderstanding increased the conflict between the two countries. In the auto situation, the opposite was the case. Indeed, there are few examples of policymaking on complicated subjects where there was as little disagreement between the major agencies of the U.S. government as there was in the early period of the auto case. What undoubtedly helped this consensus to develop was the interagency consultation that occurred prior to the congressional hearings in March, 1980, and the fact that bureaucratic decision making was kept relatively free of political interference. In the textile case, the bureaucracy was faced with a presidential decision to advance the interests of one group in the economy. In the auto case, the bureaucracy was given scope to determine what policy would be to the best advantage of the nation as a whole. It is instructive to note that the latter procedure appeared to produce the more liberal policy in international trade and, consequently, the least amount of friction in U.S.-Japanese economic relations.

On the Japanese side, there were important differences between the textile and auto cases that helped to produce smoother relations in the latter problem. Essentially, these involved the role of the MITI in Japanese trade policymaking. In the textile case, the MITI took a strong stand in defense of the domestic industry, and it did not cooperate in the more conciliatory and internationalist policies pursued by the Ministry of Foreign Affairs. However, over the years, the MITI has become much more internationalist, in the sense that it is now more willing to accommodate the interests of

Japan's major trading partners instead of trying to defend the narrow and immediate interests of the industries under its jurisdiction. The auto situation was proof of this generalization, because the MITI took the lead in dealing with this problem on the Japanese side, and its position on the issues negotiated was generally receptive to the concerns advanced by the Carter administration.

There were reasons why the passage of time may have better equipped MITI to deal with Japan's trading partners. For one thing, the MITI had already dismantled most of the trade barriers under its jurisdiction and, therefore, it had more yoyu (scope) than before to talk about and promote free trade. Of course, the new internationalist position of the MITI is not always synonymous with trade liberalism, because, while the MITI has called for more liberalization on the agricultural products on which Japan has restrictive policies, it also talks about the need for orderly marketing or orderly exporting arrangements to avoid conflict with trading partners. This was the case in the auto situation of 1980. Another reason for the MITI's new internationalism is that many of Japan's manufacturing industries have become stronger, and the comparative advantage they enjoy over their U.S. and European counterparts is now obvious to the world community. This was clearly the case with automobiles, and, as a result, the MITI had considerably more flexibility to press for accommodative solutions than it might otherwise have had. Finally, the MITI has recognized that the structure of international trade among OECD nations has become more interdependent and that this requires countries to coordinate economic policies among themselves. The MITI apparently has become more aware over time of Japan's place in the world economy, and, therefore, it is more ready to make policy that is consistent with international economic interdependence than it previously was. This posture helped improve relations with the United States during the negotiations over the auto situation.

Another reason the auto case was handled more smoothly than textiles was that the role of the Japanese Diet in the auto problem was negligible. In the textile case, the industry was widely represented in the Diet, and the Dietmen exercised strong pressure on the government on behalf of the industry, thereby making compromise with the United States all the more difficult. The auto industry, however, is not well represented in the Diet, in part because the industry is regionally concentrated. In this sense, the auto industry is quite unlike the textile industry or agriculture, which are both fragmented and widely distributed throughout Japan, and which employ larger numbers of Japanese workers. It is true that Japanese automakers, such as Toyota, met with the Liberal Democratic Party (LDP) leadership to explain their concern over U.S. demands for overseas investment, and presumably they sought whatever support the leadership might have been prepared to offer. However, the fact was that the political leadership was more concerned with the overall state of U.S.-Japanese relations than with defending what might have appeared to be narrow constituency interests. The industry did attract vocal support from the rank-and-file Dietmen, but, in the end, this did not amount to effective political pressure for the industry's interests. Unlike in the textile case, the Dietmen did not have any political incentives to get involved in the auto problem, nor did the government's handling of the problem apparently create any such incentives on its part.

Finally, in the auto issue, there were some fortuitous circumstances not under the government's control that helped the Japanese and U.S. governments to avoid a repetition of the wrangling that had occurred previously over textiles. Largely, these circumstances had to do with the industries in question. In the textile case, the industries in both countries were unified and took essentially unreconcilable positions; throughout the dispute they were opposed to any concessions on the part of their governments that might have ameliorated the situation. Furthermore, in both countries, the textile industry exercised considerable leverage over their government's position on the issue. In the auto situation, some of these circumstances were reversed. For one thing, the auto industry appeared to have less political leverage in their respective capitals than did the textile industry, which is curious, given the paramount national importance of the industry in each country. Another point is that the auto industry was not wholly unified in either country, particularly in the United States, where the industry sought to achieve government action in its favor. General Motors, the largest U.S. producer, never supported wholeheartedly the call for import restrictions on Japanese cars, nor did it join the UAW and Ford Motor Company in the injury petition to the U.S. International Trade Commission. It is probable that the position of General Motors was motivated more by an analysis of its competitive position than by high-minded internationalism, but the fact remains that its unwillingness to press for import controls made it easier for the U.S. government to decide against such controls early in the year and more difficult for the ITC to return an injury finding late in the year. Had the U.S. auto industry been united in favor of import controls, the U.S. government would have had less running room in handling this issue with the Japanese.

Perhaps the most important difference on the industrial side between the textile and auto cases was the nature of the industries in question. The auto industry in both Japan and the United States has become a global operation, while the textile industry, particularly in the United States, was more national and even provincial in its orientation. Consequently, the auto industry has become more accustomed to international production and competition, and it is perhaps therefore less willing to expand an economic problem into a nasty international political dispute. On the U.S. side, this attitude was reflected in the relatively statesmanlike behavior of the UAW leaders, who represented a union as sorely pressed as any in recent memory, but who generally refrained from the sort of hyperbole about unfair Japanese competition that has exacerbated U.S.-Japanese trade problems in the past. On the Japanese side, an international attitude was reflected by the Japanese automakers who, after some initial foot-dragging, indicated their willingness to cooperate in orderly exporting arrangements that would help to alleviate the distress in the U.S. auto industry. This spirit of moderation will undoubtedly assist the U.S. and Japanese governments in maintaining amicable relations over autos should the automobile issue reappear on the negotiating agenda between the two countries in the future.

Epilogue: The "Unilateral" Japanese Restraint of May 1981

If the 1980 presidential campaign and subsequent election of Ronald Reagan served as one temporary watershed in the auto crisis, then the recent agreement by Japan to voluntarily restrict auto exports will likely serve as another. On May 1, 1981, with U.S. Trade Representative William Brock in Tokyo for final consultations, the Ministry of International Trade and Industry announced that Japanese automakers would cut exports to the United States in 1981 by 7.7 percent. This would mean a ceiling of 1.68 million vehicles in 1981, down from the 1.82 million shipped in 1980—a reduction of approximately 140,000 units. The Japanese plan will extend for two years beyond 1981, but future export levels will be based in part on the amount of growth that occurs in the U.S. market. Japanese auto companies denounced the agreement, but industry spokesmen indicated that they would have little alternative but to cooperate.

The Japanese action produced immediate relief in Tokyo, where it lifted one cloud threatening the Suzuki-Reagan summit meeting the following week, and in Washington, where the negative finding of the ITC in November 1980 had not succeeded in putting the auto-import issue to rest. The House Trade Subcommittee had moved quickly with a resolution authorizing the president to negotiate an orderly marketing agreement with Japan—this authority had been in doubt when the ITC failed to find imports a substantial cause of serious injury to the U.S. industry. The resolution passed the full House on December 2, by 317 to 57, but quota opponents used procedural means to block Senate action prior to adjournment. In January, as U.S. auto sales continued sluggish, the Senate Trade Subcommittee held further hearings on the auto situation, and, in February, its new chairman and ranking minority member, Jack Danforth and Lloyd Bentsen, introduced a bill to impose annual quotas of 1.6 million on Japanese car imports for three years (compared to the 1.2 million being urged by some in the industry). They threatened to press their bill unless Japan agreed to export restraints, and General Motors joined Ford, Chrysler, and the UAW in calling for import relief.

During his election campaign, President Reagan had moved from his original free-trade position—that the auto industry's problems were in Washington, not in Japan—to a promise "to try to convince the Japanese that . . . the deluge of their cars into the United States must be slowed." Once in office, he found his cabinet sharply divided: his secretaries of Transportation and Commerce pressed trade restraint, while his economic and budget advisors thought special benefits for the auto industry ran counter to the administration's central goal of reducing government intervention in the economy. The resulting request that Japan take the initiative was very much the product of compromise on the U.S. side, but it also reflected a clear White House decision to seek some visible action on imports. Notwithstanding the unilateral form of the final action, it was in fact a negotiated arrangement. The Brock visit clinching the agreement was preceded by earlier intergovernmental discussions at the cabinet and working levels. Moreover, Brock had been in regular consultation with congressional leaders, as evidenced when he publicly assured the Japanese, in Tokyo, that, in light of the restraint plan, he now saw no prospect of legislation passing Congress. President Reagan had earlier stated that his administration opposed legislated quotas, but that he would find it difficult to veto such a bill.

It is tempting to conclude that the Japanese action on automobiles resolved the crisis of 1980-1981, but such a conclusion is not likely. In the first place, in a market that has averaged around 10 million units per year, the reduction is not large enough to make an appreciable dent in the underlying economic problem. It is probable that only General Motors, which reported a profit in the first quarter of 1981, will benefit much from the reduction. Meanwhile, the position of the remaining U.S. companies— Ford, Chrysler, and American Motors Corporation—is reported to be so bad that even the import levels of the Danforth-Bentsen bill would not in themselves have led to significant sales increases for these companies. For these reasons, it is difficult to avoid the conclusion that the Reagan request for voluntary restraint was largely a symbolic action by the U.S. government, done mostly because it was one of the few things the U.S. automakers, the UAW, and the government could agree upon. Above all, it allowed the U.S. government to avoid dealing with the substance of management decisions in the U.S. auto industry or the issue of high wages in the UAW.

Second, the Reagan administration may have compounded its problems by adding a diplomatic dimension to what hitherto has been a domestic economic problem. The Japanese government may have agreed to restrain exports in order to avoid the possibility of congressional action, but it will now have to deal with a hostile industry to make the restraints work. In these circumstances, one might expect the Japanese government to interpret the restrictions as favorably as it could to its own industry. For example, already there are problems of interpretation about whether existing dealer inventories should be counted in the 1981 quotas and whether exports to U.S. dependencies, such as Puerto Rico, are subject to the restraint. If Japan interprets these and other issues in favor of its own industry, there will undoubtedly be charges of bad faith to which the U.S. government might eventually have to respond. Thus, the implementation of a voluntary restraint agreement could in itself become a source of difficulty between the two countries. Should this occur, it would be entirely consistent with the history of textile restraints between the United States and Japan.

The diplomatic problem is further compounded by the means the Reagan administration chose to deal with the Japanese. The auto question produced a controversy in the Reagan cabinet between those who supported protection versus those who insisted that no action be taken. The resulting decision was a compromise whereby, first, the Japanese would be asked through informal channels to cut back exports, but, second, the U.S. government would not publicly specify the amount of the cutback desired. Procedurally, this arrangement worked badly, because it encouraged bureaucratic actors (notably the secretary of State and the U.S. trade representative) to send conflicting signals to the Japanese. But even the form of the arrangement was unfortunate. It made the Japanese government appear to be taking an initiative without a clear request from the U.S. government, which might have served as a mandate of sorts for what was an unpopular action in Japan. This arrangement will likely make relations between the government and the auto industry in Japan more difficult than they might have been, which will make bilateral relations between the two countries more difficult as well.

More serious, however, are the antitrust implications of the Reagan procedures. It is likely that if the Japanese automakers agree to reduce exports, they will have to implement these reductions through market-sharing agreements that violate provisions of the Sherman antitrust Act that prohibit collusion in restraint of trade. If this were the case, U.S. importers of foreign autos would certainly sue the Japanese companies. Antitrust implications might be avoided if the Japanese automakers were to act under explicit orders of the Japanese government, but initiating such orders under, for example, Japan's little-used export control laws would be contrary to the consensual decision-making style that predominates in Japan. Had the U.S. government transmitted explicit requirements for reductions to the Japanese government, the companies might have been cleared of any possible lawsuit, but then the U.S. government itself might have been acting illegally. As things now stand, the Japanese have been pressured into taking an action that the U.S. government was unwilling to take responsibility for and that might bring them into conflict with U.S. law. It should not be surprising if these procedures create resentment on the Japanese side.

Finally, the policies adopted by the Reagan administration will likely internationalize the auto problem beyond the U.S.-Japanese relationship. What impact this will have on world trade is unclear at the moment. In the short run, the U.S. action will make other importers of Japanese cars, notably the Europeans and the Canadians, anxious to arrange a similar deal in order not to have their markets surfeited with exports that might have gone to the United States. There is a further possibility that some nations might resort to punitive quotas against Japanese automobiles, which could in turn lead to a retaliation affecting other industries. Such a spectre was recently raised by West German Minister of Economics Otto Lambsdorff, who warned a U.S. audience that auto protection in the United States could lead to a spiral of restraint actions that might damage some stronger U.S. export industries, such as chemicals or synthetic fibres. At this time, such a pessimistic scenario seems unlikely, because the auto problem has been handled in isolation from other trade issues. However, the prospect that protectionism on autos might trigger a general trade war is too real for nations to take it lightly.

There is a curious possibility that internationalizing the U.S. problem now might lead to a broader adjustment of the international trading system in the longer run. The auto industry is heading into a period of chronic overcapacity, which some predict will result in a substantial reduction in the number of firms now operating. Undoubtedly, this will cause severe dislocations in some countries. Because the auto industry plays such a vital role in many national economies, it is probable that governments in those nations will take an increasingly larger hand in promoting the interest of the industry. Thus, the immediate auto crisis, which is largely a U.S. problem, might serve as an occasion to consider the wider structural problems facing the industry—before those problems reach crisis proportions on a world scale. It is possible that the world will eventually move to a regulated trading regime in autos, such as it has had for some time in textiles. Such a regime could promote stability in auto production, employment, and trade, and, although it would bring with it the sort of costs to economic efficiency that are associated with any trade-restrictive arrangement, it might still be preferable to the crisis-prone ad hoc procedures now being applied to the industry.

References

In addition to interviews conducted during the spring and summer of 1980, this chapter draws on the following sources. Factual information not otherwise referenced is generally taken from the last two sources listed.

Newspapers

Asahi Shimbun, Tokyo.
Mainichi Shimbun, Tokyo.
Nihon Keizai Shimbun,, Tokyo.
The New York Times.
Sankei Shimbun, Tokyo.
Yomiuri Shimbun, Tokyo.
The Wall Street Journal, New York.
The Washington Post.

Other Publications

"Special Report: Auto Industry Crisis." *Congressional Quarterly*, May 10, 1980, pp. 1262-1266.

U.S. Congress, Senate, *Congressional Record*, 96th Cong., 2d Sess., 1980.

Destler, I.M. "U.S.-Japanese Relations and the American Trade Initiative of 1977: Was This 'Trip' Necessary?" In *Japan and the United States: Challenges and Opportunities,* edited by William J. Barnds. New York: New York University Press (for the Council on Foreign Relations), 1979, pp. 190-230.

Destler, I.M.; Fukui, Haruhiro; and Sato, Hideo. *The Textile Wrangle: Conflict in Japanese-American Relations, 1969-1971.* Ithaca and London: Cornell University Press, 1979.

Hormats, Robert D. Statement to the U.S. House Committee on Ways and Means, Subcommittee on Trade. In *World Auto Trade: Current Trends and Structural Problems* (Washington, D.C.: Government Printing Office, 1980), pp. 186-191.

Ikema, Makoto. "Nichibei Jidosha Masatsu," *Genda: Keizai* (Summer, 1980), pp. 35-49.

Japan Automobile Manufacturers Association, *Motor Vehicle Statistics of Japan,* Tokyo, 1980.

Japan Economic Institute, *Japan Insight,* January 23, 1981 and February 2, 1981.

Metzler, Ronald J. "Color-TV Sets and U.S.-Japanese Relations: Problems of Trade-Adjustment Policymaking." *Orbis*, Summer 1979, pp. 421-446.

Raftery, William A. Statement of March 7, 1980 in House Ways and Means Committee. In *World Auto Trade: Current Trends and Structural Problems* (Washington, D.C.: Government Printing Office, 1980), pp. 128-131.

U.S. Congress, House, Committee on Ways and Means, *Auto Situation: 1980,* 96th Cong., 2d Sess., 1980, Report of the Subcommittee on Trade. (Washington, D.C.: Government Printing Office, 1980).

U.S. Department of Transportation, News Release, August 1980.

Ward's Automotive Yearbook. 42nd ed. Michigan: Wards Communication, Inc., 1980.

Agricultural Trade: The Case of Beef and Citrus

Hideo Sato and
Timothy J. Curran

Traditionally, a trade issue between Japan and the United States involved increasing Japanese imports to the U.S. market that invoked domestic industry opposition. However, in the past few years, another pattern of trade-issue initiation has emerged. As the United States has lost its comparative advantage in numerous manufacturing industries and as the trade imbalance with Japan has visibly increased, the U.S. government has turned its attention to the opening of the Japanese market for those U.S. products for which the United States believes it still enjoys comparative advantage. These include agricultural commodities and high-technology manufactured products such as telecommunications equipment, semiconductors, and computers. It was in this context that the United States asked for an expansion of Japan's beef and citrus imports in connection with larger bilateral trade negotiations in 1977 and, in 1978, within the framework of the MTN or the Tokyo Round negotiations. During each of these two phases, bilateral talks broke down a number of times, producing a high level of tension between the two countries.

Economics cannot fully explain this clash over citrus and beef trade. As items in the overall U.S.-Japanese trade relationship of over $40 billion and in the bilateral agricultural trade relationship of about $4 billion, citrus and beef products are clearly insignificant. As table 4-1 shows, U.S. exports of these products accounted for approximately $60 million in 1977 and $139 million in 1978. Moreover, estimates of trade potential in these products, given a completely free market in Japan, amount to only $500 million—still a small factor in the broad trade relationship.

Of course, the U.S. domestic industry was not without justifications for wanting to expand its beef and citrus exports to Japan. Between 1964 and 1971, citrus acreage in the United States expanded rapidly at an annual rate of 50,000 to 70,000 acres (see figure 4-1). As a result, orange production increased from less than 4 million tons in 1964 to well over 10 million tons in 1976. Many of the citrus trees are less than fifteen years old and, even without any more acreage increase, the United States's citrus-production growth rate for the coming decade will continue to exceed its population growth rate. At the same time, per capita consumption in the country seems to have already leveled off at around 54.4 kilograms (Ministry of Agricul-

Table 4-1

Major U.S. Agricultural Exports to Japan, Calendar 1977-1978

	Quantity (in metric tons)		Value (in thousands of dollars)	
	1977	1978	1977	1978
Total	—	—	$3,856,739	$4,435,253
Soybeans	3,410,346	3,854,953	937,682	980,747
Soybean meal	267,695	267,343	54,667	57,749
Corn	7,829,154	8,486,066	811,927	914,884
Sorghum	2,424,590	2,359,204	240,819	231,821
Wheat	3,315,084	3,275,901	374,490	431,910
Raw cotton	206,902	267,570	309,710	343,445
Whole cattle hides[a]	8,414,349	8,788,978	186,034	233,304
Unmanufactured tobacco	61,429	46,385	259,953	226,911
Tallow	102,539	88,164	40,709	39,930
Alfalfa meal and cubes	248,286	311,286	29,205	29,969
Peanuts	26,852	24,519	20,789	19,138
Refined cottonseed oil	19,026	23,029	11,822	13,866
Beef and veal	20,159	33,588	52,364	116,729
Pork	21,887	24,110	59,936	86,974
Poultry	31,608	38,774	35,972	49,800
Lemons	104,823	120,239	40,882	67,680
Grapefruit	148,992	131,963	35,501	36,227
Oranges	22,257	49,151	7,415	22,411
Almonds	10,748	11,941	23,862	34,208
Raisins	7,259	15,978	9,509	21,867

Source: U.S, Department of Agriculture, reprinted in the United States-Japan Trade Council, *U.S.-Japan Agricultural Trade: What's Ahead in the 1980's* (Washington, D.C.: 1980), p. 4.
[a]Quality in number of pieces.

ture, Forestry, and Fisheries, 1978, p. 186). Meanwhile, fresh-orange exports declined from 479 million tons in 1974 to 398 million tons in 1976. In particular, exports to Europe were cut in half (to 77 million tons) during this same period (U.S. Department of Agriculture, 1978, p. 221). There is a similar situation in the beef trade. Although the United States is the world's largest importer of grass-fed beef, it is also the only major exporter of grain-fed high-quality beef. However, as figure 4-2 shows, U.S. beef exports have not been growing steadily because Canada—once the largest customer—has substantially reduced its importation of U.S. beef in recent years.

Considering only these domestic-industry conditions, one remains still puzzled as to why the U.S. government invested so much time and energy in seeking Japanese concessions, particularly when the Japanese beef and citrus industries themselves were in a difficult situation.

Since around 1973, Japanese citrus growers have been faced with a serious problem of overproduction. Japanese citrus production has been increasing (from 1.6 million tons in 1965 to 2.9 million tons in 1976), but its

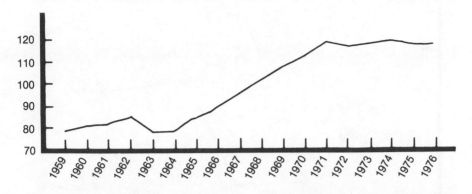

Source: Ministry of Agriculture, Forestry, and Fisheries, *Nichibei Keizai Kankei Shiryo* [Japan-U.S. Economic Relations Data] (Tokyo: International Planning Division of the Economic Affairs Bureau, 1978), p. 186.

Figure 4-1. U.S. Citrus Acreage Trend (unit: 10,000 acres)

per capita consumption has been decreasing since 1973 (see figure 4-3). As a result, citrus growers implemented a 20 percent acreage reduction. Moreover, Japan was importing more citrus products than it was exporting (24,400 tons of imports versus 19,900 tons of exports in 1976). As for Japan's beef industry, it had suffered a major crisis in 1973-1974, when the doubling of beef imports was followed by a drastic reduction of domestic demand in the wake of the OPEC oil embargo. In 1977, the industry was still recovering from that crisis.

These Japanese industry conditions aside, one might rightly argue that, because Japan's beef- and citrus-import quotas were clearly against GATT rules, it was quite natural for the United States to seek their elimination, especially as part of the Tokyo Round negotiations, the major purpose of which was to reduce nontariff barriers to free trade, including residual import quotas as such. This was in fact a basic assumption behind the U.S. government's position on the issue. (Although not through residual quotas against GATT rules, the United States, too, restricts its importation of beef and oranges (mikan or mandarin oranges). The United States sets a beef-import quota under Public Law 88-482 (the Meat Import Act). The quota for 1978, including 90,000 additional imports allowed in to offset the domestic beef shortage, was 681,000 tons (Ministry of Agriculture, Forestry, and Fisheries, 1978, p. 154). Fresh mandarin oranges from Japan can be imported into only six U.S. states (Alaska, Hawaii, Washington, Oregon, Idaho, and Montana), presumably to prevent the spread of a citrus disease called citrus canker, to which mandarin oranges are considered to be resistant and U.S. valencia and navel oranges are not.

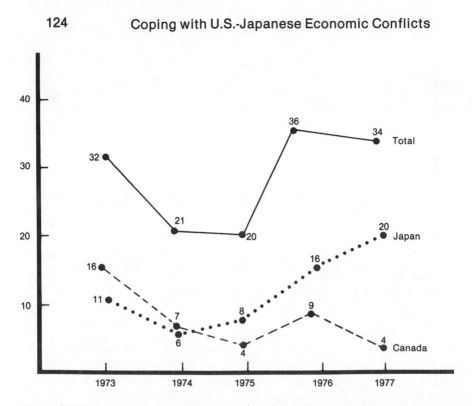

Sources: U.S. Department of Agriculture, *Agricultural Statistics of 1978* (Washington, D.C.: U.S. Government Printing Office, 1978), pp. 346-347, and Ministry of Agriculture, Forestry, and Fisheries, *Nichibei Keizai Kankei Shiryo* [Japan-U.S. Economic Relations Data] (Tokyo: International Planning Division of the Economic Affairs Bureau, 1978). p. 155.
Note: Unit = 1,000 tons.

Figure 4-2. U.S. Beef Exports

A more important reason for the U.S. actions was that the administration was trying to diffuse the bilateral tension that had built up as the result of a large U.S.-Japanese trade imbalance and trying to generate support for multilateral trade liberalization during a period of heightening protectionism (particularly with regard to Japan). This reason goes a long way toward explaining why the U.S. government paid so much attention to beef and citrus. Both products are represented by important political constituencies in the United States. Indeed, salient factors behind the U.S.-Japanese agricultural trade dispute in 1977 and 1978 were rooted in the domestic politics of both countries. In Japan, the disproportionately strong political power enjoyed by the agricultural sector explains why the Japanese government could not easily concede, even though concessions might not have seriously damaged farmers and would certainly have been in the interest of consumers.

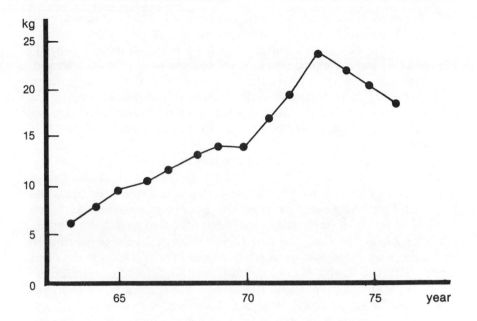

Source: Japan Fruit Growers Cooperative Association, *Nihon no Kankitsu Jijo* [The Citrus Fruit Situation in Japan] (Tokyo: April 1978), p. 11.

Figure 4-3. Per Capita Consumption of Mandarin Oranges in Japan

This chapter will deal not so much with the economics of the U.S.-Japanese beef-and-citrus-trade issue of 1977-1978. Rather, it will focus on the politics of the policymaking in both countries and of the negotiations between them in the course of reconstructing the issue as accurately as possible. Specifically, we intend to examine how the issue was initiated, how it was handled or mishandled within and between the two countries, what channels were used and what misperceptions arose in the course of the negotiations, and how the issue was finally resolved. Before turning to this task, we will briefly elaborate on the major political constraints in both countries.

Agriculture and Politics

The agricultural sector in the United States has long been export oriented. However, a general balance-of-payments crisis for the United States in the late 1960s and early 1970s increased the importance of agricultural products as export items. Compared with the manufacturing sector, whose relationship with the governments has often been that of an adversary, agriculture has enjoyed "more careful government attention and generous funding" (GAO, 1979, p. 188). The increasing bilateral trade imbalance with Japan in 1976 and 1977 naturally made the U.S. government want to expand agricultural exports to that country. In the Tokyo Round, the U.S. government was determined more than ever to bring agricultural products under the free-trade regime. This determination was directly related to the administration's domestic strategy for ensuring congressional passage of the MTN package.

Unlike previous multilateral trade negotiations, the Tokyo Round was unique in the major emphasis it placed on negotiating the reduction or elimination of nontariff barriers. In previous rounds, where the focus was on tariffs, Congress granted the president, prior to negotiations, authority to cut U.S. tariffs in response to reciprocal reductions by other countries. Upon completion of these tariff negotiations, any cuts the president had authorized were automatically in effect in the United States. On the other hand, NTBs often involved domestic laws, and Congress could not extend the executive authority to amend these laws automatically in the course of negotiation. Instead, a special procedure was designed as part of the Trade Act of 1974 to reconcile the executive's authority to negotiate with foreign governments and the Congress's authority as lawmaker. This procedure required the president to give Congress ninety days' notice before concluding any negotiations and to provide Congress with a copy of the agreement and a statement of how it affected U.S. interests. Congress then had ninety days to act on the legislation. It could not amend, table, or otherwise delay the bill. However, if unsatisfied with the results of the negotiations, Congress could, of course, refuse to ratify the agreement.

This procedure, therefore, did not eliminate at all the possibility of a U.S. repudiation of the MTN. And, indeed, throughout the negotiations, U.S. negotiators were aware of the danger that existed if the agreements they reached in Geneva were unacceptable to major U.S. interest groups, who could subsequently bring pressure to bear on Congress to reject the settlement.

Gaining the support of the agricultural sector was central to the construction of an effective pro-MTN coalition. In doing so, the special trade representative (STR) had to identify the major components of the agricultural sector, and either win their support or neutralize them. Two major trouble spots loomed: the grains and dairy sectors. The STR knew that, by satisfying the grains sector, they would effectively neutralize virtually the entire midwestern United States—and in the process go a long way toward securing the passage of the MTN. The problem was that not much could be done by the STR for the grains people. Their major complaints concerned foreign NTBs, which were not negotiable, such as the

European community's variable levy system or the Japanese government's artificially high selling price of imported U.S. wheat. As a result, STR officials decided to eliminate effectively the grains sector from the MTN by placing discussions on the grains commodity in the context of negotiations on a new International Wheat Agreement. These negotiations were the responsibility of the U.S. Department of Agriculture, and not the STR. Thus, the outcome of such negotiations was not directly tied to the MTN.

The dairy sector presented a bigger problem for two reasons. First, the United States does not have a comparative advantage in this sector and, hence, could expect foreign pressure. The United States is a net importer of dairy products, and other countries sought increased access to the U.S. dairy market during the negotiations. Particularly difficult for the United States were Scandinavian and European Community (EC) requests for access to the U.S. market for cheese. The United States was forced to make concessions in this area in order to gain concessions from the EC in areas of relative U.S. comparative advantage.

The cheese concessions, however, were vigorously opposed by the U.S. dairy industry, which is extremely well-organized and which had the potential to mount a campaign to scuttle the negotiations. Once the STR decided on the necessity of dairy concessions, they knew they would lose the support of dairy interests and probably face the opposition of this powerful lobby. Therefore, they tried to minimize the loss by balancing the dairy sector's opposition with the support of other agricultural groups that also exercised substantial political influence. The citrus and beef industries were among them. The citrus industry was represented by ninety-eight senators and representatives from Florida, Texas, Arizona, and California. The beef industry was strategically located in key agricultural states in the Midwest and the Southwest, and over twenty U.S. legislators were individually identified as beef-industry supporters by the Japanese agricultural ministry in 1978 (Ministry of Agriculture, Forestry, and Fisheries, 1978, p. 65).

In Japan, agriculture in general does not enjoy comparative advantage because of a lack of large arable land. However, the government has emphasized a policy of national food self-sufficiency in addition to maintaining the income level of Japan's rural population. As in the case of many other countries, the devices through which these objectives have been pursued have included domestic subsidies to producers and import protection from more economically efficient foreign producers. Farmers have exercised enormous political power to sustain these protective policies.

The political influence of the Japanese agricultural sector is derived from a number of factors. First, Japanese farmers have had unusually strong political clout because rural, agricultural areas have provided a haven for political conservatism and, therefore, are a bastion of strength for the ruling Liberal Democratic Party (LDP). Indeed, as Masumi Ishikawa's analysis shows, there has been a close correlation between the postwar trend in the percentage of those gainfully engaged in farming and the trend in the percentage of electoral votes received by the ruling conservative party (Hemmi, 1981, pp. 7-3).

Second, despite the considerable demographic changes in Japan in the last three decades, little adjustment has been made in the electoral district system, which is skewed in favor of rural districts and, therefore, in favor of LDP candidates. (In the December 5, 1976, Lower House election, for instance, an LDP candidate with 37,107 popular votes in the agricultural Niigata third district was successfully elected, whereas a Japan Communist Party candidate with as many as 114,662 votes was only a runner-up in the urban Osaka third district.)

Third, most of the important agricultural policy positions in the Diet and the party are usually held by politicians from agricultural areas.

Last but not least, Japanese farmers are effectively organized by Nokyo, or the Agricultural Cooperative Association. Virtually all of Japan's five-million farm households belong to this organization, which has a nationwide network of well over 10,000 local agricultural cooperatives. Although only 400,000 Japanese farm households (8 percent of the total) raise beef cattle and only 340,000 households (6.8 percent) grow citrus, most of their national-level political activities, including antiimport campaigns, are orchestrated by Nokyo's national peak organizations, such as Zenchu (National Central Union of Agricultural Cooperatives) and Zenno (National Federation of Agricultural Cooperatives). Specialized cooperative federations, such as Nichienren (Japan Fruit Growers Cooperative Association) and Zenchikuren (National Livestock Cooperative Federation) also play their parts (George, 1980, pp. 10-69).

Now we are in a slightly better position to understand why the Japanese government could not easily give in to U.S. pressure on the beef and citrus issue. However, if Japanese farmers are so politically influential, then why did Japan end up making substantive concessions not just once but twice? A similar question can be asked about the U.S. side. If the citrus and beef lobbies were so important in the politics of U.S.-Japanese relations and of the MTN in 1977 and 1978, why did the U.S. government manage to settle the bilateral agricultural trade issue short of total, or at least more comprehensive, liberalization of Japanese beef and citrus imports? These and other questions will be addressed in our following discussions of the actual negotiations.

First Phase, 1977

The Carter administration's effort to open up the Japanese market for U.S. agricultural products came as early as February 1977, when Vice-President

Mondale asked, during his Tokyo visit, for the lifting of Japan's import control on citrus fruits containing certain preservatives, such as OPP and TBZ. On his visit to Japan in June, Secretary of Agriculture Bergland suggested that Tokyo buy more beef for hotel use as well as liberalize the importation of cherries. In September, a delegation of officials from the Special Trade Representative's office visited Japan to discuss the upcoming MTN negotiations.[1] The leader of the delegation, Alan Wolff, expressed U.S. interest in expanded agricultural exports and in eliminating Japan's nontariff barriers to U.S. products, particularly on citrus, beef, and other agricultural products. Wolff pointed out to the Japanese that many agricultural products were politically sensitive in the United States. Cherries, he said, are a major crop in Oregon, which is the home of Al Ullman, chairman of the powerful Ways and Means Committee. As for citrus products, Wolff noted the strong interest of Florida and California. Florida growers, for example, had, through their representative, Senator Richard Stone, urged the government to pressure Japan to eliminate barriers to Florida's citrus exports. A similar suggestion was made during the U.S.-Japanese subcabinet-level consultations of September 12-13, which focused on the growing bilateral trade imbalance.

Japan at that time was not particularly responsive. Officials of the Ministry of Agriculture, Forestry, and Fisheries (MAFF)[2] argued that Japan could not make any substantive concession on beef and citrus imports because domestic demand for beef was not catching up with increasing domestic production and Japanese producers of mikan or mandarin oranges (which were considered to compete directly with imported U.S. oranges) were already facing a serious problem of overproduction. Moreover, the government was discouraging the production of rice and encouraging farmers to shift to other types of farming, such as livestock and horticulture. The ministry was under pressure from domestic beef and citrus producers and their spokesmen in the Diet, who were contending that the agricultural sector should not be punished or sacrificed for the surplus trade in Japan's manufacturing sector. Japanese concessions on beef and citrus, it was also argued, would be far from sufficient for redressing the bilateral trade imbalance.

Toward the Rivers Mission

Economic-policy officials in the United States were quite disappointed with the lack of Japanese response. They were convinced that the continuation of the high-level tension between the two countries, as well as a series of public confrontations and bickering on specific products and issues, such as they had just experienced over color televisions, could do serious damage to the overall U.S.-Japanese relationship. Robert Strauss in the STR was also concerned that a wave of anti-Japan sentiment could generate a congressional protectionist surge, which would scuttle the slowly reviving MTN. They came to realize that the United States needed to present a very specific set of demands—rather than general admonitions—to produce more response from the Japanese. Japanese officials, particularly in the Foreign Ministry, concurred with this analysis. They encouraged U.S. officials to push quickly on the offensive. These Japanese and U.S. officials believed that, by identifying a series of highly visible targets, particularly visible Japanese barriers to trade, and negotiating quickly to remove them, they could get a jump on the protectionist forces and bring under control the economic situation.

High on the list of barriers were Japanese restrictions on agricultural imports, including beef and citrus. Although Japanese concessions on beef and citrus would be too small to correct the trade imbalance between the two countries, by obtaining symbolic concessions from Japan on these and other matters, U.S. officials believed that congressional attacks on the Carter administration would be eased.

Two interagency groups of officials immediately set to work, one at an assistant-secretary level, chaired by Deputy STR Wolff, and the other at a deputy-assistant-secretary level, chaired by Erland Heginbotham of the State Department, to support the former. By early November, the working-level interagency groups had prepared a package of proposals to be presented to Japan. On November 9, the cabinet-level Economic Policy Group met under Treasury Secretary Michael Blumenthal's chairmanship to review these proposals. It was decided then to send a mission to Tokyo to present the proposals, but there were differing opinions as to who should head the mission. Someone suggested that Special Trade Representative Robert Strauss head the mission. In October, Japanese officials had privately urged Strauss to come to Tokyo in order to conclude a broad agreement on some of the enumerated targets. Strauss, however, was reluctant to make the trip until the substance of the talks was a bit clearer. Other officials at the meeting felt also that the United States should maintain a low profile when dealing with the Japanese—in order to avoid publicity and a negative emotional reaction there. Strauss was considered too high level and too visible, as was his deputy, Wolff. So the decision was to send the next ranking STR official, General Counsel Richard Rivers. The Economic Policy Group met again on November 17 in the presence of President Carter to finalize the U.S. negotiating position.

As the Rivers mission was about to depart for Japan, a delegation of Komeito politicians, headed by Secretary General Jun'ya Yano, had a series of meetings with top U.S. policy officials, including Mondale, Strauss, and Wolff. Mondale reportedly told the delegation that the economic relationship between the United States and Japan was in a very serious situation. He also asserted that, despite Prime Minister Fukuda's promise made at the Bonn Summit to reduce Japan's trade surplus, the U.S.-Japanese trade imbalance was actually increasing. Strauss expressed his hope that Japan would make meaningful adjustments in its economic policy in order to arrest the growing tide of protectionism in Congress. As recounted by Yano in his press conference, Strauss was supposed to have said that the kind of economic policy measures being considered in Japan (such as tariff reductions on imports of automobiles and motorcycles), as reported in the U.S. press, would be taken as a joke by Congress. The evening edition of *Nihon Keizai*, dated November 17, reported on the Komeito meetings with U.S. officials with the heading, "STR Says Japan should Set a Timetable for Turning the Current Account into Deficit."

Rivers arrived in Tokyo on November 17 and stayed there for five days. With him were Heginbotham and Japan Country Director Nicholas Platt of the State Department. Rivers warned the Japanese government that its continuing substantial trade surpluses with the United States as well as other nations seriously threatened relations between Washington and Tokyo. The U.S. officials strongly suggested that Japan publicly announce, within three weeks, its commitments to drastically cut its current-account surplus, increase its imports, restrain export promotion, and produce a specific list of immediate and long-term measures to restructure its trade problems. To overcome local Japanese resistance to such steps, which threatened to further depress a virtually stagnant domestic economy, the Americans said they hoped Japan would seek a real economic growth rate of 8 percent during the next fiscal year (far higher than the 6 percent that the Japanese prime minister had envisioned). They told the Japanese that President Carter himself would be closely watching Japan's economic performance in the days ahead. On agricultural trade, Rivers talked mostly with Nobuo Imamura, MAFF's director of the Economic Affairs Bureau. In response to the U.S. request for the liberalization of agricultural imports, particularly beef and citrus, Imamura emphasized that Japan had expanded farm imports from the United States 2.3 times during the preceding five years (*Asahi Shumbun*, 19 November 1977).

The Rivers mission did have some impact on MAFF officials, however. While continuing to resist full agricultural liberalization, MAFF officials began to consider an expansion of slightly beyond 20 percent of the import quotas. Although the ministry did not, in its earlier announcements, include oranges and citrus juices in the quotas-expansion scheme, it was indicated now that MAFF officials were also considering an expansion of the orange and citrus-juice quotas as well. In regard to liberalization (total elimination of quotas), the ministry maintained a firm position of outright opposition. Ministry officials explained that orange- and citrus-juice import liberalization—at the time mikan oranges were overproduced and their prices were going down—would cause a serious situation in the mikan-producing areas of the country and might create a social problem. As regards beef liberalization, one MAFF official had this to say:

> Implementation of beef import liberalization would require a revision of the present law. Even if a bill to change the existing law were to be introduced in the Diet it would not be passed. For the ruling LDP and the opposition parties are united in their opposition to such legislative change. Even incremental expansions of the import quota would be difficult.

While Rivers was in Tokyo, Zenchu and Zenno issued statements opposing any expansion of beef and citrus imports and sent copies to top Japanese agricultural policy officials, including Minister Zenko Suzuki, Director Imamura, and LDP politicians in the agricultural committees.

Outwardly, the Japanese government remained calm in the face of what amounted to a stern lecture from the United States. Privately, however, Japanese officials expressed shock at what they regarded as a U.S. ultimatum. The prime minister called Rivers "the most famous person in Japan" when he showed up with Ambassador Mansfield on a courtesy call.

Reading about emotional Japanese reactions to the Rivers overture, as reported in the U.S. press, President Carter apparently became worried. He called Strauss and asked him if the United States was not putting too much pressure on Japan. Strauss said he did not think so, but he sent a cable to Mansfield in Tokyo to check his judgment. The ambassador's reply was that the United States was on the right course (although he subsequently changed his mind).

Fukuda Reorganizes His Cabinet

The first thing Fukuda did after the Rivers mission was to reshuffle his cabinet. There were some important changes in the cabinet make-up. First of all, in order to smooth out Japan's foreign economic relations, Fukuda created a new post (minister for External Economic Affairs) and appointed to the post a veteran diplomat who had substantial economic expertise—Nobuhiko Ushiba, former Japanese ambassador to the United States, former foreign vice-minister, and former director of the MITI's International Trade Bureau. In view of the fact that Ushiba was not a Diet member, it was a very unusual appointment. Another notable appointment was that of Ichiro Nakagawa as the MAFF minister. Although substantially younger than his predecessor, Suzuki, Nakagawa was known for his strong leadership quality within the party. As a leader of Seirankai, he represented the voice of an outspoken intraparty group of twenty-two "Young Turks," many of whom came from agricultural areas in the country. Kiichi Miyazawa, an internationalist, was appointed director-general of the Economic Planning Agency. Another economic expert, Toshio Komoto, was made head of the MITI.

The first meeting of the new cabinet, on November 29, created an intra-cabinet group, called the Economic Ministers Group (Keizai Kakuryo Kaigi), to promote comprehensive domestic and foreign economic policies. The group consisted of eleven cabinet members: from Economic Planning, Foreign Affairs, Finance, Agriculture, International Trade and Industry, Transportation, the cabinet secretariat, the prime minister's office, and External Economic Affairs. It was to be chaired by EPA Director Miyazawa, whose role was to coordinate interministerial economic policies. In view of the pending trade imbalance issue with the United States, Fukuda asked the group to prepare a trade promotion package by December 6. He also asked Nakagawa to come up with beef-import measures that would help domestic consumers and have a positive impact on the government's attempt to correct the trade imbalance. In his press conference after the cabinet meeting, Nakagawa agreed to reconsider Japan's beef-import policy, saying, "The lowering of beef prices will help increase beef consumption" (*Asahi Shimbun*, 30 November 1977). He alluded to his desire to take dramatic action on the citrus problem as well. Ushiba was even more forthcoming. He said that Japan should make a decisive move toward agricultural import liberalization to persuade the United States that Japan was making a serious effort to reduce the bilateral trade imbalance. He then added that he had a lot to expect from the new MAFF minister in this respect.

The first meeting of the Economic Ministers Group was held the next day in the presence of Fukuda and three top party leaders. The atmosphere of the meeting was basically forward-looking, reflecting the determination of the goverment to resolve the trade imbalance dispute with the United States. Fukuda told those attending the meeting that, while the group had to deal with both domestic and foreign economic policies, it should focus on an improvement of the U.S.-Japanese trade relationship, which required immediate attention. Foreign Minister Sunao Sonoda emphasized the need for substantial concessions to the United States in view of the fact that the Rivers mission apparently went back unsatisfied. Miyazawa asked for the maximum possible concessions from each ministry concerned, saying that, while the remaining import barriers were all very difficult ones to remove, the government should seriously explore every possible move toward liberalization; even partial liberalization should be given serious consideration. After agreeing to let the bureaucratic-level officials work out the details of a Japanese trade-promotion package, the group decided to assign to Ushiba the task of carrying the package to the United States and negotiating a settlement of the trade dispute with Strauss and other U.S. officials.

In order to help build intraparty consensus for concessions to the United States, Fukuda met with party elders (including former prime ministers Kishi and Miki and former Lower House speakers Ishii and Maeo) on December 2 and asked for their cooperation in settling the pending dispute with the United States. He told the elders that the government would send Ushiba to the United States after December 10 and would like to increase emergency imports beyond $700 million. Speaking at the Foreign Correspondents Club in Tokyo the same day, Ushiba hinted that he would take to the United States a package of Japanese concessions that the Americans would appreciate, including concessions on agricultural imports.

Meanwhile, working-level consultations and deliberations on the Japanese package had been going relatively smoothly, except for agricultural imports. The Foreign Ministry and the EPA were advocating liberalization of the key import items such as beef and oranges, in which the United States had been particularly interested. But the MAFF was only willing to implement partial liberalization of certain fishery products and a 20 percent expansion of the agricultural products under residual import quotas. As table 4-2 shows, herring and cuttlefish (which the MAFF suggested that it might liberalize) were only subitems, and their liberalization would not eliminate any of the twenty-two agricultural import quotas. The Gaimusho suggested that the MAFF implement at least seasonal liberalization of orange imports (free imports during the off-season months of June through August for mikan) as well as full liberalization of tomato-ketchup imports. The MAFF's response was that seasonable liberalization would be practically the same as full liberalization because present-day refrigeration technology can keep imported oranges fresh more than six months. As regards beef, the MAFF said it could not expand the overall quota because 5,000 tons were already being added to 35,000 tons for the later half of fiscal 1977; the only possibility would be an expansion of the special quota for beef for hotel use. In fact, due to interministerial disagreements, agricultural imports were left outside of the final eight-point EPA guidelines for the Japanese trade-promotion package, which was announced on December 4. Agricultural imports were to be taken up at the cabinet level on December 6.

On December 5, Miyazawa met with Nakagawa and MITI Minister Toshio Komoto separately and agreed that, while keeping the basic framework of the twenty-seven residual import quotas, they should liberalize imports of some subitems within such quotas. The Japanese package approved by the Economic Ministers Group on December 6 offered to liberalize smoked herring and ten other subitems. Under the conditions of the package, Japan would double the importation of beef for hotel use and increase orange-juice imports to 2,000 tons for fiscal 1977 (ending in March); double the orange import quota for the latter half of fiscal 1977 to 6,500

Table 4-2
List of Japanese Commodities: All "Residual" Agricultural Import Quota Items and Four Government Trade Items

BTN[a] Code	Commodity
Agricultural "residual" items	
02.01	Beef (011-100, 610)[b]
03.01	Herring, cod, cod roe, yellowtail, sardine, mackerel, jack mackerel, and saury, live, fresh, chilled, or frozen (031-131, 142, 143, 152, 161, 192)
03.02	Herring, cod, cod roe, yellowtail, sardine, mackerel, jack mackerel, and saury, salted or dried and smoked herring (031-212, 221, 229, 230)
03.03	Squid and cuttlefish and scallop (031-314, 315, 323)
04.01	Milk and cream, fresh (022-300)
04.02	Milk and cream, evaporated, condensed, or dried (022-111, 112, 121, 122, 190, 210, 222, 223, 224, 230, 240, 299)
04.04	Cheese and curd, except natural cheese (024-010, 020)
07.05	Beans and peas, dried (054-210, 220, 230, 240, 250, 260, 290)
08.02	Oranges and tangerines, fresh (051-110, 120)
08.11	Oranges and tangerines, temporarily preserved (053-632)
11.01	Cereal flour (046-011, 012, 020; 047-011, 019)
11.02	Cereal meals and groats (046-030, 040; 047-023, 029; 048-112, 119)
11.07	Malt (048-200)
11.08	Starches and inulin (599-511, 512, 513, 514, 519, 520)
12.01	Peanuts (221-100)
12.08	Laver and other seaweeds and konjak (054-871, 872, 879, 880)
16.02	Prepared or preserved meat, except bacon, ham, and sausages (013-811, 819, 820, 891, 893, 899)
17.02	Sugars and syrups, except those of beet and cane (061-911, 912, 920, 931, 941, 942, 949, 950, 960, 970, 981)
20.05	Fruit purees and pastes (053-330, 340)
20.06	Fruit pulp and prepared pineapple (053-911, 919, 962)
20.07	Tomato Juice and fruit juices (053-511, 513, 514, 521, 529, 530, 541, 542, 543, 545, 549, 550)
21.04	Tomato sauce and ketchup and seasonings mainly containing sodium glutamate (099-041, 042)
21.07	Food preparations containing sugar and prepared milk, seaweeds, and cereals (099-084, 091, 093, 094, 098, 099)
Government trade items	
04.03	Butter (023-000)
10.01	Wheat and maslin (041-000)
10.03	Barley (043-000)
10.06	Rice (042-110, 120, 210, 220, 290)

Source: *Genko Yunyu Seido Ichiran* [The List of Curent Import System] (Japan: Agency for Research on Industry and Trade, 1974). Taken from William R. Cline, et al., *Trade Negotiations in the Tokyo Round* (Washington, D.C.: The Brookings institution, 1978), p. 166, Reprinted with permission.

[a]Four-digit numbers are BIN codes.

[b]Six-digit numbers in parentheses are Japanese Trade Classification (JTC) Codes.

tons; and increase the annual importation of oranges in fiscal 1978 and after by 50 percent (to 22,500 tons). Moreover, tariff reductions would be carried out on ninety items; the tariff on autos would be cut from 6.4 percent to zero; on computer terminal equipment; from 22.5 percent to 18 percent; and on color film, from 16 percent to 11 percent (*Nihon Keizai Shimbun*, 7 and 15 December 1977). Apparently not satisfied with the content of the Japanese package, Ushiba told the press that it would be difficult to persuade the United States to accept the Japanese plan.

However, even this limited Japanese package created a lot of opposition from and resentment among some groups within the Liberal Democratic Party. In fact, because there was so much opposition expressed regarding the government package at the December 6 meeting of the party's Executive Council, another Executive Council meeting had to be held the next day in the presence of Miyazawa, Nakagawa, and Ushiba. Nakagawa explained the government position that, in view of the strong U.S. pressure for import liberalization, Japan would have to make at least some effort, even if it did not contribute very much to the reduction of the overall bilateral trade imbalance (*Nihon Keizai Shimbun*, 8 December 1977).

Takami Eto, an outspoken representative of agricultural interests, contended that he was opposed to liberalization of agricultural imports if it did not contribute to the elimination of the trade surplus. He went on to ask the question: "Miyazawa as EPA Director once implemented the liberalization of lemon and grapefruit imports. As a result, producers around the Inland Sea severely suffered. Can we feel assured that you will not do the same thing again?" (*Nihon Keizei Shimbun*, 8 November 1977). Nakagawa interjected by saying, "I believe a statesman must make a balanced judgment," implying that he must sometimes make a decision against domestic interests. In any case, the government leaders agreed to behave cautiously, respecting the intraparty sentiment. But there was still more commotion within the LDP before the Japanese package was finally approved by the party. At one time, all the directors of the relevant bureaus from the Foreign Ministry, the MITI, and the MAFF were asked to appear at a joint meeting of the party's Comprehensive Agricultural Policy Research Council (CAPRC), Agriculture and Forestry Section, and Fisheries Section. These bureau directors were severely assailed by agricultural politicians. The latter approved the Japanese package only after repeatedly clarifying with the Executive Council that there would be no more Japanese concessions on agricultural imports.

Ushiba Visits Washington

On December 8, announcing that Minister Ushiba would begin trade talks with U.S. officials on December 12 in Washington, the Gaimusho (foreign ministry) expressed its view that it would be difficult to conclude the U.S.-Japanese trade negotiations unless Japan could show an import liberalization plan, at least with regard to beef, oranges, citrus juices, and tomato ketchup—those products in which the U.S. side maintained a particularly strong interest. This could be interpreted as the Gaimusho's last-minute attempt to seek more concessions from the MAFF. Interministerial differences were also reflected in the fact that some groups within the government were opposed to the designation of Ushiba as the Japanese government's representative for negotiations with the United States, saying that such negotiations should involve all the economic ministries and should not be left to Minister Ushiba alone.

Even before Ushiba left for the United States, U.S. officials were disappointed with the Japanese package as it was reported in the press. In background briefings with U.S. correspondents, they said the slim Japanese package showed that a wide gap remained to be bridged. They said that they realized the Japanese government was going through a delicate process of balancing conflicting domestic and foreign forces but that the final Japanese plans had to be substantial. "We want to be able to go to the Congress," said one official, "and tell them, 'The Japanese are no longer part of the problem; they are working with us.' " "Unfortunately," one American added, "I think [the Japanese] perception of the seriousness of the situation is on the short side." According to Andrew H. Malcolm of *The New York Times*, the current trade controversy had much to do with cultural differences. Stating that the Japanese package that was being prepared by Tokyo's economic bureaucrats and politicians did not contain a real response to U.S. demands, he wrote that these Japanese officials were drafting what they thought of as "concessions" and "presents" to "satisfy" U.S. critics, to "restore harmonious relations" and to prove Japan's "sincerity." This, to the Japanese mind, was far more important in "clearing the atmosphere" and "refreshing" relations than the specific steps the Americans would like them to take. And, Malcolm continued, it underlined the deep "cultural chasm" that still separated the mysterious East from what the Japanese regarded as the equally mysterious West (*The New York Times*, 8 December 1977). Although there was perhaps some truth to this argument, the Americans also did not fully understand the severity of the domestic constraints facing Japanese officials.

Although he had expressed disappointment with the Japanese package domestically, Ushiba defended the Japanese position in his interview with Western correspondents. Saying that there would be no public commitment to seek a current-account deficit by a specific date, he added: "Who can do that? No country in the world. You know exporting and importing are done by private companies." He said there were some improvements in Japan's economic offerings, but that "You cannot expect something dramatic"

(*The New York Times*, 8 December 1977). Much of his presentation, he said, would consist of his outlining for U.S. officials the economic and political problems and constraints of Japan, such as its strong domestic opposition to trade liberalization.

On December 11, Ushiba left for the United States amidst Japanese news forecasts that the coming talks would be very difficult in view of the wide gap existing between the two countries' positions. In order to provide some moral support, Prime Minister Fukuda entrusted Ushiba with a letter addressed to President Carter, which expressed Fuduka's hope for an early and amicable solution. Also to bolster Ushiba's position, Foreign Minister Sonoda stated the day after Ushiba's departure that the proposals Mr. Ushiba was presenting in the United States represented the maximum possible package Tokyo could offer at the moment.

Ushiba made his first presentation of the Japanese proposals to Robert Strauss and other U.S. officials on December 12. Strauss promptly said Ushiba's offers fell short "of what I sought as minimum goals" (*The New York Times*, 13 December 1977). On the specifics of the package, Strauss pointed out that the proposed expansion of beef imports (as well as the proposed reduction of tariffs on film and computers) was too small. Later, in his meeting with Ushiba, Agriculture Secretary Bergland specifically asked Japan to increase its annual importation of beef for hotel use by 10,000 tons and also pressed for an elimination of import barriers against citrus. Altogether, Ushiba had sixteen meetings with Strauss and other U.S. officials in four days, but these talks did not produce any agreement. In a joint press conference after a luncheon meeting with a group of twelve U.S. senators on December 15, Strauss stated that, while there had been a constructive exchange of views between the two sides, they had not reached a final agreement. But Strauss did not want to give an impression that the talks had failed completely. He said that Ushiba "hasn't hit a home run with us, but he hasn't struck out, either." Later the same day, Ushiba met with President Carter who, among other things, asked for Japanese cooperation so that U.S. agricultural products would receive fair treatment. Fortunately, while Ushiba was in Washington, the Japanese cabinet in Tokyo announced a new growth target of 7 percent, and Ushiba announced this on the last day of his visit. Strauss dubbed it promising. Nevertheless, it did not solve his problems. The Ushiba visit had heightened the tension Strauss needed to quell if the MTN were to move forward. Strauss still needed his visible targets and a major agreement in which to display them. In any case, both governments decided to continue their talks in the near future. It was tentatively agreed that Strauss would go to Japan for the final round of talks before January 19, when the increasingly protectionist Congress was to reopen.

Despite his failure to reach an agreement, Ushiba's straightforward style of presentation was highly regarded by U.S. officials. The STR and other U.S. officials went so far as to say that Ushiba opened a new pattern of U.S.-Japanese negotiations, because they thought his outspoken approach had contributed a great deal to mutual understanding. Strauss came to respect him. On his return to Tokyo, Ushiba stated that protectionism and anti-Japanese sentiments were unexpectedly strong in the United States and that the view of Japan as unfair was prevalent in Congress. "Anti-Japanese feelings," he said, "are much more deep-rooted today than at the time of the U.S.-Japan textile negotiations." He then pointed out the need for producing greater Japanese concessions on agricultural imports and other specific economic issues, as well as the need to expand and deepen contact with the U.S. Congress.

Despite the United States's impression of the Japanese press as being sensationalistic and as arousing emotional reactions to the U.S. pressure, *Nihon Keizai*, Japan's leading economic journal, was rather philosophical about the latest round of trade talks between the two countries. In its December 17 editorial, it actually urged the government to make more concessions on agricultural imports, critical as it was of the U.S. pressure on Japan to achieve a higher economic growth without itself doing anything to stabilize the dollar. The paper called for seasonal liberalization of orange imports and expanded importation of beef for hotel use, contending that such steps were necessary for the benefit of domestic consumers as well as for U.S.-Japanese relations.

After Ushiba's return from the United States, the Japanese government began to reexamine its package of economic concessions. As part of this effort, Eiichi Nakao, the LDP's chairman of the Agriculture and Forestry Division (Norin Bukai), left for the United States on December 21 on a fact-finding mission. Nakagawa and other government leaders realized the necessity of making further concessions to the United States, but, at the same time, they faced increasing opposition from within the party. The Parliamentary League for the Promotion of Livestock Industry (the beef caucus), headed by Sadanori Yamanaka, held an emergency meeting, with Ushiba attending, on December 20, and it unanimously passed a resolution saying that there was no reason to make any more concessions to the United States. This was followed three days later by a similar resolution passed by the Fruit Promotion Parliamentary League (the fruit caucus), headed by Tokutaro Higaki. Normally, when resisting an expansion of agricultural imports, the MAFF would welcome such support from agricultural politicians. However, the U.S. pressure seemed too strong, and noncompliance might jeopardize the entire U.S.-Japanese relationship. Thus, agreeing that further expansion of orange and beef imports would hurt domestic producers, Nakagawa expressed the need to submit an additional reply to the United States. He said the government was expecting to receive specific counterproposals from the United States in a few days. Japan's response would be determined after receiving those proposals and after hearing Nakao's report about his trip to the United States.

The United States Submits Its Counterproposals

Four economic ministers, Nakagawa, Ushiba, Miyazawa, and Komoto, were asked to respond to questions at an Upper House Budget Committee meeting on December 21. Asked by the Japan Communist Party's Takeshi Watanabe if the United States were going to demand an increase of annual hotel-use beef imports to 10,000 tons and an increase of oranges and citrus juices worth $60 million, Nakagawa responded that such a request would be too much for Japan to accept. The domestic demand for hotel-use beef, he said, was 4,000 tons, and therefore it would be impossible for them to accept 10,000 tons. Excessive imports of oranges and citrus juices would seriously hurt domestic producers, who were already suffering from unusually low prices of mikan at home.

Shortly before Christmas, an STR official quietly went to Tokyo with a concrete list of U.S. demands, which included an increase in the hotel beef quota to 10,000 tons (Ushiba had offered 2,000), an increase in the juice quota to 50,000 tons (Japan had previously offered 2,000), and seasonal liberalization of oranges. On December 22, this request list was formally delivered to the Foreign Minisry by Minister Jack Button of the U.S. Embassy in Tokyo. Button explained that the U.S. package contained the minimum conditions that would be necessary if Strauss were to conclude the bilateral negotiations during his visit to Japan. Nakagawa called the U.S. demands unreasonable, saying that, to absorb them, Japan would have to build 2.5 times more hotels and double the size of each Japanese stomach. On December 25, Zenchu and Nichienren (Japan Fruit Growers Cooperative Association) held massive rallies against import expansions in Tokyo. Agricultural politicians, both within and outside of the LDP, began putting enormous pressure on the government not to concede to the United States. The LDP's Comprehensive Agricultural Policy Research Council and Agriculture and Forestry Section held an emergency joint meeting on December 23, and issued a resolution that Japan should reject the unreasonable U.S. demands. On December 26, Zenchu and its fruit- and dairy-policy divisions sent representatives to the prime minister's official residence to present their case to Fukuda. They told the prime minister that Japan's agriculture should not be sacrificed any further for the sake of reducing trade surpluses caused by exports in the manufacturing sector, and they urged him to reject the unreasonable U.S. demands. Fukuda sympathized with the plight of Japanese farmers, but he asked the agricultural representatives to render some assistance in view of the seriousness of the situation with regard to U.S.-Japanese relations. Nonetheless, Nokyo groups held a massive antiimport rally in Tokyo the next day and sent copies of their resolution to all major policymakers in the Japanese government.

Diet members from beef- and citrus-producing constituencies were naturally receptive to the antiimport campaigns of the Nokyo organizations. Their immediate concern was that, if they antagonized these groups, they would receive a painful backlash at the next general election. One LDP Diet member from an agricultural area went so far as to say that whether or not he was reelected in the next election depended entirely on his response to this particular agricultural import issue. These politicians visited the prime minister's residence one after another and participated in the antiimport rallies organized by Nokyo. Many received numerous cables each day (as many as 60 sometimes) from beef or citrus producers, who were asking the politicians to cooperate. Some of the cables contained messages threatening that, if the farmers were ignored, the politicians should be prepared to lose in the next election.

Under these circumstances, even the Foreign Ministry, which had been calling for substantial concessions to the United States, became cautious and refrained from making statements in favor of concessions. In view of the unreasonable nature of the U.S. demands, some MAFF officials wondered if Ushiba had really conveyed to the Americans the very difficult situation facing Japanese agriculture. Thus, their initial surprise at the U.S. counterproposals turned to a distrust of Ushiba. They said it was a mistake that only the chief of the Gaimusho's First North American Affairs Division had accompanied Ushiba, and they stated that an MAFF bureau director should also have been on the trip. In reality, Ushiba did repeatedly explain the difficult domestic situation in Japan to Strauss and other U.S. officials, but the Americans were naturally more concerned with their own domestic problems.

Meanwhile, some Japanese had been working to soften the U.S. position. On December 21, for example, an LDP Dietmen mission left for the United States to meet with Strauss and, hopefully, convince him of the sensitivity of the citrus and beef question. The leader of the group, Eiichi Nakao, explained to Strauss the LDP's long support of close defense and political relations with the United States. He also said that angry farmers could destroy the party if the LDP were forced to make excessive concessions regarding agriculture.

The same point was stressed in a later visit by Nokyo representatives, who were led by Chairman Saburo Fujita of Zenchu. In a meeting with STR officials, Fujita concluded that liberalization would result in significant unrest in Japan's rural sector and in a weakening of farm support for the LDP.

However, Strauss was determined to press on. He had identified his targets and, in doing so, had highlighted the confrontation with Japan. Now he needed a visible success in order to quiet the protectionist forces in Congress. In his meeting with Nakao, Strauss reportedly pressed the Japanese politician very hard by demanding significant concessions. Should Japan fail to make an appropriate response to the latest U.S. demands, Strauss said, an anti-Japanese import-control bill would be passed by Congress and Japanese products would be pushed out of the U.S. market within ninety days. Nakao came out of the meeting frustrated. He even confided to a friend later that evening that, this time, Strauss was really hitting Japan where it hurt. Upon his return to Japan in late December, Nakao reiterated that the U.S. position was extremely rigid.

Japan Prepares Its Response

Intragovernment efforts to formulate Japan's response to the demands the United States had made on December 22 were far from easy. Although many officials thought that Japan should make further concessions, the U.S. demands were simply too severe. Some believed that the United States must be bluffing. But it was soon decided that Japan would resume negotiations with the United States within the year so that the final agreement could be reached during Strauss's scheduled visit to Japan in January 1978. In order to gather more first-hand information about the U.S. situation, the LDP sent another mission, headed by Takami Eto, to the United States on December 26. Government leaders decided to prepare the Japanese response while keeping in communication with Eto's mission in the United States.

Sandwiched between external and internal pressures, the MAFF had been placed in a difficult position. This problem was exacerbated by the fact that MAFF officials had trouble in obtaining correct readings of the U.S. intention due to a lack of reliable information. Immediately after they received the U.S. demands on December 22, some ranking MAFF officials concluded that USDA officials would not submit such unreasonable demands because they were sufficiently knowledgeable about the reality of Japanese agriculture. If the demands had been formulated by STR officials who were ignorant about the Japanese situation, the Japanese officials thought that they might very well modify these demands by working through the USDA. This was, of course, a serious misunderstanding of the U.S. trade policymaking and negotiations, which had been orchestrated by the STR in consultation with relevant departments. Such optimistic perceptions were changed somewhat after Japanese officials heard Nakao's subsequent report on his visit to the United States. As Nakao explained, Strauss was determined to obtain major concessions from Japan on agriculture; the STR was in control of the issue and the USDA's influence over the negotiation process was rapidly declining.

Throughout this period, Nakagawa was working furiously to urge the bureaucrats in his ministry to increase their concessions. Finally, on December 28, the Japanese presented their second offer in a private meeting between Minister Nakagawa and Ambassador Mike Mansfield. Concerning beef products, they offered a hotel quota of 3,000 tons. This was 1,000 tons better than the December offer but well below both U.S. demand for 10,000 tons and the potential market if the quota restrictions were removed. The orange-juice offer was doubled from the previous 2,000 tons, but again was well below the 50,000 ton request. The orange issue was the trickiest. Nakagawa refused to consider either total liberalization or seasonal liberalization. The best he could offer was to increase the previous offer of 22,500 to 45,000 tons. Mansfield expressed appreciation for Nakagawa's offer, but he said that the decision to accept or reject this offer remained with Strauss.

Both the beef and citrus proposals presented problems to Strauss and the STR. The beef problem was simple—he needed Japan to import more. The citrus problem was more complicated. The 45,000 ton figure that the Japanese were offering might have been sufficient as an interim agreement before the actual MTN bargaining took place. Nevertheless, the monthly division of the quota presented problems. Florida and California ship their oranges at different times—Florida in the winter and spring and California year round.[3] If the offered 45,000 tons were to be imported during the summer months the offer would not satisfy Florida. Senator Richard Stone of Florida was not about to let that happen. He decided to go to Tokyo to negotiate a deal for himself. The problems caused by this Florida-California split were to plague the situation throughout the negotiations.

In early January, Stone arrived in Tokyo. He held talks with Ushiba, Nakagawa, and certain Japanese citrus-fruit importers, all held in an effort to explore the citrus situation in Japan. Stone's meetings with Nakagawa were most crucial. Meeting in a private hotel, Stone and Nakagawa discussed Florida's special concerns. Drawing diagrams on table napkins, the two men worked out a deal. The largest part of the new quota offer, 22,500 tons, would be designated for the traditional importing season of June, July, and August. However, rather than allocating the remaining 22,500 tons evenly over nine months (2,500 tons per month), 7,500 tons would be specially allotted in April and May. This agreement guaranteed Florida shippers a slice of the pie and prevented California, whose growers could easily ship the entire 45,000 tons, from taking the entire quota. The arrangements, when plotted as a graph, show a sharp vertical increase during the summer and a lesser rise during April and May. This came to be known as Stone's Hump. Apparently, as a result of this Nakagawa-Stone agreement, the Japanese government was able to announce, on the evening of January 4, that it had reached virtual agreement with the U.S. side. Earlier that day, the Eto mission had come back from the United States. Eto reported that the mission had met with various U.S. government and congressional leaders but had not been able to reach any fundamental understanding with them. He suggested that Japan might have to accommodate the U.S. demands to some extent, saying that the final decision was up to the Japanese government. It appears that, having been exposed to U.S. pressures directly during his mission, Eto, a hardliner, was forced to modify his own position.

Toward the Strauss-Ushiba Agreement

Deputy STR Wolff, accompanied by Rivers and other U.S. officials, arrived in Tokyo on January 8 to pave the way for the conclusion of the trade negotiations before Strauss's arrival. At the airport, Wolff expressed an optimistic view that, this time, the two countries would be able to reach agreement. Nevertheless, in his subsequent meeting with Japanese officials, he stated that the United States was not fully satisfied with Japanese concessions on agricultural imports, and he urged the Japanese government to undertake additional measures during the Tokyo Round negotiations that were to follow. Strauss arrived on the evening of January 11 and stated at the airport that, while Wolff's negotiating efforts in Japan had improved the atmosphere of the bilateral relationship, it was quite another thing whether the two countries could reach agreement—a somewhat more cautious statement than Wolff's arrival statement. Asked if he had any hope for agreement, Strauss said that he did not entertain any expectations. In the past, he said, he had frequently developed an expectation only to be disappointed at a later date. In fact, according to Hobart Rowen's article, published in *The Washington Post* on February 2, 1978, Strauss was rather pessimistic about the success of the latest talks. On his way to Tokyo, he called President Carter from Anchorage and told him that there was a possibility of the talks breaking down. Later, seeing the first draft of the joint communique that had been worked out between Wolff and Japanese officials, Strauss reportedly told the Japanese that he would have to call up the president and inform him of the failure of the negotiations. This caused a panic among Japanese officials.

Strauss opened negotiations with Nakagawa with a public, pro forma reiteration of U.S. demands and further haggling over the Japanese offer of December 28. Strauss refused to accept the earlier offer of an increase in the hotel beef quota to 3,000 tons. He pressed Nakagawa very hard to meet the U.S. demand of 10,000 tons. Nakagawa was equally hard pressed to refuse the demand. Opposition from within the party had been intense enough before and after the previous meager increase. Yet, under Strauss's pressure and under the threat of a breakdown, Nakagawa made a final small concession. He agreed to make every effort to increase demand within Japan so that high-quality beef imports would increase to 10,000 tons. Thus, on the twelfth, substantive agreement on the joint communique was finally arrived at. However, a conceptual problem appeared to be arising between the two sides. The U.S. officials viewed the measures, expected to be modest, as only the beginning of a major long-term economic restructuring aimed at opening Japan far more to foreign goods and making the country play a greater global leadership role economically. On the other hand, Japanese officials (except perhaps Ushiba) tended to see the settlement as an end in itself and were resisting U.S. demands for future trade commitments. "As long as we can get the Strauss visit over with and get the settlement," one Japanese official reportedly said, "then we can get United States-Japan relations back on an even keel."

On the evening of the twelfth, Ambassador Mansfield invited Strauss, Ushiba, Miyazawa, and Senator Edward Kennedy (who was visiting Tokyo at the time) to dinner at the ambassador's residence. All major substantive issues had been resolved during the daytime, but there was still some work remaining on the wording. After dinner, Kennedy left the scene, saying he had been invited for tea elsewhere. Then the four officials worked on the wording of the communique late into the night to maximize its positive impact.

The next day, the United States and Japan were able to announce the joint communique, or the Strauss-Ushiba agreement, on a package of bilateral economic measures that were intended to open a new and more liberal era in the trading relationship between the two largest economic powers in the noncommunist world. The steps, agreed to after six months of increasing tensions over Japan's mounting trade surplus, covered the Japanese's decisions to reduce tariffs on about 300 items and stimulate the domestic economy so that it could achieve a 7 percent growth rate for 1978.

On beef and citrus, Japan agreed to the following: an increase in the importation of high-quality beef for hotel use to 10,000 tons on a global basis beginning in fiscal 1978; a threefold increase in orange imports to 45,000 tons; a fourfold increase, to 4,000 tons, in the quota for citrus juice; and the formation of an interindustry citrus group to study the current and future developments in the citrus situation, including juice blending and seasonal quota, and report to their governments by November 1, 1978.

As if to dramatize the event to allay the growing protectionist sentiment in the United States, Strauss sounded very enthusiastic about the agreement once it was reached. "We have really redefined the economic relations between our two great nations," he said at a news conference before his return to Washington. "This agreement represents a change in direction and philosophy." Japanese officials, who faced strong domestic protectionist forces themselves, were considerably more restrained. "I do believe," Ushiba said of the likely adverse reaction in Japan, "that, whatever present dissatisfaction or confusion there may be, Japan can overcome it" (*The New York Times*, 14 January 1978).

Second Phase, 1978

Emergence of New U.S. Pressure

Japanese agricultural producers and many MAFF officials thought that the U.S.-Japanese agricultural trade issue involving beef and citrus had been settled once and for all in the bilateral trade negotiations culminating in the Strauss-Ushiba agreement. However, new U.S. demands regarding beef and citrus surfaced in the spring of 1978 in the context of the Tokyo Round negotiations.

Although the January agreement defused the larger trade crisis, it also contributed to a heightening of U.S. producer interest and resolve that made the following MTN negotiations more difficult. As we have noted, producer interest in the Japanese market for citrus and beef existed before the larger trade crisis. The dynamics of the September-through-January trade dispute between Japan and the United States did not, therefore, create U.S. producer interest in the Japanese market for citrus and beef.

The dispute did, however, help intensify their interest and heighten their expectations. In the minds of many Americans, the trade crisis clearly made citrus and beef symbols of Japan's closed market, thanks to frequent remarks by U.S. officials to this effect. Typically, Alan Wolff, speaking before the House Subcommittee on International Economic Policy and Trade on April 4, said that citrus and beef "are of more symbolic significance than of major commercial value to our nation as a whole." Japan's willingness to open U.S. citrus and beef markets, he continued, "will indicate whether Japan, which believes in allowing the theory of comparative advantage to operate in areas in which it has proven itself strong, in steel and automobiles, for example, will play the game fairly and allow U.S. producers to sell to Japanese consumers the beef and citrus they demand" (*The New York Times*, 5 April 1978).

Once citrus and beef came to be viewed as symbols of a closed market, Japan's failure to open these markets was of interest to a wider audience than just producers. This fact was not lost on the producers, and they began to press for the elimination of Japan's quotas—because they now could argue that it was not only in their own interest, but in the national interest as well. The pre-January bilateral beef and citrus talks also aroused Congress and alerted its members to the symbolic importance of these commodities.

The realization of this new situation made Strauss and other U.S.-administration officials feel strongly that further Japanese concessions on beef and citrus would be necessary to secure congressional support for the MTN. They also seemed to have concluded that the way to deal with the Japanese was to pressure them. For instance, on February 1, Strauss testified before the International Trade Subcommittee of the Senate Finance Committee that the STR had been able to take a strong stand in the recent trade negotiations with Japan thanks to the tough congressional pressure on the Japanese, adding that it would be necessary to continue to exert such political pressure on Japan.

The Japanese government received its first signal in February, when Yutaka Yoshioka, an advisor to the MAFF, visited the United States. The need for further concessions was stressed again on April 10 in Geneva, when Strauss asked Minister Ushiba for further expansion of the import quota for beef and other agricultural products. He made clear that the United States would not accept Japan's January concessions on citrus and beef as final. Strauss stressed that U.S. demands for total liberalization of citrus and beef remained on the table and that the United States fully expected Japan to respond to them within the context of the MTN. The MAFF officials were quite surprised, and domestic producers were enraged, by this U.S. move. They thought they had just made all the necessary concessions they could possibly make considering the difficult circumstances surrounding Japanese agriculture.

By April 19, MAFF officials had concluded that they might have to make additional concessions—but only within the context of the MTN negotiations and for a few years ahead, not for fiscal 1978. Sensing what was happening within the ministry, on April 21, Zenchu gathered together in Tokyo representatives of agricultural producers from all over the country and passed a resolution against any further expansion of agricultural imports. They thought they had made all the possible concessions in January and bitterly resented the fact that the United States was asking for more and that MAFF officials were inclined to acquiesce.

A summit meeting between President Carter and Prime Miniser Fukuda had been scheduled for early May. As the summit approached, Senator John Glenn's Subcommittee on Asian and Pacific Affairs held a hearing on Japan on April 27. Deputy STR Wolff and Deputy Assistant Secretary of State Heginbotham testified that the United States should ask for more Japanese agricultural concessions at the coming summit.

Prime Minister Fukuda, who arrived in Washington on May 1 for the summit, had a breakfast session the next day with Treasury Secretary Blumenthal, Strauss, and a few other U.S. cabinet members. At the meeting, Strauss took the opportunity to ask for more Japanese MTN concessions on agriculture, saying that the Japanese offers in that area were not satisfactory.

He specifically suggested that Japan eliminate import quotas on beef and citrus, arguing that success in the ongoing Tokyo Round negotiations was essential if the current protectionist trend in Congress were to be arrested.

Fukuda met with Carter on May 2 for two-and-a-half hours. The agriculture issue did not seem to become a major part of the discussion, but they agreed that the MTN should be concluded by mid-July, in time for the seven-nation summit in Bonn. Afterward, the prime minister visited Capitol Hill and saw some thirty members of both houses. During his visit, Fukuda was asked, among other things, to expand Japan's agricultural-import quotas. He replied that Japan could not implement further expansion of agricultural imports because the nation's agricultural population was already a bare 11 percent of the total population and therefore should not be diminished any more by increased imports.

Referring to Fukuda's discussions on agricultural import expansion with U.S. senators and congressmen, MAFF Minister Nakagawa stated (perhaps for domestic consumption only since the statement was made at the Japan Correspondents Club in Tokyo on May 6) that the agricultural trade issue had been settled in the form of a joint communique in January and that the government had no intention of further expanding imports of beef and oranges.

Strauss-Ushiba Discussions Leading
to the Starkey Memo

Ushiba saw Strauss in Los Angeles on May 24 and was told that the United States was most keenly interested in a further expansion of Japan's beef- and citrus-import quotas, along with tariff reductions on about eighty agricultural products. As reported by Ushiba on his return to Tokyo two days later, these agricultural problems, being the United States's main preoccupation, would have to be resolved if the Tokyo Round negotiations were to be concluded by the time of the seven-nation summit in mid-July. In his talks with Strauss, Ushiba sensed that the United States was more interested in citrus than in beef. For one thing, in the recent working-level discussions, the Japanese side had already indicated that Japan would gradually expand beef imports in accordance with an increase in the domestic demand. It was speculated in Tokyo that the United States was overproducing oranges (just as Japan was overproducing mikan) and U.S. senators and congressmen from citrus-producing states (such as California and Florida), with an eye on the off-year elections in November, were putting pressure on the executive branch. Nakagawa was astonished at the tenacity of the United States in demanding Japan's agricultural import expansion. He and Ushiba agreed that Japan would have to make further concessions but they should take utmost caution so as not to arouse emotional reactions on the part of domestic producers. However, domestic agricultural producers were quick to react. On May 12, six national agricultural cooperative organizations—Zenchu, Zenno, Nichienren, Norin Chuo Kinko (Agricultural Central Bank), Zenchikuren, and Zenkaren (National Federation of Fruit Juice Cooperative Associations)—held a joint national rally in Tokyo and issued a resolution against import expansion. The resolution was then presented to key agricultural policy officials in the government and the party. On May 30, Zenchu instructed its prefectural affiliates to send antiimport cables to all the key government and party officials.

The idea of gradually increasing beef imports as domestic consumption increased was reiterated by Nakagawa in his press conference on June 13. However, he made it clear that Japan would not agree to the further expansion of orange and citrus-juice imports because domestic producers had already had to cut back production of mikan by 20 percent. The only thing he could possibly say to the United States would be that, if circumstances should change, Japan would be willing to reconsider the matter. Meanwhile, the U.S.-Japan Inter-Industry Citrus Group, created by the Strauss-Ushiba agreement, had met twice—on April 3-5 in Tokyo and on June 2 in Washington. The group's meetings, consisting of six to eight representatives of citrus producers and dealers from each side, roughly paralleled discussions at the intergovernmental level. The U.S. side asked for complete liberalization of citrus imports by Japan and the Japanese side refused, emphasizing the fact that Japanese mikan producers were themselves suffering from overproduction. The group decided not to meet again, agreeing only that each side separately submit a report to its own government by November.

Japan again received a strong message from the United States on agriculture when Ushiba saw Strauss in Washington for three days (June 18-20). (He also met with Wilhelm Haferkamp of the EC Commission.) Ushiba's repeated explanations to Strauss about the difficulty of making further agricultural import concessions fell on deaf ears. He reiterated his remarks at a luncheon held on June 20 under the sponsorship of *National Journal.* He said the difficulty Japan was facing with regard to agricultural imports was the same as the difficulty the United States was facing with regard to steel and auto imports. Upon his return to Tokyo, he reported that, while there were some major issues remaining to be resolved, the European Community, Japan, and the United States might be able to draft an outline of MTN agreements by the time of the seven-nation summit in July. He emphasized, however, that no serious negotiations had been held on agricultural imports and that Japan would have to formulate its position on beef and citrus imports by early July. He said that no MTN agreement would be possible without the settlement of the agricultural trade issue.

The Economic Ministers Group met on June 23, and both during and after the meeting Ushiba asked for his colleagues's cooperation in resolving the agricultural and other issues remaining in the Tokyo Round.

Intragovernment discussions on beef and citrus imports continued at various levels, but without much progress. Ushiba saw Nakagawa on the afternoon of July 5 and discussed Japan's position, which was to be presented in Geneva a few days later. Because of strong sentiments among domestic producers, the two ministers concurred that Japan could agree to try to increase beef imports in the context of the growing domestic demand (by 5 percent annually) but that Japan could not agree to any more orange or orange-juice imports. Japan's mikan growers were in the midst of a drastic acreage reduction, which would not be complete until 1983. While it was underway, no further imports could be discussed. Future imports would depend on the success of the acreage reduction. This position was approved the next day by Prime Minister Fukuda.

On July 10, President Carter sent a letter to Prime Minister Fukuda, asking for an expansion of Japanese agricultural imports. When the cabinet-level negotiations opened in Geneva that same day, one week before the meeting at Bonn, the U.S. and Japanese positions were far apart: on citrus, the United States wanted total liberalizations, while Japan was offering no increase in imports at all for three years. In meetings between Strauss and Ushiba, the U.S. side expressed its complete dissatisfaction with Japan's offer. Strauss emphasized that it would be impossible for him to sell the trade package to Congress without concessions for the citrus growers.

Working against these demands was the U.S. desire to reach a settlement. The timetable called for a conclusion of the major negotiations before Bonn, and the progress made during the week of cabinet-level negotiations indicated that the goal might be achieved. The Japanese, for example, had, during the week, made major improvements in their industrial tariff offer. The remaining industrial problems, particularly Japan's tariff offers on computers and color film, were close to settlement and apparently could be finalized with a decision by the Prime Minister at Bonn. Thus, with regard to Japan, the major stumbling block to achieving a pre-Bonn settlement was agriculture, particularly the political items, citrus and beef.

In order to break this impasse, the United States apparently showed a willingness to settle for significantly less than originally demanded. Near the end of the week of negotiations, Strauss, together with his deputy, James Starkey, met in closed session with Ushiba and MAFF officials. Strauss stressed his desire to settle the talks. When the discussion moved to citrus, the most difficult issue, Strauss reportedly turned to Starkey and said, "What will it take to settle this?" Starkey penned out on the back of an envelope the United States's bottom-line position. The precise figures mentioned are not available, but apparently they were well below previous U.S. requests for total liberalization. This represented a major concession by the United States and one that had the potential to create difficult political problems within the United States. As we noted earlier, because of the different production schedules in Florida and California, any settlement below total liberalization would discriminate between these two states. However, if the Japanese off season for mikan shipments (or the season for greater orange imports) could be extended beyond the June-August period, the interests of Florida would be partly accommodated. Florida would also benefit from an expansion of the orange- (and grapefruit-) juice quota. Apparently, this was the substance of the Starkey memo. The Japanese press subsequently described the U.S. position as follows: the expansion of U.S. beef imports by Japan to one-fourth of Japan's total beef imports; the extension of the off-season (or summer) quota for oranges from June-August to April-September and the implementation of off-season liberalization at the earliest possible date, and immediate liberalization of grapefruit-juice imports (*Nihon Keizai Shimbun*, 18-29 July 1978).

In any case, Starkey emphasized that this was a bottom-line position, presented only in the hope of sticking to the timetable and settling all remaining questions before the Bonn summit took place.

Ushiba apparently did not have the authority to agree to even these scaled-down U.S. terms. But he and other Japanese officials became substantially more optimistic about settling this citrus issue now that the U.S. side had retreated from its position in favor of full liberalization. In any case, the ministerial conference ended without agreement between the United States and Japan on agriculture (although Strauss and Ushiba, together with Haferkamp, signed a general "Framework of Understanding"). In an unusual move, however, both Ushiba and Strauss traveled to Bonn and continued the negotiations. In a private meeting between Strauss and Prime Minister Fukuda, the final difficult unresolved issues were discussed. Fukuda personally authorized major Japanese concessions on computer and color-film tariffs and, as a result, the industrial sector talks were concluded. However, the settlement of the agriculture issue, the prime minister said, would require a major political decision by Minister Nakagawa. When the United States suggested that Japan send Nakagawa to Washington in September to make that decision, the prime minister agreed. The summit itself did not apparently get into details of MTN negotiations, and the seven leaders simply agreed to conclude the MTN by December 15, several months later than had been planned initially.

Higaki Heads a Mission to the United States

Having read about the U.S. position, as reported in the Japanese press, heads of prefectual agricultural cooperative associations from mikan-producing areas assembled in Tokyo on July 27 and discussed ways of effectively opposing Japanese government concessions to the United States. These and other agricultural organizations intensified their lobbying campaigns on the government and the LDP. Faced with these circumstances, the LDP decided to send a group of four LDP Diet members, headed by Tokutaro Higaki, on a ten-day mission to the United States. The purpose of the mission was to not only gather information about the nature of the U.S. demands, but also, and more importantly, explain the difficult situation facing Japanese citrus and beef producers to U.S. political and agricultural leaders. The other three Diet members were Jun Shiozaki, chairman of the LDP's Foreign Affairs Division; Moriyoshi Sato, member of the party's Executive Council; and Isao Maeda, member of the Upper House. These politicians were accompanied by six representatives of agricultural producers. The mission left Japan on August 5. In the United States, the mission met with twenty members of U.S. Congress, including Senators Richard Stone, Abraham Ribicoff, Herman E. Talmadge, S.I. Hayakawa, Lloyd M. Bentsen and Representatives Bill Frenzel, James R. Jones, John Krebs, and Al Ullman. They also met with Bergland, Wolff, and other executive-branch officials.

In their talks, the mission members emphasized the following points: trade in the agricultural sector was not the cause of friction between the two countries and the overall trade-balance issue between them could not be solved by an expansion of Japanese agricultural imports; Japanese beef producers had been threatened by declining prices and citrus growers had been driven into a corner by stagnant prices caused by overproduction; if beef and citrus producers suffered hardships, the political stability of Japan would be threatened; and if the LDP lost the support and trust of the farmers, it would be very difficult for the party to stay in power and maintain a pro-United States government.

The mission members were surprised by the fact that all the U.S. leaders they met with spoke with one voice; that is, they all emphasized the same points, as if they had been closely briefed in advance by the STR. (Some even suspected that Japanese Foreign Ministry officials must have briefed them, but this accusation was denied by the Gaimusho. Some Gaimusho officials said that, while they did not encourage frequent visits to the United States by Japanese politicians and agricultural representatives, they did not discourage them, either. They thought that the exposure of these people to direct U.S. pressures might soften their rigid stands against concessions.)

Some of the points made by the U.S. officials were (Liberal Democratic Party, "U.S. Mission Report," 1978, pp. 23-30):

1. As long as the big bilateral trade imbalance continued, congressional protectionist pressures would persist and so would their demands for opening up the Japanese agricultural market.
2. The trade imbalance was a product of Japan's unfair trading practices, and agricultural protection was a symbol of such unfair competition.
3. Industries lacking competitive power would naturally decline, and agriculture was no exception. It was of no use to talk about special political problems involving Japanese agriculture because the United States, too, had such political problems.
4. Japan should import more U.S. beef so that U.S. beef would constitute one-fourth of Japan's total beef imports. Japan's importing only the difference between domestic demand and domestic production was not good enough.
5. Japan should extend the off-season from June through August to April through September for orange imports, expand the import quota, and implement seasonal liberalization at the earliest possible opportunity. Grapefruit juice should be immediately liberalized, the seasonal tariff of 40 percent for December through May should be abolished, and a flat 20 percent tariff should be instituted instead.
6. Import quotas on beef, oranges, and citrus juice were violations of GATT rules, and the United States might file a suit with the GATT.

Toward the Nakagawa-Strauss Talks

The schedule for the Nakagawa-Strauss talks had been set for September 5-7. As the top-level talks approached, the Japanese government again faced stepped-up domestic pressures against import expansion. Yukio Tashiro, an Upper House member and a director of Nichienren, met with Chief Cabinet Secretary Shintaro Abe on August 31 and handed him an antiimport petition from domestic citrus producers. Abe's response was that the government would respect the position of Japanese farmers and would not accept the U.S. position as it was then formulated. That same day, Higaki's fruit caucus met and discussed ways and means of preventing further expansion of orange imports. A week earlier, Chairman Saburo Fujita of Zenchu and several top Nokyo leaders met with Mansfield and expressed their opposition to further expansion of agricultural imports in view of the difficult situation facing Japanese agricultural producers. The ambassador said he understood the plight of the Japanese farmers, but he emphasized that what the United States wanted from Japan was considerably restrained and would not cause very much injury to Japanese producers. It was necessary, he said, to settle the pending agricultural trade issue to arrest the tide of rising protectionism and solidify a cooperative relationship between the two countries. The proposed expansion of the import period for U.S. oranges was not unreasonable and Japan's domestic demand for citrus could easily take a further increase in the orange importation. (Meanwhile, the Ehime Fruit Growers Cooperative Association, which represented Japan's largest mikan-producing prefecture, with 15.8 percent of domestic production in 1977, placed a one-page advertisement entitled "Please Listen to Us" in *The Washington Post* and *The Los Angeles Times* on August 18, asking the U.S. people to understand the plight of Japanese mandarin-orange growers, who were undergoing a 20 percent acreage reduction to cope with the overproduction problem as well as the problem of import expansion based on the January agreement. The two ads, which cost $22,500 [about 4.2 million yen], were paid for by donations from Ehime mikan growers.)

Domestic pressures notwithstanding, the Japanese government was already preparing to make partial concessions in order to meet the U.S. demands. Nakagawa was anxious for a settlement. He had spent the period since Bonn consulting with his bureaucrats, colleagues in the Liberal Democratic Party, and members of the agricultural cooperatives in an effort to generate a consensus on a concessional offer to the United States. The Japanese position gradually evolved and its outline became public on September 2. While rejecting the U.S. demands for an extension of the import period for U.S. oranges and for the immediate liberalization of grapefruit-juice imports, the government decided to increase, by about 10 percent each year, imports of oranges and citrus juice after fiscal 1982, with the existing import quotas for oranges and juice remaining unchanged until then. Furthermore, the government decided to consider a slight increase in the importation of high-quality beef (about 5 percent per year), depending on changes in demand and supply in the country. Nakagawa apparently thought that the offer he was carrying would be acceptable to the United States. He had tested it out in a general fashion on Ambassador Mansfield in Tokyo and the response had been good. Leaving Tokyo, he privately told aides that the agricultural problems could be solved during his meeting with Strauss.

Unfortunately, however, between July, when U.S. negotiators presented the conditional terms of a settlement to Japan, and early September, when Nakagawa arrived in Washington, the political situation in the United States had changed, and this complicated the ensuing negotiations. The complications involved leaks of the U.S. negotiating position, rumors of a political scandal in Japan concerning oranges, and private channels of information between U.S. citrus producers and the importers of their products in Japan.

Although the United States had pulled back from its position for full citrus liberalization in July—in hopes of obtaining a settlement before the Bonn summit—U.S. producers had been kept in the dark about the substance of this new U.S. offer. They assumed that the U.S. government was still pushing for full liberalization. But, as we saw earlier, the substance of the Starkey memo was printed in the Japanese press soon after the Bonn summit and became known to the representatives of U.S. citrus producers stationed in Japan.

The leaked information angered both the Florida and California citrus industries. The California industry, dominated by Sunkist, held to the goal of full liberalization. Florida, while pushing for full liberalization as its primary goal, was willing to accept seasonal liberalization, provided that the liberalized season be extended to include at least April and May. The U.S. position, as reported in the Japanese press, called for seasonal liberalization but did not specify any particular date for implementation. Also, although it asked for an expansion of the off season for greater Japanese citrus imports from June through August, the U.S. position did not state that the seasonal liberalization called for at the earliest possible date included April and May as well. As a result, some U.S. producers became highly suspicious of the STR. They were convinced that U.S. trade officials were either not pushing Japan hard enough or, worse, were selling out to the opposition.

The confusion and rivalry between Florida and California, which was heightened by these new developments, was further intensified by rumors of a scandal in Japan concerning orange imports. As with most controlled import items, the laws of supply and demand dictate whether oranges are a lucrative business: if demand is high and the supply is artificially limited, the price is high. USDA figures, for example, show that a carton of U.S. oranges, which costs the Japanese importer about $10, sells at retail for about $50. The huge profits that accrue from the sale of these oranges go mainly to the importers. In 1978, the largest and most influential of these privileged importers was Kazuo Fujii, who headed the Japan Citrus Importers Association's fifty-four licensed importing companies. Fujii's own company—Fujii Trading, Inc.—controlled 15.18 percent of orange imports directly and approximately 30 percent indirectly. There were allegations that he was using the huge profits of his orange imports to buy influence in the LDP. He was also reported to be using his influence to gain control over the distribution of other fruits and, not surprisingly, to severely limit the number of importers with orange-import rights. This point was particularly disturbing to Florida because Fujii was reported to have strong ties to California (although his relationship with Sunkist was not all that good). Florida producers feared that, even if the orange quota were increased, Mr. Fujii might use his influence to keep Florida out of Japan.

The Fujii group first tried to form a united front with Japanese mikan producers to oppose orange-import expansion and liberalization. His group was opposed to the substantial expansion of orange imports because, as more oranges were imported, it would become more difficult to sell them at unreasonably high prices in the domestic market. The group was against full liberalization because large general-trading companies could easily take over the business if the market became fully open. In any case, domestic citrus producers refused to work with this group that benefited from orange imports. On the other hand, it was in the interest of those importers without orange-import licenses to support an expansion of orange imports. Their rationale was that, with increased imports, the MITI would be more likely to increase the number of orange-import licenses (which was then limited to ninety-one). Unlike large trading companies, the non-license-holders who were operating small-fruit import businesses would not necessarily benefit from full import liberalization. However, they called for full liberalization as part of their strategy to challenge the monopoly of the Fujii group. (They may also have thought that full liberalization would not be realized in the near future anyway.) Believing that they were not politically powerful enough to influence Japanese policies directly, these Japanese importers took an indirect route, working with U.S. orange producers and their supporters in Congress.

Among such importers was Kin'ichi Yamazaki, who headed a small company called Japan Fruits, Company, Ltd. He organized an organization (rival to the Fujii group) called All-Japan Citrus Importers Association by bringing together approximately one hundred importers without orange-import licenses. This group sent a petition to Strauss, U.S. agricultural politicians, and nearly twenty U.S. orange producers' organizations, emphasizing the importance of opening up Japan's orange-import market, currently dominated by the Fujii group, which was profiteering at the expense of Japanese consumers. This group apparently worked closely with Florida citrus producers and dealers, who had shared a common interest in changing the existing Japanese orange-import system. A small Kyoto-based citrus-importing concern was also known to be working closely with Senator Stone's office, providing data to be used for pressuring Japan to liberalize orange imports. A good bit of information about the Fujii group also flowed between Japan and the United States through one particular U.S. shipping company, American Mercantile. This firm, based in California, ships Florida oranges to Japn. It was and still is well connected to those Japanese importers who would like to see Fujii's alleged control of the market broken. On the U.S. side, the firm is well-connected to Florida producers.

Although the Japanese government was far more concerned with the impact of imports on domestic producers and, ultimately, with the electoral impact of these producers on the LDP, rumors of a scandal involving importers in Japan had a strong impact in the United States. They were easy to understand, and they seemed to go a long way toward explaining Japan's tough bargaining position. Their effect was to heighten the outrage of U.S. producers, who considered themselves to be unfairly locked out of Japan's market. It is important to note these rumors were impossible to stop. They appeared more likely the longer negotiations dragged on, and they inevitably complicated the task of resolving the dispute.

As a result of these rumors and the leaked information concerning the U.S. pre-Bonn bargaining position, pressure on the STR increased during August and September. Through their representative Senator Richard Stone, Florida interests were especially forceful in their efforts to pressure the STR into pressing Japan for total liberalization. Meanwhile, there had been stepped-up pressure from beef producers as well. Their interest for exports to Japan had been increasingly aroused after the Strauss-Ushiba agreement. The Beef Cattlemen's Export Association was created as a result of this intensified interest in the export business. They even wanted Japan's complete import liberalization, although the USDA had reminded them that Australia would likely take over the Japanese market in the event of full liberalization. As a result of these pressures, the STR changed its position and returned to its original demands. Hence, when Nakagawa sat at the negotiating table with Strauss on September 5, he faced a different situation and a different set of demands than had been shown to Japanese negotiators only a month and a half earlier in Geneva.

Accompanied by Ushiba, Nakagawa had arrived in Washington the day before. The negotiations opened on a low note. The Japanese side explained the plight of Japanese farmers and presented the latest Japanese government plan. For his part, Strauss dwelt on the seriousness of the growing bilateral trade imbalance and, in tones that reportedly shocked and upset Nakagawa, he called Japan's offer completely unacceptable. Nakagawa, who had been hoping to narrow the differences between the two countries in a man-to-man session with Strauss, was put off by the latter's sharp repudiation and businesslike tone. On the other hand, with domestic producers watching the negotiations carefully, Strauss had to present a tough image and press for concessions that would satisfy the different seasonal producers. On the second and third day, the Japanese offer improved somewhat, with slow, incremental increases in the quota tonnages allowed. Strauss, however, continued to insist that these increases were insufficient. He also criticized Japan's refusal to expand the definition of off season beyond June through August, and, apparently for the first time, he raised the problem of import licenses and the U.S. interest in breaking the monopolistic hold on the market of certain importers. Finally, Strauss insisted that the question of liberalization—apparently not only for citrus but also beef (particularly high-quality beef for hotel use)—had to be addressed before a settlement could be made. Under these circumstances, the two sides could not reach any substantial agreement.

Nakagawa and Ushiba attributed the failure of these talks to the sudden toughening of the U.S. position. Despite the July agreement not to demand full liberalization, the U.S. side had backed down in September and revived the question of liberalization, introducing what seemed like a completely new set of arguments. On the other hand, in a statement publicized on the evening of Thursday, September 7, Strauss issued a warning to the Japanese, saying that "it should be clearly understood that the U.S. expects Japan to undertake the responsibility of all industrial nations to open her markets to imports of both agricultural and manufactured goods." In a closing comment that implied a delay and a possible collapse of the MTN, Strauss said, "We did not achieve our basic negotiating objective for American agricultural exports—and until we do, there's no deal" (*The Washington Post*, 8 September 1978).

The atmosphere changed, however, on Friday morning. In an unexpected additional comment, Strauss said that he and Japanese negotiators had come very close to reaching a conclusion on agricultural trade issues. The brighter tone with which Strauss approached the negotiations was the result of an unannounced and unscheduled visit Strauss had paid to Nakagawa at his hotel on Friday morning, just as the Japanese minister was preparing to leave Washington. Strauss was upset at the way the talks with Nakagawa had ended. On Thursday evening, he had received reports from intermediaries that Nakagawa was equally upset at what was being reported in the Japanese press as the failed mission. In an effort to change this mood, Strauss visited Nakagawa alone to discuss ways to break the deadlock. He reportedly thanked Nakagawa for the effort he had made to present a reasonable offer, but he reiterated the critical importance of addressing the liberalization question and of expanding the definition of off-season. Strauss said that the language regarding liberalization was even more important than the tonnages involved: the more explicit the commitment on liberalization, the less would be needed in the way of increased tonnages. During the meeting, Strauss and Nakagawa agreed to pursue these questions in a series of administrative-level negotiations in Geneva.

The private meeting between Strauss and Nakagawa did not settle any of the remaining difficult questions. However, it did prevent an awkward sense of breakdown in the talks. The warmth and skill of Strauss's gesture reportedly impressed Nakagawa and the Japanese delegation and set a constructive tone for the talks to follow. One Japanese source said that Strauss's gesture "was very Oriental" (*The Washington Post*, 9 September 1978).

There was a curious episode involving Minister Nakagawa and Senator Stone during the former's stay in Washington for the three-day agricultural talks with Strauss in September. The senator had an informal meeting with Nakagawa and asked the Japanese minister to help increase exports of Florida oranges, in the event Japan's orange-import quota was expanded, by giving new orange-import licenses to those Japanese fruit importers who had not maintained close ties with U.S. citrus exporters on the West Coast, including Sunkist. Not many Florida oranges had been exported to Japan, the senator believed, because most of the Japanese importers who then had orange-import licenses were tied to West-Coast producers and exporters. (Another important reason was that Florida oranges are not as suited for fresh consumption as California or Arizona oranges because they were not as tasty and rot more easily for lack of acidity. Florida oranges are better consumed as juice.) Nakagawa consented to Stone's request on the condition that the senator call up Strauss and ask him not to press for full liberalization of orange imports by Japan. The following day, Nakagawa asked Strauss if he had received a phone call from the Florida senator. Strauss smiled and said yes, but he insisted that he was the government negotiator, not Stone, and it was up to him to decide whether to push for full liberalization. Later, Strauss called up Stone and reprimanded him for interfering in the negotiating process.

Zenchu Contacts U.S. Farm Organizations

On September 19, Chairman Fujita sent a letter to three major U.S. farm organizations—the American Farm Bureau Federation, the National Farmers Union, and the National Council of Farmer Cooperatives—requesting cooperation and understanding for the Japanese farmers' position. He and other Japanese farm executives had assumed that, since Japan was the best overseas customer for U.S. agricultural products, those U.S. farmers and farm organizations benefiting from agricultural exports to Japan might help persuade domestic beef and citrus interests not to pressure Japan. However, this strategy did not work, because the basic assumption was wrong. The agricultural sector in the United States is export oriented (although the manufacturing sector had been domestic-market oriented). While there are many differences of view among U.S. farm organizations, particularly on the extent of allowable government interventions, they are fully united in their support of export expansion. Consequently, all three major U.S. farm organizations supported the U.S. cattlemen and citrus industry in expanding exports to Japan. In fact, grain dealers in Chicago went so far as to say that, even if the Japanese beef industry should decline as a result of import liberalization, which would lead to a major decline in feed-grain imports by Japan, the overall demand for U.S. feed grains would not be affected very much because there would then be a greater domestic demand for feed grains in the United States for producing extra beef to be exported to Japan. Domestically, Japan's agricultural organizations continued to lobby against further agricultural concessions. Fujita saw Nakagawa on September 22 and asked him to take a firm stand regarding the United States in the next round of agricultural talks "so that the interest of domestic farmers would not be sacrificed" (*Nihon Keizai Shimbun*, 23 September 1973). Nakagawa's response was that, in view of the persistent U.S. pressure, Japan would have to concede to some extent. A few days later, Prime Minister Fukuda made a similar statement in the Diet, adding, however, that the coming agricultural talks would not produce an outcome that would seriously damage the interests of Japanese farmers.

Preliminary Talks Postponed

Working-level consultations took place in Washington on September 26-27. Director Jun Shimura of the MAFF's International Economic Affairs Department and Counselor Hiroshi Oki of the Gaimusho's Secretariat met with Deputy STR Wolff and other U.S. trade-policy officials to make arrangements for the working-level preliminary talks that were to lead to the final Nakagawa-Strauss agreement. These officials decided to postpone, from late September to October 16, the preliminary talks scheduled to take place in Geneva. In large part, this postponement was due to the inability of the two governments to narrow the wide gap still remaining between the two sides. Domestic consultations in both countries were taking longer than expected, and the positions of the two governments even seemed to be toughening. While MAFF officials had thought beef and citrus were the only remaining issues, the United States had just communicated a new position, demanding further tariff reductions on forty agricultural products. Earlier, the MAFF had noticed that a part of beef cattle's internal muscle (called inside skirt) had been imported freely to Japan—between 10,000 and 20,000 tons annually—as part of the intestines that were outside the beef-import quota. Consequently, the MAFF decided to put this inside skirt under the quota as of October 1, 1978. This particular administrative problem had an unexpectedly serious impact on the bilateral negotiations. Some say that Strauss asked for liberalization of beef imports for high-quality beef in reaction to the MAFF's decision on inside skirt.

As the date of the talks approached, domestic producers intensified their antiimport campaigns. Particularly active were mandarin-orange producers, who feared that the government might end up making major concessions in the face of the U.S. pressure for at least seasonal liberalization. On October 11, Nichienren, or the Japan Fruit Growers' Cooperative Association, held a special assembly of its members in the Upper House office building, apparently through the courtesy of Tokutaro Higaki, who headed the fruit caucus. Both Higaki and Nobuo Imamura, Japan's chief working-level agricultural negotiator, had been asked to speak at the assembly. As President Matsutaro Goto of Nichienren put it, the purpose of the meeting was to wish Imamura Godspeed and plead with him against orange-import expansion and liberalization on the eve of his talks in Geneva with Deputy STR Alonzo McDonald, his U.S. counterpart. "Coming from Ehime," Imamura replied, "I understand the plight of mikan growers and the difficulty facing Japanese agriculture." But he reminded the Nichienren members that he would not be able to simply say no to every U.S. demand because "agriculture cannot exist in isolation from the Japanese economy as a whole" (*Nihon Keizai Shimbun*, 12 October 1978). He promised to do his best in the negotiations so that Japan's overall agricultural policy would not be jeopardized and the stability of the agricultural economy would not be threatened.

Basically, Higaki shared the same view and talked about the increasingly severe and rigid nature of U.S. demands. He was in a particularly difficult situation. He not only headed the fruit league in the Diet, as we noted, he also chaired the party's Comprehensive Agricultural Policy Research Council (CAPRC). As the caucus head, he had to defend the immediate interest of domestic citrus growers. But, as chairman of the CAPRC, he had to emphasize the overall interests of Japanese agriculture and economy, which were closely tied to the interests of viable U.S.-Japanese relations. After all, Japan was heavily dependent on the United States as the largest supplier of such important products as soybeans, wheat, and feed grains. His past efforts to strike a happy balance between meeting the interests of citrus and beef producers and not threatening U.S.-Japanese relations did not please some farmers. When he stood before the rostrum at this particular gathering, he heard somebody shout, "Kill him, kill him!" Nichienren issued an antiimport resolution and later handed a copy to all the Diet members from mikan-producing areas. Some of the leaders subsequently attended Higaki's Dietmen citrus caucus as observers. In a tense and heated atmosphere, members expressed their views against conceding to U.S. demands. Even Higaki went so far as to declare the United States was like a greedy moneylender, demanding higher interest each addditional day.

Imamura-McDonald Talks

Imamura arrived in Geneva on October 14 accompanied by a few other MAFF officials. The next day, he began his talks with McDonald to pave the way for a Nakagawa-Strauss agreement. Before negotiations started, McDonald made it clear that he was negotiating ad referenda; any agreement reached in Geneva would have to be cleared through Strauss in Washington. McDonald also stressed that there must be no leaks, because any premature or partial leaking of negotiating terms would undoubtedly alert and confuse U.S. domestic constituent groups and make it difficult for Strauss to win support for the settlement.

The talks held between October 16 and 21 focused mostly on oranges and beef. The major problems encountered concerned the definition of the off season, a future date for liberalization, increased tonnages, and the question of quota allocation in Japan (the import-license problem). The United States, of course, continued to ask for liberalization. However, as a result of the September talks, it became clear that Japan could not concede on this vital point. Instead, the United States hoped for an expanded off-season period (to include May and possibly April) and the setting of a specific future date when liberalization (for both oranges and beef) would be achieved. In addition, the United States wanted a guarantee from Japan that any increased orange imports would be allocated to new importers not under the control of the dominant Fujii group.

The Japanese were unable to accede to these demands. Liberalization had become a political buzz word in Japan, and any government leader who conceded it would probably have suffered serious political damage. Similarly, the Japanese were unwilling to extend the off-season period, because of the competition this would present to mikan growers.

McDonald, of course, knew that both these issues, liberalization and the April-May extension, were politically important in the United States. However, since he was convinced that the Japanese would not move on these points, he negotiated around them. With regard to liberalization, McDonald pushed the Japanese to agree to a continuation of negotiations in 1982 with the objective of providing an open-market situation in the off season. There was no guarantee that the objective would be achieved, but McDonald believed that a firm statement of the objective and a definite commitment to at least negotiate toward it was the best he could get.

The question of expanding the off-season period, which the Japanese argued would be politically difficult to do, was also negotiated. The Japanese agreed to lump a large proportion of the seasonal quota (September-May) in the April-May period.

The question of import licenses was especially difficult. U.S. officials made it clear that they were aware of the huge profits made by Japanese orange importers and of the various alleged political and commercial improprieties of the dominant importer, Mr. Fujii. (Apparently, these discussions had a light touch: the U.S. officials joked that, if the Japanese government would just award a few of these lucrative import contracts to the U.S. negotiators, they would be willing to settle on any terms.) The Japanese maintained that the question of import-licensing systems was a domestic matter, the sovereign right of any government to decide, and not the subject of international negotiations. The United States, however, continued to insist that, although the system itself was Japan's concern, the result of that system was of legitimate interest to them. The present system, the United States argued, was an additional restraint on trade and one, moreover, that created particular domestic political problems in the United States. In the end, the Japanese promised to give new importers import opportunities on a fair and equitable basis under a new system.

Another problem concerned increased tonnage quotas. The U.S. team was unable to win the politically appealing doubling of the fresh-orange and beef quotas. However, they did get enough of an increase on these items, as well as substantial increases in the orange-juice and grapefruit quotas, to apparently satisfy them.

On October 21, Imamura and McDonald ended six days of talks, having made substantial progress on the difficult problems concerning beef and citrus. The two governments agreed that another round of working-level talks should be held between these two negotiators in early November to prepare for the final agreement at the ministerial level in mid-November. Throughout the talks, Japanese officials wondered what was the true intention of the United States behind its demand for full liberalization of beef and citrus imports. Was the demand part of its strategy to squeeze Japanese concessions in other areas, or was it simply the United States's basic, unchanged position? Meanwhile, the U.S. House of Representatives had passed the revised Beef Import Law to reduce imports at the time of increased domestic production. Japanese officials and producers were critical of the United States's hypocritical attitude of demanding Japan's beef-import liberalization when the United States itself was restricting beef imports.

The Japanese government reviewed the Imamura-McDonald talks at a meeting of the Economic Ministers Group, with Fukuda attending, on October 24. The meeting was held to prepare Japan's position for the Ushiba-Strauss talks, which were scheduled to take place first in Orlando, Florida, on October 30 and later in Geneva. The group reaffirmed Japan's opposition to full liberalization of orange and beef imports. However, Ushiba told reporters afterward that he remained optimistic about the possibility of the MTN talks being concluded within the year, despite the tough U.S. position against Japan on farm-produce trade and the Common Market's dissatisfaction with the U.S. position on the waiver of countervailing duties. This view was echoed by the STR, which issued a statement in Washington on October 23, saying that a framework for agreement existed, and the remaining issues would likely be resolved within a month. At approximately this time in Geneva, McDonald told reporters that Japan and the United States had agreed on a broad framework for the final agreement and only six issues remained unresolved. If the MTN could not be wound up by the December 15 deadline, he said, there might be a possibility of political explosion.

On October 26, the Japanese press reported that broad agreement had been reached between Imamura and McDonald during the October 16-21 talks. Apparently based on a leak from certain MAFF sources, the story cited the following terms: that orange imports for 1980 would be expanded to 60,000 odd tons, including 30,000 tons during the June-August season, with a 10 percent annual expansion of the quota thereafter; that the full liberalization question had been shelved for the time being (to be brought up again at the mid-point of the eight-year Tokyo Round implementation period that was to start in 1980); that a special quota for U.S. beef—around 30,000 tons a year—would be set by 1983; that the orange-juice import quota would be expanded to 5,000 in 1980, with a 10 percent annual expansion thereafter; and that the grapefruit quota would be expanded to 3,000 tions in 1980, with an annual addition of 1,000 tons until 1983. Domestic agricultural producers immediately reacted to this disclosure. On the morning of October 27, top leaders of four peak agricultural cooperative organizations, led by Fujita of Zenchu, paid a visit to Ushiba's office in the Foreign Ministry building and questioned the validity of the press report. Ushiba denied the existence of the broad agreement reported in the press, saying that the United States was still demanding full liberalization. After a meeting with Ushiba and Chief Cabinet Secretary Abe, Nakagawa, too, emphasized that the question of liberalization was still pending. Nevertheless, citrus and beef producers throughout the country were suspicious and angry about what they thought was a serious deception by Nakagawa and Ushiba. When the top-level talks had broken down in September, they had thought that these Japanese negotiators understood the plight of domestic producers. Now they found it incomprehensible that these same people had apparently made secret concessions to the United States—concessions that ignored the position of domestic farmers. The October 30 issue of *Nihon Nogyo Shimbun*, a Japanese agricultural daily, carried the headline, "Suspicion and Anger Rising Among Producers."

On the U.S. side, too, the leaked information that appeared in the Japanese press made an already difficult situation worse. Throughout October, U.S. producers had been concerned that their interests were not being protected—from both the Japanese and competitors in the United States. For example, an internal STR report noted that in California rumors were rampant that Ambassador Strauss was conspiring with Senator Stone to force a change in the import-licensing system to the benefit of Florida producers. Sunkist producers in California had reportedly received cables from the Fujii group in Japan to the effect that, as a result of pressure from Strauss and Stone, Japan had agreed to allot 55 percent of the orange-import

licenses among 400 Japanese banana importers who had close ties to the
Florida grapefruit industry. In response to this kind of information,
California producers and their representative made it clear to STR officials
that they wanted seasonal liberalization, immediately if possible, and if not,
then they wanted at least a guaranteed future date for its realization.
California also opposed any changes in the licensing system that would
favor Florida.

Florida producers, on the other hand, continued to fear that the Fujii
group would use its control of the market to circumvent any settlement that
was reached. A memo from one source close to the Florida industry noted,
"Fujii correctly cautioned that fresh oranges are in such limited supply and
in such high demand that the greengrocer who controls distribution of fresh
oranges can effectively control the distribution of any other fresh fruit or
produce." This memo concluded that "if measures are not taken to correct
Fujii's apparent stronghold, there is a very real danger that these monopolistic trade practices will be extended to the full range of the potential U.S./
Japanese fresh fruit and produce export/import trade activities." Florida
interests pressed the STR to gain liberalization and, barring that, to insist
that any settlement reached with Japan break Fujii's monopolistic control
of the market.

In the midst of this commotion, the Japan Citrus Situation Study
Group—the Japanese side of the U.S.-Japan Inter-Industry Citrus Group—
submitted its report to Minister Nakagawa on October 27. The report emphasized that further expansion of citrus imports would have a devastating
impact on the Japanese citrus industry; that producers were worried about
their future because of the 20 percent acreage reduction; that citrus juice
was also overproduced and import liberalization would be disastrous; and
that producers strongly resented new U.S. demands for import expansion
and liberalization because they thought the issue had been settled in the
January agreement. The report recommended that the government make
serious efforts to get the United States to understand the Japanese citrus
situation and that it maintain the position for no expansion of liberalization
of citrus imports. Earlier, the U.S. side had submitted its report to Strauss,
recommending that Japan eliminate its citrus-import quotas. It suggested
that the group might ask the president to take necessary countermeasures if
Japan failed to do so.

Prelude to the Final Agreement

Ushiba and Strauss met in Orlando, Florida, on October 30, primarily to
check whether their January agreement was being followed through. The
two leaders ended up, however, spending considerable time discussing

MTN problems. Apparently reflecting stepped-up domestic-industry pressure, Strauss insisted that Japan achieve full liberalization of beef imports and at least seasonal liberalization of citrus imports. Considering the political nature of these remaining problems, it was decided that Nakagawa visit Washington again after the trilateral ministerial-level MTN meetings scheduled for November 15-17. In contrast to the official position of the Japanese government and domestic producers against liberalization, major Japanese newspapers had a somewhat different position. For instance, *Asahi Evening News* stated in its November 7 editorial that Japan would do well to outline steps for opening the Japanese beef and citrus market to an internationally acceptable level. The same day, the Japan Economic Research Council (Nihon Keizai Chosa Kyogikai), a study group for the business community, published a report with a set of recommendations on Japanese food policy. The report, entitled "The Role of Food Industry in National Economy," recommended, among other things, that Japan eliminate import quotas for agricultural products and that the quotas be substituted by deficiency-type payments to producers (financed by somewhat higher tariffs). This recommendation was immediately, though informally, rejected by MAFF officials, who argued that such a system would only increase Japan's food dependence on other countries and put Japan's agriculture into jeopardy.

At about this time, Prime Minister Fukuda and top LDP leaders were increasingly preoccupied with the first primary election for the LDP-party presidency, which was to take place toward the end of the month. The primary was to select the top two contenders out of the four candidates for the party presidency—Fukuda, Masayoshi Ohira, Yasuhiro Nakasone, and Toshio Komoto. Fukuda, Nakagawa, Ushiba, and Abe met on November 7 and talked about the latest Ushiba-Strauss meeting. Ushiba conveyed Strauss's desire to meet with Nakagawa again to settle the agricultural trade issue, and the leaders agreed on the necessity for such a meeting. Afterward, Nakagawa told reporters that Nakagawa-Strauss talks would probably take place toward the end of November or in early December, after the results of the Imamura-McDonald talks going on in Geneva and the Ushiba-Strauss-Haferkamp meeting that was scheduled to take place from November 15 to 17 were known.

Imamura and McDonald met in Geneva from November 6 to 7. Although the issue of orange and beef quotas had been settled generally in October, its final settlement was contingent on the outcome of the discussion on other MTN issues, particularly agricultural tariffs. Japan was especially cooperative in the agricultural tariff talks because of their desire to protect the orange settlement. Significant reductions (40 to 50 percent) in tariffs were offered for lemons, grapefruit, chicken legs, raisins, almonds, prunes, herring, pollack, crab, wine, and pine lumber. Sizable reductions were also offered for grapes, walnuts, canned peaches, fruit cocktail, and plywood. The reductions on lemons, grapefruit, raisins, almonds, and prunes were especially important because these appealed to Florida, Texas, and California interests and might therefore balance the fresh-orange settlement.

Agricultural producers in Japan had their eyes set on the Geneva talks, wondering if Imamura would defend the interests of Japanese farmers or sacrifice them for the sake of U.S.-Japanese relations. In fact, on November 8, Chairman Fujita of Zenchu and a few other agricultural leaders sent cables to Imamura in Geneva, urging him to do his best in the interest of Japanese farmers. Fujita himself flew to Wellington, New Zealand, immediately thereafter to attend a meeting of the International Federation of Agricultural Producers (IFAP) and made a presentation to the effect that Japan was already importing a great deal of agricultural products from abroad and could not expand agricultural imports any more for fear of causing injury to Japanese agriculture. Back in Japan, he and other leaders of peak agricultural organizations saw U.S. delegates (including S.I. Hayakawa) at the first symposium of the U.S.-Japan Parliamentary Political Council, held on November 15, and explained the difficulty of increasing beef and citrus imports.

Ministerial consultations among Japan, the United States, and the European community took place on schedule from November 15 to 17 in Geneva. There, Ushiba, Strauss, and Haferkamp announced their decision to conclude the Tokyo Round talks before Christmas. Ushiba stated in a press conference that Japan and the United States were close to an agreement on their negotiations. He predicted that their farm-trade dispute, stemming from U.S. demands for wider access to the Japanese market, would be settled in early December. Ushiba's optimism was based on the fact that he and Strauss had reached consensus on a general outline of the final agreement and only the details remained to be worked out between Immaura and McDonald.

Soon afterward, Imamura and McDonald, assisted by their subordinates, began to work on the details, and, by November 18, they had reached a formula for agreement. However, before the formula was agreed upon, there was a last flurry concerning soybeans. Japan annually imports about $1 billion of U.S. soybeans at zero duty. However, the zero duty rate is unbound, meaning it could be raised in the future if, for example, Japan wanted to raise its own soybean production. A U.S. request to bind the soybean duty at zero would have been relatively painless for Japan, and it would have counted for enormous trade coverage. However, the United States had withheld its request for the binding for precisely this reason. If they had made the request early and the Japanese had granted it, additional requests for other items could have been turned away on the grounds that a concession amounting to $1 billion in trade coverage was sufficient. When the United States finally made the request in the final meeting, the Japanese delegation expressed some surprise, but they granted the binding. Thus, the total agricultural offer made by Japan, including soybeans, came to $1.5 billion.

Although this settlement did not meet some important U.S. demands, McDonald was convinced that it was all he, or anyone else, could obtain from the Japanese at this point. Moreover, in spite of the deficiencies, McDonald felt he had balanced the package sufficiently to satisfy critics in the United States, especially the Florida interests. He had achieved language that suggested opening and expanding import licensing, an agreement to lump the yearly orange quota in April and May, and an expanded orange-juice quota. On the tricky subject of liberalization, McDonald felt the best he could get was a promise to sit down again in 1982 with the objective of an open-market situation clearly defined.

McDonald was able to exercise this judgment in large part because the talks were held in Geneva. The GATT negotiators stationed in Geneva shared certain qualities: an esprit de corps, isolation from the daily pressure of interest groups, and a tendency—almost the necessity—to negotiate beyond instructions when piecing together final deals. All of these qualities were present during the McDonald-Imamura meetings. Familiarity among the negotiators allowed them to joke about the potentially explosive import-license question. More importantly, without the pressure of interest groups watching and questioning every move, McDonald was able to exercise his judgment in assembling the pieces of the final package, balancing a good offer on tariffs, for example, against a weak offer on fresh-citrus quotas. Had the talks been held in Washington under congressional scrutiny (or in Tokyo), it would have been much more difficult for the negotiators to reach agreement.

The settlement in Geneva was indeed a big step, but it was not the end of the journey. The agriculture negotiations had been rooted in domestic politics from the start. This was where they would have to end. It was decided, therefore, that the final agreement would be concluded at the political level between Nakagawa and Strauss in Washington in early December. Before that, the settlement package had to be successfully sold to domestic producers and politicians in both Washington and Tokyo.

Although Japanese officials did not particularly anticipate any difficulty (now that they managed to prevent citrus- and beef-import liberalization), there were, however, some tense moments due to an immediate leak of the settlement formula to the press. The December 4, 1978, issue of *Newsweek* (put on the market on November 27) sensationally referred to a secret agreement between the two governments. In a paragraph headed "War of the Oranges," the U.S. journal wrote that the Japanese had finally agreed to double their annual orange-import quota and that this agreement, while far less than Strauss's original demand for full liberalization, would probably upset Japanese farmers and was therefore being kept secret in view of Prime Minister Fukuda's December bid for reelection as LDP president.

This news was reported in the Japanese press on the evening of November 27 and created emotional reactions among domestic producers. MAFF officials refrained from any direct comment, saying they were not in a position to comment on every news report.

The evening edition of November 29 *Nihon Keizai* gave more detailed information about the agreement formula: Japan would aim at the realization of an open market with regard to citrus imports; increase its orange-import quota to 68,000 tons (35,000 tons in the mikan off season) in 1980 and 82,000 tons by 1983; increase orange-juice imports to 5,000 tons in 1980 and 6,500 tons in 1983; increase grapefruit-juice imports to 3,000 tons in 1980 and 6,000 tons in 1983; and increase the beef-import quota gradually to 30,000 tons in 1983 (after 1983, the quotas were to be renegotiated).

Meanwhile, there was an important political development in Japan. Prime Minister Fukuda unexpectedly lost the primary election (held on November 28) for the party presidency to the party secretary general, Ohira, and announced his intention to resign as prime minister. Consequently, he decided to settle the agricultural import issue with the United States on December 5, a day before his formal resignation. Nakagawa stated later that, since it had become difficult for him to visit the United States for talks with Strauss (because of the latest political development in Japan), he would ask Deputy STR Wolff to come to Japan so that the MAFF minister could settle the issue with him and Ambassador Mansfield.

In the United States, the STR had quieted many of the fears of domestic industry groups by late November and had generated some support for the settlement negotiated in Geneva. For instance, Strauss had met with citrus industry representatives on November 28, and explained to them that, compared to the same time the year before, great progress had been made. Quotas had been substantially increased and tariffs had been sharply reduced. The Geneva package contained something for all elements of the citrus community. Moreover, it contained a mechanism for the eventual achievement of quota liberalization. Strauss also stressed the fact that the package was not yet final. He noted that the STR had come under considerable criticism for the attention it was paying to citrus. The citrus issue had almost collapsed the Strauss-Ushiba agreement, and it was the cause of the break-off in July and September. Moreover, no concessions were obtained from Japan on other agricultural items until after the citrus issue had been taken of. Many said this attention to citrus was excessive, but Strauss said he thought it had been worth it.

Industry complaints continued to center around four concerns: a specific date for the achievement of off-season liberalization; an expansion of the off-season period to include April and May; improvement of the import system for orange juice to ensure that all quotas were fully utilized (there were indications that the major orange-juice quota holder was not utilizing it fully in order to protect his other mikan interests); and, finally, the loosening of Mr. Fujii's apparent monopolistic control of the orange-import market.

The industry was generally favorable to Strauss's presentation, although there were some, particularly Florida fresh-orange producers, who expressed strong dissatisfaction. All the producers, however, urged Strauss to make one last attempt to satisfy their demands. Based on this expression of support, Strauss decided to send Alan Wolff back to Tokyo to conclude the negotiations on the most favorable basis possible.

Final Agreement Reached

Wolff arrived in Japan on December 1, but he immediately retreated to Kyoto to avoid publicity. That same day, Zenchu held a mammoth rally in Tokyo, opposing any further expansion of beef and citrus imports. The Ehime Fruit Growers Cooperative Association held a breakfast meeting on December 3 at the LDP headquarters with the presence of all (but one) LDP Diet members from Ehime, including Higaki and Isamu Imai, parliamentary vice-minister for agriculture, forestry, and fisheries. Ehime citrus leaders asked these politicians to reject the unreasonable U.S. demands. The only thing Higaki and others could say to assure the citrus producers was that the government was not going to approve seasonal or full liberalization.

The final agricultural talks between Nakagawa and Mansfield started on the afternoon of December 4. Ushiba and Wolff also participated. At the outset, the two sides confirmed the broad agreement that had been reached through working-level consultations in Geneva. Subsequent discussions produced no change in the overall numbers but Wolff was able to get the Japanese to clarify a number of points of interest to U.S. producers. The Japanese clarified, for example, that three-fourths of the yearly on-season quota would be imported during April and May. In a separate eight-hour technical group meeting with MITI and MAFF officials, three short papers were worked out providing for more equitable allocation and utilization of quota licenses. An agreement that committed the Japanese government to preventing anticompetitive behavior, such as using control of the orange trade to influence the trade in other citrus products, was also signed.

The talks, however, hit a snag when the U.S. side demanded a program for opening the Japanese market. The U.S. side also demanded that Japan extend the season for orange imports. Under the broad agreement, Japan was to gradually increase its annual import quota for oranges to 82,000 tons in 1983 and review the figures in early 1983. However, the U.S. side insisted that Japan present a timetable for liberalizing orange imports. At one point, as a Japanese negotiator told the press, the U.S. side called the package unsubstantial and said that it would not satisfy Congress.

The Japanese negotiators were indeed surprised by this toughening of the U.S. position, because they had thought that the December negotiations were going to be mostly ceremonial and that the Japanese and U.S. negotiators were going to shake hands to finalize the agreement. One Japanese interpretation of this sudden change in the U.S. position was that certain U.S. legislators, not satisfied with the formula for agreement, demanded complete elimination of import quotas, putting Strauss and his staff on the spot. Another interpretation was that representatives of domestic producers in the United States expressed strong opposition to the settlement formula and the U.S. government asked for additional Japanese concessions in order to look tough. Still another Japanese interpretation was that Wolff, who brought up the question of liberalization, had been bluffing in order to squeeze last-minute concessions and claim credit for obtaining conditions more favorable to domestic industry. As one official put it, "He was not happy just to sign his rival McDonald's agreement."

None of the above interpretations were entirely correct. As noted earlier, the Imamura-McDonald agreement was an ad referenda, subject to reconsiderations in Washington (as well as in Tokyo). Based on Strauss's earlier talks with domestic-industry representatives, Wolff needed to make one last attempt to satisfy their complaints. Indeed, Wolff had come to Tokyo determined to press U.S. demands for the improvement of Japan's offer. It had not been an idle trip in his mind nor in the minds of U.S. producers watching back home.

On December 5—the second day—the U.S. side withdrew its demand for orange-import liberalization, full or seasonal, after the Japanese side insisted on its inability to make such concessions. "I am about to be fired and can't do anything any more," said Nakagawa. "There would be no agreement unless you took back your demand for liberalization." Mansfield explained to Wolff that the Geneva accord represented the best effort possible by the Japanese government. Mansfield argued that to reject the settlement in the hope of negotiating a better deal with the incoming Ohira cabinet offered no real chance of success and could seriously delay and disrupt the MTN, and Wolff concurred.

At long last, therefore, an agreement was finally reached between the two countries, and its contents were basically the same as the terms disclosed before. Japan would gradually expand its annual orange-import quota to 82,000 tons (from the current 45,000 tons) by fiscal 1983 and its quality-beef-import quota from 16,800 tons to 30,000 tons, also by fiscal 1983.

Japan woud also gradually increase its annual orange- and grapefruit-juice imports to 6,500 tons and 6,000 tons, respectively. In addition, it would lower import tariff rates on other agricultural products, such as broilers, by an average of 40 percent. Under the agreement, the two nations were scheduled to hold talks again in the spring of 1983, the midway point in the proposed eight-year multilateral trade agreement, on Japan's liberalization of orange and beef imports.

Emerging from the talks, Ushiba told reporters that great significance should be attached to the conclusion of the prolonged talks because rules governing U.S.-Japanese farm trade in the future had been firmly established. Nakagawa said that the agreement on orange imports would not affect domestic orange growers because the import quota would be increased gradually in off-season months. He stressed that Japan did not commit itself to extending the seasonal orange-import period from June-August to April-September. Wolff, for his part, stated at a press conference that the bilateral agreement on farm-trade issues had both symbolic and economic value at a time when trade between the two countries was heavily imbalanced.

Concerned as they were about the possible impact of the new agreement on domestic beef and mikan prices, Japanese agricultural leaders claimed victory in that they had prevented the full (or seasonal) liberalization of beef and citrus imports for which the United States had been so persistently pressing Japan. They attributed this success to the most active antiimport campaigns they had ever staged in the course of the bilateral agricultural talks. Some were thankful to Nakagawa and other government leaders for resisting liberalization.

In July 1979, the U.S. Congress voted overwhelmingly to approve the results of the multilateral trade negotiations. Support came from all quarters. The farm community was a particularly early and enthusiastic supporter of the trade package. Allan Grant, president of the important American Farm Bureau, announced his support on January 25, 1979— even before the final results of the negotiations were clear. Spokesmen for the citrus and beef industries also endorsed the trade package during congressional hearings. Both the specific producer groups and the general farm organizations cited satisfaction with the negotiations with Japan as the reason for their support. When the vote came in the Congress, only a few representatives—mainly from dairy states—voted against ratification.

Conclusion

Management of the Dispute

The U.S.-Japanese agricultural trade dispute of 1977-1978 could have, if mishandled, escalated into a serious bilateral crisis. Although beef and oranges were not as economically important as wheat, soybeans, and feed grains in bilateral agricultural trade, they were considered symbols of the economic strife between the two countries. The textiles issue was a relatively minor economic one between the two countries in the late 1960s (with Japanese man-made textile imports constituting less than one percent of U.S. domestic consumption), but it escalated into a major political crisis in 1971, culminating in the U.S. threat to invoke the Trading with the Enemy Act. Indeed, further prolongation of the agricultural dispute might have provoked major congressional protectionist actions against Japan and might also have crippled the MTN, as Strauss and other U.S. officials had warned the Japanese. Difficult as it was, the issue was resolved in time and in a way acceptable to both Japanese and U.S. producers, at least for the time being. This outcome, however, was clearly far from inevitable. In fact, based on the opening positions of both nations, and the fervor with which domestic groups pursued their goals, the successful outcome was somewhat startling. How did it happen?

Answers can be found in the relatively effective management of policymaking and negotiating by the governments of both countries; they were sufficiently sensitive to the interests of both domestic groups and the other country.

For a democratic government to make and implement bold concessions to a foreign country in order to settle an international issue, it must win support or at least acquiescence from those influential domestic groups whose interests are most directly affected by such government actions. In both the United States and Japan, government leaders were essentially successful in obtaining such domestic support or acquiescence. There was both an institutional and a personal side to this successful political management.

Institutionally, on the U.S. side, the system of advisory committees established to advise the STR and Congress concerning the negotiations succeeded in bringing divergent groups into the negotiating process and giving them a stake in the outcome. STR officials like to say that this advisory committee system made domestic interest groups "accomplices to the crime." The committee system gave interest groups an opportunity to participate in the formulation of early request lists, to observe closely the course of the negotiations, and to evaluate the results before they went to Congress. As a result, the significant concerns of particular interest groups did not go unnoticed. And, even if some of these concerns were not fully satisfied, the domestic groups affected could be assured that at least an effort had been made on their behalf.

On the other hand, the fact that domestic interest groups had such a say in the formulation of the U.S. position in the negotiation made it very difficult indeed for the STR to devise any significant concession to Japan. Here one cannot overemphasize the personal role played by Robert Strauss, who combined "immodesty, profanity, sensitivity . . . a taste for good whiskey, and deft persuasiveness" on almost any political matter (*Time*, 27 April 1978). Strauss was sensitive to the needs of U.S. producers and their representatives. He kept in close touch with these people through the advisory committee system and through his own highly developed network of contacts. When an issue such as the Japanese import-licensing system for oranges or the concerns of winter and spring citrus producers came to him, he raised the issue with the Japanese and pressed for its resolution. Strauss's sensitivity to producer concerns also contributed to another of his important characteristics: credibility. Producers and congressmen believed him. As Russell Long said, "We have a man in charge of our trade policy who we . . . in Congress can trust." Strauss was open with producers and congressmen and honest about the limits of negotiation. As a result, when he went before the producer groups in November, and again in December, to tell them he had squeezed the last concession possible out of Japan, they believed him.

Indeed, his inborn political talent, assisted by his familiarity with U.S. domestic politics and his strong presidential base, made it possible for him to sell a bad deal to domestic interest groups and Congress from time to time. He and his STR staff were also sufficiently effective in coordinating and unifying intraexecutive-branch views on the agricultural trade expansion issue with Japan and did not have the problem of a divided bureaucracy sending different messages to the Japanese side.

One of the major problems with the textile negotiations of 1969-1971 had been that there were several different channels (Maurice Stans's official channel, back channels involving Kissinger and Stans's emissary, the State Department's channel with the Foreign Ministry, and Donald Kendall's private channel) existing at the same time, each communicating different messages to the Japanese. Consequently, only the most convenient message was perceived to be true by each major Japanese actor or group involved. The Japanese actors who believed only moderate messages expected that the United States would eventually make major concessions when, in fact, the U.S. position had remained basically unchanged throughout the course of the issue. Thus, the resolution of the issue was delayed, unnecessarily escalating tension between the two countries.

By contrast, the agricultural negotiations of 1977-1978 were well orchestrated in the sense that consistently tough messages were sent to Japan. Accordingly, most Japanese officials involved in the negotiations believed that the United States was not simply bluffing in demanding major Japanese concessions on beef and citrus.

As I.M. Destler noted, while Strauss is sui generis, "he represents the culmination of a trend; the movement of the special trade representative into the position of overall trade broker" (Destler, 1980, p. 203). As such, future STRs will be responsive first of all to the domestic politics of trade policy rather than to the more general concerns of foreign policy. The more effective these future STRs are as trade brokers, the more likely it is that trade disputes will be settled successfully.

As for the Japanese side, how was it possible for the government to win necessary domestic concessions in view of the enormous political clout usually associated with Japanese agricultural interests?

First of all, there was no intensive, widespread public support for protecting Japan's agricultural interests from import expansion, although there was no articulate consumer movement to support import liberalization either. While strongly criticizing the high-handed U.S. negotiating approach, major Japanese newspapers including *Asahi* and *Nihon Keizai*, expressed the need for some Japanese agricultural concessions. Big business groups, another pillar of support for the ruling Liberal Democratic Party, also advocated concessions to the United States to further broaden bilateral economic interests. Some went so far as to propose a total elimination of the import quotas, substituting them with deficiency-type payments to producers (financed by slightly higher tariffs). On the other hand, one agricultural politician warned Nokyo that farmers, bureaucrats, and politicians must unite in opposition to import liberalization in order to protect the interest of less than a million beef and citrus farmers against the interest of more than 110 million Japanese.

Farmers did unite under the banner of Zenchu and held numerous antiimport national rallies and delivered petitions to government leaders. However, Zenchu leaders themselves were not fully confident of Nokyo's ability to resist a relative expansion of the import quotas (as contrasted with full or seasonal liberalization). Some citrus and livestock producers thought Zenchu (and Zenno) did not make as serious an effort as they could have in opposing the expansion of beef and citrus imports because they were primarily preoccupied with rice.

Within the government bureaucracy, the MAFF was not in an easy position. It still maintained twenty-two residual import quotas (as compared to the five the MITI maintained), and the beef and citrus quotas had been made symbols of the closed Japanese market. Thus, the ministry was under pressure from the MITI, the EPA, and the Foreign Ministry to reduce such import barriers as quickly as possible. It was also increasingly exposed to direct external pressure for liberalization as it began to take the lead role in international agricultural negotiations. Because Japan was so heavily dependent on the United States for supplies of many important agricultural products, the ministry could not afford to ignore U.S. demands completely. More importantly, there was increasing consensus among top-party and government leaders that Japan should make some substantive concessions to the United States in the interest of the overall U.S.-Japanese relationship.

Despite the notion of dominant bureaucratic influence in Japanese government policymaking (which is popular among U.S. social scientists specializing in Japan), it would be next to impossible for Japanese bureaucrats to ignore a prevailing sentiment among the top political leaders in the party and the government.

Agricultural politicians were not necessarily united in the intensity of their opposition to U.S. pressure. Some members of the citrus and beef caucuses were only nominal ones, and those who were actively involved in the antiimport campaign were not particularly influential. Some of the politicians most influential on the beef and citrus issue were advocates of *sogo nosei* (comprehensive agricultural policy) and were in a position of having to consider the country's overall agricultural interest at the same time. They were thus prepared to make some concessions to the United States, on whose agricultural supply Japan depended heavily. Tokutaro Higaki concurrently headed both the citrus caucus and the LDP Comprehensive Agricultural Policy Research Council (CAPRC). Another member of that council, Eiichi Nakao, headed the Lower House Agriculture and Forestry Committee. Takami Eto (who headed the LDP Agriculture and Forestry Section), Sadanori Yamanaka (who headed the beef caucus), and other powerful agricultural politicians gradually acquiesced to the dominant party and government position in favor of concessions.

Despite all these factors, the Japanese government would not have been able to settle the agricultural trade issue with the United States had it not been for the effective political leadership exercised by Nakagawa and the seasoned diplomatic caliber provided by Ushiba, coupled with the unified support of other top government leaders. Being an agricultural politician himself, Nakagawa enjoyed credibility among fellow Dietmen from rural areas and Nokyo leaders. He dealt with these people straightforwardly and came to be respected for his sincerity in working out a reasonable trade off between agricultural and other interests. He was helped by Higaki and other *sogo nosei* politicians in persuading the LDP rank and file in the direction of concessions to the United States. Prime Minister Fukuda himself was strongly supportive to Nakagawa, and Chief Cabinet Secretary Shintaro Abe maintained close contact with the MAFF minister. Ushiba effectively supplemented Nakagawa with his rich experience and expertise in the area of international trade negotiations. Moreover, Ushiba kept in close contact with EPA Director Miyazawa, who, as head of the Economic Ministers Group, worked at interministerial coordination as deemed necessary. The smooth, mutually supportive relationship between Ushiba and Nakagawa was replicated at the working level. MAFF officials in the Economic Affairs Bureau kept closely in touch with Ushiba's office, keeping the latter informed of the MAFF's internal disscussions and its occasional consultations with domestic producers. The Economic Affairs Bureau of Gaimusho (the Second

North American Affairs Division) also provided assistance to the Ushiba office, keeping the latter posted on the U.S. domestic situation.

Mismanagement of the Dispute

Although the U.S.-Japanese agricultural trade issue was generally managed well, given the difficult circumstances involved, the handling of the issue by the two countries was far from perfect. For one thing, the issue might have been settled much earlier. Contrary to popular expectation, if the United States and Japan take more and more time to discuss an issue, it does not become easier to settle. Indeed, just the opposite may be true. The prolongation of an issue tends to bring new actors and information into the negotiation process, thus complicating discussions. Moreover, the prolonged process itself often intensifies emotions, leading to unnecessary politicization.

It was appropriate for the United States to raise the agricultural trade issue relatively quietly first at working-level discussions, then adding pressure as time went on. But the lack of specificity in the initial U.S. demands prevented a speedy settlement of the issue. The U.S. side should have presented specific quota-expansion figures as soon as initial explorations revealed that the Japanese were unlikely to accept full or even seasonal liberalization. Because the Japanese had become accustomed to responding to external signals—instead of taking direct initiatives—in their postwar foreign relations, such signals should have been specific enough to assure specific Japanese responses. Japanese officials also needed specific U.S. requests so that they could get an early start on the domestic consensus-building process, which is essential and usually very time consuming in Japan. In the first phase of the agricultural dispute, the United States did not present specific quota-expansion figures until Ushiba's visit to the United States in December 1977 and in the second phase, until the Geneva talks in July 1978. Generally, the sooner the bottom line is presented by both sides, the better will be the chance of arriving at a necessary compromise.

A related but more serious problem arose because the United States often changed its position and disregarded what had been offered previously. As we noted, one of the most unfortunate shifts in the U.S. negotiating position occurred in September 1978, when Nakagawa and Ushiba visited the United States for talks with Strauss. If Strauss had not reintroduced the question of liberalization at that time, the two countries might have been able to settle the issue much more quickly. Of course, this problem was closely related to the sensitivity of the STR to domestic industry's concerns and congressional sentiments—the sensitivity crucial to the domestic support for (or acquiescence in) the U.S. negotiating position, as noted above.

In view of the fact that the STR was eventually able to settle the issue short of full liberalization, one might logically argue that Strauss and other U.S. officials could have exercised a little more leadership in selling them the July 1978 position as expressed in the Starkey memo.

On the other hand, as discussed earlier, two things done by the Japanese side made it more difficult—although still not impossible perhaps—for the STR. The premature leaking of the substance of the Starkey memo in the Japanese press and the flow of biased information from competing Japanese fruit importers (notably the Fujii and anti-Fujii groups) to U.S. citrus producers intensified the rivalry between California and Florida producers and hardened their attitude toward the STR (and the Japanese government). Indeed, the alleged profiteering and scandal involving some Japanese importers seemed to have given U.S. producers and officials alike a kind of moral justification to press Japan harder.

In addition to the prolongation of the issue, negotiation tactics per se and the noise surrounding the negotiations seem to have contributed to the high level of tension and emotion between the two countries. Japanese officials directly or indirectly involved in the issue resented what they thought of as cavalier U.S. pressure tactics and found Strauss's personal style too crude. (Some may argue that Strauss's personal style was inseparable from his effectiveness as a trade broker. But it is hard to believe that one has to be necessarily cavalier in dealing with a foreign government in order to remain sensitive to legitimate domestic interests and thus maintain credibility at home.) U.S. officials apparently believed that the Japanese would not respond unless pressured by the United States.

Pressure tactics may be useful in winning Japanese concessions in the short run, but they may bring serious backlash on the bilateral relationship in the long run. To some extent, however, the Japanese themselves are responsible for the U.S. perception that Japan needs to be pressured into action. Some Japanese officials encourage the United States to exert pressure on Japan to get reluctant domestic groups to cooperate. If not encouraging U.S. pressure, others often advise domestic-industry concessions because the United States wants them, not because such concessions are important on their own merits. During the agricultural trade negotiations, few Japanese officials called for expanded beef and citrus imports from the standpoint of lowering the domestic prices of these products for the benefit of Japanese consumers. In addition to avoiding the encouragement of or the dependency on U.S. pressure, it is advisable for Japanese officials to anticipate potential issues with the United States and try to nip them in the bud, so to speak. Moreover, to the extent that particular U.S. demands are considered reasonable, Japanese officials would do well to pay serious attention to even quiet U.S. messages communicated at the working level.

There was also a problem of "scapegoating" that was not entirely unrelated to U.S. pressure tactics. Many Japanese felt that U.S. criticisms of the Japanese trading practices were exaggerated, unfair, and one-sided. For instance, U.S. officials criticized the closed Japanese agricultural market but often failed to take note of the fact that Japan was the world's single largest customer of U.S. agricultural products, importing more than $4 billion worth at the time, or the fact that the United States itself had been restricting beef and citrus imports from abroad.

When U.S. officials made statements to the press or to a group of Japanese visitors, that were highly critical of Japan, these remarks were immediately reported back to Japan. Some of these remarks were specifically directed to the Japanese. Others were made for domestic consumption but often had an unfortunate effect of promoting an air of confrontation between the two countries. U.S. legislators were more responsible for such statements than were executive-branch officials. As one Japanese observer put it, "Congressmen would only say things and do things back home which would sound pleasing to their constituents." These are the people who are, as Neustadt put it, "booed and booted out at home or cheered and re-elected there," and what Japanese and other foreigners may think about them is often considered irrelevant. Thus, even if the legislators sufficiently understood the Japanese situation, they would still be inclined to make exaggerated or one-sided statements for domestic consumption. One Congressional aide explains the position of U.S. legislators: "They often make statements highly critical of Japan, but you have to understand the dynamics of domestic politics. They have to identify themselves with particular issues and try to get as much attention as possible from the domestic audience." Of course, the same thing applied to Japanese legislators. However, because of the so-called attention gap existing between the two countries, the U.S. side of the problem was usually more pronounced.

If U.S. officials tended to make one-sided statements about Japan, for domestic consumption or with the intention of pressuring the Japanese, the U.S. media painted an almost uniformly negative view of Japan during the course of the agricultural negotiations. Even in the midst of the controversial textile wrangle of 1969-1971, the press in the United States demonstrated a wide variety of views, including those critical of the Nixon administration and supportive of the Japanese position. In 1977 and 1978, however, anti-Japanese press coverage was predominant. One might say that this was because Japan's import quotas were against GATT rules and against the free-trade principle. But a similar critical attitude was evident in the news coverage of the steel and color-television issues in 1977, which had to do with U.S. protectionism. A unifying theme during this period of increasing bilateral trade imbalance was that of an unfair Japan. Japan was either unfairly closing its market, or unfairly promoting exports. Very few

U.S. press reports mentioned the Japanese liberalization that had already been accomplished. *Business Week* reported in its January 30, 1978, issue that "U.S. and Japanese officials signed an agreement aimed at opening Japan's tightly protected market." The June 4, 1978, issue of *The New York Times*, reporting about "a great shortage of beef" in the United States and the Carter administration's decision to slightly relax the U.S. beef import protection, made no mention of the inconsistent U.S. demand that Japan totally liberalize its beef-import market. In a related context, a Japanese official observed: "Most American news correspondents stationed in Japan have preconceived ideas about Japan and it is difficult to change them. Also, news articles critical of Japan are more likely to be accepted by the editors at home in view of the current state of affairs."

However, the Japanese press was also guilty of some sensational reporting. Although major newspapers sometimes expressed the need for Japanese agricultural concessions in their editorials, they tended to make too much news out of every negative public statement about Japan that U.S. officials made—even though many of the statements did not have much political significance in the United States.

More generally, the problem of communication between the United States and Japan seems to be exacerbated by the fact that, while the Americans employ an adversary style of bargaining, emphasizing all the negative aspects of the other side (as lawyers do in court), the Japanese tend to remain reticent. In such a context, the Americans are likely to conclude that the Japanese have admitted their own guilt. In turn, U.S. actions based on that assumption breed further Japanese resentment. In order to avoid repeating this pattern, it will be necessary for Japanese negotiators to counter such U.S. charges as squarely as possible. Ushiba was rather effective in this regard. U.S. officials should be more sensitive to the traditional Japanese negotiating style, but more and more Japanese officials would do well to learn to bargain in the U.S. style to minimize the misunderstandings that often produce unnecessary tension.

We do not mean to say that any bilateral tension (or friction) is bad by definition and therefore must be avoided. Indeed, a certain level of tension may be inevitable between the world's two largest market economies, which are closely interdependent. Some tension may be even necessary to get things done. The important thing is to prevent bilateral tension caused by a particular issue getting out of control and spilling over into other policy areas, thereby detrimentally affecting the overall relationship. In this sense, the agricultural trade issue was well-managed—despite some difficulty involved in attaining its conclusion.

Notes

1. The MTN had broken through a major impasse and sprung to life during the summer of 1977. In July, STR Robert Strauss reached a compro-

mise with the European community on the subject of agricultural negotiations in the MTN. Until that time, the United States had insisted that
agriculture be negotiated on the same basis as industry—that is, subject to
formula reductions in trade barriers. The Europeans rejected this approach,
and the failure to reach an agreement produced the impasse. In July,
Strauss made a major concession to the EC by agreeing to negotiate the
agricultural and industrial sectors separately on the condition that the
negotiations produce substantial results for U.S. agriculture. As a result of
this compromise and a subsequent agreement on a speeded-up timetable for
the MTN, the negotiations moved forward. Later in the same month, the
agriculture subgroup of the negotiations agreed on a "request-and-offer"
procedure for agriculture. Requests were to be submitted by November 1,
1977 and offers were due by January 15, 1978. Hence, by late summer and
early fall, the MTN as a whole began to move forward, forcing U.S. negotiators to finalize their strategies regarding Japan and other countries.

2. The ministry's formal name then was the Ministry of Agriculture
and the Forestry (MAF), but it was changed a few months later, during the
second Fukuda cabinet, to the current Ministry of Agriculture, Forestry,
and Fisheries (MAFF). For the sake of expediency, we will use the current
name throughout this study.

3. Citrus production in the United States is essentially divided between
Florida, California and Arizona, and Texas. These areas contribute 73, 23
and 4 percent, respectively, of total U.S. citrus tonnage. This output is comprised of oranges (71 percent), grapefruit (19 percent), lemons (6 percent),
and tangerines, tangelos, and limes (4 percent).

Florida is the center of orange production, providing roughly 74 percent of total U.S. production. Florida oranges are grown under near-tropical
conditions and are ideal for orange-juice processing. Ninety-four percent of
the Florida crop is processed for shipping year round. The fresh crop is a
winter variety and, although it can be stored, the bulk is ready for shipment
during the winter and spring, which is the period from January through May.

California and Arizona produce nearly one-quarter of the orange
crop. These oranges are ideal for eating because of their higher sugar content, and two-thirds of the crop is shipped fresh. The timing of the
shipments depends on the variety: Valencia oranges (the bulk of the crop)
are shipped during the summer months (June, July, and August) and the
navel variety from Southern California are shipped during the winter (U.S.
Senate Committee on Finance, 1979, pp. 66-91).

References

Interviews

The authors conducted approximately eighty interviews with government
officials and agricultural leaders in Japan and the United States between

July 1978 and July 1980. In the text, direct quotations not specifically cited are taken from those interviews.

Newspapers and Journals

Asahi Evening News, 7 November 1978.
Asahi Shimbun, September 1977-December 1978.
Business Week, 30 January 1978.
Newsweek, 4 December 1974.
The New York Times, September 1977-December 1978.
Nihon Keizai Shimbun [Japan Economic Journal], January 1977-December 1978.
Nihon Nogyo Shimbun (Japan agricultural daily), September 1978-December 1978.
Time, 27 April 1977.
Tokyo Shimbun, 7 December 1977.
The Washington Post, 7 December 1977; 2 February, 18 August, and 8-9 September 1978.

Books, Articles, and Reports

Cline, William R., et al. *Trade Negotiations in the Tokyo Round*. Washington D.C.: The Brookings Institution, 1978.
Comptroller General of the United States. *United States-Japan Trade: Issues and Problems*. Washington, D.C.: U.S. Government Printing Office, September 1979.
Destler, I.M. "United States-Japanese Relations and the American Trade Initiative of 1977: Was This 'Trip' Necessary?." In *Japan and the United States: Challenges and Opportunities*, edited by William J. Barnds. New York: New York University Press (for the Council on Foreign Relations), 1979, pp. 190-230.
_____ . *Making Foreign Economic Policy*. Washington, D.C.: The Brookings Institution, 1980.
George, Aurelia D. "The Strategies of Influence: Japan's Agricultural Cooperatives (Nokyo) As a Pressure Group." Ph.D. dissertation, Australian National University, 1980.
Hemmi, Kenzo. "Agriculture and Politics in Japan." In "U.S.-Japanese Agricultural Trade Relations: Determinants and Prospects," edited by Emery N. Castle and Kenso Hemmi. Unpublished manuscript. Washington, D.C.: Resources for the Future, 1981.

Japan Fruit Growers Cooperative Association. *Nihon no Kankitsu Jijo* [The Citrus Fruit Situation in Japan]. Tokyo: April 1978.

Liberal-Democratic Party. "Nichibei Nosanbutsu Boeki Mondai ni kansuru Hobei Kiroku" [U.S. Mission Report on Japan-U.S. Agricultural Trade Issue]. Tokyo: 15 August 1978.

Ministry of Agriculture, Forestry, and Fisheries. *Nichibei Keizai Kankei Shiryo* [Japan-U.S. Economic Relations Data]. Tokyo: International Planning Division of the Economic Affairs Bureau, 1978.

United States-Japan Trade Council. *U.S.-Japan Agricultural Trade: What's Ahead in the 1980's*. Washington, D.C.: 1980.

U.S. Department of Agriculture. *Agricultural Statistics of 1978*. (Washington, D.C.: U.S. Government Printing Office, 1978.

U.S., Congress, House, Committee on Ways and Means, Subcommittee on Trade, *Task Force Report on United States-Japan Trade*, 96th Cong., 2d sess. (Washington, D.C.: U.S. Government Printing Office, January 1980).

U.S., Congress, Senate, Committee on Finance, Subcommittee on International Trade, *MTN Studies: Results for U.S. Agriculture*, 95th Cong., 2d sess. (Washington, D.C.: U.S. Government Printing Office, June 1979).

Zenchu (National Central Union of Agricultural Cooperatives). "Nosei Renraku Joho," no. 1540. Tokyo: 5 December 1978.

Politics and High Technology: The NTT Case

Timothy J. Curran

In recent years, trade disputes between the United States and Japan have revolved around items higher and higher on the technological scale. From the confrontation over textiles at the start of the seventies, we found ourselves, by the end of the decade, quarreling over steel, automobiles, and telecommunications. Disputes in these higher-technology sectors have involved complicating new factors. In addition to the particular trade issue at stake in these disputes—be it Japanese exports to the United States or the United States's inability to penetrate the Japanese market—U.S. anxiety over a Japanese challenge to a major U.S. industrial sector has complicated discussions between the two countries. This problem will endure. Japan is committed to developing its high-technology industries, including computers, semiconductors, robots, and telecommunications. As these Japanese industries gain strength, competitive friction between the United States and Japan is likely to increase. It is important that both nations learn how to manage this friction and keep it from sparking repeated confrontations. A close look at how one recent dispute in the high-technology sector developed, how it produced a major confrontation, and how it was resolved may thus provide clues for better management of similar issues in the future.

This chapter deals with the dispute over the procurement practices of the Japanese state-owned telephone monopoly, Nippon Telephone and Telegraph Company (NTT). Specifically, during the course of negotiations for a code on government procurement in the Tokyo Round of multilateral trade negotiations (MTN), the United States requested that Japan place NTT under the code—that is, subject NTT's procurement practices to the competitive bidding procedures called for in the new code. The Japanese at first refused, citing as their reason the fact that most telephone systems in the world use a form of closed, negotiated contract system similar to that used by NTT. Detailed and complex negotiations throughout late 1978 and early 1979 failed to bring a solution. By the turn of the year, congressional actors in the United States had focused on the issue and were calling NTT's closed bidding system a symbol of Japan's closed market. Tempers on both

The author would like to acknowledge the contribution Yashusi Hara, of the *Asahi Shimbun*, made to this paper. Hara provided an important interpretive analysis of the negotiations.

sides of the Pacific rose. As the dispute festered, it became entangled with the preparations for two summit meetings to be held in mid-1979. When a series of highly publicized negotiations collapsed on the eve of the first of those summit meetings, many feared a major confrontation between the two countries.

Fortunately, a procedural solution allowed the dispute to be smoothed over until after the summit meetings had passed. Low-level discussions resumed in July 1979 and continued through 1980. Finally, in December 1980, an agreement detailing procedures for U.S. access to the NTT procurement market was signed. In seeking to analyze and explain the crisis that occurred over NTT, this chapter will concentrate on the events leading up to the clash that took place on the eve of the 1979 summit meetings.

Telecommunications in the United States and Japan

Outside of the United States, telecommunications networks in the developed world are similar to each other in their organization and operation.[1] Usually, a government monopoly provides all telephone services and controls the access of any supplier to the telecommunications market. In the United States, however, the primary suppliers of services and equipment are private corporations subject to regulation and oversight by an independent government agency, the Federal Communications Commission (FCC).

Two companies dominate the U.S. market. American Telephone and Telegraph Company (ATT), which is the largest company in the world, has the controlling share, while General Telephone and Electronics (GTE) is a small second company. About two-thirds of ATT's equipment is procured from Western Electric, a subsidiary of ATT; the remainder comes from other suppliers, including foreign firms. In this sense, ATT's relationship with Western Electric is similar to the relationship found in other countries between the government telephone monopoly and a network of preferred local suppliers.

However, in the United States, a major difference exists in that ATT, although the primary supplier, is no longer the sole supplier of telephone equipment and services. In recent years, several other corporations have challenged ATT's near-monopoly control of the market for telephone services, and a number of other firms, including several Japanese companies, now supply equipment to private end-users, who plug into ATT's central network. These changes have been brought about by important court decisions.

Prior to 1956, complete end-to-end phone service in the United States was supplied by operating telephone companies that owned all the telecommunications equipment. In the 1950s and 60s, two companies that had developed telephone attachments designed to plug into ATT's network filed suit against ATT's prohibition of the devices. The courts ruled in favor of these companies, thus opening the way for a broad range of terminal (end-user) equipment to be attached to the telephone system. In response to these changes, in 1974, the FCC established a registration program for terminal equipment. Under this program, if a manufacturer's equipment meets the necessary standards to protect the system and end-users from harm, the FCC issues a license that allows the direct connection of the equipment to the phone system. These decisions effectively broke ATT's monopoly of the telecommunications market. As the recent General Accounting Office (GAO) report states: "The effect of these decisions on the U.S. telecommunications market has been to open the market substantially to direct competition in both mainline and interconnect/peripheral equipment" (1979, p. 63).

A similar opening of telecommunications markets has not taken place in either Europe or Japan. Government operation of telephone services in Europe entails state involvement in the approval and purchase of telephone equipment. In most countries, market access to imported telephone and switching equipment depends on post, telephone, and telegraph authority (PTT) approval. Telecommunications policies in the EEC, reinforced by these PTT approval procedures, generally require local sourcing of equipment. According to the International Trade Commission (ITC), U.S. exporters report that their shipments of telephone terminal and switching equipment to Europe are restricted to second sourcing. (Equipment is procured from a second-source company only when the approved primary supplier is unable to provide it, due to a strike or bankruptcy, for example.) Documentation of approved technical characteristics and standards in European countries is often undefined or unavailable, and type approval procedures are time consuming, thus further hindering U.S. exports.

In Japan, NTT is the government telephone monopoly empowered to approve the use of communications equipment supplied by any company—Japanese or foreign. NTT's policies, like European policies, encourage domestic suppliers and severely restrict the purchase of imported telephone equipment. Technical specifications are based on design rather than performance and are written to favor the specific products of a small group of local suppliers known as the "NTT Family." Because NTT does not have a manufacturing subsidiary (such as Western Electric), it obtains virtually all of its equipment for the exchange and transmission markets from members of this family of suppliers. NTT has never permitted foreign firms to join this family. NTT's practices of procuring equipment from a relatively small group of trusted suppliers is not unusual, because most Western-European phone systems are supplied in the same way. However, the practice of excluding foreign firms, even foreign firms with local subsidiaries, is unusual.

In Europe, for example, a large volume of equipment purchases by various national phone systems are made from local subsidiaries of International Telephone & Telegraph (ITT), a major U.S. telecommunications manufacturer. In Japan, however, all foreign companies are excluded, including long-established and locally based firms such as IBM Japan. This divergence seems to reflect a greater European dependence on U.S. technology, a more liberal investment climate for U.S. firms in Europe, and Japanese policy decisions favoring the development of indigenous technology.

Entrance into the terminal or interconnect market is also difficult. Although theoretically open, in fact, this market appears to be restricted by NTT regulations and standards. As the recent ITC report stated: "NTT considers standards to be proprietary information, and although foreign firms are required to meet certain specifications for approval, it is NTT's policy not to divulge what the standards are" (1979, p. 33).

As a result of these divergent domestic telecommunications policies, the United States suffers an increasingly large bilateral trade deficit with Japan in the telecommunications sector. Table 5-1 shows the bilateral balance of trade in this sector through the first half of 1980. Table 5-2 presents the global U.S. balance in this sector for 1977.

Table 5-1
Telephone Terminal and Switching Equipment: U.S. Imports, Exports, and Balance of Trade with Japan
(dollar amounts in thousands)

Type of Apparatus	1976	1977	1978	1979	½ of 1979	½ of 1980	Increase 1980 over 1979 (percent)
Switching equipment and parts:							
Imports	$10,805	$14,828	$135,580	$47,967	$21,535	$30,283	—
Exports	90	128(E)	534	364	105	437	—
Balance of trade	− 10,715	− 14,700(E)	− 35,046	− 47,603	− 21,430	− 29,846	39.3
Telephone instruments:							
Imports	6,311	4,772	13,140	10,639	4,314	8,349	—
Exports	111(E)	157	121	314	200	455	—
Balance of trade	− 6,200(E)	− 4,615	− 13,019	− 10,325	− 4,114	− 7,894	91.9
Other telephone apparatus:							
Imports	9,928	15,567	24,520	23,964	10,232	17,844	—
Exports	1,256	1,885	3,113	4,887	1,816	1,235	—
Balance of trade	− 8,672	13,682	− 21,407	− 19,077	− 8,416	− 16,609	97.4
Total:							
Imports	27,044	35,167	73,240	82,570	36,081	56,476	—
Exports	1,457(E)	2,170(E)	3,768	5,565	2,121	2,127	—
Balance of trade	− 25,698(E)	32,997(E)	− 69,472	− 77,005	− 33,960	− 54,349	60.0
Ratio imports to exports	18.6	16.2	19.4	14.8	17.0	26.6	—

Source: Official Statistics of the U.S. Department of Commerce, reprinted in U.S., Congress, House, Committee on Ways and Means, Subcommittee on Trade, *United States-Japan Trade Report,* 96th Cong., 2d. Sess., (Washington, D.C.: Government Printing Office, 1980), p. 27.

According to these figures, the United States ran a global surplus of $1.27 million in telecommunications equipment trade in 1977, which was a slight increase over the $1.25 million posted for 1976. The bilateral balance with Japan, however, has been in deficit and is growing. The deficit has gone from roughly $25 million in 1976, to $33 million in 1977, $69 million in 1978, and $77 million in 1979. The figures clearly indicate that U.S. sales to Europe have been only slightly higher than those to Japan. However, the scale of the Japanese penetration of the U.S. market has given rise to tension. As the GAO report concludes, "the furor over access to the Japanese market arises over the scale of the imbalance in our telecommunications trade with Japan" (1979, p. 79).

Tension over this issue has increased because of fears that Japan is gaining an early foothold in one of the significant industries of the future. A recent congressional study of the issue noted that "by developing all of its own equipment in a a closed market, NTT serves as a mechanism of advancing the technology and quality of Japan's . . . telecommunications companies. Growing under the 'hothouse' protection of NTT procurement practices these . . . companies are moving into the position of being major exporters of telecommunications equipment." On an ominous note, the report concludes that "telecommunications is clearly one of the industries of the future, and Japanese efforts to restrict our sales while building theirs are unacceptable" (U.S. House of Representatives, Committee on Ways and Means, 1980, p. 27).

Table 5-2
U.S. Imports and Exports of Telecommunications Equipment by Principal Source/ Markets for 1977
(dollars in 000s)

	U.S. Imports[a]	Percent of Market[b]	Exports[c]	Share of U.S. Exports (percent)
Telecommunications equipment				
Total	106,791	100	156,372	100
Canada	50,164	47	46,898	29
Japan, Korea	35,633	33	2,343	1
France, Germany, Sweden, Italy	4,801	4	9,290	6
Iran	0	0	20,626	13
Mexico	6,294	6	6,250	4
All others	9,899	9	70,965	45

Source: Comptroller General of the United States, *United States-Japan Trade: Issues and Problems* (Washington, D.C.: U.S. Government Printing Office, September 1979), p. 78.
[a]Imports include telephone instruments, switching equipment, and parts.
[b]Figures may not add due to rounding.
[c]Exports include telephone terminal and switching equipment.

It is clear, therefore, that a growing trade imbalance in this high-technology sector has produced increasing friction. The trade imbalance does not explain, however, why the subject was initially raised in discussions between Japan and the United States, nor why it sparked a major confrontation in early 1979. In order to answer these questions, we must turn to a detailed reconstruction of the NTT negotiations between the two countries. Specifically, we will look at how the issue was initiated, how it was handled or mishandled within and between the two countries, what channels of communication were used and what misperceptions arose during the talks, and how the dispute was finally resolved.

The confrontation with Japan over NTT moved through three rough and sometimes overlapping phases. In phase one, the spring and summer of 1978, the forum for negotiations was the Tokyo Round talks on a government procurement code. At this stage, the United States was interested in the amount of NTT's annual purchases. It requested, therefore, that NTT be placed under the code, but the Japanese government was unable to comply. In phase two, during the winter in 1978-1979, influential members of the U.S. Congress requested greater access to NTT's market for telecommunications equipment. When NTT flatly refused, the issue became highly public, particularly in Japan. Phase three, which lasted through the spring of 1979, was the most important and is treated here in considerable detail. As the Japanese government made belated but determined efforts to force NTT to concede, the issue was complicated by the broadening of U.S. interest, which now focused not only on the amount of NTT's purchases, but also on the content of those purchases, particularly its purchases of high-technology equipment. In addition, tension was increased by the entanglement of the NTT negotiations with two approaching summit meetings. The most serious clash took place on the eve of the first of these summits, when negotiations temporarily collapsed because a Japanese offer was rejected by U.S. officials.

Phase I: Expanding Japan's Procurement Offer

Initial U.S. Requests

Throughout 1978 and 1979, the NTT problem began and ended within the context of the negotiations for a code on government procurement in the Tokyo Round of multilateral trade negotiations, sponsored by the General Agreements on Tariffs and Trade (GATT). The issue was raised by the U.S. government in the hope of expanding world trade in a heretofore closed sector. Many governments have "buy-national" laws or policies designed to favor domestic producers in the countless purchases made by government institutions, from missiles for the defense department to mail trucks for the postal service. Discrimination against foreign producers in the area of government procurement had not been discussed in previous trade negotiations. In the late 1960s, however, discussions about an international regime to govern trade affected by various "buy-national" policies began in the OECD. The start of the Tokyo Round in 1973 provided an arena in which these discussions could be continued. In July 1976, the GATT members participating in the Tokyo Round agreed to establish a subgroup to open discussions on a government procurement code.

Due to the world recession and international economic instability, the Tokyo Round as a whole moved slowly. By July 1977, however, a major impasse between the United States and the European Economic Community (EEC) was broken and the timetable was speeded up. In December 1977, the GATT secretariat prepared a "Draft Integrated Text for Negotiations on Government Procurement." Up until that time, there had been no agreement either on the provisions of the code or on procedures for negotiating which entities of each government would be subject to it. Following the submission of the secretariat's draft, extensive consultations began on both these questions, and some progress had been made by the summer of 1978. In June, it was agreed that the question of entity coverage would be handled on an offer/request basis. Rather than negotiate on a product-by-product basis (for example, purchases of electric typewriters by my Health Ministry for purchases of concrete by your Highway Department), it was agreed to limit discussions to entities. In addition, reciprocity was to be measured in total coverage, rather than in matching entities. With this agreement, offers began to come forward in July 1978.

The provisions of the code itself were also gradually narrowed. In July, a "Draft Integrated Text" that reduced alternative passages in the text of the code was introduced. Negotiations on this text continued after the summer recess, with the focus on certain outstanding issues: threshold limits, entity coverage, tendering procedures, and dispute settlement. Intensive bilateral and multilateral discussions took place on these issues from November 1978 to February 1979.

The dispute between the United States and Japan centered around the question of entity coverage but included questions concerning two provisions of the code as well. The United States used a twofold standard to judge the value of foreign entities: (1) How much do they buy?, and (2) What do they buy? It was against this yardstick that the United States found Japan's offer to be inadequate, but each criterion was important at a different time. When Japan presented its offer in July 1978, the answer to "How much do they buy?" was too low for each of the entities included. Japan's original offer included only central government ministries—the Ministries of Finance, Transportation, and so forth. The combined yearly purchases of these entities totaled only approximately $3.5 billion. This was well below both the EEC's original offer of approximately $10 billion in entity coverage and the United States's initial offer of $16 billion. At this early stage, there was no agreement either between governments or within the United States on a formula for determining what would constitute a sufficient Japanese offer. Given the disparity between Japan's offer and those of the United States and the EC, however, U.S. officials believed Japan's offer was too low and should be improved.

In order to achieve some measure of reciprocity, the United States requested that Japan include in its offer purchases by the nation's public corporations. There are approximately 112 such corporations officially listed by the Japanese government, and these are subdivided into various types. The largest are the three kosha (public corporations): Nippon Telephone and Telegraph (NTT), the Japan National Railways (JNR), and the Japan (Tobacco) Monopoly Corporation. These three employ about 85 percent of the total 919,743 persons employed at all the 112 public enterprises. Among the three kosha, NTT is the largest, with yearly purchases of over $3 billion.

During the first phase of the dispute, therefore, the United States was interested in NTT not because of the public corporation's purchases of high-technology equipment, but because of the sheer size of its purchases. NTT was viewed as the only Japanese government entity with sufficient purchasing power to bring Japan's Tokyo Round offer into reciprocity. Indeed, NTT might never have developed into a problem if Japan had tabled a better offer. Some officials from the Office of the Special Trade Representative (STR) have suggested that if Japan had found a way of increasing its offer by including the other public corporations but excluding NTT, a settlement could probably have been reached. As it was, Japan was unable to do this because of the relatively small size of the other public corporations and because of NTT's role as the pacesetter. If NTT, as the largest and most powerful of the public corporations, could refuse to submit to the code, then the other public corporations apparently could refuse as well.

NTT and the Government of Japan

Why was the Japanese government unable to make an offer including NTT during this early stage of negotiations? The basic reason was that the government lacks direct control over all the public corporations. This was difficult for U.S. officials to understand. Superficially, the question of Japanese government control over NTT seems simple. NTT is a public corporation that was created by national law with 100 percent government capitalization. Its rates, budget, and wages must be approved by the Japanese government, and the majority of its senior administrative body, who are known as the management committee, are appointed by the cabinet.

In Japan, however, legal authority does not always mean actual control. NTT was established in 1952 as a quasi-governmental public corporation. The law establishing NTT granted to the new public corporation all responsibility for operating the nation's telephone, telegraph, and other telecommunications services. These operations had previously been carried out by the Ministry of Postal Services. The law also delegated to the (renamed) Ministry of Posts and Telecommunications supervisory control over the new corporation. This authority, however, has not enabled the ministry to effectively control NTT because the laws establishing public corporation generally provide only broad legal guidelines to the ministry with supervisory control. The public corporations are granted wide discretion in their day-to-day operation. Particularly in the area of procurement, government control of NTT is weak. Hence, the company enjoys almost complete freedom in procurement decisions.

Apart from statutory authority, the Japanese government often exercises control over both public and private corporations through a variety of informal mechanisms, one of the most famous and effective of which is called "amakudari" (descent from heaven). This refers to the practice of placing retiring government bureaucrats (who generally retire at 55) in senior positions in the public and private sectors. Over time, an informal network develops linking a particular ministry with many of the companies under its jurisdiction. The Ministry of Finance, for example, places a significant number of retiring officials among the major city banks. This facilitates a free flow of information and ideas and provides an avenue for influence—albeit both ways.

In the case of NTT, however, this informal control mechanism is missing because the Ministry of Post and Telecommunications has not been able to place many of its retiring officials in NTT. The degree of independence this creates for NTT is enhanced by the traditional sense of superiority NTT enjoys over the ministry, a result of the fact that, when the two were split, many of the better officials are said to have joined the public corporation.

NTT's sense of independence from government control is reinforced by the structure of relationships NTT has created with certain suppliers. The NTT family consists of four major companies (Nippon Electric, Fujitsu, Hitachi, and Oki Electric) and a considerable number of more specialized Japanese manufacturers. Virtually all of NTT's $3 billion in annual procurements are made from this family of firms. Because NTT has no manufacturing facilities, it usually negotiates procurement contracts with one or more of its major suppliers. These firms subcontract with the more specialized family firms, many of which depend almost exclusively on NTT contracts. Members of the family are thus sure of steady orders and reasonable profits. Entry into the approved family of suppliers is extremely difficult and has appeared totally closed in recent years. Once in, however, firms enjoy a secure future. One executive of a family firm said that getting into the NTT family is more difficult than getting into Tokyo University. But, he remarked, "Once you are in, nobody flunks out" (*Nikkei Sangyo Shimbun*, 4 April 1979).

It is a common practice for retiring NTT officials to enter these family firms. NTT thus creates its own system of amakudari, insulating itself from government control and also creating an intimate set of relationships with its suppliers. The result is a common outlook on the part of both NTT and its suppliers concerning attempts to open up the system. Naturally, the suppliers are anxious to protect their exclusive-procurement preserve, while NTT officials are interested in protecting their postretirement landing spots. The result is a reinforcement of the sanctity of the status quo.

Two other concerns of NTT relate to the procurement dispute: the family provides for the protection of indigenous technology and the rehabilitation of the weaker firms. As a public corporation, NTT sees its mission as providing low-cost, high-quality service to the Japanese public. It has not been preoccupied with profits. Working closely with its family suppliers, NTT has striven to develop the most sophisticated forms of telecommunications technology, many of which are at the frontier of technology. NTT is now afraid that, if it is forced to comply with the open-bidding procedures stipulated in the government procurement code, it will lose control over this development process. Worse, the fear exists that information concerning computers and microprocessors will leak to U.S. competitors. Hence, it is not surprising that NTT wants to remain closed.

A second concern relates to the small suppliers of the NTT family. As previously noted, many of these firms subsist solely on NTT contracts and, as a result, have weak or nonexistent marketing and research and development capabilities. For years, the major job of many of these firms has been the production of simple telephone instruments. Until the early 1970s, demand for telephones far exceeded supply, so the business of these firms was good. In the mid-seventies, however, Japan reached a saturation point and the demand for telephones leveled off. Many of the smaller firms that were dependent on this business suffered. Without the marketing or research capabilities to branch out into new products, they faced a difficult future. NTT has tried to help these companies by bringing them in at the development stage of slightly more sophisticated technology. Because this is the area that NTT feels would be most vulnerable to foreign competition, the company and its small suppliers have naturally resisted change.

In summary, while NTT is a government corporation, it is resistant to the formal and informal control mechanisms normally used in Japan, although, ultimately, the cabinet can dismiss the corporation's president for insubordination. Moreover, it has insulated itself from government control by developing its own network or family of supplier firms. This fact was apparently not well-understood by U.S. officials dealing with the government procurement negotiations. As a result, the Japanese government's inability to offer NTT in the early stage of the talks was generally perceived by U.S. officials as a conscious decision not to cooperate.

The Foreign Ministry Gets the Job

Despite NTT's independence from direct government control, the negotiations with the United States still might have been productive in the early stage if a strong Japanese government ministry with an interest in the problem had made a determined effort to build a consensus with the company on the need for some concessions. This did not happen, partially because the job of persuading NTT fell almost by default to the government ministry least able to do the job—the Ministry of Foreign Affairs (MFA).

Other ministries with potentially more leverage in domestic economic policymaking were unable or unwilling to get involved. We have already noted the weakness of the Ministry of Posts and Telecommunications. In addition to its traditional weakness with regard to NTT, the ministry was further handicapped by a lack of awareness of the problem. As an almost exclusively domestic agency, the Ministry of Posts and Telecommunications had little institutional understanding of the problems raised in the Tokyo Round and thus had little interest in confronting the government procurement issue.

The Ministry of Finance might have been expected to exert leverage over the public corporation through its control of the budget. Here too, however, NTT enjoys a considerable degree of independence. Since 1977, when NTT began generating large surpluses, it has not had to rely on government loans to operate. Hence, the leverage created by financial weakness—such as exists over another public corporation, the deficit-ridden Japan National Railways—does not exist in NTT's case. Moreover, it is precisely because NTT is profitable that the Ministry of Finance was reluctant to move against the public corporation. In a period in Japanese financial history when national government deficits were a major problem, the Ministry of Finance did not want to do anything that might have weakened NTT and thus increased the government's burdens.

Finally, why was the Ministry of International Trade and Industry (MITI) unable to influence NTT? During the 1950s and 1960s, the MITI was notorious for the control it exercised over Japanese industry. Despite a decline in the MITI's relative strength in recent years, it is still said to have considerable influence in the business world. Regarding the computer industry, for example, the MITI can exercise influence through its control of budgetary allocations for research and development. Nevertheless, NTT has remained independent of this type of control, preferring to develop technology in its own laboratories or in conjunction with its major suppliers. One MITI official remarked that NTT had become so strong that it was now "beyond the reach of MITI's industrial policy" (*Nikkan Kogyo Shimbun*, 6 April 1979).

The task of persuading NTT thus fell to the officials in the Foreign Ministry who were responsible for the overall Tokyo Round negotiations. The MFA was handicapped in its efforts to deal with the company in two ways. First, like most foreign offices throughout the world, the MFA has a weak domestic base in Japan. Its clients, after all, are foreigners, not Japanese. Second, the MFA was handicapped by the technical nature of the issue. When NTT argued, for example, that technical problems prohibited competitive bidding in the procurement of telecommunications equipment, the MFA was without the technical expertise to refute the company's arguments. Instead, the Foreign Ministry officials had to rely on general admonitions about the need to successfully conclude the MTN or about the isolation Japan would feel if excluded from the code. These warnings were not enough to move the company, given NTT's strength and independence and internal reasons for resistance.

In addition to these structural weaknesses, the MFA also committed a tactical mistake that reduced its effectiveness in persuading NTT. Yasushi Hara of the *Asahi Shimbun* has pointed out, in his discussion of the NTT negotiations, that the MFA acted late in sending sufficiently high-level officials to persuade NTT to make some concessions. Hara notes that, throughout the early stage of the dispute, the MFA assigned only middle-level officers (section chief and below) to the NTT problem. The point is not that these men were inactive. In defending the MFA's action, former Minister of State Ushiba, for example, has noted that, "an official from the responsible section of the MFA was at NTT throughout the spring and summer of 1978. One evening he spent the entire night trying to persuade NTT officials. The NTT people were very impressed with him." In Japan, however, where status has deep implications, the level of officials sent to convince the company may have conveyed a message of insufficient urgency. Thus, senior officials should have been involved from the very beginning in order to convince NTT of the seriousness of the problem. Ushiba admitted as much when he said, "It would have gone more smoothly if someone higher than a mid-level officer had done the job" (Hara and Ushiba, 1979, pp. 102-105).

One important reason for the MFA's failure to assign sufficiently high-level officers to the NTT problem lies with the United States. Throughout the first stage of talks, as previously noted, U.S. officials couched their requests for NTT's inclusion under the code in ambiguous terms. No direct request for NTT was made. Rather, it was simply a demand for an overall improvement in Japan's offer that was made. By making its request in this way, the United States made the MFA's job of convincing NTT to make some concessions more difficult in two ways: first, the lack of specificity may have deceived even Foreign Ministry officials into believing that NTT was not the central U.S. concern. Second, the lack of a specific request surely complicated the job of convincing NTT that it was necessary to make painful sacrifices.

To sum up, when the United States made its initial requests for NTT in the summer of 1978, the Japanese government was not in a position to force NTT to concede. Moreover, because of a weak effort at persuasion, the public corporation was not alerted to the seriousness of the issue. As a result, in the second stage, when U.S. congressional actors showed an interest in the procurement issue and thus began to probe for flexibility on the part of NTT, they ran into a stone wall.

Phase II: Symbol of a Closed Market

The Trade Facilitation Committee and NTT

Beginning in 1975, the United States began to run large and apparently chronic balance-of-trade deficits with Japan. From a small deficit in 1975, the United States moved to a $5.3 billion deficit with Japan in 1976. The deficit increased to $8 billion in 1977, and it jumped to over $11 billion in 1978 (Commerce Department figures). These deficits raised the visibility of the United States's economic relationship with Japan and contributed to the intensification of what might otherwise have been relatively low-level trade frictions. In addition, the trade imbalance and the series of economic initiatives that resulted from it gave rise to two new institutions that helped focus U.S. attention on Japanese trade barriers, particularly NTT. The first was the U.S.-Japan Trade Facilitation Committee (TFC), and the second was the U.S.-Japan Task Force on Trade of the Subcommittee on Trade, Committee on Ways and Means, U.S. Congress.

The TFC was formed on September 27, 1977 by agreement between the Secretary of Commerce and the Minister of International Trade and Industry. Its job was to facilitate the growth of Japan's imports by identifying barriers faced by U.S. exporters and seeking their removal.

(Although the committee is the brainchild of Commerce Department officials, bureaucratic politics almost interfered with its creation. In the fall of 1977, as the U.S. trade deficit with Japan grew and as tension between the two countries increased, officials in the State and Treasury Departments began planning a bilateral subcabinet meeting at which various economic problems could be discussed. Stanley Katz, undersecretary of Commerce, was determined to have the Commerce Department included in the meeting. He told Frank Weil, assistant secretary for Industry and Trade, to make sure he got himself invited. Weil proposed the idea to the organizers in the State and Treasury Departments. He argued that, since most of the officials with expertise in Japanese trade affairs were in Commerce, it was natural that a representative be included. The State and Treasury Departments, hoping to keep the meeting small, replied that, if they made an exception for him, other agencies would want to get on board and the mission would become unwieldy. Weil returned to the Commerce Department and drafted a letter from Commerce Secretary Juanita Kreps to Secretary of State Cyrus Vance, requesting Commerce's inclusion in the meeting. Weil got the Commerce Secretary to sign it. Before sending it, however, he had Katz quietly phone the State Department to tell them it was coming. The State Department was on the phone inviting Weil to come along. The Trade Facilitation Committee (TFC) resulted from meetings between Weil and MITI officials during that September 1977 subcabinet meeting.)

The TFC's mode of operation was to solicit complaints from U.S. exporters who had encountered barriers in Japan and present these complaints, along with appropriate documentation, to the Japanese for discussion. The TFC hoped that a favorable resolution would be attained. The TFC staff included career Commerce Department officials with long experience in Japan. In reviewing cases brought to the committee for action, these officials were particularly interested in ones that held significant trade potential. They thought that, too often, the United States had wasted its political leverage in removing trade barriers of little consequence to overall trade flows. (Automobile standards are a case in point. Even if Japan removed the last remaining barriers to U.S. autos, exports could not be expected to significantly increase because of the incompatibility of large U.S. cars with narrow Japanese streets.) Telecommunications was a different story. It represented a major market and one in which the United States was highly competitive. Moreover, the practices of NTT, the major purchaser of telecommunications equipment, were clear barriers to trade. One official remembered that, during his tenure in the U.S. Embassy in Tokyo between 1975 and 1977, businessmen had often come to him with complaints about NTT. Hence, with the formation of the TFC, staff members were anxious for a test case to force open the NTT market. In late 1977 and early 1978, a number of cases came to the TFC. Although none were directly related to NTT's procurement practices (the subject under discussion in the GATT negotiations), they did focus attention on NTT and its monopoly position. A case brought by General Datacom, Inc., for example, charged that NTT was using its rate structure to discriminate against the equipment produced by this company. The Control Data Corporation case alleged that NTT was using its monopoly position to restrict Control Data's ability to service the Japanese data-transmission market.

TFC staff members used these cases to alert senior Commerce officials to NTT's restrictive practices. In April 1978, for example, after a briefing by the TFC staff, Assistant Commerce Secretary Frank Weil protested NTT's rate-structure discrimination to the Japanese economic minister in Washington, D.C. Once alerted, Weil pursued the issue independently, both within the context of the TFC and during his October 1978 trip to Japan as a member of a U.S. export mission. Both these latter incidents helped contribute to an increased visibility for the NTT issue.

In August 1978, Weil was given an opportunity to raise the NTT issue during a TFC meeting in Tokyo to review outstanding cases. Prior to his departure, Weil was thoroughly briefed by TFC staff personnel, particularly concerning the unresolved case of General Datacom. (General Datacom's market for high-speed modems used to connect computers to telephone lines had been wiped out by NTT's introduction of a new rate structure that favored a domestic manufacturer's product.) Weil's briefing book noted that "NTT . . . has not responded favorably to any of our efforts to seek an acceptable solution." The briefing book also contained an account of a meeting between the president of NTT and Japan's prime minister. In that meeting, the NTT official asserted that he wanted to continue to use only domestically produced equipment. During his stay in Tokyo, Weil met with NTT officials and asked about the General Datacom case and NTT's procurement policies. He was reportedly disappointed with the results of the meeting.

In November 1978, Weil returned to Tokyo as cochairman of a U.S. export mission that had been mandated in the Strauss-Ushiba Agreement of January 1978. As a result of both his earlier bad experience at NTT and the presence on the mission of telecommunications firms interested in NTT, Weil made another trip to NTT. This visit was equally disappointing, but Weil's reaction to the encounter received considerably more press coverage, particularly in Japan. In "excited" interviews, Weil was reported in the Japanese press as accusing the public corporation of "stonewalling" and of engaging in "double talk" (*Sankei Shimbun*, 5 April 1979).

NTT's rigid response to the TFC's complaints seems to have reflected a strategic choice by the public corporation. Prior to the U.S. interest in penetrating NTT, the corporation had been under considerable domestic pressure to open its procurement contracts. Well-known electronics firms such as Sony, Matsushita (Panasonic), and Toshiba, which to date have not been able to bid on a significant amount of NTT procurements, pressured NTT to allow new members to join the procurement family. NTT was slowly and very cautiously beginning to react to this pressure when U.S. demands threatened to disrupt the entire corporation. Apparently, the combination of pressures from these divergent directions seems to have overwhelmed NTT. One Foreign Ministry official who worked on the NTT issue said that, just as NTT was beginning to think about a slow and controlled opening to nonfamily Japanese suppliers, it saw its entire procurement system threatened by U.S. demands. The corporation concluded, this official explained, that the best way to deal with the pressure was to dig in its heels and refuse to move any further toward opening. This attitude was also present in NTT's response to the task force on U.S.-Japanese trade, which visited Japan in mid-November.

The Task Force on U.S.-Japanese Trade

Congressional interest in U.S.-Japanese economic relations was stimulated by the growing trade imbalances that became highly visible in 1977 and 1978. Congressional concern was heightened as a result of a series of highly publicized negotiations between the two countries in late 1977 and early 1978, which culminated in the Strauss-Ushiba Joint Communique of January 1978. Certain members of Congress, alarmed at the problem, felt that Congress should help ensure that the provisions of the communique were observed by establishing a body to monitor the communique's implementation. Congressman James Jones of Oklahoma was a driving force in this effort. Jones had become interested in the problem of U.S.-Japanese trade in 1977 as a result of his efforts to expand the market in Japan for Oklahoma beef. He feared that, if a protectionist movement were to develop in the United States, the major source would most likely be U.S. anger at the growing trade deficit with Japan. Recognizing that the joint communique would be useful in reducing the trade deficit only if there were pressure for its fulfillment, Jones proposed the formation of a task force to monitor the agreement.

The task force on U.S.-Japanese trade was appointed in April 1978 by Congressman Charles Vanik, chairman of the House Subcommittee on Trade. Its goals, according to the task force's report published in January 1979, were to "monitor the implementation of the Strauss-Ushiba Agreement of January 13, 1978, and to advise the subcommittee on United States-Japanese trade problems" (U.S. House of Representatives Committee on Ways and Means, 1979, p. IV). One staff member saw the task force as having two further goals: "to give a kick in the butt to the U.S. bureaucracy enforcing the agreement and to do the same to the Japanese."

The task force received information and briefings from the State Department, the STR, and the TFC. It was the TFC, however, that was particularly important in alerting the task force to the problems surrounding

NTT. Task-force staff members received almost weekly reports from the TFC on its "score card" of cases and especially on the status of NTT-related cases. The impact of these briefings can be seen in the task force's second interim report, issued on August 8, 1978. In language almost exactly duplicating the briefing book prepared for Assistant Secretary Weil, the report drew attention to NTT. It cited the meeting between the NTT president and the Japanese prime minister, which, as we noted earlier, was also pointed out in Weil's briefing book as evidence of NTT's uncompromising attitude. It noted that Japanese officials had said earlier in the year that the procurement practices of NTT, Japan's quasi-governmental telecommunications monopoly, would fall under the January cabinet order, which opened such procurement to foreign competition. However, during a May 17 meeting between NTT President Akigusa and Prime Minister Fukuda, confirmed reports in the Japanese press quote Akigusa as saying that "NTT uses only domestically produced equipment—and wants to keep it that way!"

The Task Force Goes to Japan

In November, members of the task force visited Japan to see for themselves the extent of Japanese trade barriers and to look for the causes of the U.S.-Japanese trade imbalance. Even before they arrived, however, their appetites were whetted for an encounter with NTT because of the problems the TFC had had with the company. However, as we noted, NTT was not prepared to meet these members because a consensus on the need for some concessions had yet to be attained. Predictably, the meeting between task-force members and NTT officials was a disaster. First, the congressmen felt that they were being insulted. On the day they were scheduled to meet with NTT's President Akigusa to discuss ways to increase U.S. sales of telecommunications equipment in Japan, Akigusa was unavailable. NTT officials explained that he had been suddenly called to the Diet, but task-force members did not believe this explanation. They were sure they had been deliberately snubbed.

At another point during the U.S. officials' stay in Japan, Akigusa was reported to have said that the only thing NTT would buy from the United States was "mops and buckets." Whether or not Akigusa actually said this is still uncertain, but the effect of the reported statement on the task force was electric. It conveyed to the Americans a feeling of condescension and intransigence on the part of NTT. The mops-and-buckets story was widely circulated, especially in Japan, and, for the U.S. officials, it came to symbolize NTT's uncompromising attitude, even though Japanese officials maintained that Akigusa had been misquoted.

The reaction of the congressional members of the task force to this encounter with NTT was predictable. Writing in their final report issued in

January 1979, they noted that their meeting with NTT officials was "one of the low points of our visit in Japan." NTT, the report stated, "does not appear to have any awareness of the incredibly serious trade problems between our two nations or that NTT procurement policies in particular are one of the sorest points in our bilateral trade" (p. 33). The report recommended that the U.S. government take action to change these practices or find ways to retaliate against them. It also warned that the task force would raise the issue of NTT when it reviewed the government-procurement-code implementing legislation that the STR planned to submit to Congress in early 1979.

As a result of the task force's very negative characterization of NTT and its system of procurement, the public corporation came to be seen in the United States as a symbol of Japan's closed market. This generated considerable resentment in Japan, particularly among some of the MFA officials who had been handling the issue. One MFA official explained his reaction to U.S. criticism this way: "NTT is being called a 'symbol' of Japan's closed market, but in fact NTT is not symbolic of anything. Practically every other telephone system in the developed world uses a procurement system similar to NTT's."

Congress, the MTN, and NTT

In December 1978, the United States and Japan had settled all their remaining differences in the MTN, including the troublesome agricultural problem, and had signed a bilateral agreement. However, as a result of the impasse reached with NTT by late 1978, it was decided to exclude government procurement from the bilateral agreement and to negotiate further on the subject in the new year.

Unfortunately, the new year saw developments that made the already difficult NTT issue even more difficult to resolve. For one thing, STR officials were frustrated. Negotiations with the Japanese during the MTN had been long and difficult, particularly the agricultural negotiations, which had ended in December. U.S. officials who had handled these talks felt that, in spite of the painfully slow and difficult negotiating process with Japan, the results were meager. Many U.S. negotiators saw Japan's negotiating strategy as one of conscious delay designed to wear down the opponent (as one STR official put it "they try to frustrate the hell out of you until you do something irresponsible"). Many saw the same process shaping up in the handling of the NTT issue.

In addition to the frustrations generated by Japan's negotiating style, STR officials reacted very strongly to the arguments used by NTT to justify its exclusion from the code. These were of two types: technical arguments about the difficulty of adapting Japan's unique procurement system to the multilateral code and quality arguments concerning the superiority of Japan's phone system. The first the STR officials found untrue and tiring. After U.S. officials repeatedly demonstrated that the code would not require vast changes in Japan's procurement system, NTT officials refused to budge. Not only was NTT's intransigence frustrating in itself, but the apparent failure of responsible Japanese government officials to intervene and explain the code to company people angered the STR. The latter argument, implying that U.S. telecommunications equipment was inferior, produced an expected reaction among U.S. officials.

If the new year brought increasing frustration, it also brought added complexity to the domestic U.S. decision-making process, which had a direct impact on how U.S. officials viewed the continuing NTT negotiations. With the bulk of multilateral negotiations concluded by late 1978, the STR entered 1979 gearing up for the long and expectedly difficult process of ratification. This put Congress and domestic interest groups in a pivotal position and forced the executive branch to see NTT in a new light.

In previous efforts at multilateral trade negotiations, such as the Dillon and Kennedy Rounds, the major focus of negotiation was tariffs. In order for the United States to participate in these talks, Congress granted the president authority to reduce U.S. tariffs in return for reciprocal reductions by other countries. After the negotiations were concluded, these reductions went into force automatically. In the Tokyo Round, however, the major focus of negotiation shifted away from tariffs (now a relatively minor barrier to trade) and toward nontariff barriers (NTB). Because NTBs include domestic laws with purposes other than trade regulation (food and drug standards that inadvertently discriminate against foreigners, for example), the Congress could not give the president blanket authority to change these laws during the negotiations. Instead, a system was devised in the Trade Act of 1974 whereby the president could negotiate with foreign governments on a variety of NTBs. When finished, the president was required to present the entire package to Congress, which then had ninety days to accept or reject the president's package.

However, in order for Congress to know whether the acceptance of the package was in the national interest, it needed the advice of those directly affected by its results. Therefore, the Trade Act of 1974 created a system of private-sector advisory committees composed of industry, labor, and agricultural representatives. Their job was to advise both the STR and Congress concerning the private sector's objectives in the negotiations and their evaluation of its results. The Trade Act also provided that each of these committees was to "grade" each portion of the Tokyo Round package by reporting its views to Congress before ratification. As one specialist has noted, "The political leverage this gave to the advisory committees was not lost on negotiators."

In early 1979, as the advisory committees began to look at the government procurement code, attention focused on Japan. This was particularly the case for the industrial-sector committee concerned with telecommunications and the labor committee, of which the Communications Workers of America (CWA) were members.

Industry and Labor Focus on NTT

The industry-sector committee had had direct contact with NTT in December 1978. Prior to that, STR officials had been having a difficult time refuting some of the technical arguments NTT officials had presented in defense of their closed-bidding system. In order to counter these arguments, STR officials requested that a group of telecommunications-industry representatives go to Japan to meet with their counterparts in NTT. The trip was organized by John Sodolski, vice-president of the Electronics Industries Association and a member of the Telecommunications Advisors Committee. The industry that Sodolski represented had been growing increasingly concerned about the threat of Japanese competition. In 1977, for example, there was what one representative called the "C-B Fiasco," in which imports of Japanese citizens-band radios had surged. Also in 1977, there were a significant number of purchases of Japanese telephone equipment by U.S. firms. The industry did not, however, see the government procurement code as the way to cope with the situation.

This notion changed, however, when the group organized by Sodolski visited Japan in December. The group of industry people was comprised of very senior technical and policy executives from the major U..S telecommunications makers, including Western Electric, GTE, and ITT. Led by Sodolski, they met for two days with NTT officials in Tokyo. The meetings did not go well. In their opening meeting with Akigusa, the president of NTT, it is reported that Akigusa openly declared that NTT had no intention of purchasing foreign equipment. In a follow-up meeting with technical people, NTT officials presented their technical reasons for excluding foreign equipment, including its incompatibility with the NTT system, its poorer service, and its higher failure rate.

The U.S. industry reportedly found these technical arguments to be "hogwash." As one U.S. participant remarked, "They may have been able to sell these arguments to our embassy people, but they're talking to technicians now and it just won't work." The general attitude among the Americans was that the arguments posed by NTT were similar to those presented by ATT in defense of its monopoly rights during a domestic court case. ATT lost that case, and the introduction of non-ATT equipment had not compromised the integrity of the phone system.

The industry group returned to the United States with their interest in NTT thoroughly aroused and with their sights set on the government procurement code. They were, as one remembered it, "exhausted and angry at Japanese intransigence." This sentiment gradually filtered into the STR's thinking.

The labor sector also provided input on the NTT problem through the actions of the Communications Workers of America (CWA). The CWA, a member of the AFL-CIO, represents the employees of ATT, Western Electric, and about ninety other firms in the communications field. It is a strong and politically popular union. As one congressional staffer said, "Every member of Congress has phone company people in his district." The CWA was represented in the STR advisory structure at all levels. Its chairman, Glenn Watts, was a member of the presidential committee. In addition, union representatives served on the policy-level and advisory-level committees.

The CWA became interested in the question of imports in 1976, when congressional legislation turned their attention to the domestic interconnect market. They noticed that a number of foreign firms, including Japanese firms, were establishing themselves in the U.S. market. The trend was disturbing. In an attempt to get information, the CWA, acting through the House Subcommittee on Trade, requested that the ITC conduct a study of the domestic telephone industry. Released in February 1979, the ITC study reported that over 17 percent of the domestic interconnect market had been captured by imports, with Japan taking a large share.

The report also noted the closed nature of many foreign markets, which contrasted with the openness of the U.S. market. It pointed out that, in Japan, imports of communication equipment from all countries represented only 1.5 percent of the domestic market. The reason was that "Japan's telecommunications policies encourage domestic suppliers and severely restrict the purchase of imported telephone equipment." NTT's restrictive policies were particularly noted: "As a general rule, only equipment designed by [NTT] . . . qualifies for approval for sale in Japan" (ITC, 1979, pp. 19-21).

The report stated that the "enactment of meaningful liberalization and cessation of discriminatory government practices in the government procurement code should lead to increased U.S. exports." It added, however, that "Japan . . . indicates an intention to exclude its domestic telephone service [NTT] from the provisions of the code." The report concluded (rather dryly) that "this action would not improve U.S. export opportunities to Japan" (ITC, 1979, p. 36).

CWA officials on the advisory committee expressed their concern about Japan and the government procurement code during the early part of 1979. They argued that the U.S. telecommunications market was open to foreign producers, yet Japan's was closed. In addition, they learned that NTT was the largest entity in Japan's government structure. They pressed STR officials to ensure that, before the government procurement code was settled, the problem with Japan, and particularly NTT, should be solved. The extent of CWA's concern was made clear in a letter to STR Robert Strauss in which CWA "expressed its strong concern on government procurement activities, urging that the United States government keep our domestic market closed to Japanese bidders in telecommunications equipment and other goods and services until there is substance in any agreement on the subject between the governments of Japan and the United States" (CWA, 1979, p. 3).

The concerns of these private-sector groups became important to the STR in its planning and negotiation, not because of the direct pressure they exerted on the executive branch, but because their collective voice was amplified and given weight by the mechanisms that Congress had designed for the ratification and implementation of the MTN. One analyst has noted, "STR continued to be sensitive above all to the domestic politics of trade policy, chastened by the recognition that . . . Congress would ultimately have to approve the MTN results."

The STR's sensitivity to Congress and the domestic politics of trade policy helped to dramatize two elements of the negotiations with Japan. The first was the dollar amount of Japanese concessions, and the second was the need to appear tough with Japan. With regard to the former, Strauss was aware that, by emphasizing the large trade gains that U.S. firms could be expected to make by penetrating the Japanese market, he could favorably impress congressional reviewers of the MTN package.

This was a particularly important concern with regard to the government procurement code, which Strauss and other STR officials considered the "prize" of the MTN. This code could potentially provide the largest trade gains in the negotiations. In hearings before the Senate Governmental Affairs Committee, Strauss noted that the code would open an estimated $20 billion in new markets for U.S. products, depending, as he put it, on the negotiations with Japan. It was an important code because it would open markets in areas where the United States is highly competitive (computers, sophisticated office machines, scientific instruments, and other high-technology items), and would therefore have immediate implications in real-dollar terms. However, STR staff members anticipated trouble. In order for the United States to adhere to the code, it would be necessary to abolish the "buy America" preference granted in many government contracts. A successful code would have to find a way to compensate or negate the countless beneficiaries of buy America contracts. One way was to offer very visible trade gains to the United States; another was to make these gains in areas that had the greatest political impact. A senior STR staff member pointed out that "the high-technology people—computers, telecommunications, etc.—are the backbone of the free-trade movement in this country. We had to give them something to cheer about."

A second element of the negotiations made more prominent by the STR's sensitivity to Congress was the need to appear tough with Japan. As noted earlier, since 1977 there had been increased concern on Capitol Hill about the growing trade deficits with Japan and the seemingly closed nature of the Japanese market. In early 1979, similar fears were again growing. The trade figures for the second half of 1978 (which became available in December 1978) were very bad, indicating a growing imbalance. These fears were amplified and focused in January, when the Jones Report, which emphasized the closed nature of Japan's markets, was published. On telecommunications equipment in particular, the Jones Report pointed out that Japanese exports to the United States were surging, thus creating a serious imbalance. The report concluded that, during the drafting of the government-procurement implementing legislation, Congress would focus on ways to open Japan's telecommunications market. Hence, any agreement that STR delivered to Congress that did not appear tough on Japan or that did not guarantee access to Japan's markets, particularly the telecommunications market, was bound to run into trouble.

Both these elements—the need to demonstrate real market opportunities in the code and to be tough with Japan—figured in the series of negotiations that resumed in early 1979. Both were at least the indirect result of congressional and private-sector participation in the domestic decision making for the MTN. In order to achieve success in the ratification fight, Strauss would have to deal with them. One STR staff member summed up Strauss's strategy for dealing with the problem when he said, "Strauss didn't have a complicated formula for dealing with NTT, but he instinctively knew two things: that big numbers look good and that you can't lose being tough with Japan."

Phase III: Ticket to the Twenty-First Century

U.S. Interest in NTT Expands

As we have noted, throughout 1978, the STR's interest in NTT resulted from the sheer size of the company's procurements and the impact their inclusion would have on Japan's government procurement offer. However, late in 1978 and increasingly in early 1979, the STR's focus shifted to the nature of NTT's purchases, particularly its purchases of high-technology equipment. Staff analysis by the STR, the TFC, and the National Telecommunications Information Agency (which, coincidentally, has its offices on the same floor as the STR) all pointed to the growing importance of the Japanese market in telecommunications. Slowly, this staff work began to filter up to higher levels and influence the thinking of senior STR policymakers.

The telecommunications market combines three previously separate fields—communications, computers, and electronics. It is a rapidly growing field and one in which the United States has long held a competitive advantage. However, in recent years, the Japanese telecommunications sector has made important advances. U.S. officials feared that, behind NTT's closed doors, Japanese companies would be able to generate sufficient economies of scale and to move down the learning and experience curves fast enough so as to pose a threat to U.S. industry. Recently, Japanese companies had succeeded in penetrating not only the U.S. interconnect market, but also the market for central switching equipment as well. (Southern New England Telephone, for example, has been a major customer of Nippon Electric Company's central office switches.) STR officials believed the most effective way of blunting the Japanese advance on the U.S. market was to force open NTT. By opening NTT's closed market, the United States could eliminate some of the economies of scale enjoyed by NTT's suppliers and thus blunt their export drive to the United States.

STR officials felt that this strategy of market penetration via the government procurement-code negotiations was imperative if the United States were to maintain its predominance in this increasingly important field. But STR officials also knew that this was precisely why Japan resisted. Both countries see telecommunications as a vital sector for future industrial development. As one senior official put it, "Telecommunications is the ticket on the twenty-first century express, and both we and the Japanese want to ride first class."

In January 1979, the United States and Japan reopened the negotiations. Until that time, the United States had requested that Japan place NTT under the code in its entirety, and Japan had flatly refused. The nature of this U.S. request—asking that all of NTT procurements be placed under the code—reflected the formula of the multilateral negotiations, which proceeded on an entity-by-entity basis. Without explicitly changing its request that all of NTT be opened immediately, in January, the United States showed some flexibility. Reports indicate that the U.S. position was: First, major telecommunications equipment was the focus of U.S. interest, but it did not need to be put on an open-bidding system immediately. Second, the U.S. was not interested in NTT's procurement of office equipment and supplies. Third, all new products developed by U.S. firms should be allowed to compete in Japan through open bidding. Finally, open bidding should be permitted immediately for all terminal and other accessory equipment.

In late January, the United States pressed its demands in a meeting with Nobuhiko Ushiba, Japan's representative for the Tokyo Round. The official Japanese position was still that NTT could not be opened, but Ushiba brought back to Japan reports that the United States was dead serious about NTT and that the failure to settle the matter could disrupt the MTN.

He urged the prime minister to find a solution before the April signing of the trade talks. In addition to the demands outlined above, the focus of the January and February talks became a dollar figure. U.S. officials pointed out that the U.S. offer in the government procurement talks was to open approximately $12.5 billion to international open bidding. The EC was offering $10.5, and Japan was offering only $3.5 billion. In order to bring the talks to a successful close, Japan would have to raise its offer to between $7 to $8 billion. This $7 to $8 billion figure was the result of a complicated formula based on the size of Japan's gross national product (GNP) and the share of government procurement within it. Despite the apparent rationality of the formula, U.S. officials admitted that the figure decided upon for Japan was a rather arbitrary one, based on their calculation of what was necessary to force NTT's inclusion in Japan's offer. U.S. officials knew that, in order to reach the stated figure, NTT's purchases of expensive high-technology equipment would have to be included. The large figure had the added attraction of looking good on the Hill.

The temperature was raised in early February with the visit of Takeshi Yasukawa, Japan's special ambassador for economic affairs. In meetings with administration and congressional figures, Yasukawa was strongly pressured to take actions to reduce Japan's surplus. His sessions on the Hill were particularly rough. Congressional figures, with some encouragement from elements within the administration, really "nailed" Yasukawa. As a staff member who sat in on one meeting put it, "it was a very unpleasant session. I doubt Yasukawa will be back any time soon."

Also at this time, Senator Lloyd Bentsen, chairman of the Joint Economic Committee, raised the possibility of an import surcharge against Japan. In a statement released on January 25, Bentsen said, "If . . . the Japanese are retaining nontariff barriers to American goods, then I think we should start looking very carefully at a surcharge or other barriers to their imports, and I think there are a lot of members of Congress who feel the same way." Although Bentsen's statement was not specifically connected to the NTT problem, it was a further indication of the growing frustration on Capitol Hill over trade problems with Japan.

The Japanese Cabinet Discusses NTT

The visit to the United States by Special Ambassador Yasukawa marked a turning point in the Japanese government's thinking about the NTT problem. As noted earlier, prior to this time, the NTT problem was the responsibility of the Foreign Ministry officials in charge of the MTN. Although high-level officials had been assigned to the case in the late fall, and although renewed efforts had been made to convince the company to make some concessions, the matter continued to be seen within the context of the MTN. In this context, discussions within the MFA and between the MFA and NTT were burdened by a perceived lack of reciprocity in the negotiations. In particular, NTT argued that it would not agree to come under the code unless the European PTTs were also included. (Europe's PTTs were refusing to do so, and the United States was not pressing the issue because the EEC's overall government procurement offer was satisfactory.)

Since the turn of the year, however, some officials in the MFA were arguing that the NTT problem had clearly become a bilateral matter. These officials argued that, whatever the merits of Japan's case within the MTN context, some sort of accommodation with the United States had to be worked out before congressional protectionist pressure became too great. After the return of the Yasukawa mission, these officials assumed a leading role in internal MFA policymaking.

This change was partially a result of the report Yasukawa brought back with him from the United States. During his meetings with congressmen and executive-branch officials, Yasukawa had been impressed with these officials' level of interest in and knowledge about the NTT problem. Interestingly, Yasukawa and the members of his party were also impressed by the civility of their exchanges with U.S. officials. Nevertheless, upon returning to Japan, Yasukawa reported on the seriousness of the issue and on its high visibility in Congress. He was able to then alert senior political and administrative leaders to the importance of the NTT problem and to impress upon them the need for government action.

The move toward government action was given further impetus after a second Ushiba trip to the United States in mid-February. As late February approached, there were signs that the Japanese government was preparing for action. Inside the MFA, position papers were being drawn up that presented reasons for a Japanese concession on NTT. One paper refuted NTT's claim that open bidding would result in a leakage of secret technology that could weaken the national security. The advanced technology obtained from abroad through open bidding, the paper pointed out, might actually strengthen Japan's national security. Another paper detailed the effects on Japan if the government-procurement-code negotiations collapsed and Japan was thus excluded from bidding in other countries' procurement markets.

More important than the shift within the Foreign Ministry was the new attention given to the issue by senior political leadership. For instance, on February 14, Minister of International Trade and Industry Masumi Esaki noted before the Lower House Commerce Committee that, while NTT's reasons for resisting were understandable, "Japan must make every effort to achieve a free and open market." The newspaper *Asahi* noted that this was the first time a senior government leader had criticized NTT (15 February 1979). On the following day, the press reported that Toshio

Komoto, chairman of the Liberal Democratic Party's (LDP's) research council, had summoned both former State Minister Ushiba and NTT's President Tokuji Akigusa and had asked them to make every effort to solve the NTT dispute with the United States (*Nihon Keizai, Shimbun*, 16 February 1979).

Most important was Prime Minister Ohira's decision on February 16 to call a special cabinet session of economic ministers to discuss the NTT problem. Ohira made this decision after hearing the reports of Yasukawa and Ushiba, both of whom had informed the prime minister of the growing seriousness of the matter. Ushiba reportedly told the Prime Minister in his report that the NTT issue had become a symbol of Japan's closed market in the United States. He said that the atmosphere in U.S.-Japanese relations was worsening and that there was increased talk of an import surcharge against Japan (*Asahi Shimbun*, 17 February 1979).

This special economic cabinet meeting was scheduled to convene on February 20. A hint of which direction the cabinet was going to move with regard to the NTT problem was provided the night before in a speech by LDP Secretary General Kunikichi Saito. He declared that NTT had become a symbol of Japan's closed market and that Japan should work to change this symbol, "so as to pave the way to smoother U.S.-Japanese relations," (*Asahi Shimbun*, 20 February 1979). At the cabinet session the following day, the assembled ministers reached the same conclusion, deciding that "it is in Japan's general interest to remove trade barriers" (*Nihon Keizai Shimbun*, 20 February 1979). In order to move in this direction, most of the ministers agreed that NTT would have to make some concessions.

Nevertheless, the meeting was not without dissension. As expected, Posts Minister Jinkichi Shirahama protested the decision, remarking that any opening of NTT would damage the company. More importantly, some ministers who apparently agreed with the decision to seek concessions from NTT complained about Japan's passive response to unilateral U.S. demands. Transportation Minister Moriyama, for example, said that Japan should not limit the improvement of U.S.-Japanese relations just to the trade imbalance problem. He felt it was also important to address issues in which Japan had grievances, such as the air agreement and the nuclear-energy agreement. "Negotiations in which the U.S. alone takes the initiative are a problem," Moriyama noted (*Nihon Keizai Shimbun*, 20 February 1979).

The cabinet meeting on February 20 was important because it marked the first time that Japan's senior political leadership publicly declared their intention to settle the NTT problem. They had not, of course, indicated how far they were willing to go to satisfy U.S. demands. Nevertheless, the meeting was an important part of the domestic decision-making process, signalling to NTT and its supporters that the end was drawing near. The slow process of consensus building had thus begun, with the government in-dicating the direction in which it wanted to move.

Unfortunately, there is no evidence that U.S. officials responsible for the NTT negotiations appreciated the start of this consensus-building pro-cess. Granted, Japan's position at the bargaining table was still a rockhard refusal to include NTT under the code. Nevertheless, had U.S. officials understood more clearly the Japanese decision-making process and seen that there was indeed movement toward a settlement in Japan, they may have been able to soften the growing sense of frustration among Americans.

NTT Counterattacks

With the return of Yasukawa and Ushiba in February, and with the moves inside the government to resolve the issue, NTT and its supporters launched a campaign to win over public opinion and rally support for their side within the various political parties. The first public move came on February 13, when the telecommunications trade association ran a full-page adver-tisement in Tokyo's most influential dailies. Splashed across the page in bold type was the word *komatta*—"We are in trouble!" The copy charged that the United States was trying to destroy Japan's phone system, and the association appealed for public support in its defense against this U.S. at-tack. A few days later, NTT's affiliated unions also began protest activities. On February 19, the day before the cabinet meeting, the Communications Workers of Japan (Zendentsu) announced its opposition to any concession by NTT. That evening, the political bureau of the union requested the help of the Japan Socialist Party (JSP)—with which the union has strong ties—in pursuing the support of government leaders in the Diet. As a result, on February 22, government officials were badgered with questions from JSP members about the government's planned moves regarding NTT. Ac-cording to the union journal, *Zendentsu,* the JSP's pursuit of the govern-ment in the Diet greatly shocked the Ohira cabinet and forced the MFA and the MITI to change their plans about giving in to U.S. demands (1979, p. 13). Actually, union activities did not seem to seriously hamper the govern-ment, but it did provide another reason for Japanese officials to proceed with caution. This was especially true because the chairman of the Lower House Communications Committee was a JSP member and a former union leader at one of NTT's major suppliers.

The most serious and effective channel of resistance open to NTT ran through the LDP. If the company could rally LDP back benchers to their defense, it could potentially create serious problems for the senior party leadership and force a reevaluation of the government's decision to make concessions on NTT. On Freburary 23, NTT formally opened this channel by meeting with members of the LDP communications division (Tsushin Bukai) and appealing for their help. The bukai members were realistic about the problems facing NTT and supportive of the company's position. They decided that the company's system of negotiated contracts should be continued. Before deciding on a formal position, however, the members decided to wait for the report of a foreign ministry official who was then visiting the United States. The bukai members also decided to send a delegation of LDP members to the United States in order to explain Japan's position more fully and to see for themselves the strength of U.S. demands. Hedging their bets a little, the LDP members said they were willing to investigate the possibility of using the negotiated contract system to buy more telecommunications equipment from the United States.

On March 16, the LDP group that had visited the United States delivered its report. They noted the severity of U.S. demands and the need for a resolution of the issue. After hearing this report, the LDP communications division approved a statement of the members' attitudes concerning the NTT problem. The language in the draft had been worked out the night before in a meeting between senior NTT officials and LDP members close to the company. The statement, entitled "Regarding NTT's Procurement in the GATT Tokyo Round," read as follows:

> The procurement of communications equipment and facilities by competitive bidding can greatly hinder the functioning of the telecommunications network. As a result, even in the other advanced countries, a system of procurement through negotiated contracts such as used by NTT is the norm.
>
> Even in the event that it becomes necessary to have NTT become subject to the government procurement code in order to facilitate a speedy conclusion of the GATT Tokyo Round, NTT's procurement of plant and equipment must follow the same pattern found in the EC; they must not be subject to the provisions of the government procurement code which are based on the principle of competitive bidding.

On March 22, the above declaration was delivered to the senior party leadership at a meeting of the Policy Affairs Research Council. It was acknowledged by the party leaders, who said they would use this "EC parity" principle as the base from which to conduct the upcoming negotiations. However, because the negotiations involved international affairs and Japan's foreign policy, the LDP members of the communications division entrusted the negotiations to the senior leaders. This provided the party some flexibility in its talks with government leaders on how to respond to the United States. The party would have to proceed with caution, but their hands were not tied (*Tsushin Kogyo,* April 1979).

Despite these moves by NTT and its supporters in the LDP, unions, and trade associations, the effort to prevent movement toward a resolution of the issue failed. In addition, NTT's counterattack backfired, particularly in the public eye. After the "komatta" advertisement on February 13, for instance, the press ridiculed NTT for its excessive egoism in putting its own interests before those of the nation. In an editorial on March 2, the authoritative *Nihon Keizai* admonished NTT to be more reasonable. The paper said that Japan's telecommunications industry was sufficiently competitive and that it had nothing to fear from open bidding. Not all U.S. demands were justifiable, the paper stated, but NTT should accept some of the U.S. requests because the issue had become politicized. The paper criticized NTT's clumsy handling of the issue, warning that NTT's plans for a political campaign—pressuring the political parties and industrial circles—were too late because the United States had already stiffened its position.

Government leaders were equally critical of NTT's activities. After the trade-association advertisement was run, MITI Minister Esaki, for example, said, before a Lower House committee, that the printing of this kind of advertisement in a charged U.S.-Japanese atmosphere "can only make matters worse," (*Asahi Shimbun*, 15 February 1979).

Although NTT was not successful in stopping the movement toward concession, the public corporation was able to cast the United States and its demands in a very negative light. One example gives a good illustration. Early in 1979, the Japanese press began to speculate openly that the force behind the United States's desire to crack the NTT market was IBM. The rumor seems to have originated in a vague response to a question about IBM in a press conference given by NTT President Akigusa. Respected Japanese newspapers and magazines ran articles attributing the U.S. request to the fact that a number of former members of IBM's board of directors were now members of President Carter's cabinet. The *Oriental Economist*, for example, wrote that IBM, which had "sent in " four cabinet members to the Carter administration, was interested in obtaining NTT's advanced communications technology in order to better compete with ATT in the expanding U.S. telecommunications market. The journal noted that many Japanese sources believed this was the real reason the United States was so insistent on an open-door policy for NTT (April 1979, p. 9).

These reports had a great impact on the attentive public who were following the NTT negotiations. (However, the reports do not seem to have been taken seriously by Japanese government officials.) Nevertheless, the United States did nothing to refute the charge. No statement was made challenging the rumors, nor was any real effort made to articulate for the Japanese public why the United States was interested in NTT or to point out the facts concerning U.S.-Japanese trade in telecommunications. Indeed, until very late in the negotiations, the U.S. public position was that NTT had to be included under the code simply to improve Japan's overall Tokyo

Round offer. As a result of this vague bargaining position, the Japanese public and press were receptive to conspiracy theories explaining U.S. motives. Thus, while the press criticized NTT's egoism, it had no enthusiasm for what was seen as an attempt by the giant IBM to swamp a growing but still weak Japanese industry.

Japan Prepares an Offer

At the cabinet meeting on February 20, the Japanese government decided that more information concerning the U.S. demands was needed before an offer could be assembled. Thus, they ordered a senior foreign ministry official, Hiroshi Oki, to visit the United States in order to continue preliminary talks. Oki arrived in Washington the first week of March and opened talks with Deputy Special Trade Representative Alan Wolff.

In these meetings, U.S. trade officials stressed their desire for meaningful competitive trade opportunities in NTT. They wanted a total Japanese offer of approximately $7.5 billion, and they wanted the offer to be within the framework of the MTN, which meant the offer should include a list of open entities, not simply open products. While stressing their demand for meaningful competitive opportunities and a dollar sum, United States also showed some flexibility about accommodating NTT. STR officials who participated in the talks with Oki reported that a number of alternative plans, which would have allowed Japan to include NTT under the code while continuing to protect some of its relationships with favored suppliers, were presented to the Japanese representative.

U.S. officials stressed that what they meant by meaningful competitive opportunities were high-technology items. Their flexible approach was designed to allow Japan to include these items in its offer without completely destroying NTT's present procurement system. At this point, the United States did not, however, specify in which particular high-technology items it was interested.

Oki gave no indication of what Japan was prepared to offer, primarily because his was really only a reconnaissance mission. U.S. officials might have misunderstood this, because one official indicated that "our requests and flexibility fell on deaf ears." Whether or not Oki clearly perceived U.S. intentions is also unclear. However, he seemed encouraged about the possibility of a successful solution, as indicated by his statements to the Japanese press. Oki noted that, while the United States did not abandon its position that NTT represented the closed nature of the Japanese market, as a result of their talks, he believed U.S. officials "came to understand Japan's position on the problem" (*Nihon Keizai Shimbun,* 16 March 1979). Upon his return to Japan, Oki reported on the new flexibility in the United

States, adding that it now seemed to understand that all of NTT's procurements could not be open to competitive bidding. "The question now is," he concluded, "how far does 'partial opening' extend?" (*Asahi Shumbun,* 7 March 1979).

On the evening of March 10, Prime Minister Ohira summoned some of his top aides and cabinet officials to discuss the NTT problem. They decided that the government should immediately start to formulate a new Japanese offer—this time including NTT. They felt that the U.S. demand for $7.5 billion was unreasonable, but the officials hoped to improve Japan's present offer of under $4 billion to between $5 and $6 billion. Ohira decided to dispatch Ushiba to settle the issue with Strauss in late March.

After hearing the reports of two Japanese groups that had visited the United States in connection with the NTT problem (the LDP group and an industry group), the Japanese Foreign Ministry was able, after working closely with the LDP, to put together an offer. As the deadline approached for Ushiba's departure, government sources said that the offer he would carry, which was expected to be about $5.5 billion, would be Japan's last.

MFA officials worked feverishly to increase the amount offered by NTT and the two other public corporations, JNR and the tobacco monopoly. On March 24, NTT officials conveyed to the Foreign Ministry their decision to allow $600 million of the company's $3 billion annual procurements to be subject to open bidding. On March 26, government leaders and senior officials of the LDP met to finalize Japan's offer. Ushiba then apparently delayed his departure from Japan by one day because of his dissatisfaction with NTT's contribution to the total offer. If he made any attempt to have it increased, however, it was unsuccessful, because he carried to the United States a total offer of approximately $5 billion, including NTT's $600 million. Ushiba noted that, because the U.S. offer in the government procurement talks was not the $12.5 billion declared but closer to $10 billion, a Japanese offer of about $5 billion should be sufficient (because the Japanese GNP is about one-half the U.S. GNP). Publicly, the Japanese government seemed to agree, and officials stated that this would be Japan's final offer.

Despite the claim by some government officials that Ushiba's offer would be Japan's last, there is evidence that some officials were aware that the offer would not satisfy the United States. Some noted frequently that they expected rough sailing in the meeting with the United States. Others noted that the quality of Japan's offer was probably below U.S. expectations. As noted, even Ushiba was reported to have been unhappy with NTT's contribution and doubtful of the trip's success.

The evidence thus indicates that the Japanese government was divided regarding the outcome of Ushiba's upcoming talks. A constructive and effective U.S. response to this difference within the Japanese government would have been a firm but calm rejection of Japan's offer, an acknowledgement of the effort that had been made, and a request for more. This would have aided allies in Tokyo, who were working toward a solution by signalling to the hardliners that more concessions were needed. Yet, it would not have been harsh enough to generate a counterproductive backlash. Unfortunately, the needs of Tokyo politicians did not match those of their counterparts in Washington.

The March Breakdown

On March 29, after only one day of negotiations, the talks between Ushiba and Strauss were abruptly broken off. U.S. officials remarked that the Japanese offer was not even worth discussing and that it was of decidedly poor quality. NTT was included for the first time, but the items it was offering for open bidding were all nontelecommunications equipment, such as computer paper, typewriters, and telephone poles. In addition, some officials were upset with what they called Ushiba's "juggling" with the numbers in his reference to the U.S. offer, which he indicated was less than the stated $12.5 billion.

Ushiba was reportedly upset with the United States's termination of the negotiations and especially with its curt rejection of Japan's offer. He was also upset at the treatment he received on Capitol Hill, where legislators were highly critical of Japan's offer. Ushiba is reported to have said, "They treat Japan as if it were some banana republic." He is also reported to have been carrying a second, fall-back offer. In reaction to the STR's abrupt rejection of his first offer, however, he left Washington without presenting a second offer. He said later that the two countries' positions were so far apart that there was no point in continuing the negotiations (*Sankei Shimbun,* 5 April 1979).

The manner in which the talks with Ushiba were terminated was highly public, almost theatrical, and seemed to have been directed toward Congress. In a press release issued after the breakdown, Strauss called Japan's offer "wholly inadequate," the acceptance of which would "allow Japanese firms to bid on a broad range of U.S. government contracts, but would exclude U.S. firms from bidding on key contracts in Japan, such as purchases made by Japan's nationwide Nippon Telephone and Telegraph Company." Strauss was sensitive to the fact that congressional committees were just then holding hearings on his MTN results, and he was conscious of the need to impress them. Therefore, Strauss said in a press release that he would not work for the approval of an unequal agreement. The press release stated that "trade must be a two-way street. When [trade] does not work both ways, there will be no agreement. I do not plan to give Congress a bad agreement. There are too many good things in our trade package to jeopardize it with something which is patently unfair, like the Japanese proposal on government procurement" (STR, 1979).

Privately, Strauss was even harsher, ridiculing the Japanese offer. In meetings on the Hill and with business leaders, he portrayed it as a deliberate attempt to be intransigent. To one group he said, "now how many steel telephone poles do you think we'll sell in Japan, with their steel business. What the hell good does that do us?"

Elizabeth Drew, in a long, in-depth article on Strauss and his operating style, speculated that Strauss wanted a breakdown with Japan at this point. On the day after the talks failed, she noted that Strauss was "particularly interested" in how the press played the story of the breakdown.[2] (It played well: The April 16, 1979 edition of *Business Week* called Japan's exclusion of key NTT contracts "a brilliant bit of evasion.") Drew wrote that "Strauss actually did not want the Japanese to be more forthcoming as yet—that he did not mind having an opportunity to criticize the Japanese." Criticizing Japan served a broad political purpose for Strauss (John Connally seemed to be getting mileage out of it) and was useful in his larger MTN strategy as well. Added Drew, "Strauss saw breaking off the talks as a good move after he had gotten the countervailing duty bill through Congress" (p. 62). Because Strauss was under attack in the House concerning the government procurement code, he may have thought he could help bolster his credibility by giving the Japanese a difficult time.

Although Strauss's congressional concerns seem to have dictated the way in which the March talks broke off, the reason they collapsed was that Japan's offer did not include high-technology equipment. By 1979, as we noted, this had become the STR's major interest in NTT. U.S. officials believed that they had indicated this interest through their frequent request for a meaningful offer from Japan. In talks with the Japanese, STR officials indicated that meaningful meant high-technology telecommunications equipment, but they would not specify for Japan precisely the kinds or types of equipment in which they were interested. There were several reasons for this lack of specificity. First, the government procurement talks to date had been held on an entity, rather than a product-by-product basis. Second, close observation by domestic industry groups had robbed the STR of the flexibility to indicate priority, because that would have meant choosing among the groups. Third, the STR preferred to talk in terms of large, total-dollar figures in order to impress congressional observers. Finally, STR officials did not want to indicate the United States's bottom-line position to the Japanese, believing that it would result in a reduced Japanese offer. Nevertheless, despite this ambiguity in U.S. demands, the interest of these officials was clearly in high technology. The fact that none of these items was included in Japan's offer led to the breakdown.

The Summit Linkage Becomes Important

When the negotiations between Ushiba and Strauss ended in failure, time began to run out, and this worked against the quiet resolution of the NTT dispute. One important approaching deadline was the completion of the MTN, which was scheduled for mid-April. Japanese and U.S. officials hoped to complete the NTT negotiations in time for the signing of the MTN package in Geneva because NTT was the last remaining issue between the two countries. Its resolution would allow both countries to sign the agreement in complete accord.

More important than the mere approach of the MTN deadline, however, was its coinciding with a major U.S.-Japanese bilateral summit meeting, scheduled for the first week of May. Ironically, it seems that neither President Carter nor Prime Minister Ohira was enthusiastic about the May meeting. Japanese press reports as late as February, for instance, indicated that Ohira was reluctant to make the trip, believing it was unnecessary because he would see the president at the Advanced Industrial Nations Summit in June (*Japan Economic Journal,* 27 February 1979). President Carter seems to have shared these sentiments. Nevertheless, once the bilateral meeting was scheduled, it became a deadline NTT negotiators could not ignore—albeit for different reasons.

Japanese officials were anxious to avoid any discussion of the NTT issue at the summit. They felt that a relatively minor trade problem such as this should not be the subject of a meeting of heads of state. More importantly, they were anxious to protect the prime minister and avoid an embarrassing confrontation. Because summit meetings are politically important events in Japan, it would damage Ohira if he were seen as capitulating to U.S. pressure in such a public forum. Hence, the Japanese wanted either to settle the issue before the summit (the preferred route because it would set a good tone for the meeting) or somehow postpone its resolution until after the bilateral session. The Americans, on the other hand, could not fail to see the tactical advantage in Japan's desire to settle the issue before the summit. This awareness was particularly strong among the line officers in the STR who were handling the NTT negotiations.

Contributing to the tension created by the chronological linkage of the NTT negotiations and the bilateral summit meeting was a set of unrelated macroeconomic issues between the two countries, which were to be discussed at the bilateral meeting and which thus increased the summit's importance. Specifically, U.S. economic officials feared that the Japanese government that had taken office in December 1978 was changing Japanese macroeconomic policies in a way that might contribute to a worsening bilateral trade balance. In December, at his first news conference, the newly elected prime minister seemed to abandon the important 7 percent growth-rate pledge that former Prime Minister Fukuda had made at the Bonn summit. U.S. officials had viewed Japan's growth pledge as part of a multilateral package that had been negotiated at Bonn, and they believed that the multilateral bargain lost its meaning if one country could renounce its commitments unilaterally. Administration officials believe that, unless they could convince Japan of the growing U.S. concern about these problems and could get a Japanese commitment to change course, political strain between the two countries would inevitably increase.

Congressional activity and anger at the worsening bilateral trade problems added to these administration fears. The White House believed that, during this period, the danger lay in the fact that the Congress might pass a very strong anti-Japan resolution, such as Senator Bensten was threatening to·introduce.

White House officials, particularly Ambassador Henry Owen, who was then coordinator for international economic policy, felt that the administration would not be able to stay on top of this developing domestic political problem unless it could get a strong commitment from the Japanese to take corrective economic action. Owen believed that constant U.S. pressure on Japan to correct a variety of specific trade problems could damage their relationship. Yet, before the administration could let these issues pass, they needed a Japanese commitment to deal with the key macroeconomic policy issues. Using the May summit as the deadline to force the Japanese to take action, Owen tried to negotiate the language of that commitment with Japanese officials.

The Japanese Cabinet Meets Again

There was one positive outcome from the failed Ushiba-Strauss talks: for the first time, U.S. negotiators stated explicitly what they wanted from NTT. Until then, Japan had been responding to vague U.S. requests for a meaningful offer. Many Japanese officials, particularly political leaders, had felt that just the fact that NTT was mentioned in the offer was sufficiently meaningful, especially considering NTT's strong resistance to any offer whatsoever and the pressure the government had had to apply to obtain what they did get. Hence, when the offer failed—or more precisely was said to be totally inadequate—these officials were surprised. The prime minister, for instance, speaking before the Upper House Budget Committee, said that he was shocked at the failure of the talks, adding that he had expected the dispute to be settled at the negotiations (*Daily Yomiuri,* 3 April 1979).

One initial reaction to the breakdown was resistance on the part of some Japanese who believed that Strauss had deliberately caused the collapse of the talks in order to gain a tactical advantage. This group initially wanted to postpone any further discussion of the matter until after the summit meeting in order to remove this form of U.S. leverage. Supporting this view was an article in the evening edition of the *Asahi* newspaper, which reported on March 30 that Strauss's intention was to use the U.S.-Japanese summit to press Japan for new concessions in order to appease Congress and get the MTN passed. The newspaper noted that there were elements within the government that wanted to deny Strauss this chance. It reported growing sentiment for postponing the final resolution of the NTT problem until 1981, when the government procurement code was scheduled to take effect. On the other hand, there were those in the government who believed that the festering dispute might disrupt the prime minister's trip. On March 30, the chief cabinet secretary admitted as much at a press conference, where he acknowledged that the government was worried about the collapse and its effect on the summit (*Asahi Evening News*, 31 March 1979).

In order to assess what had gone wrong, Prime Minister Ohira huddled with his advisors, including Ambassador Yasukawa and senior MFA officials. These officials described to Ohira what they saw as an increasingly harsh anti-Japan attitude in the U.S. Congress and advised that something needed to be done soon to alleviate it. The prime minister did not express any concrete opinions at this point. Instead, he decided to postpone the formulation of a formal response until after listening to a detailed account of the failed talks from Ushiba, who was due to return on April 1 (*Nihon Keizai Shimbun,* 31 March 1979). The press speculated that any further concessions by Japan would be difficult because of NTT's determined opposition.

The prime minister met with Ushiba on April 2. Foreign Minister Sonoda was also present for part of this meeting. Ushiba reported that U.S. demands had been strong, particularly for high-technology goods such as computers. The talks failed, he said, because Japan did not indicate whether NTT would allow foreign manufacturers to bid on any mainline telecommunications equipment. Ushiba also said that, if Japan could improve its offer to about $6 or $6.5 billion by including some high-technology goods, the negotiations could be settled (*Japan Times,* 3 April 1979). Based on his conversations with Ushiba, Prime Minister Ohira ordered the foreign minister to explore further the U.S. position during his scheduled visit to Washington on April 5. He especially asked the foreign minister to look for ways to finally settle the procurement matter. This policy was confirmed the following day at a cabinet meeting, which was convened in order to hear Ushiba's report and discuss the NTT problem.

At this point, Ohira was apparently leaning toward making further concessions to the U.S. request for the inclusion of high-technology goods in Japan's government procurement offer. The foreign minister hinted at this during the cabinet meeting, when he asked the assembled ministers for their cooperation. He said that, because Japan faced the difficult task of improving its offer in terms of both quantity and quality, he would need the cooperation of all related ministries (*Nihon Keizai Shimbun,* 3 April 1979). However, no decision was reached at this point. The cabinet adjourned with the agreement to await the foreign minister's return from the United States before formulating a response.

Despite the appearance of flexibility in Japan, there was still some uncertainty in official circles concerning the U.S. officials' motives and sincerity in their negotiations. The feeling was that, if the United States were interested in settling the problem and willing to compromise to achieve that goal, Japan would improve its offer. However, if the United States continued to view the negotiations in terms of the domestic political advantage to be gained, then Japan might not move any further. The foreign minister alluded to this continuing uncertainty in an interview on the eve of his departure for the United States. He said that it was necessary for Japan to find out whether it was better for domestic purposes for both sides "to be fiercely pitted against each other," or whether it was better to strive for an early solution, with both sides making compromises. If it turned out that it was better to continue the confrontation, then Japan could "toe the mark" for a while and look for a solution after the Tokyo summit and U.S. presidential elections. On the other hand, Sonoda said that if it appeared better to settle the problem quickly, then it would be his job to carefully read U.S. aims, especially concerning the monetary amount and the extent of mainline liberalization to be offered (*Yomiuri Shimbun,* 5 April 1979).

Thus, when the foreign minister arrived in Washington, he was looking for signals. In other words, he wanted to know if the United States wanted a settlement and if they were prepared to accept a compromise in order to achieve one. During his meetings with senior U.S. officials, Sonoda believed that he received affirmative answers to both questions.

During four days of talks, Sonoda met with Secretary of State Vance, Treasury Secretary Blumenthal, Commerce Secretary Kreps, and Special Trade Representative Strauss. In all these meetings, Sonoda was asked to convey back to Tokyo a sense of urgency about the escalating trade problems. In particular, he was urged to try to settle the NTT problem before the prime minister's visit (*The Washington Post,* 11 April 1979).

The meeting with Trade Representative Strauss was especially crucial. Sonoda pressed the STR for a list of products the United States wanted included in Japan's procurement offer, as well as an indication of priority. Sonoda indicated that this information was an essential ingredient in the consensus-building process back in Japan.

Under instructions from Strauss, an STR staff official compiled a list of U.S. demands regarding NTT, which consisted of all the major high-technology items procured by the company. This included switching equipment, carriers, transmission equipment, cables, data-transmission equipment, telegraph equipment, and PBX exchanges. Strauss read the list to the foreign minister, but he would not indicate which were priority items. Instead, he is reported to have commented that "these are the kinds of things your offer should include."

Apparently as a result of Strauss's refusal to indicate some priority in the request list, Foreign Minister Sonoda returned to Tokyo confident that, as long as Japan assembled a reasonable package that included some of the items Strauss had mentioned, a settlement could be reached.

The Final Drama Begins as Japan Prepares its Offer

With the return to Japan of Foreign Minister Sonoda, the effort to convince NTT to make the necessary concessions began. This difficult task fell to the politicians—particularly Prime Minister Ohira, his chief cabinet secretary, and the chairman of the party's research council.

The key meeting was held on Friday, April 13, the day after the foreign minister's return. When the cabinet met to hear his report in the morning, Sonoda told the ministers that the U.S. attitude toward the NTT matter was extremely strong and that something had to be done before the prime minister's trip to Washington. Sonoda stressed the need for further concessions. The posts minister, however, continued to vigorously oppose the idea of any further concessions by NTT. He said that there was still strong opposition within the party to opening NTT's high-technology contracts and that any further opening would seriously damage many small- and medium-size suppliers. This attitude may have reflected increased political protests by NTT's related trade associations and unions. In any event, as a result of Shirahama's opposition, the meeting ended without conclusion.

However, after the inconclusive cabinet meeting the discussion continued when Shirahama met privately with Research Council Chairman Komoto. Komoto, who had been in close contact with Chief Cabinet Secretary Rokusuke Tanaka, applied strong pressure on the posts minister, reflecting the fact that the senior party leadership had decided that the issue must be settled. Komoto insisted that NTT must open up $900 million in contracts in addition to the $600 million already offered. Komoto also insisted that the items to be included in the additional offer should be of a high-technology nature.

Komoto's intervention was the result of his institutional responsibility as coordinator of internal party decision making. However, he also seems to have had strong personal views on the NTT issue and, more generally, on the need for Japan to develop greater international competitiveness through open competition. As a businessman-turned-politician, he was said to be concerned about the overcartelization of Japan's economy. As a former businessman, he also had confidence in Japan's technology and was aware that open bidding would not result in a swamping of Japanese companies by foreign competitors. On this latter point, he is reported to have remarked favorably on Nippon Steel's attitude toward government procurement. The large steel company had taken the position that, since it was allowed to bid on government contracts throughout the world, foreigners should be allowed to bid in Japan. "This open spirit was important," Komoto said, "living in a hothouse is no good" (*Nikkan Kogyo Shimbun,* 19 April 1979).

Thus, following his meeting with Komoto, Posts Minister Shirahama contacted NTT President Akigusa to suggest that he begin formulating a concrete list of items that could be opened. Shirahama left the choice of items required to meet the supplemental goal of $900 million up to the NTT president. In a meeting with his vice-president, Akigusa suggested that they make an offer composed largely of electronic cable. The vice-president concurred, noting that the inclusion of central phone equipment, such as computers and switching equipment, must continue to be excepted. Later that evening, NTT officials tried to gather support for their proposed new offer by meeting with eight LDP Dietmen who were sympathetic to their cause. Meanwhile, Posts Minister Shirahama met with business figures from NTT's major supplier firms, including the presidents of Oki Electric, Sumitomo Electric, NEC, and Hitachi to ask them to prepare for open bidding. He met strong opposition. The businessmen argued that it was a national disgrace that unilateral U.S. pressure was forcing Japan to become the only advanced country in the world to use an open-bidding system for its telephone network (*Nikkan Kogyo Shimbun,* 16 April 1979).

At this point, one factor complicating the internal Japanese negotiations was the extremely technical nature of the issue. By now, the discussions between both the United States and Japan and between the LDP and NTT had begun to revolve around the definition of what constituted mainline telephone equipment. Until this point, NTT had argued that, for technical reasons, no mainline equipment, which it described as phone-to-phone or anything directly used in transmitting telephone calls, could be opened to competitive bidding. When it became apparent upon Sonoda's return that some of this equipment would have to be offered, discussions centered on defining further the term *mainline.* Shirahama noted that, because U.S. demands were now suggesting the inclusion of mainline items in Japan's offer, the relevant cabinet officials would have to decide how far mainline extends technologically and then try to convince NTT to make the necessary concessions (*Nihon Keizai Shimbun,* 14 April 1979). Because these men were politicians who were not versed in the technical problems surrounding telephone procurement, however, they had difficulty in convincing NTT.

After the meeting between Shirahama and Komoto, NTT deliberated for five days on what to include in its supplemental offer. NTT's offer was finally ready by April 18, less than two weeks before the prime minister's departure for Washington. NTT's new offer was presented to Shirahama, Sonoda, and Komoto by ten LDP Dietmen. NTT had produced the requested $900 million, but whether or not it was sufficient to satisfy the senior leadership remained to be seen.

Apparently, the offer was not sufficient, because Komoto phoned Akigusa the following morning to tell him that more was needed. Komoto told the NTT president that it would not be necessary to include computers but that more electronic cable, carrier equipment, and microwave transmitters and receivers were required. These last items were part of the mainline NTT had vowed to protect, and it was apparent that more pressure would be needed in order to force the inclusion of these items into the offer. Thus, the stage for direct intervention by the prime minister had arrived.

On the morning of the twentieth, Chief Cabinet Secretary Tanaka, apparently under direct orders from Ohira, summoned NTT President Akigusa to the prime minister's residence and told him to include an additional $400 million in the offer, including the items Komoto had mentioned the previous day. Akigusa accepted the government's request, and a new NTT offer was conveyed by letter later that afternoon to the Foreign Ministry, where the complete negotiating package was being assembled.

The next morning, in a traditional Japanese response, the corporation president offered his resignation as a gesture of accepting responsibility for the trouble he had caused the government with his recent adamant opposition.

Although Akigusa's resignation could have created delicate political problems for the Ohira government, most government officials were relieved that the company had finally capitulated. At last, with the inclusion of these important mainline high-technology items, Japanese officials believed they could settle the negotiations with the United States. Japan's offer had now improved in both quantity and quality, and the total government procurement offer was now close to $7 billion, including NTT's $1.9 billion and increased offers from the other public corporations. With the inclusion of the high-technology items, government officials felt they were being responsive to the signals they had received at the Ushiba-Strauss and Sonoda-Strauss meetings. Thus, confident that a settlement was near, Hisashi Owada, a senior Foreign Ministry official, left Tokyo on the evening of April 20 to carry the new offer to the United States.

The Final Negotiations

On Monday morning, April 23, little more than one week before the prime minister's arrival, the talks began with a Japanese presentation of the list of items that they were prepared to open to competitive bidding under the rules of the government procurement code. STR officials spent the entire day reviewing the offer, a complicated one that was presented in very great detail. STR officials checked it for what was not being offered in order to determine what was being excluded. Even these STR officials were now anxious to reach a settlement, because they were under pressure from officials in the State Department and the White House, who were arguing that the Japanese offer was a good-faith effort and one that, if rejected, could disrupt the prime minister's visit. Said one STR official who participated in the review process, "there was none of the late March theatrics involved here. We all wanted to reach a settlement, but we couldn't accept anything less than a good offer." After careful review, the officials decided it just was not an acceptable offer. Key elements, including central switching equipment, were missing. Despite the size of the offer, the absence of these elements made it impossible to justify a settlement to industry and congressional critics, who were worried about being locked out of Japan's high-technology markets.

U.S. officials from the STR argued that the U.S. telecommunications market was open to Japanese products while Japan's market remained closed. Acceptance of Japan's latest offer would not rectify this situation, and it would effectively shut out U.S. products in precisely those areas in which the United States was most competitive, namely digital switching equipment and computers. It was especially disturbing, they said, that Japan's offer indicated no intention of opening these areas to competitive bidding in the future.

Japanese officials responded that their offer had been put together after careful consideration based on the outcome of the Ushiba-Strauss talks held in March. They said it represented Japan's best offer and that it had been made under difficult circumstances. To have it rejected by the United States was most unusual. In addition, they said, compared to the offer made by the EC and other countries, Japan's offer was very generous. Finally, they noted that, to date, the United States had said nothing firm about digital switching equipment and computers and that to introduce these new demands at such a late date was highly irregular.

Strauss responded that, while this final point was technically correct, the United States had believed all along that Japan understood that these high-technology items were the object of U.S. interest. The United States also recognized, Strauss said, that Japan's offer was good compared to others, but a special effort by Japan was needed because Japan enjoyed such a large trade surplus with the United States, particularly in the telecommunications sector.

On the evening of the second day of talks, April 24, Japanese officials in Tokyo were informed of the United States' dissatisfaction with Japan's offer and of Strauss's new demands for computers and switching equipment. This new information started an important train of events. Upon hearing of Strauss's new demands, an official in Prime Minister Ohira's inner circle made one last effort to force NTT to capitulate—such was the desire for a settlement. Meeting with NTT's president in a Tokyo hotel, the prime minister's representative pressed NTT to make a final concession on computers. This effort failed, however, when NTT refused to include any further items in its offer.

Meanwhile, some officials in the Japanese government reacted angrily to the rejection of Japan's offer and the introduction of Strauss's last minute demands. This attitude was partially revealed in an article in *The Washington Post* on April 26. "Top officials of the Japanese government," the newspaper reported, "have been uncharacteristically blunt in conversations with American reporters, insisting that the U.S. demands are unreasonable and claiming that they amount to direct intervention in domestic affairs."[3] This same attitude was also present in the Diet where, on April 25, Prime Minister Ohira was strongly criticized by the socialist members for making too many concessions in the face of unreasonable U.S. pressure.

At eight o'clock on the evening of April 25, Prime Minister Ohira gathered in emergency session with some of his closest advisors, including Chief Cabinet Secretary Tanaka, Ambassadors Yasukawa and Ushiba, and other Foreign Ministry officials. Ohira had called the meeting in order to assess the situation and to respond to a cable from the Japanese embassy in Washington requesting further instructions. The consensus of the meeting was that no further concessions could be made by Japan. The assembled officials felt they had made every effort to make a good offer that was responsive to U.S. signals. Any further concessions by Japan on the eve of the summit would put the prime minister in a politically untenable position. The answer to further U.S. requests had to be no. Although this was not a formal cabinet meeting, it was reported as such in several Japanese dailies the following morning.

Strauss, upon hearing of the apparent Japanese cabinet decision, was reported by one high official to be livid. Working with officials in the State Department and White House, however, Strauss made one final effort to save the negotiations by conveying a new U.S. proposal to the Japanese. The United States would accept Japan's latest offer, provided Japan would pledge to move toward a full opening of the NTT market by 1985, at which time the government procurement code was scheduled for review. The Japanese embassy, apparently under instruction from Tokyo, replied that the negotiations had ended and did not formally recognize Strauss's proposal. Thus, five days before the prime minister's arrival an impasse had been reached.

The breakdown of talks produced a harsh response in Congress. On April 26, Senator Robert Dole called Prime Minister Ohira's refusal to make further concessions "untimely, ill-advised, and provocative." He warned that the prime minister's action could lead to a "legislative backlash" that could jeopardize not only U.S.-Japanese trade relations, but the political alliance as well. Congressman James Jones, chairman of the House Ways and Means Committee Task Force on U.S.-Japan Trade, said the breakdown was caused by a Japanese "attitude of intransigence" that could only heighten protectionist sentiment in Congress. On the House floor, Representative Bill Frenzel, a member of the task force, said that the impasse on government procurement could produce "the most serious trade crisis in this country . . . since I have been in Congress". The United States, he said, "was running out of patience," and the Congress would have to deal with the problem legislatively if it were not solved soon (*Congressional Record,* 26 April 1979, pp. S4828, H2357, H2358).

Strauss may have partly contributed to this outburst. On the day after the talks broke down, for example, in a closed session before the Senate Governmental Affairs Committee, Strauss described the negotiations in terms that reflected unkindly on the Japanese. At a luncheon with a group of reporters on April 25, moreover, Strauss used colorful language to describe his problems with Japan. "I'm doing the bastards a favor," *The Washington Star* reported him as saying, "If I take their deal to Congress, Congress will kick them in the ass and raise sanctions against Japanese imports."[4] While perhaps not unusual for the special trade representative, this language nevertheless angered those Japanese who heard reports of it.

One reason for Strauss's strong reaction was undoubtedly simple frustration at the collapse of a long and difficult negotiation. Another may have stemmed from rumors that the Japanese had wanted a collapse because they hoped to be able to negotiate a better deal with Strauss's successor (Strauss had been appointed special ambassador to the Middle East the previous week). According to reports of private conversations of the STR, these rumors apparently bothered Strauss. *The Washington Post,* for example, reported him as saying, "The Japanese are misreading the situation. They seem to feel that if I step out of the [trade negotiations] picture, they will have someone easier to deal with, but Congress will be even tougher on them."[5]

By Friday, April 27, however, Strauss had changed his tone, making a strong effort to change the mood of the breakdown. In testimony before the House Subcommittee on Trade, he tried to calm the congressional storm over NTT. "It is my genuine and sincere belief," he said, "that the Japanese have tried and are trying very hard to meet our minimal requirements." He remarked that the press's treatment of the breakdown had been "skewed" and "misconstrued." The Japanese had genuinely tried to meet U.S. demands, he concluded, but they had been unable to do so "because of the same kind of political pressures that we face in this country."

Strauss's efforts to calm the waters he himself had muddied resulted from a number of factors, including Strauss's inevitable calming down and realization that the Japanese had made a good-faith effort to negotiate. Congressional concerns were also important in shaping Strauss's new attitude. In particular, Strauss received private assurances from the Congress that the implementing legislation for government procurement would be written to require reciprocity with Japan and so he was able to hint at this legislative escape route when he testified before the Senate on April 27. He said, "We will solve that problem of government procurement somewhere, somehow, sometime. If we don't, we will deal with it in this country to see that the agreement works equally both ways or not at all." He made similar comments before the House, noting that the United States "will resolve or deal with the problem here at home in the implementing legislation" (*The Washington Post,* 28 April 1979). The solution was found in the language of the Trade Agreements Act of 1979, which empowered the President to close U.S. procurement opportunities to countries that do not reciprocate in the area of appropriate goods, which the Congress defined as heavy electrical, telecommunications, and transportation equipment. Confident that this legislative route was open to him, Strauss was better prepared to compromise.

Fortunately, the groundwork had also been laid. Since the collapse of the talks on April 24, State Department and White House officials had been working to reach a compromise solution before the summit. Particularly important was a meeting between Henry Owen and Hisashi Owada shortly after the breakdown. At this meeting, it became clear to both sides that it would not be possible to reach a substantive solution before the summit. Politically, the Japanese could not make further concessions, and the United States could not accept Japan's current offer as final. The answer, these officials believed, was in some form of procedural solution—some form of agreement that could point the way toward a settlement after the tension of the moment had subsided. In order for this solution to be made possible, it was imperative for Strauss—the only one among the Americans who could make the decision—to have another chance to meet with the Japanese. Since Owada, who had previously been an effective negotiator, had returned to Japan shortly after the above-mentioned meeting, State and White House officials urged the Japanese to have Owada return to the United States with the prime minister. This was an unusual request, considering Owada's close association with Ohira's rival, former Prime Minister Fukuda. However, the Japanese agreed to the request, thus indicating the extent of their desire for a settlement.

On Sunday morning, April 29, three STR officials, including Ambassador Alonzo McDonald, deputy special trade representative, met with Henry Owen to discuss a possible solution to the NTT problem. Although some line officials in the STR were reportedly still favoring a hardline U.S. position, the consensus of this meeting was that a compromise was needed if a settlement of some sort was to be reached before the summit. The idea for a procedural type of solution, which had first come up at Owen's meeting with Owada, was the most promising. At this point, Ambassador McDonald, who was well-versed in the NTT problem and who had a strong business background, played a central role in translating the general idea into specifics to fit the case at hand. The compromise position these officials worked out called for Japan to agree to the specific negotiating objective of mutual reciprocity in access to each other's markets, and it committed the Japanese to establishing a work schedule for negotiations to reach that objective before January 1, 1981. The proposed compromise agreement also called upon NTT to prepare for the eventual implementation of this mutual-reciprocity agreement by taking steps to facilitate the purchase of U.S. telecommunications equipment. If the Japanese could agree to this U.S. compromise plan, the summit meeting between the president and the prime minister could proceed undisturbed.

On Tuesday, May 1—the day before the summit—Strauss and Owada met in secret session to discuss the U.S. proposal. At this meeting, a tentative agreement was reached whereby mutual reciprocity would be the objective of future negotiations to be opened after the summit meeting. Thus, with just hours to spare, as one close observer recalled, a compromise was reached—an agreement to agree, it was called later—and the bilateral summit would begin.

Agreeing to Agree

At the meeting on May 1, Strauss expressed his understanding that Japan had various domestic difficulties that prevented a rapid or sudden opening of the total telecommunications market at the present time. Accordingly, the United States was ready to accept Japan's offer of April 24, including the portion offered by NTT. However, Strauss also noted that, if Japan did not indicate a future willingness to open the market for products in which the United States was most competitive, it would cause him difficult domestic problems. Hence, he wanted Japan to agree to the continuation of negotiations with the object of attaining mutual reciprocity in access to each other's markets by January 1, 1981.

Owada explained this new U.S. proposal to the prime minister and foreign minister. They decided that the problem needed careful study and that there was insufficient time for this before the bilateral summit, which was scheduled to begin the following day. Ohira agreed, therefore, only to continue negotiations. In his meetings with President Carter, he indicated that he would try to solve the problem before Carter's scheduled visit to Japan in June. This permitted the bilateral summit to proceed without a major confrontation over NTT.

Returning from a trip to China on June 2, 1979, Strauss stopped in Tokyo to sign an agreement on NTT and on other related items. The agreement was based on the offer made by the United States to Japan on May 1, but its details had been ironed out in mid-May during private discussions between Japanese and U.S. officials. The United States and Japan agreed that "mutual reciprocity should be provided among Japan, the United States and other major countries in access of opportunities to each other's markets, including the market for telecommunications." The agreement established a work schedule for negotiations to achieve that obective. The negotiations would begin in July 1979, after the Tokyo summit of advanced industrial nations, with a view toward reaching a final agreement not later than December 31, 1980, the effective date of the code. In the event no agreement could be reached by that deadline, Japanese firms would be barred from the U.S. government procurement market, as specified in the MTN implementing legislation passed by the Congress.

This agreement cleared the way for the Tokyo summit to proceed unimpeded by the NTT dispute, but it did not settle the basic issue at stake: To what extent and for what items would NTT's procurements be bound by the rules of open bidding set forth in the government procurement code?

Epilogue: The Final Settlement

Negotiations between the United States and Japan resumed at the working level after the Tokyo summit and continued into 1980. However, little progress was made. Because at that time the deadline for reaching a settlement was a year and a half away, no immediate pressure was placed on the negotiators to reach a final agreement. In addition, a potentially serious misunderstanding between the Americans and Japanese arose concerning the interpretation of mutual reciprocity under the June 2 agreement. As noted above, the agreement applied this term to "access opportunities to each other's markets, including the market for telecommunications." It added: "The government of Japan considers the access opportunities offered by U.S. telecommunications enterprises as relevant" to the final settlement.

Japanese delegates, and particularly NTT officials, interpreted these clauses to mean that NTT should have to open its procurement procedures only to the extent that U.S. telecommunications companies were opened.

As a result, many of the post-June negotiating sessions were devoted to detailed examinations of the American Telephone and Telegraph's buying and procurement practices in an effort to determine the degree of openness in the United States's telecommunications market.

U.S. officials came to regret the reciprocity language in the June 2 agreement, at least insofar as it referred to telecommunications, because they felt it detracted from the central issue of the negotiations: the size of Japan's overall government procurement compared to that of the United States. U.S. officials believed that Japanese counterparts were mistaken in focusing on the respective degrees of openness in each country's telecommunications markets, even though they also believed that the U.S. market was in fact more open than the telecommunications market in Japan. One way that U.S. officials tried to refocus attention on what they believed to be the central issue of the negotiations was by taking the negotiating authority away from the telecommunications and electronics specialists within the STR's office and transferring it to officials whose primary responsibility had been the government procurement code.

In the spring and early summer of 1980, after the working-level discussions had been refocused on the extent of Japan's overall government procurement offer, the positions taken by the Japanese government and NTT began to soften. As the final December deadline neared, the government naturally became concerned about another embarassing blow-up on this issue. In March, Ambassador Takeshi Yasukawa, who was then special representative for trade negotiations, conferred with Prime Minister Ohira before making a trip to the United States to discuss the NTT issue with U.S. officials. At the time, Yasukawa said that prolonging the disposition of the NTT issue was not in Japan's best interests and that it should be settled as soon as possible. Prime Minister Ohira said he hoped the issue could be settled by the summer.

During this period, not only did the Japanese government's position appear to soften but the NTT position did also. There were several reasons for this change in NTT's outlook. After the signing of the June 2 agreement, the NTT issue dropped from public discussion in the United States; the press, congressional figures, and industry sources had little to say publicly on the matter. NTT apparently interpreted this quiet to indicate a lack of U.S. interest in actually penetrating the NTT market. As a result, NTT officials adopted a very tough position in the early post-June negotiations. In fact, however, U.S. officials noted that the reason for the absence of public clamor over the issue was an unusual degree of unity of purpose among the U.S. government, congressional actors, and industry leaders. In any case, by early 1980, NTT officials who were participating in the negotiations slowly came to realize the seriousness of the United States's determination. This gradual educational process apparently helped prepare NTT for the final compromise.

In addition, NTT's position appears to have softened because of increasing domestic attacks against its monopoly practices in Japan. In June, for example, the Administrative Management Agency of the Japanese government issued a report criticizing NTT for its closed procurement practices and inefficient internal management. Thus, the collapse of domestic support for its position may also have contributed to NTT's increasingly conciliatory attitude.

A final factor contributing to movement in the talks was a charge of personnel handling the negotiations in Japan. As a result of a no-confidence vote in the Japanese Diet in May 1980, the second Ohira cabinet fell and new elections were called. During the campaign, Ohira suddenly died, leaving his party leaderless. In the ensuing election, however, the LDP won a substantial majority and after ·intense internal manuevering among the party's faction leaders, Zenko Suzuki was elected as party president and prime minister. In forming his cabinet, Suzuki asked Saburo Okita, who had served as foreign minister in the second Ohira cabinet, to take the post of special representative for trade negotiations.

Okita's appointment as special trade representative was important for several reasons. First, he was able to win the trust of NTT officials. Previously, NTT officials had expressed anxiety about leaving the negotiations in the charge of Foreign Ministry officials or politicians, neither of whom had extensive experience with the many complicated issues concerning telecommunications technology. Okita, on the other hand, was an electrical engineer by training and thus brought to the negotiations a sense of the complexity of the issues involved. Moreover, Okita's father-in-law had been the first president of NTT and the founder of the NTT family system of procurement. NTT officials believed they could trust Okita's handling of the negotiations.

Another reason for Okita's effectiveness was his reputation in the United States as an international economist and his fluency in English. Okita was able to develop a good working rapport with U.S. officials, particularly Special Trade Representative Reubin Askew, who had replaced Robert Strauss, and with several congressional figures. These relationships were useful in convincing U.S. officials to accept the final settlement.

In August 1980, an important series of working-level talks opened in Tokyo between representatives of the United States and Japan. During these talks, U.S. negotiators offered the Japanese examples of complicated procurement methods used in the United States by the Defense Department—methods that allowed for open bidding and at the same time permitted the development of close working relationships with suppliers. U.S. officials believed procedures such as these would satisfy both U.S. and Japanese concerns and still be consistent with the MTN code. U.S. officials offered these suggestions as a result of a new sensitivity to some of NTT's particular concerns. The long negotiating process had proved educational for both sides.

Sometime later, the Japanese introduced a proposal for a three-track procurement system that would permit NTT varying degrees of openness, depending on the level of technological sophistication in the equipment involved. Under this system, the least sophisticated items would be procured through open-bidding procedures, while more sophisticated items would be procured from designated reliable suppliers. Qualified U.S. firms, however, would be able to become reliable suppliers. U.S. officials were pleased by this new Japanese approach and decided to use it as the basis for further negotiations.

In September 1980, Special Trade Representative Okita met with Askew in New York City to discuss the NTT negotiations. The friendly tone of the talks was indicated by the fact that the two men attended a baseball game together. On the way back to the hotel after the game, Askew asked Okita to ride with him. Privately, the two men discussed the remaining problems. Askew emphasized the importance of arriving at an agreement that allowed U.S. companies opportunities to compete on the full range of NTT's procurements. After returning to his hotel, Okita had a long session with his staff, at which it was agreed that further efforts should be made to bring the talks to a successful conclusion.

In early October, the Japanese government revised its proposal to open NTT's procurements. The three-track system introduced earlier was maintained. Procurement would be divided into three parts: competitive bidding, negotiated bids, and joint research and development leading to procurement. Although it retained the original basic framework, the new offer raised the amount of procurement to be made under the competitive-bidding heading and eased the language for foreign participation in negotiated bids and for research procurement. Under the previous plan, Japan had offered to place $600 million of equipment under competitive bidding, but none of the equipment offered represented sophisticated telecommunications equipment. In the new proposal, this amount was raised to approximately $1.5 billion by including a substantial portion of the high-technology equipment that had previously been earmarked for inclusion in the negotiated bid portion of the new procurement system.

This new proposal was discussed at a second Okita-Askew meeting in late October. At that time, the U.S. side maintained its position that all NTT procurement must be opened to foreign competition, but it added that, with modifications, the Japanese three-track system would be acceptable. Thus, the two governments were gradually narrowing their differences and approaching a final settlement. However, domestic problems in both countries threatened to upset the talks until the very last moment.

In the United States, representatives of the electronics and telecommunications industries were unhappy with the evolving settlement. They were particularly concerned about the complexity of the proposed Japanese package, fearing that it would provide NTT with sufficient means to continue to exclude U.S. firms from their market. Congressional figures were also reportedly concerned about the extent of NTT's willingness to allow U.S. firms to become involved in research and development projects. As a result of suspicion over the reliability of Japan's new offer, some U.S. industry representatives preferred that no deal be reached. In that case, Japanese firms could be excluded from the U.S. government procurement market under the terms of the 1979 MTN-implementing legislation. Japanese officials tried to ease these U.S. concerns. They lobbied their U.S. counterparts to accept the emerging package by arguing that the NTT negotiations were between governments, not with NTT, and that the Japanese government would stand behind any agreement that was reached and would see that it was faithfully implemented. In the end, this argument seems to have won the day, and U.S. government officials were able to persuade domestic actors to accept the deal.

In Japan, an even stickier problem developed. When the Japanese government submitted its Tokyo-Round-implementing legislation to the Diet for ratification in 1979, it had promised several important committees that, in return for prompt ratification, it would see to it that the formal government procurement code would not be applied to the full range of NTT procurements in any eventual settlement of the NTT matter. (This was a sensitive point for the Diet because neither the United States nor any of the European countries were putting their telecommunications entities under the code.) The United States, on the other hand, had long been committed to full coverage under the multilateral code. This issue was finally resolved through semantics: In the final agreement, one-half of NTT's procurement is formally under the provisions of the code; the other half is subject to the full obligations of the agreement but is not formally under the code. This formula was greeted with some skepticism in the United States, where it contributed to the fears concerning NTT's sincerity in implementing the agreement. In the end, however, the solution to the problem was accepted by both sides.

After a final series of negotiations in November, at which the last details were ironed out, and a meeting between Okita and Askew in Williamsburg, Virginia, a final agreement settling the government procurement issue was reached on December 18. As a result of this agreement, Japan offered to open more than $8 billion of government procurement to international competition on a nondiscriminatory basis. Of this total, $3.3 billion was accounted for by NTT purchases. About $1.5 billion of this was included under the first track of the three-track system: competitive bidding procedures subject to the final provisions of the MTN code. The remainder of NTT procurement, about $1.8 billion, was divided between the negotiated bids and joint research and development. These categories were not under the formal code, but instead were covered by a bilateral agreement between the United States and Japan.

Conclusions

To sum up, the confrontation between the United States and Japan over NTT was not initiated as a result of the inherent importance of the industry involved. Telecommunications is an industry of the future and one in which the United States is highly competitive. Japanese companies are also competitive, and, in recent years, they have been able to make important inroads into the U.S. market. However, when the United States initially raised the subject of NTT in July 1978, during the course of government procurement negotiation, U.S. interest in NTT was not focused on telecommunications or high technology, per se. Rather, as we saw, the request for NTT's inclusion in the code resulted from the United States's desire to have Japan's overall offer improved.

Nevertheless, as the negotiations dragged on, U.S. officials and labor and private-sector leaders became concerned about the implications of Japanese competition in this high-technology sector. This concern, together with frustration at the slow pace of negotiations, contributed to the crisis that developed in April 1979. How did this happen? There are lessons to be gained in each phase of the dispute's development.

In the first phase, the U.S. request for the inclusion of NTT under the code assumed an ability on the part of Japanese government to deliver the requested concessions. When that government did not deliver NTT concessions, U.S. officials believed Japan was deliberately being uncooperative. As we saw, however, the Japanese government has limited influence over NTT, even though it is a wholly owned government corporation. This fact suggests two lessons for the United States: first, it must learn patience when dealing with Japan, and second, it must learn more about Japan—about the structure of power and influence within the Japanese government and between the government and the public corporations. When requesting changes in long-standing Japanese practices that act as informal barriers to trade, the United States should not expect too much too soon. The infamous Japanese monolith, "Japan, Inc.," does not exist. Japanese government officials cannot order public corporations—much less private corporations—to change practices that the companies consider to be in their best interests. This does not mean that the Japanese government should do nothing. The Japanese must work to remove barriers to trade by using the levers of pressure and persuasion available to any market-economy type of government. It is particularly important that the Japanese government make these efforts in the high-technology sector, where a protected market can contribute to significant competitive advantages. However, at the same time, the United States must recognize that making these changes, if they can be made, will take time.

A corollary lesson exists for Japan. It is a lesson that, if followed, would have slowed the escalation of the dispute. Specifically, the Japanese government must start the domestic process of persuasion earlier and in response to less overt forms of U.S. pressure. Although NTT is isolated from most forms of direct government control, it is not immune to high-level and persistent persuasion. Unfortunately, the Japanese government generally sent only mid-level officers to negotiate with the public corporation during the summer of 1978. This was a time when U.S. demands for NTT were still unfocused and more flexible. If higher-level officials had perceived the importance of the issue more clearly and had made greater efforts to persuade NTT to be flexible during this early phase, a number of subsequent difficulties could have been avoided. U.S. frustration at a perceived lack of Japanese government action, for example, might have been muted. More importantly, early action to persuade NTT might have helped avoid some of the confrontations that took place in the second phase.

In particular, if NTT had been better prepared, or softened up, before its meetings with the TFC group and the congressional task-force members, the confrontations that occurred in those meetings could have been avoided. A more reasonable position by NTT at that point might also have eliminated the symbolic importance attached to the issue by these U.S. groups.

In the early part of the third phase, we saw that the Japanese government began belated but very determined efforts to pressure NTT to concede. The United States should have done all it could to aid those efforts. Specifically, the United States should have been more attentive to the dynamics of the Japanese decision-making process. Had it done so, the growing sense of frustration found in the United States might have been alleviated. In February 1979, for example, U.S. officials were frustrated when Foreign Ministry Official Oki had nothing to offer during his trip to the United States. Closer attention to Japan's decision-making process, however, would have revealed that Oki was on a reconnaissance mission designed only to test the strength of the United States's resolve.

The United States could have helped the Japanese government in its efforts to persuade NTT by making specific demands whenever possible and by refraining from changing or increasing its demands during the course of the negotiations. This would not always have been easy. As previously noted, there are often legitimate reasons for avoiding specificity (the reluctance to choose between the demands of competing constituents) and for changing demands (the availability of new information or analysis). Nevertheless, a specific demand repeated in a firm and unyielding, but noninflammatory, style would help those Japanese leaders favoring concession in their job of persuading reluctant Japanese to concede.

In the third phase, as we saw, it became impossible to quietly resolve the NTT dispute once it became linked with the approaching summit meetings. Although this linkage was partly accidental and not the product of a conscious strategy, its presence in the final stage of the talks added to the strain between the two nations. In the future, similar linkages between a specific negotiation and a broader Japanese goal, such as a successful summit meeting, should be avoided where possible, because they generate widespread resentment in Japan. The United States should work to avoid any perception of linkage because it is counterproductive. A summit linkage, for example, limits the maneuverability of those Japanese leaders who are working for concession. In April 1979, Prime Minister Ohira risked his political credibility in forcing concessions from NTT shortly before the May bilateral summit. When Japan's offer proved insufficient, however, the prime minister was constrained from doing more by the presence of the summit meeting. These meetings are politically important events in Japan, and for the prime minister to have capitulated to the final U.S. demands on the eve of the summit could have been politically damaging.

A summit linkage, such as the one present in early 1979, is also ineffective because it fails to target U.S. pressure specifically enough to do any good. In the case of NTT, the forces that have influence over the corporation are its four major suppliers—Hitachi, Nippon Electric, Fujitsu, and Oki Electric—all of whom are major computer and electronic firms. The perceived threats to the summit meeting provided no incentive to these companies to abandon their profitable relationship with NTT.

In order to target pressure on specific actors, the United States should use more issue-specific, quid-pro-quo styles of bargaining. In this sense, a positive development was the agreement signed on June 2, 1979, which made access by Japanese companies to the U.S. procurement market dependent on U.S. access to Japan's market. Although it is not yet possible to specify the exact impact this tactic had on NTT's willingness to compromise, it does seem to have increased the Japanese government's bargaining leverage in dealing with the public corporation. The ultimate resolution of the NTT dispute took more time using this route, but the negotiating process was far less divisive and confrontational than that of early 1979.

Finally, a word about resolving a crisis situation once it develops: As we saw, the tension that had built up before the bilateral summit in May 1979 was relieved when STR officials acquiesed in a move to put the negotiations on a separate track. This move was successfully led by State

Department and White House officials. Japan agreed at that point to send back to the United States the previously effective Hisashi Owada of the Foreign Ministry. A tentative agreement was finally reached in discussions between Owada and Robert Strauss.

There are two lessons here for Japan and the United States. First, both nations should be sensitive to the effective role that can be played by government officials who are attuned to each other's country. In the United States, for example, one of the reasons White House official Henry Owen was interested in playing the role of an honest broker was that he was aware of some of the special problems encountered in negotiating with Japan. In the future, both countries should ensure that such officials are placed in appropriate policy positions.

The second lesson concerns ensuring the effectiveness of officials attuned to the other nation's problems. Trade and economic relations between the United States and Japan are too important in both political and economic terms to be left to officials whose major focus is overseas. Issues of such importance must continue to be handled either by the central political leadership or by trade and economic specialists. If a country specialist wishes to be an effective guiding and moderating voice in U.S.-Japanese relations, he will have to open the lines of communication to these other decision makers. Officials in the State Department and White House, as noted, were effective in guiding policy because they were sensitive to Japan. More important, they were effective because they had the trust of the actual decision maker of the hour, Robert Strauss.

Notes

1. The following section is derived predominantly from two U.S. government reports: Comptroller General of the United States, *United States-Japan Trade: Issues and Problems* (Washington, D.C.: Government Printing Office, September 1979); and U.S. International Trade Commission, *A Baseline Study of the Telephone Terminal and Switching Equipment Industry.* Washington, D.C.: February 1979.

2. Elizabeth Drew, "Profiles: Equations (Robert Strauss)," *The New Yorker,* 7 May 1979, pp. 61-62. Reprinted with permission.

3. William Chapman, "Japan Refuses to Expand Concessions on Trade, *Washington Post,* 26 April 1979. Reprinted with permission.

4. Leonard Curry, "Japan Again Resists U.S. Effort to Open Its Market," *The Washington Star,* 26 April 1979. Reprinted with permission.

5. Hobart Rowen, "Strauss Warns of Retaliation by U.S. to 'Buy Japan' Policy," *The Washington Post,* 28 April 1979, p. 14. Reprinted with permission.

References

Interviews

The author conducted approximately fifty interviews with government officials, industry representatives, and journalists in Japan and the United States between January 1979 and July 1980. Direct quotations in the text that are not specifically referenced are based on interviews. Research in Japan, which was part of the author's doctoral dissertation, was generously supported by the Japan Foundation.

Newspapers and Periodicals

Asahi Evening News, 31 March 1979.
Asahi Shimbun, July 1978-June 1979.
Business Week, 16 April 1979.
Daily Yomiuri, 3 April 1979.
Japan Economic Journal, February 1979.
Japan Times, 3 April 1979.
Journal of Commerce, 11, 19, and 20 April 1979.
The New York Times, July 1978-June 1979.
Nihon Keizai Shimbun, July 1978-June 1979.
Nikkan Kogyo Shimbun, February-June 1979.
Nikkei Sangyo Shimbun, April 1979.
Sankei Shimbun, March-April 1979.
Tsushin Kogyo (trade association periodical), April 1979.
The Washington Post, July 1978-June 1979.
The Washington Star, 25 April 1979.
Yomiuri Shimbun, 5 April 1979.
Zaikei Shuho (financial weekly), 30 October 1978.
Zendentsu (trade union periodical), May 1979.

Books, Articles, and Reports

Communications Workers of America. *Statement on Multilateral Trade Negotiations to the Fourth Annual Convention.* July 16-21, 1979, p. 3.
Comptroller General of the United States. *United States-Japan Trade: Issues and Problems.* Washington, D.C.: U.S. Government Printing Office, September 1979.
Destler, I.M. "United States-Japanese Relations and the American Trade Initiative of 1977: Was This 'Trip' Necessary?" In *Japan and the United States: Challenges and Opportunities,* edited by William J. Barnds. New York: New York University Press (for the Council on Foreign Relations), 1979, pp. 190-230.

_____. *Making Foreign Economic Policy.* Washington, D.C.: The Brookings Institution, 1980.

Drew, Elizabeth. "Profiles: Equations (Robert Strauss)." *The New Yorker,* 7 May 1979.

Electronic Industries Association. "Electronics and International Competition." Washington, D.C.: 1978.

General Agreements on Tariffs and Trade. *The Tokyo Round of Multilateral Trade Negotiations.* Geneva: 1979.

Hara, Yasushi, and Ushiba, Nobuhiko. *Nihon Keizai Gaiko no Keifu* [The Evolution of Japan's Foreign Economic Diplomacy]. Tokyo: *Asahi Evening News,* 1979.

Johnson, Chalmers. *Japan's Public Policy Companies.* Washington, D.C.: American Enterprise Institute, 1978.

Nihon Denshin Denwa Kosha, *GATT Tokyo Raundo Seifu Chotatsu Mondai ni Kansuru Keii* [Facts Concerning the Government Procurement Problem in the GATT Tokyo Round]. Tokyo. 1979.

Oka, Shigeo. "Tokyo Round to Seifu Chotatsu Mondai: Dendenkaihokosho no Soten to Haikei" [The Tokyo Round and the Government Procurement Problem: Background and Focus in the Negotiations to Open NTT]. *Sekai Keizai hyoron.* Tokyo. July 1979.

"Press Release." Washington, D.C.: Office of the Special Trade Representative, 29 March 1979.

United States International Trade Commission. *A Baseline Study of the Telephone Terminal and Switching Equipment Industry,* Washington, D.C.: February 1979.

United States-Japan Trade Council. *Trade Roundup.* Washington, D.C.: 9 March and 4 May 1979.

_____. *Yearbook of U.S.-Japan Economic Relations 1979.* Washington, D.C.: 1980.

U.S., Congress, House, Committee on Ways and Means, Subcommittee on Trade, *Task Force Report on United States-Japan Trade,* 95th Cong., 2nd sess., 1979, (Washington, D.C.: U.S. Government Printing Office, January 1979).

_____. *United States-Japan Trade Report,* 96th Cong. 2d sess., 1980, (Washington, D.C.: U.S. Government Printing Office, September 1980).

U.S., Congress, Senate, Committee on Finance, *Trade Agreements Act of 1979,* 96th Cong., 1st sess., 1979. (Washington, D.C.: U.S. Government Printing Office, July 1979).

U.S., Congress, Senate, Committee on Governmental Affairs, *Hearings Before the Committee on Governmental Affairs,* 95th Cong. 2d Sess., 1979, (Washington, D.C.: U.S. Government Printing Office, 26 April 1979).

Locomotives on Different Tracks: Macroeconomic Diplomacy, 1977-1979

I.M. Destler and
Hisao Mitsuyu

The years 1976 through 1978 brought a growing imbalance in Japan's economic dealings with the United States and with the world as a whole. Bilaterally, Japan's trade surplus with the United States grew from $5.4 to $8 to $11.6 billion, with each figure setting a new record. Worldwide, Japan's current-account surplus increased from $3.7 to $10.9 to $16.5 billion over this same period, while the U.S. trade deficit—the most widely watched global figure for the United States—rose from $5.7 to $26.5 to $28.3 billion.

Alarmed by these trends, Carter-administration officials repeatedly pressed their Japanese counterparts for strong action to bring Japan's international accounts back into balance. Specifically, they sought changes in: (1) trade policy—opening up Japanese import markets (for an analysis of such efforts, see chapters 4 and 5); (2) exchange-rate policy—a higher value for the yen; and (3) fiscal policy—more domestic stimulus. This chapter analyzes U.S.-Japanese negotiations in the second and third categories, especially the third. Its goal is not to determine whether the U.S. campaign made economic sense, but to explain how and why the two countries came to negotiate so visibly on such normally domestic matters as Japan's target growth rate for 1978 and the budget deficit required to attain it. Beyond this, it seeks to assess the broader political impact of the U.S. campaign and to reach conclusions about whether similar efforts would be a promising approach to future economic relations.

Background: Trilateralism and the Locomotive Argument

The U.S. macroeconomic campaign has its roots, of course, in the rough voyage of the world economy in the early seventies and in how this was interpreted by that specialized community of Americans concerned with international economic relations. One early, broadly supported theme was

The authors are grateful to Timothy J. Curran for his contribution to their research and analysis on this issue.

trilateralism. The neglectful, sometimes hostile Nixon-Kissinger-Connally treatment of major allies in 1969-1972 had generated a general reaction, even a counterdoctrine, that the world's economic future depended above all on cooperative, constructive U.S.-European-Japanese economic relations. The Trilateral Commission—an organization of influential private citizens with extensive governmental experience in these countries—was established in 1973, mainly at U.S. impetus, to develop and proclaim this theme.

The crises that followed seemed to underscore the need for cooperative trilateral action. When the OPEC countries quadrupled the price of oil in 1973-1974, the sudden increase in their export earnings generated a new international financial problem: offsetting the OPEC surplus. If major industrial countries had resisted running compensating deficits, the result would have been "begger-thy-neighbor" trade policies such as had deepened the Great Depression of the thirties. Thus, the OECD countries took a trade pledge in June 1974 to eschew such policies, and they renewed this pledge in 1975 and 1976.

The exceptionally severe worldwide inflation of 1973-1974, followed by the deepest of postwar recessions, underscored the need for macroeconomic policy coordination. Internationally oriented economists in the advanced industrial countries were generally of the view that "both the inflation of 1973-1974 and the recession of 1974-1975 were aggravated by the failure of policymakers in each country to take adequate account of the cumulative effects of developments and policies in other countries" (Brookings Institution, 1977, p. iii). Because of this interdependence, the annual economic summit conferences, which the advanced industrial countries began in 1975, treated national macroeconomic policies as a major agenda item, notwithstanding the desire of all participants to protect national autonomy in this sphere.

By June 1976, the strength of economic recovery was sufficient, especially in the United States, to focus the attention of the leaders at the Puerto Rico economic summit on the need to avoid rekindling inflation. However, in the second half of 1976, recovery seemed to falter. Simultaneously, contrasting national paths to recovery were generating a new international imbalance among the advanced industrial countries.

For Japan, the overriding economic problem of the early seventies had been inflation. Spurred by a combination of expansionist economic policies and the OPEC oil shock, Japan's consumer price index for 1974 jumped 24.3 percent over the previous year, and the wholesale price index rose 31.4 percent. Combined with the threat to Japan's energy supplies, this inflation created a crisis of economic confidence requiring stringent corrective measures. By December 1973, Prime Minister Kakuei Tanaka was forced to turn to his archrival, Takeo Fukuda, to take charge of Japanese economic policies. First as finance minister, then as deputy prime minister and head of the Economic Planning Agency, Fukuda enforced a very tight monetary and fiscal regime for two years. The rate of inflation dropped sharply—the wholesale price index, for example, rose only 1.9 percent in Japan's fiscal year (JFY) 1975 (April 1975-March 1976) and only 5.5 percent in JFY 1976. For the same two fiscal years, consumer prices rose 10.4 and 9.4 percent.

A side effect of these policies was to delay Japan's recovery from recession. After more than a decade of double-digit percentage increases in real gross national product (GNP), Japan's growth was zero in JFY 1974 and only 3.2 percent in JFY 1975. When growth recovered to 5.9 percent in JFY 1976, it was led by exports. Domestic consumption, investment, and government spending remained sluggish. Corporate profits declined and unemployment actually increased.

Thus, although Fukuda's policies were greatly successful in suppressing inflation, and although the GNP was once again increasing, the lag in domestic demand was creating an international imbalance. Fukuda cautiously sought to stimulate demand in the JFY 1976 budget, but the projected spending increase was modest. Moreover, the Lockheed scandal threw Japanese politics into enormous confusion that year, delaying the formulation of the budget and Diet action on it, and absorbing Fukuda in maneuvers to remove Prime Minister Takeo Miki from office.

In the United States, the pattern of recovery was very different. Its inflation of 1973-1974 had been virulent also, but less so than Japan's. Although the U.S. economy plunged rapidly into recession in late 1974, it was bouncing back strongly by the second half of 1975. Notwithstanding the Ford administration's cautious economic policies, the U.S. recovery was driven by domestic demand. Thus, the U.S. trade balance moved in a direction opposite to Japan's—from a record surplus of $11.4 billion in 1975 to a $5.7 billion deficit the next year. Given the need to offset the OPEC surplus, U.S. Officials generally labeled this a healthy development and increasingly criticized Japanese (and Germans) for not doing likewise. As the Ford administration's final *Economic Report of the President* put it in January 1977, "The shift in the current account balance of the United States . . . contributed to smoothing the international adjustment process. . . . No such support to better international equilibrium was apparent in the shifts in the current account positions of the other two major industrial countries" (p. 124).

One focus of U.S. criticism was Japan's exchange-rate policies. In August 1976, Congressman Henry Reuss, chairman of the House Banking Committee, wrote Ambassador Fumihiko Togo and called on Japan to allow the yen to rise to counteract the imbalance. However, the yen's value remained low through 1976—at more than 290 to the dollar. Critics saw this as a result of a conscious policy by the Ministry of Finance and the Bank of

Japan, aimed at maintaining markets for Japan's export industries. Standing as evidence that the yen was being kept below where market forces would drive it was the fact that Japan's foreign currency reserves increased by $3.8 billion in 1976. Governor Teiichiro Morinaga of the Bank of Japan defended what he labeled a "controlled float" policy, but critics called it a "dirty float."

Increasingly, however, criticism also focused on Japanese fiscal policies. And this prescription—getting Japan to stimulate demand so as to attract more imports—would prove particularly congenial to the Carter administration.

In early November 1976, a group of private economists from Europe, Japan, and the United States met at the Brookings Institution. They recommended:

> . . . that Germany, Japan, and the United States should now adopt domestic economic policies geared to stimulating economic activity. Stronger economic expansion in the three countries, each of which has recently experienced a lull, need not intensify inflation problems, but should reduce domestic unemployment and provide benefits to other countries, both developed and developing. Germany, Japan, and the United States were singled out as the appropriate engines of world economic recovery because of their weight in the international economy, their relatively low inflation rates, and their comparatively strong balance-of-payments positions. A similar shift in economic policy would appear to be appropriate for a number of other countries. . . .
>
> A stronger expansion in Germany, Japan, and the United States would improve the outlook for all countries. For the European countries suffering from balance-of-payments difficulties and political strains, an opportunity for export-led expansion would be created, if they persevere with their current efforts to stabilize their economic and financial conditions and wind down their wage-price spirals. Developing countries would also benefit significantly, since a pickup in economic activity in the industrial world would increase demand for their exports and thereby reduce their swollen balance-of-payments deficits.[1]

The OECD secretariat advocated a similar approach in its December 1976 *Economic Outlook* (pp. 11-12).

By January 1977, at the Trilateral Commission meeting in Tokyo, the "engines" had become "locomotives," and the argument was winning broad endorsement. As Marina von N. Whitman put it,

> It does make a crucial difference. . . . whether economic expansion is based on domestic stimulation or on export-led growth. Since the increased exports of one country must be matched by increased imports somewhere else, export-led growth is a zero-sum game, at least in the short run, while real growth originating in the domestic sector benefits one's neighbors as

well as oneself. It is by undertaking appropriate stimulative policies domestically, rather than waiting for export expansion to restore high levels of employment and output, that Germany, Japan, and the United States can best serve as "locomotives" for global recovery.[2]

To the officials of the new Carter administration preparing to take office later that month, the locomotive argument had particular attractions. It addressed, constructively, the related problems of recovery and absorption of the OPEC trade surplus. It also offered a nice, practical application of trilateralism, combining U.S. leadership with shared responsibility. And it was a means of internationalizing the economic policy most democrats preferred domestically. Carter and his economic advisors had attacked the Ford administration for being overcautious about stimulating the economy, and when U.S. unemployment actually rose slightly in the second half of 1976, some concluded that this caution had cost Ford the presidential election.

If the U.S. stimulated its economy alone, however, it risked a larger trade deficit, stronger downward pressure on the dollar, and heightened inflation. With the locomotive approach, the United States could stimulate recovery in tandem with others and the international burden would be shared.

The locomotive approach, of course, had adherents outside the United States: the Brookings Institution report, for example, was signed by six European and five Japanese economists. Elements of the prescription were pressed also by other national governments and international organizations, as subsequent pages will show. However, the primary energy in promoting it came from the new Carter administration. Elsewhere, caution was the byword. Saburo Okita, a participant at both the Brookings and Tokyo conferences, gave the doctrine a careful personal endorsement, reflecting the views of many Japanese private economists that more economic stimulus was needed. But he added.

> . . . I am not quite sure the (Japanese) government will follow the economists' line. We have the tradition of very careful, cautious management of the economy, and some of the policy-makers are getting very nervous about the possible renewal of rapid inflation."[3]

The Fukuda and Carter Administrations

Japan's Liberal Democratic Party (LDP) resolved its protracted internal crisis on December 24, 1976, choosing as premier none other than Takeo Fukuda. He immediately promised to stimulate economic expansion through increased government spending, and his government presented a JFY 1977 budget that was up 17.4 percent over the previous year, with public-works expenditures up 21.4 percent. There was also a very small tax reduction, 432 billion yen, amounting to under two percent of the total budget. The government's overall economic forecast projected that the budget would bring overall real growth of the GNP to 6.7 percent and that increased domestic demand would eliminate the current-account surplus entirely—instead, there would be a deficit of $700 million.

Keynesian private economists in Japan were doubtful that the fiscal stimulus would prove sufficient to accomplish these targets, because they found the projections for consumer spending and private investment unreasonably high. One group of scholars, Seisaku Koso Forum (Forum for Policy Innovation), chaired by Yasusuke Murakami, predicted that the growth target could not be achieved unless public-works spending were a trillion yen above the 4.281 trillion planned and unless there was also a tax reduction totalling a trillion yen.

Officials of the new Carter administration were similarly skeptical. When Richard Cooper, soon to be undersecretary of State for Economic Affairs, met with a high MITI official prior to inauguration day and was told of the projection of a current-account deficit, he replied, "I don't believe it." However, with a number of locomotive advocates, including Cooper, in key positions, the administration moved quickly to articulate this policy approach and seek allied cooperation. Before his inauguration, Jimmy Carter was on the telephone with Prime Minister Takeo Fukuda, stressing the need to cooperate in reviving the world economy. Secretary of the Treasury Michael Blumenthal and Chief Economic Advisor Charles Schultze gave the locomotive approach prominence in early congressional testimony. When Carter sent Vice-President Walter Mondale to head a mission to Europe and Tokyo during the first week of his administration, macroeconomic cooperation was the prime policy theme. German Chancellor Helmut Schmidt got what he later reportedly disparaged as an economic-policy lecture from Cooper and C. Fred Bergsten, assistant secretary of the Treasury for International Affairs. When Mondale met Fukuda, however, the new premier's response was basically positive. He expressed understanding of Japan's locomotive role and stressed his commitment to the growth and current-account targets.

When Fukuda flew to Washington two months later for his first meeting with Carter, the two leaders reaffirmed their two countries' roles as locomotive economies, although this subject was much less prominent in their discussions than other matters (above all, the two leaders' contrasting policies on nuclear reprocessing). At the May economic summit conference in London, the United States and other participants (particularly Britain) pressed Germany and Japan on growth. The summit communique gave an obliquely worded endorsement of the locomotive thesis ("Some of our

economies have adopted reasonably expansionist growth targets for 1977''),
and the United States, Germany, and Japan committed themselves "to
adopt further policies, if needed to achieve their stated target rates and contribute to the adjustment of payments imbalances" (*The New York Times*,
9 May 1977).

The Carter administration also gave considerable early emphasis to
Japanese exchange-rate management. Both Cooper and Bergsten were convinced that Japan's market intervention in 1976 had been heavy and inappropriate. The administration stressed early and often, particularly through
Treasury-Finance channels, that it opposed such action and would not cooperate with it. When Professor Lawrence Klein of The University of Pennsylvania, a prominent Carter economic adviser during his campaign, gave
congressional testimony in February 1977 about how economic growth in
OECD countries would benefit from a rise of the yen (and the German
mark), this, too, was understandably perceived as pressure in Tokyo. Some
Treasury officials were persuaded within weeks that Japan was getting the
message, and the yen did rise—to below 290 in February and to below 280 by
April. It rose further after Secretary Blumenthal sent a public message at
the OECD meeting in Paris on June 24 calling on Germany, Japan, Switzer-
land, and the Netherlands to allow their rates to float upward. By mid-year,
the yen had risen to below 270, the highest rate since before the 1973 oil embargo.

By mid-summer, then, U.S. officials believed that they had accomplished
something on the monetary front. However, the current-account surplus
was another matter entirely—on this, they were not sure they even had a
dialogue. Responsible Japanese officials kept asserting that the current-
account balance would right itself, but it kept getting worse. At the London
summit, Fukuda took refuge in the $700 million deficit projected for JFY
1977, even though this estimate was already viewed by many, inside and
outside Japan, to be obsolete. The Japanese government was still sticking to
this forecast at the time of the OECD meeting in late June, where Tadashi
Kuranari, director of the Economic Planning Agency, argued that export
expansion was slowing, that the balance of payments would stabilize, and
that the 6.7 percent growth target was still attainable. Americans and Europeans were skeptical; the OECD secretariat was projecting a $6 billion
current-account surplus for Japan (as well as a $1.5 billion surplus for Ger-
many and a $10 billion deficit for the United States). The government and
the Bank of Japan were taking further steps to stimulate the economy, such
as lowering the discount rate and accelerating the implementation of public-
works contracts. However, the current-account surplus was $2.2 billion for
the April-June period. By early summer, Toshio Komoto, chairman of the
LDP's Policy Affairs Research Council and former minister of Finance,
called for a far more aggressive growth policy—a supplemental budget,

further lowering of the discount rate, and a larger budget deficit. Fukuda, however, kept an optimistic face as he departed in August for a visit to Southeast Asia, promising to reexamine the economic situation, if necessary, on his return.

By summer, therefore, "Things [had] drifted precisely contrary to American hopes" (Samuelson, 1977, p. 1335). Both the German and Japanese locomotives were not pulling their weight. Bonn was expected to fall far short of its growth target. Japan's current-account surplus was growing, as her government officials now recognized, due to expanding exports and sluggish domestic demand. Meanwhile, the U.S. trade deficit was getting alarmingly large—the figure for the first five months of 1977 was well above the previous record for a full year. U.S. macroeconomic officials viewed their prescription as more urgent than ever. They feared that world recovery might stall prematurely, leading to a new recession. They also worried about the political effects of the trade imbalance in the United States and its potential for protectionist exploitation. Therefore, they proposed that subcabinet-level bilateral discussions on the trade imbalance be conducted in September. The Japanese government agreed. It faced not only international, but also domestic discontent over its economic policies—the business community in particular was pressing for increased budgetary stimulus, with the MITI sympathetic, but the Ministry of Finance adamantly resisting.

Growing Pressure on Japan

Under secretary of State Cooper and Assistant Secretary of the Treasury Bergsten led the subcabinet mission. They stressed Japan's growing current-account surplus and the burden this was placing on the world economy. They emphasized that the problem was not easing, but worsening. They argued that it was not for the United States to state exactly what steps Japan should take but that allowing or encouraging the yen to float further upward and increasing domestic economic stimulus were two of the prime alternatives mentioned. (A third, of course, was trade liberalization.)

As perceived by U.S. officials, the Japanese response was inadequate. In the weeks after the mission, the rise of the yen did accelerate, but relatively cautious growth policies were still in place. As one of the mission's leaders put it in retrospect, the Japanese seemed "totally incapable of moving from the general problem to specific measures designed to resolve it. Instead, they kept asking what specific steps *we* wanted!" In an October visit to Washington, a senior Foreign Ministry official encouraged a more detailed U.S. initiative. MITI officials, reflecting the concern of the big business community, also encouraged this.

The Japanese government was, of course, already taking certain specific steps. On September 3, the Fukuda government announced another set of measures to stimulate the economy—a further increase in public-works spending and a further lowering of the discount rate. On September 20, it announced particular short-run surplus-reduction measures, including accelerated imports of crude oil, uranium, and feed grains. On October 3, it issued corrected projections: the 6.7 percent growth figure was maintained, but the current account was now reckoned at a surplus of $6.5 billion. Japanese private economists were skeptical, once again, about whether this stimulus package was anywhere near sufficient to reach the growth target.

By this time, Japan had sustained heavy international criticism at the annual conference of the International Monetary Fund, held in Washington on September 26 to 30. Dennis Healey, British chancellor of the exchequer, was particularly outspoken in arguing that Japan and Germany must grow faster to stimulate the world economy. Secretary Blumenthal suggested that the yen ought to rise further. Japanese Minister of Finance Hideo Bo made no effort to rebut criticisms of Japan's performance; instead, he was silent in the formal sessions, and, in private sessions, he referred to the new Japanese measures aimed at economic stimulus. However, Governor Morinaga of the Bank of Japan was shocked by the strength of the criticism and returned to Tokyo determined to press for major new steps.

For the Japanese, October was a month of growing economic crisis. The yen reached a postwar high of 253 to the dollar by mid-month, and it rose further to 250 by month's end. This alarmed the business community, which saw it as theatening export earnings and thus reducing growth prospects. It also exacerbated the split in Tokyo between Finance Ministry officials, who preferred exchange-rate adjustment to the loosening of fiscal policy, and the MITI-business alliance that wanted domestic stimulus—for its own sake, but particularly to arrest the rise of the yen. On October 28, Fukuda met with his economic ministers to consider a further policy package to reduce the surplus and ameliorate U.S.-Japanese trade friction. He found their proposed $700 million in additional imports insufficient and urged that it be raised to as much as $3 billion. The bureaucracy, however, saw no practical way for the government to increase imports by even $1 billion in the short run.

In Washington, October was a month of increasing attention, inside the government, to the "Japan problem": the combination of the growing surplus and a range of micro issues (specific-product issues). Officials were determined to resolve the trade and financial problem, insofar as was possible, not by restricting the U.S. market but by expanding the Japanese. They worried, however, about growing pressure from import-affected industries, particularly steel, which they saw as a threat to congressional acceptance of the multilateral-trade-negotiations (MTN) agreements being negotiated at

Geneva. And particular Tokyo officials were encouraging them to be more specific in their demands. Thus, newly constituted interagency groups met and developed a list of specific steps to be urged upon the Japanese, including removal of Japan's import quotas, especially agricultural, and even changes in the Japanese marketing system. Pervading the discussion was an overwhelming conviction of the correctness of U.S. policy goals and a determination to jar the Japanese to take the desired actions.

The action within the U.S. government shifted, in the main, from macroeconomic policy officials to the trade negotiators, in alliance with the East Asia Bureau of the State Department. Thus, the interagency group on Japan was chaired by Deputy Special Trade Representative Alan Wolff, and it was supported by a group chaired by Deputy Assistant Secretary of State Erland Heginbotham. Cooper was less involved in this stage, and Treasury officials seemed to remain largely on the sidelines. Bergsten felt that the exchange rate was the key to adjusting the trade imbalance, and although he did not oppose the negotiating initiative that was developing, he considered it of secondary importance.

However, one person with "macro" concerns was very much involved: Henry Owen. As a White House consultant, he had served as the U.S. coordinator for London summit preparation and follow-up, and he would become Carter's full-time international economic policy coordinator in early 1978. Owen was not himself a macroeconomist, and he felt personally that the United States might have stimulated its economy excessively in the first Carter year. He was, however, a trilateralist strongly committed to macroeconomic policy coordination, and he felt that Japanese (and German) growth needed to be accelerated. He also saw a political need for an umbrella agreement with Japan to counter particular protectionist pressures, and he viewed Special Trade Representative Robert Strauss as the obvious person to negotiate such an agreement.

Owen saw a specific Japanese growth-target commitment for the coming fiscal year (1978) as central to any package that might emerge. Philip Trezise, long-time Owen colleague at the State Department and the Brookings Institution, agreed with this viewpoint and (with Owen's encouragement) pushed the idea with Strauss and others. Senior Treasury officials were skeptical about negotiating such a target and were opposed to Strauss doing it, because Blumenthal and Strauss were often bitter rivals for administration foreign-economic-policy leadership. However, Owen pressed the idea skillfully and successfully—a JFY 1978 growth target of 7 to 8 percent was put on the list of what the U.S. would seek.

This proposal generated particular controversy when, in mid-November, it was broached as one of a number of U.S. demands by an interagency mission headed by STR General Counsel Richard Rivers and Heginbotham of State. (Before the mission, the U.S. embassy in Tokyo checked whether MITI officials would prove sympathetic to the 8 percent figure; they did.) Also broached was the proposal that Japan should seek, as a matter of policy, a current-account deficit, with a specific timetable for its achievement. Americans intended the mission to be forceful, but publicly quiet; hence the choice of Rivers rather than someone more senior. (A visit by Strauss himself would have to wait until the content of an actual agreement became clear.) Recognizing the particular sensitivity of the growth-rate proposal, the United States reportedly saved its formal presentation for a meeting of Ambassador Mike Mansfield and Prime Minister Fukuda (Rivers was present, but silent on this point). However, it was presented as part of a very broad overall U.S. package, including such specifics as elimination (or expansion) of Japan's residual import quotas, a major increase in imports of manufactured goods, much greater Japanese tariff reductions for the MTN, and elimination of strings on Japanese aid to LDCs. Also, the Americans made it clear that they wanted a specific response by mid-December (Destler, 1979, pp. 207-210).

The initiative inevitably leaked to the press, and its substance and timing generated an uproar. Both sides in the Japanese internal-policy struggle leaked dramatic and (to U.S. eyes) inaccurate reports of particular meetings Rivers had attended in order to generate the impression either of strong external pressure that must be accommodated or of outrageous pressure that must be resisted. And because the Japanese government was only weeks away from sharply contested decisions on the JFY 1978 growth target, the uproar involved the United States directly and inextricably in those decisions.

Because the U.S. demands were specific, the Japanese government's response had to be specific also, unlike most of the previous Japanese government communications on these subjects. The Japanese government began to differentiate between what was possible and what was not—it could not promise a current-account deficit or to double imports of manufactured goods, but it might increase its MTN tariff reductions, and, if it could not eliminate agricultural quotas, it might be able to enlarge them.

Concern about Japan (and Germany) continued to be multilateral, and an OECD economic policy committee meeting of late November confirmed the general view that among major countries only the United States was playing the desired locomotive role. However, now the pressure was almost exclusively bilateral—Japan somehow had to settle with the United States.

The Cabinet Reshuffle and the JFY 1978 Budget

On November 28, Fukuda announced a major reshuffling of his cabinet—one that demonstrated responsiveness to domestic-growth advocates and

U.S. demands. The expansionist Komoto was made minister of International Trade and Industry. Kiichi Miyazawa, an expansionist and an internationalist, was designated director of the Economic Planning Agency. Nobuhiko Ushiba, formerly Japanese ambassador to the United States, was given the newly created position of minister for External Economic Affairs and charged with negotiating outstanding issues with the United States.

With the bilateral economic crisis now a visible, urgent affair, the new cabinet turned immediately to the intertwined issues of domestic economic policy and relations with the United States. Fukuda declared that Japan faced its gravest situation since World War II and promised a large supplemental budget for the last three months of JFY 1977 (January-March 1978), as well as an expansionist budget for JFY 1978. Komoto, the MITI, and their business allies pressed very hard for the maximum fiscal stimulus and growth target; they were further alarmed when the yen rose to 240 by December 1. (The Bank of Japan then intervened to keep the yen from rising further—something it had generally avoided doing for most of the year.) The Ministry of Finance resisted the expansionists, seeking to hold to its debt ceiling of financing 30 percent of the budget through bonds. The Economic Planning Agency was in between but inclining increasingly toward the MITI-business side. In general, government bureaucrats (and many businessmen) were pessimistic about whether anything above 6 percent growth was actually attainable for JFY 1978, although many nonetheless favored the 7 percent target as a means of exerting maximum pressure for economic stimulus. Responsible politicians, however, tended to see the attainment of 7 percent as possible.

In mid-December, just as the Fukuda cabinet was making final decisions on the growth rate and related issues, Ushiba flew to Washington with Japanese proposals for alleviating the bilateral economic crisis. When, by one inside account, Treasury Secretary Blumenthal told Ushiba early in the visit that the precise target was not the most important thing, this view was quickly reported to the Finance officials pressing for the 6 percent growth. When they used this in the internal Japanese debate, their MITI adversaries urgently phoned counterparts in the STR, insisting that the United States must not retreat from its support of 7 percent. Thus had the politics of the two governments become intertwined. In any case, the Fukuda government adopted the 7 percent figure while Ushiba was still in Washington, giving Strauss something that he could label promising for the overall trade relationship. To contribute to its attainment, 37 percent of the new budget was to be financed by bonds, to Finance's dismay. The total budget was up 20 percent, with public-works spending increased by over 30 percent.

After further negotiation on a range of trade matters, Strauss and Ushiba issued a joint statement on January 13, 1978, which recorded substantive and procedural agreements on a wide range of economic issues.

In it, the "Government of Japan reiterated its recently adopted real growth target of seven percent for Japan Fiscal Year (JFY) 1978, and stated its intention to take all reasonable and appropriate measures" to achieve it. The joint statement noted the agreement of "both sides . . . that in the present international economic situation, the accumulation of a large current account surplus was not appropriate." It added that Japan had "undertaken steps aimed at achieving a marked diminution of its current account surplus," recorded Ushiba's personal assurance that the surplus for JFY 1978 would be "considerably reduced," and promised efforts at further reduction through JFY 1979 and therafter, "aiming at equilibrium, with deficit accepted if it should occur" (*The New York Times*, 14 January 1978). (For JFY 1977, Japan's surplus reached the unprecedented level of $14 billion, amply vindicating U.S. skepticism about the $700 million deficit originally projected.)

Thus, U.S. pressure did, apparently, affect Japan's domestic macroeconomic policies for fiscal year 1978, and in the directions Washington desired. Such influence was possible because the Japanese economic-policy community was deeply divided, and stagnation of domestic demand led to pressures for new government stimulus. This made it possible, for example, for the MITI and its growth-oriented new minister, Toshio Komoto, to have greater involvement in this issue than would normally have been the case. U.S. pressure succeeded essentially without the support of what would normally have been the key ministries, because the Treasury Department was on the sidelines, and the Finance Ministry was strongly opposed to the new budget. This could hardly bode well, however, for continued macroeconomic policy cooperation.

Moreover, the Strauss-Ushiba statement committed the Japanese—and, by extension, the Carter administration—to a target that many thought unlikely to be attainable. The ink was hardly dry, for example, before analysts in the U.S. Central Intelligence Agency were projecting that, despite the new package, and despite the yen's rise, the Japanese current-account surplus would grow still further in 1978.

The Strauss-Ushiba Statement also included, however, some U.S. commitments: to policies aimed at "substantial, non-inflationary economic growth"; to "reducing its dependence on imported oil and increasing its exports," thereby strengthening the dollar, which had been falling against other major currencies as well as the yen. Strauss even expressed "confidence," which events did not vindicate, that "in the next ninety days an effective energy program would be enacted by the Congress" (*The New York Times*, 14 January 1978). These U.S. pledges were inserted largely as tokens of reciprocity, but they signaled the beginnings of some modest Japanese counterpressure. And by spring, U.S. domestic economic performance was beginning to come under strong foreign attack, with allies arguing that the United States was exacerbating international economic problems through excessive oil imports and growing inflation. Indeed, the United States was bowing out as a locomotive. In May, Schultze told the OECD that the United States was now seeking to hold down growth in order to combat inflation.

The Bonn Interlude

In the months after the Strauss-Ushiba statement, U.S.-Japanese economic tensions eased. In fact, the primary target of U.S. macroeconomic diplomacy in the first half of 1978, as the advanced industrial nations prepared for the Bonn economic summit slated for July, was Germany. The United States felt German growth in 1977 had fallen well short of international needs, and it wanted a clear commitment from Chancellor Schmidt to do more. Other European allies also had particular interest in German growth, since, due to the volume of intra-European trade, their economies would benefit from German demand much more than they would from Japanese. Schmidt, however, was unwilling to have the Bonn communique refer to a specific German growth target. He had taken international heat for the shortfall from the 1977 goal he had tied himself to at London, even though Germany had, he argued, taken the promised additional stimulus steps, and no country could guarantee actual attainment of a particular rate. In addition, Schmidt was increasingly critical of U.S. policies on energy and inflation.

What emerged, after hard bargaining, was primarily a bilateral U.S.-German deal, managed, on the U.S. side, by summit coordinator Henry Owen. Schmidt promised additional stimulus measures up to one percent of the gross national product, thus committing himself to what Germany would do, but not to what the ultimate results would be. In return, Carter promised a range of fiscal and regulatory measures aimed at combatting inflation, and he made a detailed, difficult set of pledges on energy policy, including a commitment to oil-price decontrol by the end of 1980.

Japan's Bonn commitment was a supplement to the basic U.S.-German bargain. Fukuda, already facing difficulty in meeting the growth target, reluctantly agreed—under substantial U.S. pressure—to have it acknowledged in the communique, and he promised to determine "in August or September . . . whether additional measures are needed" to achieve it. He also pledged "to work for the increase of imports" and "stated that in order to cope with the immediate situation of unusual surplus, the Government of Japan is taking the extraordinary step of calling for moderation in exports with the aim of keeping the total volume of Japan's exports for the fiscal year of 1978 at or below the level of fiscal 1977." (*The New York Times*, 18 July 1978).

If Japanese policy was not the primary focus at Bonn, this did not mean that U.S. concern had abated. There was a general feeling within the U.S. government that the Japanese were really trying at last. They were even allowing the yen to rise further—to the unimagined level of below 200 to the dollar by the end of July. (It would reach a high of 176 on October 31.) However, the numbers the Americans cared most about seemed to get worse. Growth lagged—the annualized rate for the first quarter of JFY 1978 was only 4.1 percent—but the current-account surplus grew further, running above $8 billion for the first half of calendar year 1978. Much of this was the perverse short-run result of yen revaluation. The volume of Japan's exports was suffering, depressing the economy, but their dollar value was rising—hence the growing trade and current-account imbalance.

In early September, the Japanese government adopted the additional measures contemplated at Bonn—primarily expanded public-works spending—and took steps in emergency imports and foreign aid in order to address the external imbalance more directly. The United States had exerted steady pressure to encourage this package. Now government economic analysts, with Owen's encouragement, made a serious effort to analyze whether the package consisted of hard measures likely to have a real impact—in other words, measures beyond those the Japanese government was already taking. The majority of the analysts to have concluded that it did contain hard elements and that it constituted a good-faith effort to deliver on the growth-rate commitment.

This hardly assuaged broader executive-branch discontent with Japan, which was made worse by the fact that the United States was now very much on the international economic defensive. The dollar plunged further in value, and on November 1, the administration was forced to negotiate, at Blumental's instigation, a dollar-defense initiative, including a sharp tightening of monetary policy and an international program of intervention in the foreign exchange markets in which Japan was a major participant. This instigated a degree of U.S.-Japanese cooperation on exchange-rate management well beyond what had hitherto existed. It also stopped the yen's rise—from 176 on October 31, its value returned to above 200 by early 1979.

However, the trade and current-account imbalance persisted; Japan's surplus reached a record of $16.5 billion for calendar year 1978. U.S. officials were frustrated by this and the political threat it seemed to pose. The MTN was due to go to Congress for ratification the next year, and Congress was already causing trouble on textile tariff concessions and countervailing duty legislation. A continuing massive imbalance with Japan could be exploited by MTN opponents and protection-seeking interests as persuasive evidence that the United States was not getting a fair deal with its most important international trading partner. Indeed, the numbers made it look as if Japan were reneging on the Strauss-Ushiba accord. Trade and foreign-policy officials increasingly denounced the closed Japanese market, of which NTT and oranges were symbols. Professional economists indulged increasingly in exchange-rate pessimism—the remarkable rise of the yen had not yet led to the predicted reduction of the surplus, and perhaps it never would. Some argued that the composition of Japanese trade was such that export and import volumes would not adjust sufficiently to price changes to bring the current account into equilibrium. If one discounted the Japanese emergency imports, purchased to reduce the 1978 surplus, the data appeared even more alarming.

The Abandonment of 7 Percent

In Japan, meanwhile, frustration over the economy continued, although domestic demand was, at long last, beginning a strong recovery. Japanese tended to seek the international and domestic credibility of Prime Minister Fukuda as tied to the achievement of 7 percent growth, which made him a target for his party rivals, foremost among whom was LDP Secretary General Masayoshi Ohira. Fukuda, while he refused to characterize 7 percent as a binding Japanese international commitment, took the goal very seriously and continued to press it well after bureaucrats, economists, and other politicians began to label it unattainable. In November, when the LDP began its first primary to choose its party leader (who would automatically become prime minister), Ohira criticized Fukuda for overemphasis on the rate of economic growth. By the time Ohira won a surprise primary victory in early December, "it had become clear that the 7 percent growth target would not be achieved in FY 1978" (U.S.-Japanese Trade Council, 1978, p. 34).

The 7 percent growth target was hardly the cause of Fukuda's defeat, which most analysts attributed to Ohira's alliances with other LDP factions, above all that of former Prime Minister Kakeui Tanaka. Nonetheless, the target had proved a political albatross. It was not surprising then, from a Japanese perspective, that Fukuda's successor would move to keep it off his neck, particularly since it was now clearly unattainable. On December 8, Ohira did precisely that in his first press conference as prime minister. He added, as reported in *The Washington Post* on December 9, that "setting a goal . . . and driving madly toward it is not realistic." On December 13, the Economic Planning Agency officially estimated that likely real economic growth for JFY 1978 would be 6 percent.

What made sense in Tokyo, however, could not have been more ill-timed for Washington. There, Ohira's declaration was perceived as a threat to, and perhaps even renunciation of, the substantive and procedural framework for cooperation constructed so painfully over the past two years.

The White House Reacts

The White House was particularly upset with Ohira's announcement, and President Carter dispatched an unusually sharp letter to Ohira expressing personal displeasure. The timing of the letter seems to have reflected, in part, the United States's determination to weigh in strongly with the new government before it got locked into its economic policy decisions for JFY 1979. It apparently argued, among other things, that the Japanese growth commitment was part of a multilaterally negotiated package that included promises by every summit participant, and Carter could not accept any unilateral Japanese abandonment of its part in the package. U.S. officials insisted that the letter did not, as later reported, contain a threat that Carter might not participate in the next economic summit, the site of which was to be Tokyo. However, the letter was sharp enough that such an inference was not totally unreasonable for the Japanese to have drawn. In any case, the contents of the letter apparently shocked those Japanese who read it and generated resentment among them. However, U.S. sensitivity to Japanese feelings could hardly have been overwhelming at this point, because the prevailing view in the U.S. government was that the 1979 current-account figures might be even worse than those of 1978. Once again, Japanese government estimates were more optimistic, but these in turn were questioned by private Japanese forecasters.

It was in this context that an interagency group of U.S. government economists from the Treasury Department, the Council of Economic Advisors (CEA), the Federal Reserve, and the State Department traveled to Tokyo in January to meet with their Japanese counterparts. Owen had organized the meeting and selected the participants; their task was to conduct a technical discussion of the Japanese official forecast, which senior U.S. officials feared would prove a repeat of the 1977 forecast—which was wildly inaccurate. When the team arrived in Tokyo, it was prepared to find flaws. However, they concluded, after two days of formal discussions and two or three more of informal communication and investigation, that the Japanese figures made sense. This time it was the U.S. projections that needed reconsideration. They cabled their conclusions to Washington on January 26. The Japanese economy, the team believed, had already undergone substantial adjustment. Clearly, growth was now and would continue to be domestically led. The current-account surplus was beginning a very sharp turnaround and this trend was likely to continue in the coming months, although they thought a surplus might reemerge in 1980. Recognizing that their message might not find a receptive audience, the group concluded: "In anticipation of the reaction in Washington to this cable, members of the U.S. team have secured jobs as doormen in several distinguished Geisha houses here in Tokyo."

Such fears of their reception nothwithstanding, the team members did come home to Washington, and they defended their findings under highly skeptical questioning from Owen, Cooper, Undersecretary of the Treasury Anthony Solomon, and others. They stuck to their analysis, and, gradually, it won acceptance, aided by the dramatic fact that Japan's current-account figures for the early months of 1979 were running $1 to $2 billion below those of the corresponding months of 1978.

Even as this news began to reach U.S. officials, however, they faced the difficult question of managing the politics of U.S.-Japanese economic issues in 1979. Two summit conferences were approaching: Ohira was visiting Washington for bilateral talks in May, after which Carter would fly to Tokyo for the multilateral economic summit of June. U.S. officials saw themselves in a serious bind. They felt that anti-Japanese sentiment in the Congress was increasing, but that Japanese resentment of U.S. demands was increasing too. Opinions were divided about what previous U.S. pressure had accomplished in Tokyo, but few felt that continuing to "beat the Japanese over the head" over a range of separate issues was likely to prove productive. Yet 1979 was the year when Congress would have to approve the MTN.

Worried about what could be done, Owen invited a small group to dinner at his house on January 19 for a broad, informal discussion of U.S. relations with Japan. Included were Blumenthal, Cooper, Bergsten, Former Ambassador to Japan Edwin Reischauer, Trezise, and Assistant Secretary of State Julius Katz. No consensus was either sought or reached, but Owen came away impressed with Blumental's argument that the U.S. had to stop tangling with the Japanese on so many specific issues. Instead, what was needed was to reach agreement with them on general policy directions, and then if the Japanese were unable to deliver on their commitments, especially on the overall trade balance, they would risk the consequences—some form of stringent trade restrictions, for example, on anti-Japanese action by Congress. But U.S. negotiators, Blumenthal stressed, should stop pressing them endlessly on details. As a high administration official put it to Hobart Rowen of *The Washington Post* at the time of the May summit, it was necessary "to get off each other's backs" and emphasize "broad policies." According to that official, protectionist sentiment would be reduced "if we can stick to that" (Rowen, 1979).

Negotiating the May 1979 Joint Communique

Seeking to implement such an approach, Owen took effective charge of U.S. economic relations with Japan in the crucial presummit period. In March, he flew to Tokyo to prepare for the May Carter-Ohira meeting and the communique the two leaders would issue. He was not yet persuaded that the current-account shift was a real turnaround, as opposed to a temporary fluctuation, although the CEA economist who had participated in the January mission was now convinced that Japan was shifting quickly to a very small current-account surplus or even to a deficit. Owen was, however, convinced of the need to approach overall U.S.-Japanese economic issues differently, and he saw agreement on macroeconomic priorities as crucial. Paraphrasing Jean Monnet, the "father" of Europe, on the need for Americans and Japanese to sit on the same side of the table with the problem on the other, he developed the basis for a summit communique that would meet the policy and political needs of both national leaders, by recognizing, reciprocally, U.S. as well as Japanese failings and responsibilites in a way the Strauss-Ushiba statement did not. There, and in subsequent Washington discussions with Hiromichi Miyazaki, the Foreign Ministry official who negotiated for Japan on summit issues, Owen pressed for communique language that stated clearly each nation's policy commitment to redress its (now-declining) imbalance and for a means of monitoring the commitments. Miyazaki resisted the latter—particularly the word *monitoring,* which implied punitive U.S. surveillance. He also resisted the incorporation of numerical targets, to which Owen responded that what was really important was quantitative trends. On both sides, the negotiating process was driven by the fear the politics could get out of hand—particularly in the United States. The summit was complicated, as Curran noted in the previous chapter of this book, by the breakdown of negotiations on telecommunications procurement just days before Ohira's arrival. It did prove possible, in the end, to agree on language that made the reciprocity seem real.

The Carter-Ohira meeting was, by all accounts, cordial and successful. Their joint communique of May 2, 1979, contained no economic numbers at all. Concluding that "the time has come for a more constructive approach to U.S.-Japan economic relations," it proclaimed a "clear understanding about the basic policies that each will follow," with "specific actions to shape these trends . . . the national responsibility of each government." The two leaders "recognized that the current account surplus of Japan and the 1978 current account deficit of the United States were not appropriate in existing international circumstances," noted "a significant reduction in their payments imbalances during the last few months," and pledged steps toward "continued reduction." They also made policy commitments that were basically consistent with the Strauss-Ushiba statement and the Bonn summit communique: Japan was to foster domestically led growth and to open her markets to foreign goods, particularly manufacturers; the United States was to reduce inflation, restrain oil imports, and promote exports. "The present U.S.-Japan subcabinet group," would "examine [not monitor] developments and results" in each country's pursuit of these goals. Broader oversight would be exercised by "a small group of distinguished persons," the so-called U.S.-Japanese wise men (*U.S.-Japan Trade Council Yearbook 1979,* pp. 78-80). This last idea also came from Owen, who saw it as a means of exerting constructive policy pressure outside of the intergovernmental framework on both governments.

By the time of the Tokyo economic summit eight weeks later, Japanese trade and payments seemed to have vanished from the international agenda. Instead, the seven countries grappled with the impact of the new rise in oil prices, which was triggered by the revolution in Iran.

Conclusions

How does one evaluate the U.S.-Japanese macrodiplomacy of 1977-1979? One approach, not taken in this chapter, would be to assess the relative "rightness" of each country, or the officials within it, on the substance of economic policy. Was the locomotive approach reasonable in its argument that the strongest advanced economies should share the burden of the OPEC surplus by running deficits? Or was the United States guilty, through overstimulation of its demand, of enlarging that OEPC surplus and exerting upward pressure on oil prices? Was it desirable or undesirable to push for greater synchronization of German, Japanese, and U.S. business cycles, as the locomotive approach in fact did? Were Japan and Germany, in their export-led growth, guilty of preying on other nations? Or was their only fault that they were pursuing sound economic policies while their rivals were not?

This chapter, being a political rather than an economic analysis, need not answer these questions.[4] If forced to judge economic policy, the authors would come down somewhere in between: The Japanese government did very well in ending its virulent inflation, but a by-product was a huge and unintended current-account surplus. The U.S. government was reasonable in viewing this surplus as a burden on others' recovery and as the cause of a political problem within the United States. And although the Carter administration's home policies were grounds for retrospective criticism— overstimulating U.S. demand, insufficient concern about the dollar—its prescriptions for Japan—domestic stimulus, a higher yen—were appropriate to the surplus problem. Indeed, they were prescriptions that many Japanese favored, and they would have meant a smaller surplus if they had been followed earlier. Conversely, the underarticulated Japanese case against U.S. economic policy had considerable merit: The United States was contributing to world imbalance through its inflation and appetite for oil;

Americans were expecting that Japan achieve a level of economic fine-tuning far beyond what they themselves had achieved.

If, on the basis of a prudent policy assessment, there seems to have been relative balance, economic merits and demerits on both sides, this suggests one type of judgment on the politics of the macroeconomic dispute. Because the impressions it generated, particularly in its early stages, were not balanced at all. Americans pressed their definition of the international economic problem and their prescription for alleviating it; Japanese adapted to U.S. pressure, some encouraging it and others resisting it, but (unlike, say, the Germans) only weakly and belatedly presented a counter-case. The silence of the Finance minister at the September 1977 IMF meeting was a graphic example of Japanese reticence.

Why did macroeconomic policy become an important political issue between the United States and Japan in 1977? The impetus came almost entirely from within the U.S. executive branch, although the locomotive prescription had broader support in the international economic community. Congress was interested less in the overall trade balance than in product-specific issues, although the imbalance did affect the overall trade atmosphere, because it was exploited by those who saw it as evidence of Japanese inequity, which they used to strengthen their case for trade restrictions. Moreover, sustained interest in the overall balance was centered in relatively well-informed legislators, such as Representative James Jones and Senator Lloyd Bentsen, who were basically administration allies and responsive to administration counsel, or among staff international economic specialists, who obtained much of their information (and their frustration) from their executive-branch counterparts. As for broader congressional attention, it was intermittent to say the least, and a product mainly of where the administration was shining its spotlight at a particular time.

Why did executive-branch officials, particularly subcabinet-level officials, press macroeconomic concerns with Japan? To some degree, it was because they feared congressional action if they did not push and keep the initiative on U.S.-Japanese relations as a whole. More important, however, was their commitment to the policy, combined with the expectation that they could influence the world for the better. The locomotive approach was an attractive, nearly irresistable formulation not just because it was well-grounded in established Keynesian economic doctrine, but also because it provided a framework for diplomatic activism, for the selling of a particular (primarily, but not exclusively U.S.) vision to the world. When the Japanese did not respond with concrete policy changes, and when events seemed to vindicate U.S. prescriptions and fulfill U.S. fears, U.S. officials got tougher, more frustrated with the Japanese. Combined with a range of specific trade issues linked to the MTN, the overall imbalance seemed to sum up what came to be labeled "the Japan problem." Only toward the end of this period did the notion begin to spread in Washington that an important share of the blame for the state of the international economy, and for the trade imbalance, might lie with the United States.

One lesson of this macroeconomic episode, then, is that Americans should not too readily assume the rightness of their own policy visions and their capacity to sell them to the world. If countries as successful as Japan and Germany resist policies, the U.S. conceptions may well be flawed. Whatever the theoretical merit of a policy, resistance from others may render it unworkable in practice.

What about the details of U.S. macrodiplomacy? Here it is useful to distinguish between two stages: The first was the move to specifics in the fall of 1977. The second was the emphasis on general goals in early 1979.

Carter administration officials began by pointing with alarm at Japan's impact on the international economy, but they refrained from intruding into Tokyo's domestic economic decision-making process. By fall, this approach had become discredited in Washington: the surplus was growing worse, and Japanese actions were insufficient. At the same time, Japanese officials who were expansionists and/or internationalists were urging their U.S. counterparts to be more specific about what they wanted; only this, they signaled, could move the Japanese system. U.S. officials aggressively complied, pressing for a 7 to 8 percent growth target for JFY 1978, greater government borrowing to implement it, and a timetable for ending the surplus.

In the short run, this pressure seems to have been at least marginally effective. It was used by Japanese expansionists in their internal policy battle, and the JFY 1978 budget and growth target were almost certainly larger than they would have been without U.S. engagement in the issue. Whether the ultimate performance of the Japanese economy was more consistent with U.S. goals than it would otherwise have been is, of course, impossible to determine. It might be, as Gary Saxonhouse suggested at the time, that the visibility of U.S. pressure compounded "the malaise and uncertainty in which the Japanese private sector" was mired, thereby weakening aggregate demand (Saxonhouse, 1978). Still, the Japanese economy did shift from export-led growth in 1977 to domestically driven expansion by 1979, and the current-account surplus did disappear, albeit more belatedly—and then more suddenly—than anyone had expected, and only after reaching levels beyond all past experience.

Why was the United States's move to specifics at least somewhat effective? The overriding reason was that the Tokyo government was deeply divided on economic policy and the business community was frightened by the rise of the yen. This domestic struggle had, however, passed its peak after the adoption of the JFY 1978 budget and the gradual realization by Japanese businessmen that they could live with the higher yen. Meanwhile, the unattainable growth target became more and more a domestic political embarrassment for Fukuda and a problem internationally. Over this same period, it was becoming clear to the Japanese (and after a lag, to the Americans) that their would-be mentors could not put their own economic house in order. Increasingly, Japanese and Europeans joined in the view that the United States was, in its inflation and appetite for oil, a major international economic culprit—perhaps the major culprit.

The United States's continued official frustration with Japan and the fears (which proved excessive) that Congress might take strong, protectionist, discriminatory action made early 1979 a period of particular difficulty. The U.S. government might have intensified its macroeconomic demands, even though Japanese receptiveness was evaporating. Indeed, this initially happened, when Carter sent his sharp letter to Ohira. Fortunately, this letter (and the Japanese reaction) seems to have demonstrated the sensitivity of the issues on both sides, and Owen, the initiator of the letter, now took the initiative in moving matters to a more constructive plane.

This involved, in essence, a return to the emphasis on general goals that had characterized the Carter administration's early relations with Japan. There was one major difference, however, because in 1979, the aim was not just to agree on macroeconomic priorities for their own sake. The aim was broader: to employ the priorities as a framework for ameliorating overall economic tensions. As Blumenthal and Owen saw it, agreement on the large things would make it possible to ease up on the small things.

Certainly such an ameliorative approach was called for in early 1979. The Carter letter and the Japanese reaction had laid bare the sensitivities on both sides that Washington's effort to influence Tokyo's growth policies had produced. Although a number of specific trade issues had been resolved by then, the sharp April break in the NTT negotiations, days before the summit, again exposed raw nerves on both sides. The danger at this point seemed not so much the pressures in the two broader societies, but the increased reluctance of the two governments to smooth the way, to play their normal role as buffers. The joint communique offered a way out for these governments—a broader framework to which both could repair. For the United States, it included a reiteration of established U.S. goals, but, for the first time, the goals were stated in the context of a bilateral summit. For the Japanese, the communique offered the absence of numerical encumberances, reciprocity in the form and substance of national commitments, and the avoidance of confrontation on a specific issue, such as NTT—very important to any Japanese premier.

This was no mean accomplishment, but can the communique formula perhaps be credited with more? Did it prevent breakdown— of the sort that the textile wrangle had triggered in 1970-1971—in U.S.-Japanese relations? Did it establish, for the future, a more effective basis for macroeconomic policy coordination? Skepticism is warranted in considering both of these questions.

As 1979 began, a major blowup did seem possible. The 1978 Japanese current-account surplus had been a record; so had the bilateral trade imbalance. Executive-congressional relations on trade were strained, with congressional resistance to reducing textile tariffs and waiving countervailing duties a threat to the completion of the MTN. Congressional concern about Japan was on the rise, as evidenced by the Jones report and Senator Bentsen's broaching the possibility of an anti-Japan import surcharge. In this context, the two governments were beginning to prepare for the summits of May and June.

However, even as Owen and Miyazaki were negotiating their language, the situation markedly improved. Japan's current account suddenly turned around, and, although U.S. officials were initially reluctant to believe this was happening, the trend had become quite clear by May. At least as important, Strauss had by then prepared the way for ratification of the MTN by negotiating an arrangement with the U.S. textile industry and by convincing Congress to waive countervailing duties long enough to get the trade agreements signed at Geneva. Indeed, by early May, the responsible Senate and House committees were well into the process of shaping and drafting the MTN implementing legislation, which passed overwhelmingly in July (Destler and Graham, 1980, pp. 64-67). Both of these factors must be reckoned as far more important than the language of the Carter-Ohira agreement, which received—by comparison—relatively little attention, at least in the United States.

The summit, therefore, came at a particularly happy time, when the two leaders were able to ride the waves of improvement in the Japanese current account and in U.S. trade politics. Whether the summit agreement would have proved effective in a less favorable environment is uncertain, because it did not have to meet that test. Did it, however, provide a stronger base for future macroeconomic cooperation? The answer here appears to be negative, too, although for a reason outside of either government's direct control.

This reason was, quite simply, that the disappearance of the Japanese current-account surplus removed the overriding reason for high-level U.S. attention to Japanese growth policy. There was continuing concern, of course, that the current-account improvement might prove temporary; there was worry, too, after the yen began to decline, that its lower level might generate a new imbalance in the near future. However, once the Japanese current account was no longer in surplus—and the energy price explosion of 1979 pushed it deeply into deficit—U.S. officials had lost their main motivation and rationale for sustained attention to Japanese macroeconomic policies. U.S. officials watched these matters, but more sporadically and at a lower bureaucratic level. The bilateral trade imbalance was of continuing concern—it fell only modestly in 1979 and rose again in 1980—but it was hard to urge stimulus or revaluation as a response to that without the existence of a global Japanese surplus. Thus, while consultation on macroeconomic issues continued, it lacked the urgency that had characterized the locomotive era. By mid-1979, the U.S. goals regarding Japan had been largely accomplished.

This quite natural shift in priorities was reflected in the joint declaration of the Tokyo economic summit in June 1979, which began by lauding the improved macroeconomic balance, but then moved quickly to more pressing matters. The "agreements reached at the Bonn summit helped to improve the world economy. There was higher growth in some countries, a reduction of payments imbalances, and greater currency stability." But the seven countries now faced "new challenges," above all inflation and the new round of oil-price rises. So their meeting, and their final document, concentrated on these and made only a general macroeconomic pledge "to pursue the economic policies appropriate in each of our countries to achieve durable external equilibrium" (*The New York Times*, 30 June 1979). The Venice summit declaration a year later also gave overriding priority to energy and inflation.

The move to specifics in 1977 had some policy impact, but serious political costs made it unsustainable. The emphasis on general goals was ineffective in 1977, and, in 1979, it was not really tested in terms of its policy impact, because the desired adjustment was already occurring. However, since most economists attributed this adjustment primarily to the impact of the exchange rate, its coming did not necessarily vindicate the heavy U.S. pressure for Japanese growth. This suggests that a third option for macrodiplomacy may be preferable: greater U.S. restraint. Notwithstanding the policy logic that drives them, and the invitations that the Japanese may extend, U.S. officials should resist the temptation to become deeply involved in Japan's domestic economic policy process. Not all invitations should be accepted; just because Americans have strong views and some Japanese encourage their engagement does not make such engagement wise.

For the U.S. officials, such involvement runs the danger of being manipulated by Japanese actors on Japanese terrain—they will never understand the Japanese policy process as well as Japanese do. It also generates particular resentment when the subject matter evokes the essence of sovereignty. In addition, the same Japanese officials Americans see as inviting their pressure may also resent it, because the jarring style that gives the pressure impact also offends Japanese sensibilities.

Macrodiplomacy has another danger: Once U.S. officials get deeply involved Japanese internal economic disputes, they end up having to be satisfied with promises or targets. U.S. political credibility, as well as that of the Japanese, becomes attached to the attainment of these targets, despite the fact that the ultimate economic outcomes cannot be controlled, let alone fine-tuned, by either government. When things do not proceed as agreed, this generates further tension—U.S. officials see their Japanese policy as visibly failing, and some will conclude they have been deliberately misled.

What seems called for, then, on the U.S. side, is more limited aspirations. It is important to understand the Japanese economy, where it is going, and its impact on the United States and the world. Americans need to alert Japanese to the problems they see emerging; they need to discuss whether the Japanese agree with the United States's perceptions of these problems and what alternative means of addressing them may exist. All parties should beware of negotiating grand solutions. In the end, a mixture of consultations and unilateral policy adjustments may be a more promising, and less politically volatile, macroeconomic policy approach.

Notes

1. Brookings Institution, "Economic Prospects and Policies in the Industrial Countries: A Tripartite Report," by 16 economists from the European community, Japan and North America, 1977. Reprinted with permission.

2. Marina von N. Whitman, "Macroeconomic Coordination and Trade Adjustments," *Trialogue,* Winter 1976-1977. p. 4. Reprinted with permission.

3. Saburo Okita, "Remarks on Macroeconomic Coordination," *Trialogue,* Winter 1976-1977, p. 11. Reprinted with permission.

4. For an analysis that does address the economics involved, see "Cyclical and Macro-Structural Issues in U.S.-Japanese Economic Relations," by Gary Saxonhouse and Eisuke Sakakibara, in *Appendix to the Report of the Japan-United States Economic Relations Group,* April 1981, pp. 3-59.

References

This chapter draws primarily on contemporary Japanese and U.S. press accounts and interviews with most of the major U.S. officials involved. The statistics cited are from standard government sources: generally, the Bank of Japan on Japan's external accounts and the yen-dollar exchange rate, and the Department of Commerce on the bilateral and U.S. global trade balances. The careful reader will note an asymmetry—we refer generally to the Japanese *current-account* surplus but the U.S. *trade* deficit. The reason is that these were the most politically relevant figures during the period, and to insert Japanese trade and U.S. current-account figures in addition would overload the chapter with numbers. The best general reference to these statistics in the United States in the *Yearbook of U.S.-Japan Economic Relations,* cited below.

Sources Cited in the Text

Brookings Institution. "Economic Prospects and Policies in the Industrial Countries." A tripartite report by sixteen economists from the European community, Japan, and North America, 1977. Quoted with permission.

Destler, I.M. "U.S.-Japanese Relations and the American Trade Initiative of 1977: Was This 'Trip' Necessary?" In *Japan and the United States: Challenges and Opportunities,* edited by William J. Barnds. New York: New York University Press (for the Council on Foreign Relations), 1979, pp. 190-230..

Destler, I.M., and Graham, Thomas R. "United States Congress and the Tokyo Round: Lessons of a Success Story." *The World Economy,* June 1980, pp. 53-70.

Okita, Saburo. "Remarks on Macroeconomic Coordination." *Trialogue,* Winter 1976-1977, p. 11. Quoted with permission.

Organization for Economic Co-operation and Development, *OECD Economic Outlook 20,* December 1976.

Rowen, Hobart. "Carter and Ohira Reach Accord on Economic Issues." *The Washington Post,* 3 May 1979.

Samuelson, Robert J. "Lower Growth—A Recession may Be Looming for 1978." *National Journal,* 27 August 1977, pp. 1335-1336.

Saxonhouse, Gary. "Helping Japan Solve Its Economic Problems." *The New York Times,* 11 January 1978.

Saxonhouse, Gary, and Sakakibara, Eisuke. "Cyclical and Macro-Structural Issues in U.S.-Japanese Economic Relations." In *Appendix to the Report of the Japan-United States Economic Relations Group,* April 1981.

U.S. Council of Economic Advisors. *Economic Report to the President,* January, 1977.

United States-Japan Trade Council. *Yearbook of U.S.-Japan Economic Relations,* 1978 and 1979.

Whitman, Marina v.N. "Macroeconomic Coordination and Trade Adjustments: Positive Coordination Among Few, Negative Coordination Among Many." *Trialogue,* Winter 1976-1977, pp. 2-5. Quoted with permission.

Coping with Economic Conflicts

I.M. Destler and
Hideo Sato

In the end, things seemed to work themselves out. The United States and Japan reached agreement on agriculture and NTT. Macroeconomic policy conflict faded with the Japanese surplus that had brought it on. The steel issue was resolved by unilateral U.S. action, with Japanese cooperation. And the long and tortuous auto dispute was finally quieted on May 1, 1981, when Japan agreed to limit car exports to the United States for the coming two years (1.68 million units during the first year, starting April 1, 1981, and 1.68 million plus 16.5 percent of the U.S. market growth in 1981 during the second year). Other recent U.S.-Japanese disputes not examined in this book—over color-television trade, Japanese nuclear processing, and economic sanctions toward Iran—were also resolved in 1977-1980.

Why then should Americans and Japanese worry? One reason is that their leaders do, repeatedly. By early 1979, frustration was high and patience was short on both sides of the Pacific; it was not inevitable that tension could be defused. In the textile dispute a decade earlier, tension was not defused; the political dynamic became impossible for either nation's leaders to control, damaging overall relations at the very time the Nixon administration was taking other steps that the Japanese saw as threatening—the opening to China and the new economic policy. On a number of issues in 1977-1980, a major political blow-up seemed at least possible. It was not inevitable that Carter and Ohira would signal a relaxation of tension by declaring, in May 1979, that "the time has come for a more constructive approach" ("Productive Partnership," p. 11). Indeed, by that time, leaders in both governments were sufficiently worried about the volatility of economic relations that Carter and Ohira established, at the same time, the so-called wise men, a "small group of distinguished persons drawn from private life" to "submit . . . recommendations concerning actions . . . to maintain a healthy bilateral economic relationship between the United States and Japan" (Ibid., p. 18).

One threat posed by specific conflicts can be labeled the spillover effect. As the wise men put it in their January 1981 *Report*, when a bilateral economic dispute becomes especially "visible and embittered," this "jeopardizes cooperation in non-economic as well as economic fields" (p. 96). The textile dispute, for example, threatened Senate ratification of the Okinawa reversion treaty. The longer a dispute remains unresolved and prominently in the public eye, the more likely such a spillover becomes.

An issue that escalates politically can also create an overload effect, draining the time of senior officials in both capitals and reducing their capacity to address other, perhaps more important matters. In 1969-1971, the textile issue dominated officials' agendas, even as a far broader international economic crisis was growing untended. In 1980-1981, the automobile issue threatened to have a similar impact. The issue is, objectively, far more important than textiles in terms of the volume of trade and the industry's economic weight; nonetheless, the constant need to cope with the immediate politics of autos made it very difficult for officials to address other important and longer-range concerns.

Finally, a severe trade dispute can have a serious aftereffect, tarnishing perceptions and expectations on issues to come. If officials or larger publics come to feel that the other nation's government was crude, unfair, or behaved in a manner unbecoming an ally, this feeling will color future transactions. There is evidence, for example, that younger Japanese are less sympathetic to the U.S. perspective than their elders; one cause may be that they have lived through periods of what Ambassador Ushiba labels "unceasing acrimony" in bilateral trade relations, inclining them toward a more nationalistic, less accommodating posture.

What can be done to lessen or mitigate such effects? What guidance can the recent past offer the future?

The U.S.-Japanese economic disputes of the late seventies were colored, of course, by two particularly important events. The first was the climax of the multilateral trade negotiations (MTN). The second was the emergence of a record bilateral trade gap, accompanied until early 1979 by an unprecedentedly large Japanese current-account surplus (and a parallel U.S. trade deficit).

The ongoing MTN talks provided the specific context for the agriculture and NTT negotiations, influencing the timing and content of U.S. initiatives and setting the deadlines for reaching an agreement. More generally, the need for congressional ratification of the MTN made the U.S. executive branch particularly responsive to industry interests on these issues, as well as on the steel issue.

The overall trade imbalance had both direct and indirect effects. It was a major impetus for U.S. agriculture and NTT proposals, and Japan's surplus was the overriding reason for U.S pressure on macroeconomic policy. In the steel and automobile issues, the trade gap was used by U.S. industry and labor to buttress their cases for import restrictions. The trade gap also had an important indirect impact by creating, in U.S. trade politics, something of a presumption of Japanese guilt. If the balance was that one-sided, Americans were inclined to feel, then the argument that Japan pursued one-way trade policies must have some validity. This presumption made it more difficult for U.S. officials to accommodate Japanese arguments and interests without undermining their credibility at home.

Yet these two circumstances were not so atypical as to make lessons drawn from 1977-1980 irrelevant to future U.S.-Japanese economic relations. The MTN may be over, but policymakers in both countries will continue to be engaged in multilateral as well as bilateral negotiations, in which they must continue to balance domestic political pressures with the needs of U.S.-Japanese relations. The $14 billion Japanese current-account surplus is now history, but cyclical fluctuations in world trade balances will surely recur. Also, the bilateral imbalance in Japan's favor persists and is likely to continue, given the composition of each nation's overall trade. Thus, the general environment for future economic relations seems likely to resemble that of the recent past.

The resolution of future economic conflicts will also be complicated by the inevitable tension between the requirements of U.S.-Japanese relations and other equally legitimate government policy goals. On most 1977-1980 trade issues, conflict would have been reduced had the Carter administration settled for greater trade restrictions at home or less liberalization abroad. Instead, its reluctance to limit steel or auto imports raised the intensity of quota campaigns in the United States, and its pressure to open up Japanese agricultural and telecommunications markets generated controversy across the Pacific. However, its broad goal—a relatively open international trading system—served both nations. In years to come, each government will recurrently find it necessary to accept some degree of bilateral tension, at least in the short run, in order to hold to a policy objective that it values.

Thus, lessons drawn from recent cases can have future relevance. Issues differ by type, of course, and even within each type. In the future as in the past, different substantive problems will engage different groupings of actors within each capital. However, barring major institutional changes, these actors will be working within political and governmental systems basically similar to those now in existence.

To glean some hopefully useful lessons for future policymakers, we will first analyze the political patterns that developed in each of the three types of disputes covered in this book: those involving, respectively, U.S. imports from Japan, U.S. exports to Japan, and macroeconomic policy coordination. We will then move to broader findings and recommendations.

U.S. Imports from Japan

The steel and automobile cases represent the most familiar form of bilateral trade conflict, initiated when U.S. industry or labor protest Japanese imports that threaten them. In both conflicts, the positions of the governments were generally similar: Neither wanted import quotas imposed by the United States, and both wanted to mute the conflict, to find a workable compromise so that the problem would not become unmanageable politically. This does not mean that all officials agreed—U.S. officials, for example, were sharply divided on how far the United States should go in sponsoring auto-trade restraints. However, all saw the uses of some easing of import volume, and none wanted volume limits embedded in U.S. law.

Industry positions in the two countries were not as diametrically opposed as one might have guessed, given essentially opposite interests. On steel, the Japanese and U.S. industries both favored an orderly marketing agreement. On automobiles, there was no similar consensus, but the difference within each nation's industry seemed as great as that between them. The UAW had moved, by 1980, to strong advocacy of quotas, but General Motors held to a relatively liberal position, with Chrysler and Ford in between. In Japan, Toyota and Nissan were less ready than Honda to invest in passenger-car production in the United States, but they seemed more willing to restrain exports.

Thus, on each issue, the political climate appears to have been reasonably favorable for one obvious means of resolution—some form of Japanese export restraint. The U.S. government was inhibited from initiating such action, however. First of all, the government considered steel an economic and trade-policy problem, not a U.S.-Japanese relations problem—and for the most part, U.S. officials viewed automobiles the same way. Second, there were some specific impediments: free-trade conviction (reluctance to bring another industry under quota arrangements); domestic economic concern (over the inflationary impact of quotas); and legal problems (lack of clear authority to negotiate limits, making any restrictive arrangement subject to antitrust litigation). Such authority could have been provided by the International Trade Commission (ITC) had it found imports a substantial cause of serious injury to U.S. automakers, but it did not find that to be the case.

In Tokyo, the Ministry of International Trade and Industry (MITI) was prepared to support export restraint on steel if the U.S. government seriously wanted it. Otherwise, the MITI did not want to set a precedent—of appearing too willing—that might encourage orderly marketing arrangements (OMAs) in other product areas also. On automobiles, the MITI's effort to achieve voluntary industry restraint was made more difficult by a lack of a clear U.S. request. Thus, while each issue heated up, the two governments consulted, but they did not enter serious negotiations.

In the end, a workable resolution was reached on the steel issue, and one may have been reached regarding automobiles also. Prior to any resolution, however, each issue became a political event of major proportions, as demonstrated by the congressional steel "firestorm" of September and October 1977 and the unprecedented visibility of the automobile issue through 1980 and into 1981.

Would earlier Japanese initiative have brought earlier resolution? The steel industry did offer export restraint, responding to signals from U.S. counterparts, but the U.S. government rejected that option. The Treasury's finding of dumping in the Gilmore suit might conceivably have been averted if the MITI had proposed that the steelmakers make cost-of-production data available in the modified form ultimately provided for the trigger price mechanism (TPM). In general, there was no way for Japan to speed resolution until the U.S. government was persuaded of its urgency, and only steel-industry pressure would accomplish this. The auto case seems different. Toyota and Nissan could have responded several years earlier, and much more substantially, to pressures that they invest in the United States, as Volkswagen had done. Their reluctance to move to multinationally based manufacturing was unique among the world's major motor-vehicle producers, and it rendered them particularly vulnerable politically.

In the United States, strong policy leadership might have brought quieter and/or quicker resolution, but the Office of the Special Trade Representative (STR) did not dominate these issues in the same way it dominated the MTN. In 1977, even though Robert Strauss had rapidly established personal primacy in trade policy, he did not take charge of steel—instead, the political firestorm and the initial focus on dumping led to adroit adjudication by Undersecretary of the Treasury Anthony Solomon, but only after the heat had been generated. The STR was preoccupied with MTN issues until mid-1979 and was engaged in a major reorganization and leadership turnover thereafter; it did not, therefore, seriously enter the auto dispute until early 1980, and even then U.S. Trade Representative Reubin Askew had difficulty establishing his ascendancy over other administration voices, such as Secretary of Transportation Neil Goldschmidt. His successor, William Brock, had similar difficulties in 1981.

Thus, both issues tended to fester, generating for interested publics the impression of serious bilateral conflict, even though governmental positions were as much cooperative as competitive. Each country's officials were, essentially, in a coping mode, seeking more to manage and ameliorate pressures than to achieve clear, positive policy objectives.

U.S. Exports to Japan

On issues involving the Japanese market, the U.S. government was much more purposive—it wanted greater access and was prepared to press hard to get it.

Unlike steel and automobiles, both agriculture and NTT were small issues in terms of the amount of current trade affected—but they had long-term significance. Both were pressed by a U.S. government that favored trade-expanding solutions to bilateral and global trade imbalances. And both became major political issues in Japan, with a volatile mix of domestic contention and highly visible U.S. pressure. In the United States, these issues were far less visible than the automobile and steel issues, because they were not connected to current unemployment. For Americans concerned with trade policy, however, they were the type of issues where Japan appeared culpable, and each came—for a time—to symbolize the closed nature of the Japanese market.

In each dispute, Japanese political leaders and trade negotiators were inclined to meet U.S. demands at least part way, but they faced determined interests with considerable capacity to resist. Credible and persistent U.S. pressure was important in countering this resistance, in making policy change possible, and change seekers with Japan sometimes encouraged U.S. pressure. Each issue became more volatile, however, when it became linked to a broader bilateral trade crisis.

In the beef and citrus case, this linkage was more or less planned. Agricultural quota liberalization was included in the broad program of policy changes that Americans, encouraged by their Japanese counterparts, put forward in the fall of 1977 with the hope of reaching a major breakthrough on trade matters. Of the issues addressed in the Strauss-Ushiba statement of January 1978, agriculture was the most intractable. On NTT, linkage was initially accidental—the issue arose late in the MTN, and its negotiating timetable coincided with preparations for the May 1979 Ohira-Carter summit conference. Once this linkage arose, U.S. trade negotiators exploited it tactically to win concessions, but they acquiesced in the eleventh-hour, White-House-led move to put NTT on a separate track once it was clear that a presummit resolution was impossible. Japanese, more sensitive to the political and symbolic cost of a soiled summit, tended to perceive the linkage of NTT to the broader bilateral trade crisis as deliberate and calculated by U.S. officials, and the threat, amplified by the Tokyo media, generated broad resentment.

In both cases, the linkage—deliberate or accidental—proved at most only a step toward resolution. The agriculture talks continued until the end of 1978, eleven months after the Strauss-Ushiba statement. The May 1979 summit yielded only an agreement to agree on NTT by the end of 1980.

In each case, resolution was complicated by the uncertainty of the U.S. bargaining position. STR Strauss, needing to balance the demands of competing groups, was deliberately ambiguous about what the United States would ultimately accept, and he introduced what the Japanese saw as new demands late in both negotiations. This made it more difficult for Japanese negotiators to mobilize the needed consensus.

Both issues were, however, handled without a major crisis. With agriculture, a major reason for this was that U.S. decision making was well-orchestrated under Strauss and U.S. officials sent consistently "tough" signals—it became clear that the United States was not bluffing, that some concessions would be necessary even if the precise U.S. demands were not clear. In Tokyo, Nakagawa and Ushiba exercised effective leadership, capitalizing on the somewhat isolated position of agricultural interests in Japanese society, building domestic consensus for concessions while simultaneously persuading the United States to modify its demands.

Resolution on NTT was complicated by the peculiar nature of the target agency—its autonomous position within the Japanese goverment, and the technical, insular outlook of its leading officials. Government leaders had limited jurisdiction over those officials and were unaccustomed to dealing with them. And the U.S. position seemed to grow progressively tougher— beginning by focusing on the volume of NTT purchases open to international bidding, and ending by focusing on the high-technology content of these purchases. Nevertheless, adroit eleventh-hour diplomacy averted the open summit break that neither the Carter White House nor the Ohira government desired. Although their agreement did not resolve the issue, it did place it on a more reasonable, quid-pro-quo basis, with U.S. access to Japanese government procurement being bargained against Japanese access to U.S. official purchases.

The Trade Imbalance and Japanese Growth Policy

The U.S. effort to influence Japanese macroeconomic policies exhibited yet another political pattern. Here the impetus came, even more than in the export cases, from the policy convictions of members of the U.S. executive branch. One major reason for their Tokyo impact was that, in the fall of 1977, the Japanese government and business community were deeply divided over the wisdom of Fukuda's conservative economic policies. Businessmen were frightened by the impact of the yen's rise on their exports. With the normally dominant Ministry of Finance resisting change, officials at the MITI and the Foreign Ministry encouraged U.S. pressure and used it in their internal struggle. Because the government's growth and current-account projections were proving wildly optimistic, critics could seize on the obvious need for policy adjustment and were able, in part, to prevail.

In terms of policy results, therefore, the U.S. drive to influence Japanese macroeconomic policy was at least a limited success. The Japanese fiscal year (JFY) 1978 growth target was higher than it likely would have been otherwise; government economic stimulus was probably larger; and the Japanese economy did in fact shift from the export-led growth of 1976-1977 to domestically led growth by 1979. Also, the current-account surpluc did disappear in 1979, although the main cause for its disappearance, most experts felt, was not increased government stimulus but the yen revaluation (and, later, the jump in oil prices).

However, the key ministries—Finance and Treasury—were either opposed to the policy change or on the sidelines. Thus, the growth initiative did not lead to improved consultation between established policy institutions (as did the November 1978 U.S. dollar-defense initiative on monetary matters). Moreover, Japanese resentment of U.S. pressure, of being victimized by it, outlasted the fall and winter of 1977-1978; indeed, in some respects, it increased as the failures in U.S. macroeconomic management became more evident. Thus, Carter's December 1978 letter to Ohira was generally resented, and, although the letter did demonstrate that the administration cared about both the form and substance of Japan's international growth commitments, its reception made it clear that internationally negotiated, publicized commitments to specific policy targets were a burden that Japanese politicians and bureaucrats no longer wished to bear. The 1979 summit communique acknowledged this limit and skillfully made it a virtue. Bilateral talks would henceforth focus on "basic policies," with "specific actions" to be, as of old, "the national responsibility of each government."

The United States's negotiating initiatives on growth were clearly correct in their assumption that international imbalances could not be effectively addressed by trade bargaining alone, and they were correct also in their recognition that national economic policies have important international impacts. However, frustrated by slow progress, and encouraged by Japanese allies to be more specific, U.S. officials ended up intruding too deeply and visibly in Japan's domestic process. Their inevitable focus on numerical targets, on outcomes beyond the government's control, created exaggerated notions of what such negotiations could accomplish, followed by disappointment when the final numbers were different from those projected. These were among the reasons why the Japan-United States Economic Relations Group urged the U.S. government to "recognize the limitations of efforts to coordinate macroeconomic policies through . . . agreement . . . on precise growth rates and other targets" (*Report*, 1981, p. 27).

If insights can be gained by focusing on types of issues, there are also lessons to be learned by looking more generally at the dynamics of recent bilateral disputes. We conclude with such a focus, presenting findings and recommendations for future officials and policymakers to consider. Our discussion is divided into three broad categories--negotiating strategies and channels; perceptions and communications; and national policymaking institutions.

Negotiation Strategies and Channels

Pressure Tactics

One subject deserving serious attention is the unique role played in all issues by what the Japanese perceived as intense U.S. pressure. On agriculture, NTT, and macroeconomic policy, the U.S. government employed strong, visible pressure as a catalyst for Japanese policy change. Some Japanese bureaucrats encouraged or welcomed such pressure, but many others resented it, and the United States came across as a malign but overpowering force that Japan must accommodate.

From the Washington viewpoint, the high-pressure sequence unfolded roughly as follows: U.S. officials indicated their strong concern about the problem, calling for Japanese policy action, but leaving it to the Japanese to define the details of that action. Nothing happened—the Japanese neither acted nor rebutted the U.S. case. At the same time, individual bureaucrats suggested to their U.S. counterparts that the approach was much too general, that more specific proposals, more forcefully put, were needed to move the Japanese system. The U.S. officials responded with specifics, clearly but diplomatically put, but their demands were leaked, exaggerated, and distorted in the Tokyo press as competitors in the Japanese policy debate sought to turn the U.S. demands to their advantage. The U.S. officials may have come to see themselves as being used and misrepresented, pawns in a Japanese game they did not understand, their pressure simultaneously encouraged and denounced. However, results did follow—U.S. officials now saw at least some policy gains where they had seen none before.

The view from Tokyo was different. U.S. officials were clearly the dominant actors, insisting on defining the issues, talking rather than listening. And in formulating their specific positions, the U.S. officials often took cues from the "wrong" Japanese—those on the fringe of Japanese institutions whose role was to communicate with foreigners, or outsiders to a Tokyo policy process who sought to employ U.S. pressure as a way to get in. U.S. officials failed to appreciate the impact of a strong U.S. position on a society where the tradition was the opposite—one of deliberate vagueness while consensus was being sought. Thus, the same Japanese officials who Americans saw as encouraging and using their pressure also resented it—because the jarring style that gave it impact also offended Japanese sensibilities. More generally, the U.S. officials came across as either consciously exploiting Japanese vulnerabilities—the need for a conflict-free summit conference, for example—or remarkably insensitive to them.

Yet, generally, the Japanese recognize that, as part of their tradition of adapting to an uncontrollable world, external pressure (gaiatsu) plays an important role in bringing—even legitimizing—internal policy change. In a government characterized by intense competition among closely knit subgroups, each of which tends to dominate its policy sphere, internal pressure for change is hard to mobilize, whether the goal is the Finance Ministry's acquiescence in greater government borrowing or NTT's opening up a system closed not just to foreigners, but to most Japanese firms as well.

However, if such strong pressure is often effective, it is also damaging. The image of presumptive U.S. behavior is particularly offensive to Japanese now that the United States is no longer predominant economically and does not appear to be handling its own economic business very well. Over time, repetition of this high-pressure scenario will reduce U.S. credibility in the minds of Japanese, with detrimental—perhaps even dangerous—effects on all aspects of U.S.-Japanese relations. On specific issues, U.S. pressure risks polarizing national positions and amplifying negative images of each country in the minds of the citizens in the other. This increases the chances of a truly serious breakdown in relations if political leaders in one country should decide one day to exploit this negative sentiment rather than counter it.

Yet the gaiatsu scenario seems to respond to real needs in both countries—it is, after all, played out repeatedly by different officials, on different issues, and usually not by advance design. It is bilateral, two-sided, in its roots. Until the two countries learn to employ other means more effectively to achieve Japanese policy adjustment, they will continue to use this one, whatever dangers it poses. Thus, a prescription must go beyond deploring this pattern; it must look for alternatives, such as the two governments employ on other occasions.

In managing their inevitable economic conflicts, officials in both governments should work very hard to avoid employing (or seeming to employ) intense, highly visible U.S. pressure as the catalyst for Japanese policy change.

For the Japanese, the need is to respond earlier to "softer" signals (as did the steel industry in 1977) and to find alternative sources of support for internal policy change. For instance, necessary economic changes (such as liberalization of import quotas) should be argued on the basis of their own merits and supported by interest groups with stakes in an open international economy. For the Americans, the need is not to abandon efforts to influence the Japanese government, but to resist invitations to escalate those efforts. U.S. officials should be firm and persistent about U.S. aims without presuming to dominate Japanese behavior; they should look for issue-specific sources of leverage insofar as possible, rather than linking economic issues in a broad package that appears as a frontal challenge to Japan as a society. At times, as in the steel issue, a unilateral U.S. solution may be feasible, if it is adopted after consultation with the Japanese and if there is Japanese cooperation in its execution.

Intrusion in Domestic Issues

U.S. pressure is particularly resented by the Japanese when they perceive it as an intrusion in issues normally considered domestic. In 1977-1978, as we noted, U.S. officials negotiated with the Japanese on such issues as the JFY 1978 growth target, the ratio of Japanese government borrowing to total expenditure, and additional steps needed to stimulate domestic demand. This approach achieved some concrete results, but it generated a severe backlash—many Japanese were resentful of such presumption on the part of Americans, especially in a period when the U.S. seemed to be mismanaging its own economy. It also created the false impression, among attentive Americans, that the Japanese government could fine-tune its aggregate economic performance and should be held accountable for doing so.

One problem was that the U.S. officials increasingly lacked credibility on economic policy as U.S. inflation rose and the dollar's value plummeted. More important is the fact that the Japanese people have grown fiercely proud of their rise to top-level economic status. Thus, they increasingly resent foreign actions—however well-motivated—that seem to imply that Japan remains a protégé requiring tutelage or a weak nation that must submit. Americans should find this easy to understand, because they react strongly to hints of foreign intervention in their domestic policymaking. When, for example, the Japanese government suggested during the textile wrangle of 1969-1971 that the U.S. Tariff Commission investigate whether imports had injured the U.S. textile industry, U.S. officials were livid. They felt that it was totally inappropriate for a foreign government to make such a suggestion (Destler, Fukui, and Sato, 1979, p. 161).

To sum up, U.S. officials need to beware of intruding too deeply in Japanese economic decision making, particularly on issues normaly considered domestic. And the Japanese should be careful about inviting such intrusion.

When the two countries negotiate on broad economic policies, they should seek both the fact and the appearance of reciprocity. In this respect, the language of the Carter-Ohira communique of May 1979 was preferable to that of the Strauss-Ushiba joint statement of January 1978.

Congress as a Threat

The U.S. Congress played an important role in all five cases presented in this book. The congressional steel caucus and the Danforth-Bentsen bill exerted strong, perhaps decisive pressure in forcing action on the steel and automobile issues. Congressional beef and citrus interests were important to the agricultural negotiations, and congressional concern both raised the visibility of NTT and provided important backing and credibility to executive-branch efforts to resolve it. Finally, executive-branch concern about the trade and current-account balance was fueled by the sense that this was a source of trouble, actual and potential, on Capitol Hill.

Yet in only one case did the Congress actually legislate, and then only to strengthen executive-branch leverage: the implementing legislation for the government procurement code was written so that the U.S. government could exclude a country's firms from access to U.S. purchases if U.S. firms did not win comparable access in return. In the other cases, Congress was a rhetorical lion but a statutory mouse; on none of them did either house pass a single bill that would have directly restricted trade with Japan. Despite the clear constitutional primacy of Congress in the regulation of foreign commerce, and despite the fact that the seventies were a time of exceptional congressional assertiveness, with regard to U.S.-Japanese trade, legislators contented themselves with being, in effect, outside players in executive-branch decision making. Their direct target was the U.S. government. Indirectly, of course, they sought to affect the Japanese as well.

Executive-branch leaders frequently encouraged this involvement, sometimes working with congressional leaders in orchestrating it, and repeatedly used the threat of protectionist action by Congress to help win Japanese concessions. The Japanese were often understandably skeptical of the strength or imminence of this threat, but they were generally unwilling to put things to the ultimate test, and those Japanese who were seeking policy change in Tokyo found the congressional threat politically useful.

In some respects, this pattern is reassuring: it suggests that Congress has not been, on Japan issues, the sort of volatile, unpredictable protectionist force it has frequently been depicted as being. However, the more often U.S. negotiators and politicians cry "wolf" without the actual animal emerging, the less credible the threat will become. Yet congressional concern about Japanese trade issues has in fact been increasing. Let us suppose Japanese leaders say visibly and publicly one day that they do not believe Congress will act on a certain trade matter and that, in any case, it is a U.S. affair. Would congressional, even executive-branch, leaders see their credibility threatened to the point where they felt they had to deliver some anti-Japanese statutory action, or at least acquiesce in it?

The threat, "Congress will get you," is, at bottom, a variant of the gaiatsu scenario, useful to a range of policy actors on both sides of the Pacific. In the long run, however, its overuse runs serious risks. Leaders in both governments—and both branches of the U.S. government—should resist the temptation to employ Congress as the "heavy." They should avoid exaggerating or misrepresenting the breadth and depth of congressional trade concerns or the imminence of congressional action.

Scapegoating

In the steel and auto issues, as earlier noted, pressure was exerted indirectly through the Japanese reading of U.S. public statements. This sometimes made the interests involved more responsive to U.S. concerns, but it also generated resentment and a sense of being beset and victimized by Americans who lacked understanding of Japan's real situation. In turn, Tokyo was upset by what were perceived as one-sided and oversimplified presentations of reality. Indeed, the U.S. steel industry aggressively promoted the view that an "unfair" Japan was a prime source of its economic problems, even though it was Europe that was most obviously dumping steel on U.S. markets, and other U.S. manufacturers have made similar charges, especially in consumer electronics.

In the agricultural issue, U.S. officials focused criticism on the closed nature of the Japanese markets while often failing to take note of the fact that Japan was the world's single largest customer for U.S. agricultural products, with imports of over $4 billion, or the fact that the United States itself restricted beef and citrus imports. Such "scapegoating" is amplified by the Japanese media, and distracts Americans from the domestic roots of trade problems, including diminished industrial competitiveness.

In Japan, bureaucrats sometimes use the United States as a scapegoat—for example, when some used U.S. pressure in the fall of 1977 as an excuse for economic and trade-policy changes they favored on other grounds. Because of the attention gap, the Japanese perception of U.S. actions has far more impact in Tokyo than the Americans' perceptions of Japanese policy have in Washington. But in both capitals, scapegoating has nourished negative images that may poison the well of future relations. Thus, Americans and Japanese both must beware of employing the other country as a scapegoat, despite short-run political gains in so doing.

Lack of Specificity

In both the agriculture and NTT cases, the United States began by asking for full liberalization—elimination of quotas and internationalization of all telecommunication procurement. Even though initial talks indicated that this was impractical, STR Robert Strauss was slow to specify what concrete steps the United States most wanted and what it would settle for. One reason was domestic politics—he did not want to appear to be choosing between Florida and California orange growers, for example, and when a particular U.S. position in fact leaked in the summer of 1978, it angered producers in both states. Nonetheless, this reluctance made it difficult for Japanese political leaders and senior officials to begin their lengthy consensus-building process, particularly when U.S. officials kept repeating the very threatening liberalization goal. Similarly, the lack of clear U.S. signals made it more difficult for the MITI to press Japanese automobile makers for import restraints in 1980 and early 1981. Hence, when seeking trade concessions, it is important that officials be as specific as possible, as early as possible, about the actions sought from the other government.

Summit Linkage

The NTT issue came to be linked with the Carter-Ohira summit, and the Japanese saw the United States as seeking to force concessions by threatening to make the prime minister's visit to the United States a failure. In fact, this was not the overall U.S. strategy, although some officials did apparently entertain this idea. In any event, such linkage was misguided, because the United States was as likely to back down as Japan—indeed, the United States did back down, settling for a procedural compromise. Moreover, the summit offered little leverage on the politics of the NTT family; it was not likely to make Hitachi, NEC, Fujitsu, or Oki Electric any more receptive to modifying their close and profitable NTT relationships.

Summit conferences can, of course, sometimes facilitate important breakthroughs on issues, if the groundwork has been prepared at the working level. Prime Minister Eisaku Sato's talks with President Lyndon B. Johnson in 1967 and with President Richard Nixon in 1969 facilitated the Okinawa reversion in just this way. However, Sato's summit discussions with Nixon in 1969 and 1970 proved disastrous for the textile issue because the groundwork had not been laid (Destler, Sato, Clapp, and Fukui, 1976, pp. 154-157).

In short, a summit meeting cannot force the settlement of a difficult bilateral problem unless a basis for substantive agreement has been prepared in advance. Otherwise, linking an issue to a summit may only exacerbate the controversy without achieving a resolution.

Trips by Hardliners

In the course of the agriculture conflict, many Japanese farm representatives and agricultural politicians visited the United States. As a result, some of them considerably softened their position against import expansion and acquiesced in the compromise between the two governments, although their repetition of the same arguments had often exasperated the U.S. officials they encountered. Similarly, when some U.S. citizens visited Japan in 1977, they apparently became less outspoken about dumping after seeing modern Japanese steel plants. It is sometimes useful, therefore, to send domestic "hawks" to the other country on fact-finding missions, because their exposure to direct pressure from the other side (or to actual industry operations on the other side) often softens their stand.

Consultations Among Experts

The macroeconomic policy dialogue of 1977-1979 was damaged by the low credibility of the Japanese government's current-account projections—they had grossly underestimated the surpluses of 1977 and 1978, and Americans feared a repeat of this error in 1979. However, the dispatch of a special team of U.S. economic forecasters to Tokyo in January 1979 led to the conclusion that the official Japanese current-account forecast for FY 1979 was a reasonable one. The mission's success was due, in large part, to two factors: it addressed a problem of major current concern to those shaping U.S. policy toward Japan, and the team's expertise was directly relevant to the problem.

Thus, when the two governments seem to be operating on divergent assumptions about economic facts and trends, serious analytic dialogue between their senior experts can prove highly useful.

Perceptions and Communications

Obsolete Attitudes

Some Japanese still cannot overcome the *amae* (dependent) mentality spawned by the postwar relationship with the United States, which leads them to unrealistic expectations of U.S. policy. To the extent that they are aware of difficulties facing the United States, they tend to be unusually impatient with them. Some Americans, on the other hand, still seem to have the image of the United States as the senior partner of that dependent relationship, thus expecting the Japanese to accede to U.S. requests at all times and at any cost. However, economic and political trends have long since rendered the postwar father-son relationship obsolete. The reality is that both governments must deal with increasingly assertive domestic interests, at the very time when there is a greater need to coordinate their economic policies internationally. This means that, when working out a bilateral settlement, policymakers in both countries need to pay greater attention to the domestic political matrix of the other side as well as to their own. Indeed, a key to effective management of bilateral issues is reciprocal political sensitivity.

Unfortunately, current trends seem to be in the opposite direction. As an astute U.S. economic journalist has noted, "Economic pressures and rising chauvinism in each country have created an increasingly intolerant political climate toward the other."[1] This problem was present in all five cases presented in this book, but it was particularly evident in the NTT, auto, and macroeconomic policy issues. In the agricultural case, as we noted, political leaders in both countries did prove effective in demonstrating reciprocal political sensitivity, despite difficult domestic pressures.

"Japan, Inc."

The MITI is not nearly as all-powerful as U.S. officials often believe, and U.S. officials tend to exaggerate the harmony of Japan's government-business relationships. In fact, the MITI's leverage over Japanese firms has decreased since the early postwar period, and government-business consensus on policy issues seems to have weakened. The MITI worked hard to persuade Toyota and Nissan to build plants in the United States, but with limited success. Only the threat of substantial U.S. trade restrictions seems to have made Nissan move, finally, in this direction. The Japanese government has even had difficulty influencing a semigovernment organization such as NTT.

In summary, despite the still prevalent image of "Japan, Inc." in the United States, the Japanese government appears to have decreasing leverage over Japanese business firms. Thus, it is necessary for the United States to scale down the expectation that the Japanese government can easily induce such firms to respond to U.S. interests.

Japanese Reticence

The problem of misperception between the United States and Japan is usually exacerbated by the fact that, while Americans often employ an adversary style of bargaining, emphasizing the negative aspects of the other side (as lawyers do in court), Japanese tend to remain reticent. This can lead Americans to conclude that Japanese are acknowledging guilt. U.S. actions based on that assumption in turn breed further Japanese resentment.

At the IMF meeting in the fall of 1977, Japan's macroeconomic policy was severely criticized. But the minister of Finance returned to Japan without even attempting a rebuttal, and later attempts to do so by Finance Ministry bureaucrats came too late. It was only much later that Japan began to criticize the U.S. inflation, oil imports, and the benign neglect of the dollar.

In the future, Japanese negotiators should speak up more, countering U.S. criticism as squarely as possible, to minimize misunderstandings and misperceptions. When the U.S. government criticizes Japanese policy and/or makes a specific demand, the Japanese government should respond with rational explanations of its position and counterarguments—instead of saying nothing, appearing to acquiesce, or simply saying no.

Japan's Hypersensitivity

U.S. politics are vocal and decentralized, generating an enormous volume of words and actions, most without enduring impact. Tokyo media naturally select and amplify those that refer to Japan. For example, in criticizing increasing Japanese auto imports, U.S. Steel Chairman David Roderick (successor to Edgar Speer) charged that the Japanese were dumping. This comment received widespread press attention in Japan, even though Roderick was not directly involved in the auto issue and charges of Japanese unfairness had not been an important theme of U.S. auto-quota advocates. Similar statements by U.S. congressional or academic critics also tend to get wide publicity in Tokyo. This reflects the broader attention gap—a statement about the United States by a Japanese industry leader or Diet member would not normally find its way into the U.S. media at all. Very often, even the Japanese foreign minister's visits to Washington fail to be noted in the U.S. press.

Thus, the Japanese government, media, and other leaders should help their countrymen put specific U.S. comments in broader perspective. Not every congressional speech matters; not every criticism of Japan reflects a widely held view.

National Policymaking Institutions

Political Leadership

The power of special economic interests seem to be increasing in both Japan and the United States. Nor, with the partial exception of automobiles (and, for a time, steel), have consumer interests emerged as an effective counter-force. In the U.S. Congress, members complain of growing pressure from narrow interests and single-issue lobbies. Within the government, numerous agencies are involved in international economic issues. In Japan, sectionalism in the bureaucracy produces alignments with special interests that ministers have difficulty resisting. Thus, there is a particular need in both countries for adroit political leaders.

In the United States, Robert Strauss combined inborn political talent with ties to the president, Congress, and U.S. domestic politics, and he was able to take and keep the domestic initiative on trade issues. This meant that he could, usually, control the U.S. side of bilateral negotiations and prevent the proliferation of channels. His successor, Reubin Askew, found it difficult to establish comparable political dominance, as the U.S. auto policy demonstrated.

On the Japanese side, the government would not have been able to win acceptance of the agriculture agreement had it not been for the effective leadership exercised by Nakagawa and Ushiba.

In any case, it is worth stressing that both countries need strong political leaders to take charge of major trade negotiations and facilitate effective political management both at home and abroad. This need is particularly acute in the United States, given its greater dispersion of power over international economic policy.

Country Experts

A common Japanese complaint cites Washington's limited number of experts on Japan. Reciprocally, U.S. officials remark on the rareness of those Japanese bureaucrats with whom they can communicate effectively and the enormously useful intermediary role played by those who can. Both governments need to encourage the development of more such people, place them in positions important to U.S.-Japanese relations, and yet guard against them becoming labeled in their own government as advocates for the other country and thus being discounted. In other words, both governments need to expand the number of career officials who are knowledgeable about the other country and who are skilled in communicating with its officials.

Watchdogs on Bilateral Economic Relations

Political leaders and career officials who manage bilateral economic relations can be assisted by small groups of consequential figures (based in either country or in both) that combine detachment from current executive responsibilities with serious attention to bilateral economic issues.

The Task Force on United States-Japan Trade of the House Ways and Means Committee has evolved into one such group. Its second comprehensive report, published in September 1980, is an unusually balanced and informative discussion of the nations' overall relationship and particular issues within it. The task force can prove helpful in balancing the considerable flow of information from special-interest sources and in providing continuous, constructive influence on both governments.

The Trade Study Group (a private, voluntary group of U.S. and Japanese businessmen) has also been playing a useful role by conducting a broad study of nontariff barriers and making recommendations to Japanese government bodies. Another helpful group is the Japan-United States Economic Relations Group, which sponsored the research for this book. One particular value of this group has been in the completely binational nature of its membership and staff work.

Concluding Reflections: Asymmetric Interdependence

Beyond the findings and recommendations presented above, what can we say more generally about the United States's political-economic relations with Japan (and other Western industrial countries)?

Over the past decade or so, U.S.-Japanese economic interdependence has deepened. Referring to Japan's one-way dependence on the U.S. economy in the past, people used to say, "When the U.S. economy gets a cold, the Japanese economy gets pneumonia." Now if the Japanese economy gets a cold, the U.S. economy is likely to get one as well. Indeed, the five bilateral issues we have examined underscore the sensitivity of the U.S. economy to economic changes in Japan or exports from that country. (They also show that increasing interdependence does not necessarily reduce conflict and may even increase it [Koehane and Nye, 1977].) There remains, however, an undeniable asymmetry. Although Japan may now be more competitive than the United States in most major manufacturing industries, Japan is still fundamentally more vulnerable. Not only is Japan's dependence on the U.S. market substantially greater than the U.S. dependence on the Japanese market, but Japan also has fewer alternatives for its key imports. As Chairman Caldwell of the Ford Motor Company implied in the statement quoted in chapter 1, the United States could make or buy elsewhere—if often less efficiently—practically all of the items it currently imports from Japan. Japan's dependence becomes even clearer when one considers the political and security dimensions of the overall bilateral relationships.

The United States has often used this asymmetry—real and perceived— to make demands on Japan. Thus, it comes as no surprise that, in all five cases covered in this volume, it was the United States—government or industry—that initiated the issue. Yet the U.S. government, particularly the executive branch, proved strongly resistant to protectionist solutions for these cases. To many, this will come as a surprise, because, with the decline of the cold war beginning in the late 1960s, the United States became more responsive to economic interests and less willing to subordinate them to foreign-policy considerations. Thus, the U.S. government often yielded, at least partially, to protectionist pressure from specific industries facing import competition. Examples include the 1969 voluntary restraint agreements on steel with Japan and the European community, the 1971 textile agreements with Japan and three other Far Eastern countries leading to the multifiber arrangement (MFA) of 1974, the 1976 import quota on specialty steel, and the 1977 orderly marketing agreement on color-television imports.

Why then did the executive branch resist protectionist pressure on the steel issue in the spring and summer of 1977 and on the auto issue in 1980? Did the U.S. government revert to the earlier policy of emphasizing free trade for foreign-policy considerations? The answer seems to be no. U.S. trade policymakers have continued to maintain a preference for free trade, even with the decline of the cold war. However, they have leaned less on foreign-policy arguments and interests—free trade for the free world—and more on classical economic ones. In the last few years, inflation has been a major preoccupation among U.S. economic policy officials, and this has tended to reinforce their basic free-trade orientation. Tension has been heightened in U.S. politics because, at the same time, domestic interest groups have increased their assertiveness, demanding protection from import competition. This in turn is a reflection of the economic plight of the United States and the declining productivity of U.S. industries. Thus, ironically, governmental resistance to protectionist solutions has led to the prolongation and escalation of U.S.-Japanese trade disputes. It was the resistance of the executive branch to the demands of the domestic industry (backed by congressional allies), and not to Japanese intransigence, that raised the visibility and volatility of the steel and auto issues.

Two decades ago, the United States advocated free trade primarily to strengthen the free-world coalition. Today, the United States increasingly promotes free trade to help itself—to eliminate foreign barriers to U.S. products. This is consistent with the trade-expansionist position the U.S. government has taken on the agriculture and NTT issues, as well as on the MTN as a whole. The U.S. government has taken the initiative in opening up the market of Japan (and of the European community) for U.S. agricultural and high-technology products—even if it has meant creating some friction with Japan (and the EC).

What might be the implications for U.S.-Japanese relations of a new cold war between the United States and the Soviet Union in the 1980s? A return to the immediate postwar pattern seems most unlikely: The United States is relatively much weaker, and much more dependent on trade, than it was in the 1950s. Rather than moving toward accommodation of the allies' economic interests, U.S. policymakers will likely increase demands on Japan and the European community to share burdens and assume larger responsibilities—economically, politically, and militarily. This is exactly what happened after Iran took U.S. hostages and after Soviet troops invaded Afghanistan. However, the United States does not always offer reciprocal cooperation, as evidenced by the Reagan administration's failure to consult its allies before deciding to lift the embargo on Soviet grain sales.

We seem to be seeing a reemergence of defense issues as sources of U.S.-Japanese controversy, but without the muting of economic conflicts that characterized the fifties and sixties. The reversion of Okinawa to Japanese control in 1972 ushered in a near-decade of unprecedented quietude in U.S.-Japanese security relations. The mutual security treaty of 1960 finally won broad acquiescence in Japan; the two countries increased their low-keyed military cooperation and pursued similar policies towards China and the Soviet Union. This security harmony provided something of a cushion, absorbing or limiting the effects of the economic disputes.

Events of the spring of 1981 brought this period to a halt—perhaps temporarily, but more likely for years to come. The episodes themselves seemed idiosyncratic. A U.S. nuclear submarine accidently collided with a Japanese freighter and then failed either to rescue the stricken passengers or to report the incident promptly so others could do so. A dispute within the Japanese cabinet over the wording of the Reagan-Suzuki joint communique, and the briefing of reporters on its content, led to the resignation of the foreign minister and the prime minister's public retreat from the communique's commitment to even greater Japanese defense efforts. Then, less than two weeks after Suzuki's return from Washington, an interview with former Ambassador Edwin Reischauer, reported by *Mainichi Shimbun*, confirmed that U.S. vessels regularly kept nuclear weapons on board when they made calls at Japanese ports, contrary to the public impression determinedly cultivated by successive Japanese governments, with U.S. acquiescence. Reischauer's comments, confirmed and reinforced by statements of others on both side of the Pacific, triggered a political storm in Tokyo, which continued as the Suzuki government sought to hold to the minimum disclosure policy of its predecessors (for background, see Destler, Sato, Clapp, and Fukui, 1976, pp. 55-60).

The defense policies of the Reagan administration will likely mean continued pressure on Japan to do more militarily, even though the administration began by wisely downplaying what the Carter administration had emphasized: the size of Japan's defense budget. The Japanese reaction to the events of spring 1981 suggests that, if public resistance to the U.S. defense connection has weakened considerably since the sixties, there has not developed any strong positive consensus for an expanded and more overt Japanese security role.

In the early postwar period, it was defense issues that caused the major political conflicts between Japan and the United States. In the seventies, it was economic issues. In the eighties, we are likely to see both issues predominate. If the United States continues to resort to pressure tactics to resolve the issues, strong resentment among the Japanese, who feel psychologically more and more equal to the United States, will be engendered—even if, in specific cases, Japanese officials invite the pressure. Although increasing interdependence has made the U.S. economic system more sensitive to economic developments in Japan, it has not yet made the U.S. political system sufficiently sensitive to political conditions in Japan, and vice versa.

The management of U.S.-Japanese economic conflicts, therefore, will continue to be a formidable political task. We can take some comfort, however, from the fact that we got through the seventies as well as we did. None of the five issues chronicled in this book was easy to resolve. Nor were several other issues not given extensive treatment here. In a number of specific respects, officials in both governments might have done better—at least this chapter so argues. However, all these issues ended with workable resolutions and without serious and lasting side effects, insofar as can be presently measured. And this made it easier for the broader U.S.-Japanese economic and political relationship, so crucial to both countries, to survive and prosper.

Notes

1. Robert J. Samuelson, "U.S., Japan Find Old Relationships Have Unraveled," *National Journal*, 30 June 1979, p. 1070. Reprinted with permission.

References

Destler, I.M.; Sato, Hideo; Clapp, Priscilla, and Fukui, Haruhiro. *Managing an Alliance: The Politics of U.S.-Japanese Relations.* Washington, D.C.: Brookings Institution, 1976.

Destler, I.M.; Fukui, Haruhiro; and Sato, Hideo. *The Textile Wrangle: Conflict in Japanese-American Relations, 1969-1971.* Ithaca and London: Cornell University Press, 1979.

Keohane, Robert O., and Nye, Joseph S. *Power and Independence: World Politics in Transition*. Boston: Little Brown and Company, 1977.

"Productive Partnership for the 1980s," Joint Communique of President Jimmy Carter and Prime Minister Masayoshi Ohira, 2 May 1979. In U.S. General Accounting Office, *United States-Japan Trade: Issues and Problems*. Washington, D.C.: U.S. Government Printing Office, 21 September 1979, Appendix II.

Report of the Japan-United States Economic Relations Group. Prepared for the President of the United States and the Prime Minister of Japan, January 1981.

Samuelson, Robert J. "U.S., Japan Find Old Relationships Have Unraveled." *National Journal*, 30 June 1979, pp. 1068-1079.

About the Contributors

Timothy J. Curran is a research Fellow for Toyota at the East Asian Institute of Columbia University and an associate director of the Institute's Project on the United States, Japan, and Southeast Asia. During 1979, he was a guest scholar at the Japan Economic Research Center in Tokyo, where he specialized in U.S.-Japanese economic relations.

Michael W. Hodin is senior advisor for International Affairs at Pfizer, Inc., having served previously as a legislative assistant to Senator Daniel Patrick Moynihan. He received the Ph.D. in political science from Columbia University, where his dissertation investigated the steel issue as a case study in U.S. trade policymaking.

Ikuo Kabashima is lecturer of political science at the University of Tsukuba. A graduate of the University of Nebraska, he holds the M.A. and Ph.D. degrees from Harvard University and has published articles on political economy and political participation.

Hisao Mitsuyu is chief researcher, Analysis and Research Center, *Asahi Shimbun*. A graduate of Kyoto University, he was an *Asahi* news reporter before assuming his current position. In 1980-1981, he was a visiting senior research associate of the Center for International Affairs, Harvard University.

Gilbert R. Winham is professor of political science and director of the Centre for Foreign Policy Studies at Dalhousie University, Halifax, Canada. His articles on international economic negotiations have appeared in *World Politics, International Journal*, and the *Journal of World Trade Law*. He is currently preparing a manuscript tentatively entitled, "International Trade and the Tokyo Round."

About the Editors

I.M. Destler is a senior associate at the Carnegie Endowment for International Peace, where he directs the Project on Executive-Congressional Relations. A graduate of Harvard College, he holds the M.P.A. and Ph.D. degrees from the Woodrow Wilson School, Princeton University. He is the author of *Presidents, Bureaucrats, and Foreign Policy* (1972) and *Making Foreign Economic Policy* (1980).

Hideo Sato is associate professor of political science at Yale University. A graduate of International Christian University in Tokyo, he holds the M.A. and Ph.D. degrees from the University of Chicago. He was a Brookings research associate in 1973-1975, and he has coauthored (with Chae-Jin Lee) *U.S. Policy Toward Japan and Korea* (forthcoming).

Dr. Destler and Dr. Sato are coauthors (with Priscilla Clapp and Haruhiro Fukui) of *Managing An Alliance: The Politics of U.S.-Japanese Relations* (1976), and (with Fukui) of *The Textile Wrangle: Conflict in Japanese-American Relations 1969-1971* (1979).

DATE DUE

FEB 2 4 1983		APR 1 9 2000	
MAR 1 7 1983]			
DEC 6 1984			
FEB 2 0 1986			
DEC 1 2 1992			